Commentary

The Russian Way of War
Force Structure, Tactics, and Modernization of the Russian Ground Forces

Published by the U.S. Army Training and Doctrine Command G2's Foreign Military Studies Office in 2016, this book picks up where the FM 100-2 series left off and discusses Russian military structure, capabilities, and future development. You will note that we added some additional information regarding new Russian weapons at the end of the book including:

- 1K17 Szhatie (1K17 Сжатие) Russian "Stiletto" Laser Tank
- Combat Laser System (Peresvet) Russian Laser Cannon
- T-14 Armata Main Battle Tank
- T-15 Heavy Infantry Combat Vehicle
- Kurganets-25 Light Tracked Armored Vehicle
- 2S35 Koalitsiya-SV 152-mm Self-Propelled Howitzer
- VPK-7829 Bumerang Modular Infantry Wheeled Fighting Vehicle

Why buy a book you can download for free? We print this book so you don't have to.

First you gotta find a good clean (legible) copy. If you find a good copy, you could print it using a network printer you share with 100 other people (typically its either out of paper or toner). If it's just a 10-page document, no problem, but if it's 393-pages, you will need to punch 3 holes in all those pages and put it in a 3-ring binder. Takes at least a couple hours.

Unfortunately, this is the only copy of this book we were able to locate and the image quality of some of the pages is very poor, so they are difficult to read. If you have a good copy, please send us the missing pages and we will update the file.

It's much more cost-effective to just order the latest version from Amazon.com

This book includes original commentary which is copyright material. Note that government documents are in the public domain. We print these large documents as a service so you don't have to. The books are compact, tightly-bound, full-size (8 ½ by 11 inches), with large text and glossy covers. 4th Watch Publishing Co. is a SDVOSB. https://usgovpub.com

Look for the AUDIOBOOK on Audible to listen to the book while studying the maps.

Other books we publish on Amazon.com

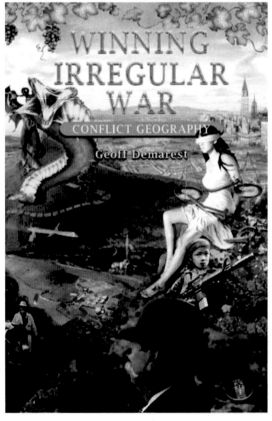

The Russian Way of War

Force Structure, Tactics, and Modernization of the Russian Ground Forces

Dr. Lester W. Grau

Charles K. Bartles

Foreign Military Studies Office
2016

Cover Design: CW2 Hommy Rosado

TG2
v1.2 (22 August 2017)

Lester W. Grau is a senior analyst and the Research Director for the Foreign Military Studies Office at Fort Leavenworth, Kansas. A Vietnam War infantryman, graduate of the U.S. Army Defense Language Institute (Russian) and the U.S. Army's Institute for Advanced Russian and Eastern European Studies, he retired from the US Army in 1992 at the grade of Lieutenant Colonel. His military education included the Infantry Officers Basic and Advanced Courses, the United States Army Command and General Staff College and the U.S. Air Force War College. His Baccalaureate and Masters degrees are in International Relations. His doctorate is in Military History. He served a combat tour in Vietnam, four European tours, a Korean tour and a posting in Moscow. He has traveled to the Soviet Union and Russia over forty times. He has also been a frequent visitor to the Asian subcontinent, especially Pakistan and Afghanistan. He was a CENTCOM Fellow.

Dr. Grau has published over 200 articles and studies on tactical, operational and geopolitical subjects. His book, *The Bear Went Over the Mountain: Soviet Combat Tactics in Afghanistan,* was published in 1996. *The Other Side of the Mountain: Mujahideen Tactics In the Soviet-Afghan War*, co-authored with Ali Jalali, was published in 1998. *The Soviet-Afghan War: How a Superpower Fought and Lost was published in 2001. The Red Army's Do-It-Yourself, Nazi-Bashing Guerrilla Warfare Manual* and *Passing It On: Fighting the Pushtun on Afghanistan's Frontier* were published in 2011. *Operation Anaconda: America's First Major Battle In Afghanistan* and *Mountain Warfare And Other Lofty Problems: Foreign Ideas On High-Altitude Combat,* co-authored with Charles K. Bartles, were also published in 2011. F*angs of the Lone Wolf: Chechen Tactics in the Russian-Chechen Wars 1994-2009*, co-authored with Dodge Billingsley, was published in 2012. *Afghanistan: Preparing for the Bolshevik Incursion into Afghanistan and Attack on India*, which is a translation of General Snesarev's 1921 classic work, was published in 2014. *From Fabric Wings to Supersonic Fighters and Drones: A History of Military Aviation on Both Sides of the North-West Frontier*, with Brian Cloughley and Andrew Roe, was published in 2015.

Charles K. Bartles is a junior analyst and Russian linguist at the Foreign Military Studies Office at Fort Leavenworth, Kansas. His specific research areas include Russian and Central Asian military force structure, modernization, tactics, officer and enlisted professional development, and security assistance programs. Chuck is also a Major, imagery, and space operations officer (FA40) in the Army Reserve at the Joint Functional Component Command for Integrated Missile Defense (JFCC-IMD). He has deployed to Afghanistan and Iraq, and has served as a security assistance officer at embassies in Kyrgyzstan, Uzbekistan, and Kazakhstan. Chuck has a BA in Russian from the University of Nebraska-Lincoln, an MA in Russian and Eastern European Studies from the University of Kansas, a certificate in Geospatial Information Systems from the University of Missouri-Kansas City, and certificates in Database Administration and Computer Programming from Johnson County Community College.

ABOUT THE FOREIGN MILITARY STUDIES OFFICE

The mission of the U.S. Army Training and Doctrine Command G2's Foreign Military Studies Office is to research and present understudied and unconsidered foreign perspectives in order to better understand the Operational Environment. FMSO was founded during the Cold War as the Soviet Army Studies Office (SASO) and charged with doing open source research and academic outreach to bring a better understanding between the armies of the two superpowers. The name and scope of the Office changed and broadened over time, but research in the source language, has remained a cornerstone of the FMSO methodology. While FMSO's motto and work continues to represent "How they think they think," FMSO does not produce official U.S. Army threat doctrine. In this regard, this book is a study of the ground forces of a major Eurasian power from its own sources.

Tom Wilhelm
Director
Foreign Military Studies Office

FORWARD

In 1984, Lieutenant General William Richardson, the commander of the U.S. Army's Training and Doctrine Command (TRADOC), authorized the creation of an office modeled after the British Army's Soviet Studies Research Center (SSRC) in order to provide unclassified material from primarily Russian sources for U.S. Army training and education. The Soviet Army Studies Office (SASO) opened at Fort Leavenworth in 1986 and was staffed with civilian academics and U.S. Army foreign area officers who were proficient in Russian, understood Russian and Soviet histories and military institutions, and had traveled, studied or lived in the Soviet Union. I was assigned to SASO at its inception and was privileged to serve as its director from 1989 to 1993, during which the office was transformed and expanded Into the Foreign Military Studies Office (FMSO). During that period, FMSO produced most of the U.S. Army unclassified studies related to the Ground Forces in Russia and the Soviet Union on training, tactics, and military thought.

In particular, I was part of FMSO's development of the study entitled The Soviet Conduct of War: An Assessment of Soviet Military Capabilities (1982-1987), which became an enduring document as the end of the Cold War shifted the U.S. military's focus elsewhere. Now, more than a quarter of a century later, FMSO has produced a new appreciation of the Russian Federation's military under the rubric The Russian Way of War: Force Structure, Tactics, and Modernization of the Russian Ground Forces. This new study combines the seasoned insight of FMSO's long-time Russia hand, Dr. Les Grau, with the exceptional skills and talent of Mr. Chuck Bartles (a younger hand) in an ambitious book that is designed to mitigate the decades-long gap in comprehensive unclassified understanding regarding how the Russian army organizes and trains to fight. In short, while acknowledging the fact that the new Russian Army is not the old Soviet Army, this study recognizes the many traditions, customs, and practices of the past that shape the present and will likely inform the future. Rather than embracing an antagonistic or adversarial point of view, this work attempts to understand an important military organization in an important global region.

David M. Glantz
Colonel, USA (Retired)
Editor, The Journal of Slavic Military Studies

Table of Contents

Charts & Illustrations

The Offense   102

Tactical Maneuver   146

Branches of Arms   208

Specialty Branches   272

Other Tactical Considerations   358

Russian Military Symbology   390

Introduction

Russia's 2014 annexation of the Crimean Peninsula, activity in Eastern Ukraine, saber rattling regarding the Baltics, deployment to Syria, and more assertive behavior along its borders have piqued interest in the Russian Armed Forces.[1] This increased interest has caused much speculation about their structure, capabilities, and future development. Interestingly, this speculation has created many different, and often contradictory, narratives about these issues. At any given time, assessments of the Russian Armed Forces vary between the idea of an incompetent and corrupt conscript army manning decrepit Soviet equipment and relying solely on brute force, to the idea of an elite military filled with Special Operations Forces (SOF) who were the "polite people" or "little green men" seen on the streets in Crimea. This book will attempt to split the difference between these radically different ideas by shedding some light on what exactly the Russian Ground Forces consist of, how they are structured, how they fight, and how they are modernizing.

Russia's actions in this regard are a continuation of past Russian and Soviet policies of achieving national objectives in the context of the current operational environment and forecasting of future war. The Russian General staff envisions less large-scale warfare; the increased use of networked command-and-control systems, robotics, and precision weaponry; greater importance placed on interagency cooperation; more operations in urban terrain; a melding of offense and defense; and a general decrease in the differences between military activities at the strategic, operational, and tactical levels. Along with these considerations of the future, the General Staff also takes into consideration Russia's unique geography, history, political and economic systems, social attitudes, weapons procurement practices, and general threat perception, altogether providing a detailed picture of what Russia's military looks like today and will look like in the future.

In terms of organization of this book we have chosen not to align it according to the warfighting functions (Movement and Maneuver, Fires, Intelligence, Sustainment, Command and Control, Protection), but have opted for a more systemic approach. In our view, there are substantial differences between the Russian and U.S. ways of warfare and how the warfighting functions are related. For this reason, we believe any analysis of this system should begin first by describing the Russian system and then proceed to an analysis of how the warfighting functions work within the system. We have also chosen to discuss Russian force structure, tactics, and modernization in one document, as we believe these issues are inextricably linked: there can be no understanding of any one of these issues without understanding all the others. Finally, the word "Soviet" appears frequently in this book. This is because the Russian system today is based on what they have preserved, modified, and improved from their former Soviet system, and that source information still best applies where indicated in this book.

---

[1] For the purposes of this book, the term "Armed Forces" will refer specifically to the Ministry of Defense, while the term "military" will refer to all of Russia's militarized intelligence and security services, including the Ministry of Defense.

We have elected to structure this book from the bottom, up. At the base of every army is its people, and so we start our discussion with the Russian personnel system. Chapter One (Personnel System) includes a description of the recruiting, training, and paying of the three personnel types found in the Russian military: the officer, contract NCO (warrant officer), and conscript. Although most discussions mention only the negative aspects (hazing, corruption, etc.) of the personnel system, we will also identify some advantages, namely specialization. Chapter Two (Structure and Echelonment) introduces the reader to the Russian system of militarized intelligence and security services and explains their differing roles, with a focus on the military forces of the Ministry of Defense. This chapter also introduces the 2008 "New Look" reforms, which, along with an influx of funding, have arguably been responsible for recent military successes. The chapter concludes with the description of Russia's primary means of force projection, it's Ground Forces, including how they are structured in tactical situations.

Chapters Three (The Offense), Four (The Defense), and Five (Tactical Maneuver) will probably be of greatest interest to Army readers. Most recent studies of Russian tactics have focused on case studies of Russian operations in Crimea and Eastern Ukraine, but we have taken a different approach. Although an examination of past Russian operations is interesting and useful for historical reference, we believe the way the Russians conducted operations against these adversaries would be much different than the way they would conduct operations against an adversary with sophisticated capabilities, such as the U.S. and/or NATO. Perhaps General Gerasimov explained this concept best when he stated: "Each war represents an isolated case, requiring an understanding of its own particular logic, its own unique character." In other words, there is no "one-size-fits-all" formula for conducting operations or understanding the operational environment. While some countries apply various models to aid in discerning operation and strategic factors for decision-making, such as Center of Gravity analysis, PMESII-PT (Political, Military, Economic, Social, Information, Infrastructure, Physical Environment, and Time), Ends, Ways, and Means Analysis, and DIME (Diplomatic, Information, Military, Economic), the Russian approach emphasizes dialectical thinking about forecasting, trends analysis, correlation of forces and means, and determining forms and methods. They are allergic to "one-size-fits-all" models.

Chapter 1
Personnel System

The Russian Federation has pursued the development of a professional enlisted component in the Russian Armed Forces since the early 1990s. The impetus for this stemmed from the conscription system inherited from the Soviets. After the Second World War the Soviets believed that the future of modern warfare would closely resemble the battles they had fought in the last years of the war, albeit with nuclear weapons. These battles would require vast numbers of troops organized in divisions, army groups, and fronts to execute high speed maneuver warfare to penetrate enemy defenses and then exploit these successes. At this time the Soviets believed that the enlisted force that would be required to fight in future battles would resemble the enlisted force that fought in the Second World War. In order to mass a large army without bankrupting the economy, the Soviets retained their universal conscription system. The intent was that all males would receive a basic level of military training during their two-year stints and would then be able to return to civilian life. These former conscripts would infrequently be called for musters, and would be called *en masse* in the event of a mobilization. This system had an unintended consequence for the strong NCO corps that the Soviets had inherited from the Tsarist Army. The two-year conscription model for enlisted personnel had no real career path for enlisted personnel who desired to serve past their initial conscription length. The strong NCO corps that emerged after the Second World War soon disappeared, as these NCOs either left the service or became commissioned officers. In the Soviet Armed Forces, officers, not NCOs, became the primary small unit leaders and trainers.[1]

This system began experiencing problems as the Soviet Armed Forces began to modernize rapidly in the 1960s and 1970s. Technically advanced equipment requires skilled and well trained labor to operate and maintain it. Since two-year conscription terms were considered insufficient time to train individuals to perform complex technical tasks, Soviet officers performed duties that would normally be performed by NCOs in Western armies. The Soviets believed this was an inefficient way of managing manpower, and decided to create "warrant officer" positions primarily to maintain and operate advanced equipment. These warrant officers, recruited from conscripts who had completed their initial tours, were generally not viewed favorably by the officer corps, since the best conscripts who wanted to continue their military service were enrolled in military academies. Russian warrant officers relieved some of the technical and small unit leadership burdens that were placed on officers, but were never well regarded as an institution and had little in common with Western NCOs and warrant officers.[2] In addition to technical positions, warrant officers filled positions somewhat similar to U.S. first sergeants (albeit with far less authority) and served as platoon leaders for maintenance and supply units. The Russian Federation abolished all warrant officer positions during the 2008 "New Look" reforms and converted all warrant officers into contract NCOs. Warrant officer billets have since been brought back. There has been little reporting about

[1] Aleksandr Pinchuk, "The University for Sergeants," *Krasnaya Zvezda* Online, 23 November 2012, <http://www.redstar.ru/index.php/2011-07-25-15-57-07/item/5984-serzhantskie-universitetyi>, accessed 1 May 2016.
For an excellent description of the professionalism of Russian NCOs in the Second World War, see:
Leonov, V.N., *Blood on the Shores: Soviet Naval Commandos in World War II*, Annapolis, M.D: Naval Institute Press, 1993.
[2] Christopher N. Donnelly, *Red Banner: The Soviet Military System in Peace and War*, first edition. (Coulsdon, Surrey: Jane's Information Group, 1988), pp. 180-182.

how warrant officer and contract NCO positions differ, but there is likely little difference.[3]

Russia has maintained a hybrid system of conscription and contract service to the present day.[4] In this system, officers, not NCOs, are the primary trainers of the platoon. In order to prepare these lieutenants, cadets usually attend four- or five-year military academies that more closely resemble a combination of the U.S. Military Academy and the officer basic course, with a strong emphasis on tactics, then anything practiced in the U.S.[5] As soon as a new lieutenant graduates from an academy and takes command of his platoon, he is expected to immediately begin training and maintaining discipline in his platoon.[6]

Soviet lieutenants filled the leadership, planning, training, and disciplinary roles of both a U.S. platoon leader and platoon sergeant, and so worked very long days. Since the Soviet platoon leader ensured small unit discipline and would leave the barracks at night to be with his own family, a very brutal system of hazing, known as *dedovschina* developed among the conscripts. This unofficial, but deeply institutionalized practice consisted of senior (second year) conscripts hazing the junior (first year) conscripts. These practices often involved theft, beatings, and humiliation, which became somewhat infamous and embarrassing to the government. Although this practice has become less common in today's Russian military, it still occasionally surfaces in the media.

Soon after the collapse of the Soviet Union, former Russian President Yeltsin mentioned abolishing the conscription system. Conscription was very unpopular due to problems with *dedovschina*, and the popularity was even further lowered due to the effects of the turbulent financial situation, which was devastating the Russian Armed Forces. Due to the economic situation, little progress was made towards full enlisted professionalization, but Russia did start its first "contract NCO" program, which allowed enlisted soldiers to serve with better pay and privileges, such as not living in barracks. Russia has maintained a hybrid system of conscription and contract service to present day.

Russia's military leadership has had mixed feelings about the replacement of conscripts with contract NCOs. Some generals have lamented the idea of abolishing the conscription system, because they believe such a reform would deprive Russia of a large strategic reserve with at least some military training. Other criticisms have involved the description of contract NCOs

---

[3] Viktor Sokirko and Denis Telmanov, "Defense Ministry Approved Positions for Warrant Officers," *Izvestiya* Online, 3 July 2013, http://izvestia.ru/news/552986#ixzz2XyXraoZW, accessed 1 May 2016.
"Warrant Officers Will Service Sophisticated Weapon Systems," *Interfax-AVN* Online, 8 April 2013.
[4] Yuriy Gavrilov, "Lining Up for the Beret: No End to Those Wishing to Serve in the VDV at the Enlistment Offices," *Rossiyskaya Gazeta* Online, 26 April 2012, <http://www.rg.ru/2012/04/26/shamanov.html>, accessed 1 May 2016.
[5] It is not uncommon for a new platoon leader in an airborne unit to join his unit after completing 45 or more jumps at the Airborne Military Academy in Ryazan. See Aleksandr Kolotilo, "VDV: The Valor of the Highest Order," *Krasnaya Zvezda* Online, 26 December 2012, <http://www.redstar.ru/index.php/siriya/item/6608-vdv-%E2%80%93-eto-muzhestvo-vyisshego-klassa>, accessed 1 May 2016.
[6] Andrey Bobrun and Oleg Pochinyuk, "To the Level of the Century," *Krasnaya Zvezda* Online, 6 July 2011, <http://old.redstar.ru/2011/07/06_07/2_01.html>, accessed 1 May 2016.
Vladimir Sosnitskiy, "Regimental Training: Hot Times," *Krasnaya Zvezda* Online, 12 July 2011, <http://old.redstar.ru/2011/07/12_07/2_01.html>, accessed 1 May 2016.

as "mercenaries," a term that is sometime used to describe the U.S. system of enlistment, the implication being contract NCOs are more interested in pay than service to the country (this argument likely carries little weight in the Russian military, as both officers and contract enlisted soldiers sign service contracts).

Probably the strongest motivator for the Russia's military leadership to support the formation of a contract NCO system is Russia's lessons learned from Chechnya and other modern conflicts. Russia has changed its view on the nature of modern and future war. Local and regional conflicts, rather than large-scale high-speed maneuver are seen as the most likely manifestation of war. In addition, warfare will also now involve "indirect and asymmetric methods" and a general blurring of the lines between the tactical, operational, and strategic levels of military operations. The implication for Russia's enlisted personnel, is that conscripts are unable to be effective warfighters on the modern battlefield, especially since the conscription period in the Russian Federation has been reduced to one year. Russia has vacillated back and forth between desiring a completely professional enlisted force, and continuing with the current hybrid system, albeit with a greater percentage of contract NCOs.[7] Due to greater costs involved with contract NCOs and the aforementioned desire to maintain a mass mobilization capacity, it is likely that Russia will utilize a hybrid system for enlisted manning for the foreseeable future. In 2015, the number of contract soldiers in the positions of warrant officers, sergeants and soldiers reached 300 thousand, for the first time exceeding the number of conscripts.[8]

There is often a Western assumption that Russian contract sergeants are distributed throughout the ranks and are placed in positions of leadership over conscripts. A more accurate term for Russian contract sergeants would probably be "contract soldier," because in the Russian system units are designated as either "conscript" or "contract sergeant," and there is apparently little interaction between these enlisted personnel types. In general, contract NCOs fill "trigger puller" positions, and positions requiring advanced skills and training. Conscripts usually fill positions that require little training, such as drivers, cooks, laborers, or tradesman. Although one-year conscription terms give little time for training, conscripts do not necessarily join the military without militarily useful skills. The Russian Federation, as did the Soviet Union, has "patriotic education," and certain rudimentary military skills (first aid, etc.) are included in the primary and secondary education curriculum for male and female students.[9]

---

[7] Charles K. Bartles, "Defense Reforms of Russian Defense Minister Anatolii Serdyukov," *Journal of Slavic Military Studies* 24, no. 1 (2011).

[8] Lieutenant General Vasily Tonkoshkurov, "Important Priority for the General Staff: Is the Current Personnel System Adequate for Modern Requirements?" *Voyenno-Promyshlennyy Kuryer* Online, 21 October 2015, <http://vpk-news.ru/articles/27609>, accessed 1 May 2016.

[9] Ilya Rozhdestvenskiy, "Parade of Children's Troops: How Children in Russia Are Taught to Love the Motherland and To Fight for It," *Medusa* Online, 7 July 2015, <https://meduza.io/feature/2015/07/07/parad-detskih-voysk>, accessed 28 March 2016. The article has been reprinted in English, and may be found at: <https://meduza.io/en/feature/2015/07/16/russia-s-littlest-soldiers>.

DOSAAF

In terms of training, Russia does have one institution with no U.S. equivalent. The Volunteer Society for Cooperation with the Army, Aviation, and Fleet (DOSAAF) is a government-sponsored sports and outdoor enthusiast organization that promotes and funds militarily useful skills, such as flying, hiking, camping, shooting, skiing, parachuting, driving, and athletics, for young people.[10] The predecessors to the organization were invaluable in the Great Patriotic War (Second World War) by providing skilled servicemen to

DOSAAF Flag
Image Courtesy: Russian Ministry of Defense

the Armed Forces. DOSAAF, in one form or another, still exists in many states of the former Soviet Union. It is particularly valuable for the conscription-based manning system that the Russian Federation utilizes to fill its rank and file, but would be an inefficient way of imparting skills to a fully professional (non-conscript) army. Conscripts who have participated in DOSAAF activities gain skills that would be difficult to impart to troops who are only drafted for one year. The DOSAAF system is so well ingrained into the Russian military system that a DOSAAF representative sits on each draft board in order to advise the state on the best way to utilize each conscript. For example, a conscript who has participated in a DOSAAF parachuting club would be more likely to be assigned to an airborne unit.[11] The DOSAAF program declined after the collapse of the Soviet Union, but in the last few years experienced a resurgence. According to a May 2015 article, about 40 percent of recruits enter the military with a military occupational specialty obtained from a DOSAAF program. The desire is that eventually all conscripts enter the military with some sort of military occupational specialty.[12]

Conscripts

The Russian Federation practices a conscription system, but this system differs greatly from the U.S. draft system with which many Americans were familiar from the Vietnam era. While Americans are familiar with the term "Draft Board," the Russian Federation utilizes military commissariats, which is the local organization of military administration responsible for not only the semiannual conscription process, but also documentation of local human and economic resources for the State's use in the event of war. Military commissariats parallel every level of the civilian administration in the military district. They are led by a lieutenant colonel or colonel, with a staff and a council of local officials. In regards to the conscription function of the commissariats, the commission usually consists of a chairman (typically an active duty colonel), doctor, and representatives from the education ministry, Federal Security Service (FSB), Internal Affairs Ministry (MVD), and DOSAAF, and possibly other members. The

10 Viktor Khudoleyev, "Toward New Standards of Mobility," *Krasnaya Zvezda* Online, 30 June 2015, <http://redstar.ru/index.php/newspaper/item/24659-k-novym-standartam-mobilnosti>, accessed 1 May 2016.
11 Ray Finch, "Patriotic Education-DOSAAF," *OE Watch* Online, May 2015
Viktor Khudoleyev, "Much Work Lies Ahead, 87 Years of DOSAAF," *Krasnaya Zvezda* Online, 23 January 2014, <http://www.redstar.ru/index.php/siriya/item/13872-vperedi-bolshaya-rabota>, accessed 1 May 2016.
12 Vladimir Mukhin "Military Commissars to Be Responsible for Service in Installments," *Nezavisimaya Gazeta* Online, 25 June 2015, <http://www.ng.ru/armies/2015-06-26/1_voenkomy.html>, accessed 1 May 2016.
"DOSAAF trains 80,000 specialists for Armed Forces annually," *Interfax*, 24 April 2013.

purpose of this commission is to determine the best utilization of the conscript. This requires sorting them for appropriate assignments. In general, the politically reliable are sent to the FSB or MVD, the physically strong to the airborne, those with language abilities to signal intelligence units, etc. The commission composition is intended to best conduct this sorting of human capital. Doctors assess physical fitness, educators describe academic performance, the FSB representative addresses political reliability, the MVD officer mentions any brushes with the law, and the DOSAAF member describes any militarily relevant activities in which the conscript may have participated.[13]

In 2013, the Russian Federation decided to take this concept a step further by creating "science companies" to best exploit the brightest and most promising recruits who are and will be entering the Russian Armed Forces. Although there have been few details about the exact role these companies will play, Defense Minister Shoygu has stated that they will become "an incubator for our institutions, scientific research institutes, design bureaus for naval, aviation, and space matters, and on other issues." There are currently twelve science companies in the Russian military, with a total of 561 service

Conscripts in the field
Image Courtesy: Vitaly Kuzmin

members. Conscripted service in the science companies is apparently a gateway to the officer corps, as already 41 former science company service members have been commissioned as lieutenants.[14] The science companies are reportedly participating in 20 research projects, and within one six-month period published 40 articles and prepared eight patent applications.[15]

Unlike the U.S. system, there is no presumption that a conscript does not have any militarily useful skills when entering the military. This difference is in part due to a slightly different civilian education system in the Russian Federation. The Russian system has some commonalities with the German system, which "tracks" students at an earlier age to university or vocational educations. The significance for the Russian military is that in some cases conscripts may already be entering military service with a few years of vocational training in a militarily useful specialty (pipe fitter, welder, machinist, etc.).

In sum, the Russian conscription system has little in common with the U.S. enlistment or draft systems, which assess a new serviceman's potential based primarily on a single test (Armed Services Vocational Aptitude Battery). Instead, the Russian system takes a more holistic approach. The implication is that although the Russian Federation has only a one-year conscription, there still is substantial value that can be had from the individual conscript.

13 Christopher N. Donnelly, *Red Banner: The Soviet Military System in Peace and War*, first edition. (Coulsdon, Surrey: Jane's Information Group, 1988), pp. 155-176.
14 "The Realization of the 'Scientific Companies' Project Begins on Friday," *Interfax-AVN*, 4 June 2015. Viktor Khudoleyev, "Serve Worthily!" *Krasnaya Zvezda* Online, 1 April 2016, <http://redstar.ru/index.php/newspaper/item/28331-sluzhite-dostojno>, accessed 1 May 2016.
15 Vladimir Ivanovsky and Oleg Falichev, "Rear Service Eagles: MTO Academy Navigates 'Invisible Bridges,'" *Voyenno-Promyshlennyy Kuryer* Online, 13 April 2016, <http://vpk-news.ru/articles/30195>, accessed 1 May 2016.

In 2016, it was reported that 20,000 of the 155,000 conscripts inducted in the spring draft already had valid military occupational specialties.[16]

Contract NCOs

The Russian Federation has practiced several different means of recruiting contract NCOs. Initially, upon conscription, conscripts were given the option of serving their conscription period or becoming a contract NCO (receiving more pay and privileges, but serving a longer term of service). There was much criticism of this method of recruiting, because many contract NCOs enlisted simply for better pay and living conditions and left the service immediately after their initial enlistments. Regulations were then changed so conscripts could opt for contract service after six months of conscripted service. In 2016, policies were again changed to allow newly inducted conscripts to immediately sign two-year conscription contracts (instead of their one-year conscription period).[17] The most likely recruiting pools for contract NCOs are conscripts who have successfully completed their conscription and civilians who have some sort of militarily useful vocation. There appears to be strong recruiting efforts at vocational schools, including for females who may fill noncombat positions. One interesting aspect of recruiting is that it is not uncommon to see the wives of contract NCOs and officers enlist as contract NCOs. These spouses often serve as uniformed cooks, admin support, and radio/telephone operators (in garrison). This is beneficial for the spouses for financial reasons, as they earn more as uniformed service members than performing the same duties as civilians, and beneficial for the government, because it does not have to provide additional housing allowances, which is a significant cost savings.[18]

In the Russian system, if a person wants to lead he should become an officer; if he desires to be a "trigger puller" or perform a vocation, he should become a contract NCO. If a contract soldier desires to be a missile crewman, he will be a missile crewman for his entire career. The Russian system encourages specialization and technical expertise. There does not appear to be any out-of-branch or broadening assignments for enlisted soldiers or officers. Such practices would be contrary to the mission to develop experts at their chosen profession. Although this appears to be a "dead-end" for Westerners, it is not so much for Russians. Russian contract NCOs appear to be content with this system, likely in part due to the Russian military pay system (discussed later), which is well structured for this contract NCO system. The Russian

Contract NCO
Image Courtesy: Russian Ministry of Defense

---

[16] Viktor Khudoleyev, "Serve Worthily!" *Krasnaya Zvezda* Online, 1 April 2016, <http://redstar.ru/index.php/newspaper/item/28331-sluzhite-dostojno>, accessed 1 May 2016.

[17] Yelena Loriya, and Dmitriy Litovkin, "Two Years for One. For the First Time, Conscripts Given Right to Turn Down Draft Service Immediately and Sign Two-Year Contract," *Izvestiya* Online, 26 February 2016, <http://izvestia.ru/news/605056#ixzz41HhAj5bx>, accessed 1 May 2016.

[18] Anatoliy Yermolin, "Russian Paratroopers' Participation in International Airborne Troops Competitions of 2015 and Preparation for 2016 Contests ," *Ekho Moskvy* Online, 28 November 2015, <http://echo.msk.ru/programs/voensovet/1666594-echo>, accessed 1 May 2016.

contract NCO system is ideal for retaining individuals who do not want to command, lead large units, or move from assignment to assignment. It is designed to retain individuals who simply want to be experts at doing their jobs.[19]

Since Russian contract NCOs fill a different niche than Western NCOs, they are trained differently. The Russian Federation has several different career paths for Russian contract NCOs (who are sometimes referred to as "officer assistants"), but the small unit "leadership" path involves the NCO graduating from an academy whose program lasts two years and nine months. (In the Russian system, contract NCOs are sometimes referred to as "officer assistants") This amount of training is comparable to the amount of education/training a new lieutenant receives while attending a military academy (4-5 years). Hence, although the Russian Federation has a different vision of enlisted professionalization, this does not mean that Russia does not value training and educating its contract NCOs.[20] One thing that does appear certain is that the Russian Federation is not interested in the U.S./Western officer/NCO model: the latter has been observed, evaluated, and rejected.[21]

Officers

If the backbone of Western armies is their NCOs, then the backbone of the Russian Army is the officer corps. Officers are the primary trainers, disciplinarians, and repositories for institutional knowledge in the Russian Armed Forces. The Russian officer education system emphasizes developing expertise in the officer's particular specialty, and begins when the officer is a cadet. Russian military academies do not impart a general university education, as similar institutions do in the West, but instead create competent leaders and experts who immediately begin leading and executing their duties after graduation. The Russian emphasis on specialization precludes such practices as branch details, branch transfers, and out-of-branch assignments.

A system that has a weak or nonexistent NCO corps and relies on a strong officer corps inherently requires a larger number of officers, but, due to this reality and a much

Airborne cadet in training
Image Courtesy: Vitaly Kuzmin

[19] "Sergeant's of a New Formation," *Krasnaya Zvezda* Online, 15 January 2013, <http://www.redstar.ru/index.php/nekrolog/item/6718-serzhantyi-novoy-formatsii>, accessed 1 May 2016.
[20] Charles K. Bartles, "Noncommissioned Officers in the Russian Armed Forces," *OE Watch* Online, March 2016. Anatoliy Yermolin, "Russian Paratroopers' Participation in International Airborne Troops Competitions of 2015 and Preparation for 2016 Contests ," *Ekho Moskvy* Online, 28 November 2015, <http://echo.msk.ru/programs/voensovet/1666594-echo>, accessed 1 May 2016.
[21] Charles K. Bartles, "Balancing: Conscription, Contract Service and a Reserve System," *OE Watch* Online, August 2015.
Vladimir Mukhin, "Military Commissars to Be Responsible for Service in Installments," *Nezavisimaya Gazeta* Online, 25 Jun 2015, <http://www.ng.ru/armies/2015-06-26/1 voenkomy.html>, accessed 1 May 2016.

different Military Decision Making Process (MDMP) these officers are distributed throughout the ranks much differently than in Western militaries. In the Russian system, units (battalions, companies, platoons, squads, etc.) tend to be smaller in order to facilitate the officer's command and control, since there is no substantial NCO leadership. Another major difference between Russian and Western armies is that Russian staffs are substantially smaller than their Western equivalents. The combination of these factors means that Russian maneuver officers get ample opportunities to lead.

The typical early years of a career for a maneuver officer will involve a succession of assignments that have the officer commanding and deputy commanding platoons, companies, and battalions. Only after mastering his specific branch of arms (motorized rifle, tank, artillery, etc.), will he be sent to a yearlong training course, such as the Combined Arms Academy, to learn the skills needed to command a combined arms unit, such as a regiment or brigade. Non-maneuver officers have similar career paths. In today's Russian Army, the practice of having relatively small staffs and the development of the institution of NCOs and warrant officers to conduct technical tasks (in conjunction with the 2008 "New Look" reforms, which condensed regiments and divisions into brigades and removed most "cadre units" from the books) has likely created a Russian Armed Forces with a ratio of officers to enlisted soldiers on par with most Western Armies.

The Russian General Staff System

One of the most interesting differences between the armies of the post-Soviet Union and the West is the presence of Prussian-style General Staffs. These general staff systems provide far more than just a planning apparatus; they also function as doctrine and capability developers. The U.S. Joint Chiefs of Staff is often equated with the Russian General Staff, but this is a great understatement of the Russian General Staff's importance. The Russian Chief of the General Staff has far more authority than any flag grade officer in the U.S. military. In terms of equivalency, the Russian General Staff has the same responsibilities for long-term planning duties conducted by the U.S. Office of the Secretary of Defense and unified combatant commanders; elements of strategic transportation performed by USTRANSCOM; doctrinal and capabilities development, as well as equipment procurement for all branches of the Ministry of Defense. It even has an

Emblem of the Russian General Staff
Image Courtesy: Russian Ministry of Defense

inspector general-like function for ensuring that its standards and regulations are adhered to.[22]

[22] The term "doctrine" in this paper refers exclusively to doctrine at the tactical and operational levels. The General Staff publishes field manuals (Боевой устав по подготовке и ведению общевойскового боя) covering these activities. Russia's official "Military Doctrine," as was published in December of 2014, much more closely resembles a U.S. "National Security Strategy" document than U.S. military documents such as "AirLand Battle." Russia's official military doctrines are produced by the Russian Security Council, albeit likely with input from the

In the Russian system, the General Staff is responsible for operational-strategic level planning. Russia has a fairly nuanced view of the differences between the tactical, operational, and strategic levels of military science. It believes that the difference between these levels is based upon the scope of mission, not simply the size of the unit. For example, a brigade fighting under an Army Group would be considered a tactical asset, but the same brigade fighting independently in a different situation could be considered a tactical-operational asset. Generally speaking, the General Staff's operational planning duties typically involve echelons above brigade level, or, in Russian parlance, "operational art."

Proponency for strategic planning resides with the Russian Security Council, which is an inter-ministerial body that is chaired by high-level officials, weighted heavily with the intelligence and security services. Although the Russian Security Council is the chief proponent of Russian strategy, the Chief of the Russian General Staff does sit on council, bridging operational art to the national security strategy. The General Staff does far more than just plan operations. It also has responsibility for the use of "foresight" to develop the theory and practice of future war.[23] In Russian military thought foresight is directly linked to military science, with military science being the science of future war.[24] The General Staff's responsibility to predict the nature of future war makes it the logical place (in the Soviet/Russian system) for doctrine and capability development for the entire Ministry of Defense.

Just as important as what the General Staff does is what the General Staff does not do. It does not have operational control of the force. Although there were Goldwater-Nichols-like reforms that removed operational control from the branch chiefs (Ground Forces, Air Force, etc.) and placed the operational control of most forces with regional commands, little has changed with the General Staff's role as operational planners and capability and doctrine developers since Soviet times. Probably the biggest change in the last several years has been downsizing to better align the size of the staff to the size of the military that it plans for, and the removal of some finance responsibilities, due to a few high profile corruption gaffes.[25] The Chief of the General Staff does have day-to-day control of the Main Intelligence Directorate (GRU), a directorate of the General Staff, which, in turn, controls the GRU Spetsnaz Brigades and several strategic assets, including the Russian Airborne, which functions as a strategic reserve. In combat however, these war-fighting assets would be operationally controlled by the appropriate field commander, not by the Chief of the General Staff.

The General Staff Personnel System: How Russia Does "Joint"
The Russian General Staff system is based upon the Prussian-style general staff system, and so has retained its personnel system. Unlike the U.S. military, officers do not rotate through "joint" assignments. In the Russian system, "joint" matters, such as operational-strategic level planning and capabilities and doctrine development, are handled exclusively by General Staff personnel. Officers who serve in the prestigious General Staff are usually selected at

General Staff.

[23] *Military Encyclopedia*, Moscow: *Voyenizdat*, 1983, 585.

[24] Dr. Jacob Kipp, *The Methodology of Foresight and Forecasting in Soviet Military Affairs*, Soviet Army Studies Office, 1988, <www.dtic.mil/dtic/tr/fulltext/u2/a196677.pdf>, accessed 30 October 2015.

[25] Charles K. Bartles, "Defense Reforms of Russian Defense Minister Anatolii Serdyukov," *Journal of Slavic Military Studies* 24, no. 1 (2011).

the major/lieutenant colonel level (late twenties/early thirties). They permanently replace their branch insignia with general staff insignia and become General Staff personnel. Since matters of military doctrine and procurement are decided by the General Staff, it is considered essential that officers break their fixation with their branch of service (Ground Forces, Navy, Air Force, etc.) and branch of arms (infantry, armor, artillery, etc.) in order to avoid the "trade union mentality" that hinders military doctrine and procurement matters in Western armies.[26] Once selected for the General Staff, a Ground Forces officer will usually spend the remainder of his career doing staff work at the Army Group, Military District, and General Staff Headquarters in Moscow. (Officers in other branches of service will have slightly different assignments.) These officers are subject matter experts about the branches of service and specialties in which they have previously served, and will be closely associated with these specialties, as planners, for the remainder of their careers (i.e., a signal officer in the General Staff, will typically always work signal issues). High level positions of leadership within the General Staff (for example, Chief of the Main Operations Directorate) are exclusively held by officers from maneuver (tank, motorized rifle, artillery, missile) branches, but specialty directorates, such as topography and electronic warfare will be led by an officer of the appropriate specialty.[27]

This system develops a caste of professional planners for handling operational-strategic matters, while freeing the remainder of the Russian Armed Forces officer corps to continue to specialize in their particular branch of service and arms at the tactical level. An obvious implication of this personnel system is that there are different career paths for officer advancement. Although selection for the General Staff is prestigious, it is not the desired path for all officers. Maneuver officers who enjoy command may best serve by not pursuing assignment to the General Staff. On this path officers get a chance to hone their tactical skills, since there is no necessity for service in joint or out-of-branch assignments. However, there still are educational requirements, such as attendance in a combined arms academy. Promotions typically happen much faster in the Russian military than in the U.S. (it is not uncommon to see a 32-year-old battalion commander), and command tours have been known to last up to six years. In this system, a brigade commander (on the tactical path) would have more years of command experience than his U.S. counterpart due to the ability to specialize in tactical leadership.[28]

Although the Chief of the General Staff is in charge of the General Staff, he does not necessarily need to be brought up through the general staff career path. Whatever career path an officer is on, if he reaches the highest ranks in the Russian military, invariably he will have several assignments in the General Staff. An interesting example of how career

[26] Although this system does alleviate many resource allocation problems within the Ministry of Defense, there are still significant battles for economic resources that the Ministry of Defense must contend with. Due to its Soviet heritage, Russia has powerful militarized intelligence and security services (FSB, Border Troops, MVD-VV, etc.) that directly compete with the Ministry of Defense for resources. This resource competition is especially acute now, because Russia no longer believes that the primary threat to its sovereignty stems from overt military invasion, but instead from social movements in the flavor of the "color revolutions," the Arab Spring, and the Maidan movement. This perception of threat could increasingly divert certain funds away from the Ministry of Defense to militarized security forces with more of a dedicated internal security mission.
[27] Donnelly, 139-145.
[28] Dr. Lester Grau and Charles K. Bartles, "Tactical Combined Arms Leadership in the Russian Army: Operational Flexibility Through Tactical Rigidity," publication forthcoming.

General Gerasimov

1977-1984	Commander of a Platoon, Company, and Battalion
1984-1987	Student at the Malinovskiy Armor Academy
1987-1993	Chief Of Staff of a Regiment, Division
1993-1995	Commander of a Division
1995-1997	Student, Voroshilov General Staff Academy
1997-2001	First Deputy Commander of the Moscow Military District
2001-2003	Deputy Commander, Chief of Staff, Army Group Commander
2003-2005	Chief of Staff of the Far East Military District
2005-2006	Chief of the Main Operations Directorate of the General Staff
2006-2009	Commander of the Leningrad Military District
2009-2010	Commander of the Moscow Military District.
2010-2012	Deputy Chief of the General Staff.
2012-2012	Commander of the Central Military District
2012-Present	Chief of the General Staff & Member of the Russian Security Council

General Makarov

1971-1977	Commander of a Platoon, Company, and Battalion
1977-1979	Student at the Frunze Academy
1979-1980	Deputy Commander of a Regiment
1980-1981	Commander of a Regiment
1981-1991	Deputy Commander of a Division, Commander of Two Divisions
1991-1993	Student, Voroshilov General Staff Academy (graduated with Gold Medal)
1993-1993	Chief of Staff of the Russian Peacekeeping Forces in Tajikistan
1993-1996	Deputy Commander of an Army Group
1996-1998	Commander of an Army Group (2nd Tank Army)
1998-1999	Deputy Commander (for Coastal Defense) of the Baltic Fleet
1999-2002	Chief of Staff, Deputy Commander, of the Moscow Military District
2002-2007	Commander of the Siberian Military District
2007-2008	Armaments Directorate Chief of the General Staff
2008-2012	Chief of the General Staff & Member of the Russian Security Council
2013-Present	Inspector General of the Ministry of Defense

General Baluyevsky

1970-1972	Commander of a Platoon, Company
1972-1974	Operations Officer on an Army Group Staff
1974-1976	A Senior Operations Officer on an Army Group Staff
1977-1980	Student at the Frunze Academy
1980-1982	A Senior Officer in the Operations Directorate of a Military District
1982-1988	A Senior Officer, then Chief of the Operations Branch of the Main Operations Directorate of the General Staff
1988-1990	Student, Voroshilov General Staff Academy (graduated with Gold Medal)
1990-1991	Special Assistant to Deputy Defense Minister Colonel-General Achalov
1992-1993	Deputy Chief of the Operations Department of the Main Operations Directorate of the General Staff
1992-1993	Chief of the Operations Department of the Main Operations Directorate of the General Staff
1993-1995	Deputy Commander of Russian Ground Forces in the Transcaucasia
1995-1997	Deputy Chief of the Main Operations Directorate of the General Staff
1997-2001	First Deputy Chief of the General Staff of the Russian Armed Forces & Chief of the Main Operations Directorate of the General Staff
1997-2004	First Deputy Chief of the General Staff of the Russian Armed Forces
2004-2008	Chief of the General Staff & Member of the Russian Security Council
2005-2006	Chief of the Joint Staff of the Collective Security Treaty Organization
2008-2012	Deputy Secretary of the Russian Security Council
2012-present	Retirement

Images Courtesy:
Russian Ministry of Defense

13

progression can occur in the Russian Armed Forces is to look at the last three Chiefs of the General Staff, noting the differences in assignments between General Gerasimov (command path) and General Makarov (command path) in contrast to General Baluyevsky (General Staff path). These officers all reached the apex of a Russian military career, by becoming the Chief of the General Staff. Although there are two different ways of achieving this end, neither path is considered better or worse, just different.

General Staff Academy, Moscow Russia
Image Courtesy: Russian Ministry of Defense

Regardless of career path, the selection process for the absolute highest levels of the Russian officer corps is very much predicated upon the officer's performance at the General Staff Academy. The top graduates receive the coveted "Gold Medal," and, although not a prerequisite, the top military positions are often held by former Gold Medal winners from the Voroshilov General Staff Academy. Any mention of General Gerasimov being a Gold Medal winner is conspicuously absent from his posted biographical information, and in this aspect General Gerasimov differs from many of his predecessors; however, his combat experience and success at a volatile time in the North Caucuses apparently have made up for any academic slights.[29]

The role of the General Staff in the Russian system is far more important than the role of the Joint Chiefs of Staff in the U.S. system. The General Staff is much more than a general's personal staff; they are an elite caste of operational-strategic planners who also guide doctrine and capability development, freeing the remainder of the Russian Armed Forces officer corps to continue to specialize in their particular branch of service and arms at the tactical level. The General Staff system allows officers to specialize as operational or tactical planners. Unlike Western officers, General Staff officers are not required to divide their time between both of these challenging endeavors. Selection for service in the General Staff is considered prestigious, and means that an officer is one of the best in his field; there is no stigma associated with "staff work" in the Russian system. This is best exemplified by the fact that the most coveted position in the Russian Armed Forces is not a senior command, but instead becoming Russia's senior operation-tactical planner, the Chief of the General Staff.

The Reserve System
The Russian Federation Ministry of Defense has been tinkering with wide-scale reforms of the military reserve system for several years. The current reserve system was inherited from the Soviet Union, and was designed for supporting a doctrine that required maintaining a large strategic reserve of troops that could be mobilized in the event of large-scale warfare. It was composed of conscripts and officers who had completed their mandatory service obligation and had been discharged from active service, with rare and infrequent call-ups to

[29] Insights from author's conversation with noted Russian military scholar Dr. Jacob Kipp on 30 October 2015.

test mobilization capabilities. Another consequence of the Soviet Union's mass mobilization doctrine was the necessity to maintain units and equipment for these mobilized reservists. These units were/are manned by small full-time cadres that would keep the equipment serviceable and maintain enough institutional knowledge to bring the mobilized reserve up to some level of combat readiness before deployment. Many of these "cadre units" were disbanded after the 2009 "New Look" reforms, as there was a belief that resources were being wasted on maintaining a mass mobilization capability to the detriment of bringing active units up to full levels of operational readiness.[30]

Lieutenant General Vasily Tonkoshkurov, Chief of the Mobilization Directorate
Image Courtesy: Russian Ministry of Defense

There has been some debate about whether Russia needs to maintain a large strategic reserve or should switch to more of an operational reserve. Opinions vary between two major camps, the reformers saying that an operational reserve would do far more to enhance security because an operational reserve would be smaller, better trained, more able to quickly become combat ready in a national emergency, and more likely to called in an emergency, while older retired senior officers believe that the capability to mass mobilize should be maintained at all costs. The first talk of an operational reserve was in 2009, when the Defense Ministry announced that 60,000 junior officers were to be dismissed from active service, but would be afforded the opportunity to contract into a reserve status that would pay on average 20,600 rubles ($870) per month. The idea of establishing an operational reserve has apparently gained some traction, based upon pronouncements by General Gerasimov. Reserve reforms may be one of the few instances in the highly controversial arena of Russian military reform, where both conservatives and reformers get what they want. Russia appears to be driving full ahead with a reserve system that maintains the large strategic reserve for potential mass mobilization, while developing a better operational reserve that can be called upon more frequently.[31]

[30] Charles K. Bartles, "Defense Reforms of Russian Defense Minister Anatolii Serdyukov," *Journal of Slavic Military Studies*, 24, no. 1 (2011): 55–80.
Yuriy Gavrilov, "The General Staff Has Been Authorized To Report: Russia Is Creating Special Operations Forces," *Rossiyskaya Gazeta* Online, 7 March 2013, <http://rg.ru/2013/03/06/sily-site.html>, accessed 1 May 2016.
[31] Charles K. Bartles, "Russian MoD Wants U.S. Style Reserve System?" *OE Watch* Online, April 2013.
"Reserve to Be Formed of Officers to be Dismissed from Service," *Interfax-AVN*, 21 January 2009.
"Laid-Off officers Will Be Put on Defense Ministry's Staff Reserve," *Interfax*, 22 October 2008.
V.A. Ordinsky, "A New System to Train and Accumulate Trained Reservists and Their Service in the Reserves," *Military Thought* 4 (2008), pp. 78–82
"Mobilization Vacuum: Military Reform Does not Guarantee the Training of a Highly Skilled Reserve for the Russian Army," *Nezavisimaya Gazeta* Online, 2 June 2010, <http://www.ng.ru/editorial/2010-06-02/2_red.html>, accessed 1 May 2016.

Interestingly, the Russian Federation appears to be experimenting with two different models for an operational reserve. The first looks very similar to the US reserve system, consisting of an active reserve component and inactive reserve component (Individual Ready Reserve), with the Russian operational reserve conducting two-week annual training requirements, receiving monthly stipends, and being completely voluntary. The intent is to maintain a cadre of officers and enlisted soldiers who regularly train with particular active units; in the event of their unit's mobilization, the reservist would be called to duty to provide support or backfill as needed. In the Vostok-2014 military exercise, Russia experimented with a new way to use an operational reserve by way of new stand-alone units called territorial-defense battalions (BTO).[32] Territorial defense units have appeared elsewhere in Eastern Europe and usually consist of relatively lightly armed infantry who are assigned to secure critical infrastructure in the rear. These forces are not intended to serve in high-intensity combat operations abroad. The intent of this form of an operational reserve is to unburden the active duty force of these duties, allowing the latter greater freedom of movement to conduct combat operations.[33] Although, Russia is still experimenting with reserve force employment options, it appears to be gravitating toward the territorial-defense unit model.

Pay in the Russian Army

The Russian Federation has a complex system for paying its officers and contract NCOs, which requires some description. The biggest difference between the U.S. and Russian systems of military pay is the concept of base salary and entitlements. In the U.S., monetary entitlements (including housing allowances) are almost always a percentage of the base salary; in Russia the base salary is merely the starting point for calculating entitlements. A few entitlements are allotted by a fixed ruble amount, but the majority are calculated by indexing the base salary by a given percentage. The total sum of these additional entitlements is always many times greater than the soldier's base salary.

The two most important criteria for pay are the serviceman's rank and position held (servicemen receive both salaries). Rank-based salaries are based on equivalent responsibility/skill levels of federal government employees, while the position salary is based upon the soldier's current duty assignment, which must be on a valid TO&E. Positional salaries are typically higher than rank-based salaries, and are set by the Ministry of Defense. (In this system, a lieutenant colonel serving as a battalion commander is paid more than a lieutenant colonel serving in a brigade staff.) Both rank and positional salary tables are pinned to the Russian Federation civilian pay scales and receive equivalent indexes for inflation. Interestingly, officers are legally considered a type of contract serviceman. Their pay and

---

[32] Charles K. Bartles, "Russia Experiments with Two-Tier Operational Reserve System," *OE Watch* Online, December 2014.
Aleksey Ramm, "It Is Time to Return the Reserve to the Formation," *Voyenno-Promyshlennyy Kuryer* Online, 8 October 2014, <http://vpk-news.ru/articles/22165>, accessed 1 May 2016.
[33] Charles K. Bartles, "Reserve Capability Development is High Priority for the General Staff," *OE Watch* Online, December 2015.
Lieutenant General Vasily Tonkoshkurov, "Important Priority for the General Staff: Is the Current Personnel System Adequate for Modern Requirements?" *Voyenno-Promyshlennyy Kuryer* Online, 21 October 2015, <http://vpk-news.ru/articles/27609>, accessed 1 May 2016.

On the March

Image Courtesy: Russian Ministry of Defense

benefits are governed by the same laws, rules, and regulations as their enlisted, non-conscript subordinates, who also serve under contract. Officers and enlisted soldiers serving on contract sign similar contracts for set periods. Although Russian officers and contract soldiers are in the same legal category, there is a sharp distinction between enlisted soldiers serving on contract and officers in the Russian Army; Russian officers are never referred to as "contract officers."

In addition to the base salary officers are paid several additional special pays, which are covered under Article 13 of the Federal Law "On the Status of Serviceman." Most special pays are based on the serviceman's base salary (rank or position). The income a serviceman receives from special pays is often many times greater than the soldier base salary. Article 13 of the Federal Law "On the Status of Serviceman" stipulates that officers receive monthly allowances for the following: length of service, location, hardship and special circumstances duty, exemplary service, and physical fitness, in addition to a supplemental subsistence allowance. There are also several one-time, lump sum payments, and meal and clothing allowances.

The most contentious issue regarding serviceman pay in the Russian military has been housing. In Soviet times, benefits of military service included higher salaries and greater access to fringe benefits, such as free vacation resorts, premium medical facilities, and more educational opportunities for children, but the biggest benefit was access to housing. Housing in the Soviet era was state controlled and difficult to obtain. Military service guaranteed access to state-provided housing while serving and during retirement. In today's Russia, this arrangement is still maintained, and has stymied some military reform efforts (such as downsizing) due to the legal requirement that officers must be provided housing (usually in the form of an apartment) before retirement. In past years housing has been in such short supply that some officers have been kept on active duty years past their planned retirement dates before housing could be provided. The Russian Federation has made great efforts to right this issue, including the development of a military-subsidized home mortgage program. This issue has been largely resolved, but occasionally embarrassing incidents still come to light. In general, Russia's economic situation has greatly improved since the early years of the Russian Federation, and the currency of stories of destitute Russian serviceman have long passed. Russian military salaries, to include the intelligence and security services, are now dependable and somewhat competitive with the civilian sector. Although the accompanying graphic is intended to display information just for enlisted MoD soldier's serving on contract, many of the pays and allowances are equally applicable to officers and other military personnel serving in other branches of government (MVD-VV, FSB, Border Troops, etc.).[34] Conscripts are paid a small fraction of what contract NCOs and officers earn, but are provided free meals and housing. In 2012, it was reported that most conscripts earned $30-50 a month, but in conjunction with special duty pays, some conscripts could earn up to $200 per month.[35]

Ethics in the Russian Armed Forces

Stomping out military corruption has been a top priority of the Russian civilian and military leadership for quite some time. Due to the Russian Federation's Tsarist/Soviet past, Russia, and by inheritance the Russian military, has developed a nuanced view towards corruption, which makes its eradication difficult. Crimes of theft against individuals are viewed the same as in the West, but crimes of theft against the state are seen as much more tolerable. Although they are seen as somewhat tolerable, they are still embarrassing The most recent high profile military corruption fiasco has involved the recent conviction and sentencing of Colonel General Vladimir Chirkin, the former Ground Troops Commander-in-Chief. Although there have been other high profile gaffes, such as Airborne Troops Commander-in-Chief Colonel General Shamanov dispatching an airborne unit to interfere in the prosecutorial investigation of a family member, the Chirkin case has garnered substantial interest, as it is unusual for such a high-ranking and prominent official to be tried, convicted, and sentenced. One of the most interesting aspects of the case is the involvement of the Chief of the Russian General Staff, General Valeri Gerasimov. General Gerasimov is an adamant supporter of General Chirkin and asked that Chirkin either be found not guilty or, if found guilty, that he

[34] Charles K. Bartles, "Pay in the Russian Military," *OE Watch* Online, November 2015.
"Military Financial Literacy," *Voyenno-Promyshlennyy Kuryer* Online, 23 September 2015, <http://www.vpk-news.ru/articles/27161>, accessed 1 May 2015.
[35] Dmitry Gorenburg, "New Pay Structure for Conscripts Announced," Blog post on Russian Military Reform, January 6, 2012, <https://russiamil.wordpress.com/2012/01/06/new-pay-structure-for-conscripts-announced/>, accessed 1 May 2016.

be given no prison time. In the Russian system, personal connections and loyalties often trump institutional governance, and this appears to be such a case. It is important to note that these views towards "relaxed morals" are not reserved solely for senior leaders, as the Russian military justice system is now being amended to allow some crimes that once required dismissal from service to now allow lesser punishments. There appears to be concern that the previous regulation was weeding out too many good officers who had a few peccadilloes. In the Russian view, it is far better to have an army with the best and brightest, albeit ethically challenged, than an army of the ethical, but less capable. Undoubtedly, as Russia continues

Colonel General Vladimir Chirkin
Former Ground Forces Commander-in-Chief
Image Courtesy: Russian Ministry of Defense

experimenting with undeclared wars and indirect and asymmetric methods, there is a need for officers who can operate in the grey area that results when what needs to be done conflicts with the letter of the law.

Perhaps the reason that the Russian military is having difficulty dealing with corruption is the view that Russia, and most Russians, have regarding the relationship between what is legally and morally right. These two concepts are very different in the West, but in Russia, whatever is considered "morally right" is usually interpreted to be "legally right." This can be seen in state asset seizures of wealthy oligarchs' property, the annexation of the Crimea, and in the conduct of an undeclared war Eastern Ukraine (in order to destabilize the Ukrainian government, a government which Russia perceives to be illegitimate and installed by the U.S.). This tendency to interpret morally right as legally right make the Russian Armed Forces, intelligence, and security services well suited to operating in the ambiguous "Grey Zone" that many operations are conducted and will occur. However, this way of thinking is certainly making the eradication of corruption difficult, as subordinates see their superiors growing wealthy from graft, and decide that it is only right to take a little for one's self. [36]

Rank Structure of the Russian Armed Forces

Some Soviet and even Tsarist uniform insignia are now being reintroduced into the Russian Armed Forces. In 2013, the Russian uniform regulations were amended so that a Russian four-star equivalent flag officer would wear one large star, instead of four smaller stars. In

[36] Charles K. Bartles, "Ethics, Military Corruption, and the Grey Zone," *OE Watch* Online, July 2016.
Charles K. Bartles, "A Russian (Pragmatic) View of Army Ethics," *OE Watch* Online, October 2015.
Sergey Shishkin, "Generals' Advocacy," *Kommersant* Online, 3 September 2015, <http://kommersant.ru/doc/2802382>, accessed 1 May 2016.
Velimir Razuvayev, "Punishment Will Be Lessened for Corrupt Army Officers," *Nezavisimaya Gazeta* Online, 10 August 2015, http://www.ng.ru/politics/2015-08-10/1_corruption.html>, accessed 1 May 2016.

Conscript and Contract Serviceman Ranks

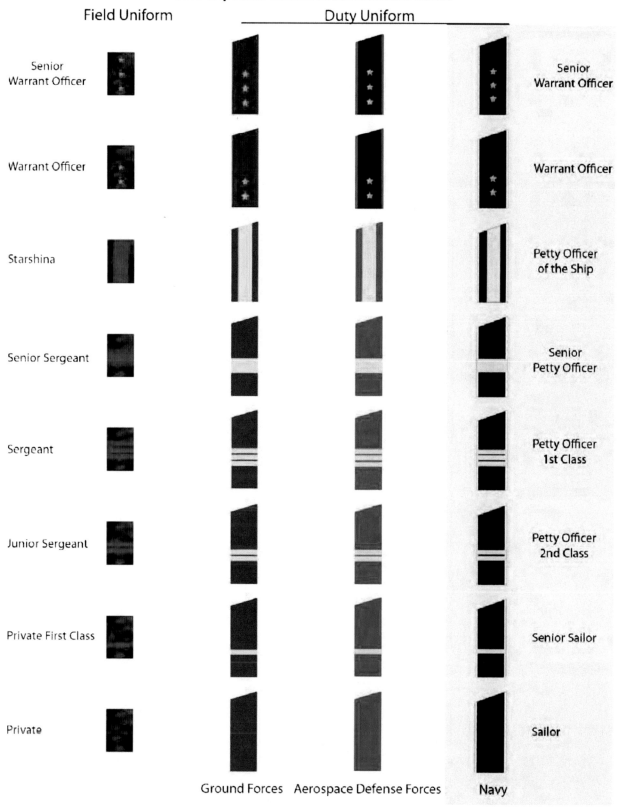

Field Uniform	Duty Uniform			
Senior Warrant Officer				Senior Warrant Officer
Warrant Officer				Warrant Officer
Starshina				Petty Officer of the Ship
Senior Sergeant				Senior Petty Officer
Sergeant				Petty Officer 1st Class
Junior Sergeant				Petty Officer 2nd Class
Private First Class				Senior Sailor
Private				Sailor
	Ground Forces	Aerospace Defense Forces	Navy	

Officer Ranks

Field Uniform	Duty Uniform			

	Field Uniform	Ground Forces	Aerospace Defense Forces	Navy	
Marshal of the Russian Federation					
General of the Army					Admiral of the Navy
Colonel General					Fleet Admiral
Lieutenant General					Vice Admiral
Major General					Rear Admiral
Colonel					Captain 1st Class
Lieutenant Colonel					Captain 2nd Class
Major					Captain 3rd Class
Captain					Captain-Lieutenant
Senior Lieutenant					Senior Lieutenant
Lieutenant					Lieutenant
Junior Lieutenant					Junior Lieutenant

Ground Forces   Aerospace Defense Forces   Navy

late 2016, the Russian Federation announced Russian officers occupying command positions would wear new badges to signify their positions. The new badge has unofficially been dubbed "wings" on account of its appearance, and is reportedly based on traditions from the Tsarist Army. These new badges are worn by commanders-in-chief of branches of the Armed Forces, commanders of military districts and branches of troops, and commanders of divisions, brigades, regiments, and separate battalions. The new symbols also appear on the uniforms of chiefs of military educational institutions and secondary educational institutions (Suvorov and Nakhimov military schools), that are administered by the military authorities. The new badge consists of the Russian tricolor with centrally placed badges of Armed Forces services (Ground Troops, Aerospace Troops, and Navy) or branches of troops (artillery, railroad, engineering, tank troops, etc.) and symbols of military units, military combined formations, and military educational institutions.[37]

Field Training
Image Courtesy: Russian Ministry of Defense

Women in the Military

General Tatyana Shevtsova
Deputy Defense Minister (Finance)
Image Courtesy: Russian MoD

The Russian Federation has a long tradition of women in uniform.[38] Women served in the Soviet military in many capacities in the Second World War. In addition to agricultural and industrial work, women served in noncombat positions such as uniformed secretaries, translators, nurses, and block wardens. Although rare, the Soviet Union was the only belligerent that utilized women in combat roles. Soviet women served as air defenders, in the infantry, and as snipers. There were also three women's air force regiments including the famous 46th "Taman" Guards Night Bomber Aviation Regiment (known as the "Nachthexen" or night witches by the Germans). In the modern Russian military, women still regularly serve, but not in combat arms roles. As previously mentioned, it is not uncommon to see the wives of contract NCOs and officers enlist as contract NCOs. These spouses often serve as uniformed cooks, admin support, and radio/telephone operators (in garrison). But women may also serve in their own right, and are often encountered as medical and communications fields, in officer and contract NCO capacities. Women do not serve in combat arms branches,

[37] Aleksey Ramm, "Officers Will Be Denoted by Wings, *Izvestiya* Online, 6 December 2016, <http://izvestia.ru/news/649705>, accessed 16 December 2016.

[38] One of the most famous was Nedezhda Durova, who disguised herself as a man and served as a Russian officer for nine years in the Mariupol Hussars. She fought in the 1807 and 1812-1814 Wars against Napoleon. Alexsander Pushkin, the famous Russian poet, disclosed her story to Russia. Her book, "The Cavalry Maiden" is well known in Russia and Indiana University Press has published an excellent translation of it.

but this does mean they only serve out of harm's way. Women serve in Russia's militarized intelligence services, and there have been reports of women fighting in various capacities on both sides of the conflict in Eastern Ukraine. Although the U.S. and Russia both utilize women in their Armed Forces, U.S. observers will notice significant systemic differences. It is important to keep in mind that Russian servicewomen serve in the Russian military in the context of a broader Russian culture. It is common for Russian women to wear high-heals and other ornamentation in field uniforms, something that would be

Contract NCOs Conducting Field Training
Image Courtesy: Russian Ministry of Defense

unacceptable in the U.S. for many reasons. They are generally treated as women first, and soldiers second. This is in stark contrast to the U.S. system, but it appears to be acceptable by all parties in Russia. Red Star [*Красная Звезда*], the daily Russian military newspaper, runs a weekly picture and short biography of "Miss Red Star," an attractive young female who is serving the Armed Services in uniform or as a civilian. Sexual harassment, in a Russian context, is apparently not an issue in the Russian Armed Forces. And although it almost certainly happens, it likely happens at no greater level than encountered in Russian civil society. In short, there are obvious differences in the way women serve in the U.S. and Russia, but Russian servicewoman are treated as professionals and serve in the Russian military in a way acceptable to the military, women, and Russian society as a whole.

Conclusion

The Russian Federation inherited a conscript system and an officer-heavy military. This system has been converted into a hybrid system of enlisted manning with conscripts and professional NCOs. Although Russia likely could not convert to a full professionally manned army for economic reasons, the Russian higher leadership seems to have little interest in achieving such an end state. While Russian conscripts serve only one year, due to a different civilian education system and the state DOSAAF program, new enlistees do not necessarily enter the military without militarily useful skills as their American counterparts. The Russian Federation still desires to maintain some large-scale mass mobilization capability that a mass conscription system supports well. In terms of the role of its officers and professional enlisted soldiers, Russia has decided to pursue a much different model of enlisted professionalization than the one practiced in the West. Except in regard to small unit leadership, leadership is the sole purview of the officer corps. At a time when the U.S. is broadening the education and experience of its NCO Corps, the Russian Federation is creating enlisted professionals who are experts in their fields, but little else. Russia does not desire to create enlisted leaders, it wants enlisted technical specialists. Russian professional enlisted soldiers' assignments invariably involve learning, practicing, or teaching their trade. In this aspect, the Russian professional enlisted soldiers mirror their officers. The Russian system is not designed to produce "jacks-of-all-trades," the Russian system is intended to create experts in a chosen military specialty for the conduct of war.

Chapter 2
Structure and Echelonment

What Kind of Military Action Does Russia Need to Prepare for?

Russia needs to defend itself against internal and external unrest or aggression and prepare to use force In support of its regional and international interests. Internal unrest and aggression may range from soccer riots to armed incursions (Dagestan) to attempted secession from the Federation (the two Chechen Wars) to civil war. External conflict may range from armed conflict (Donbass region of Ukraine) to local war (Soviet-Afghan War) to regional conflict (coalition against ISIS in Syria) to large-scale war (which may involve the territory of the Russian Federation). Additional military actions may involve humanitarian and disaster relief (Chernobyl during Soviet times), peace enforcement (Kosovo or the naval blockade and no-fly zone in Libya) or peace keeping (Golan Heights). To meet all these challenges, the Russians train the bulk of their force primarily to meet the most dangerous challenge/large-scale conventional maneuver war under nuclear-threat conditions, and then train for other contingencies. However, they do not assume that competency in conventional maneuver will transition to all climates and geography. Mountain and arctic combat pose special difficulties, and the Russians commission officers from their five-year mountain combat or arctic combat academies. These lieutenants will spend their careers in Russia's mountain or arctic brigades.

What Constitutes the Russian Military?

Russia's Soviet legacy made stove-piped militarized intelligence and security agencies the norm, as the Soviets were leery of investing all military power in a single organization or ministry, primarily due to fears of a coup. The Russian Federation inherited a system that has militarized intelligence and security services spread throughout its various ministries, services, and agencies. Often military forces that serve in ministries other than the Ministry of Defense (MoD) are labeled in the West as "paramilitary," which implies these troops are somewhat less than military. This assumption would be incorrect, as the conscripts, contract NCOs, and officers who serve in these formations are, for the most part, indistinguishable from MoD forces.[1] These non-MoD forces live in barracks and possess BTRs, BMPs, mortars, artillery, and other weapons appropriate for light or motorized rifle units. In common usage, when Russians speak of serving "in the Army" they may be referring to service in any of these organizations. Historically,

**General Sergey Shoygu,
Minister of Defense**
Image Courtesy: Russian MoD

the vast majority of the Soviet Union, and later Russia's, military forces could be found in the MoD, Ministry of Interior (MVD), and Federal Security Service (FSB-formerly the Committee for State Security or KGB) and their subordinate Border Troops.[2] In general, troops serving in the MVD and Border Troops are more concerned with internal security, while the MoD is oriented towards external threats.

---

[1] The officer academies of Russian military forces are so similar that officers can attend one ministry's academy, but be commissioned as an officer into a different ministry.

[2] In some post-Soviet states, especially where external state actors are less of a concern, these other organizations have significantly more combat power than the Ministry of Defense units.

The Assessed Chain of Command for Combat Operations

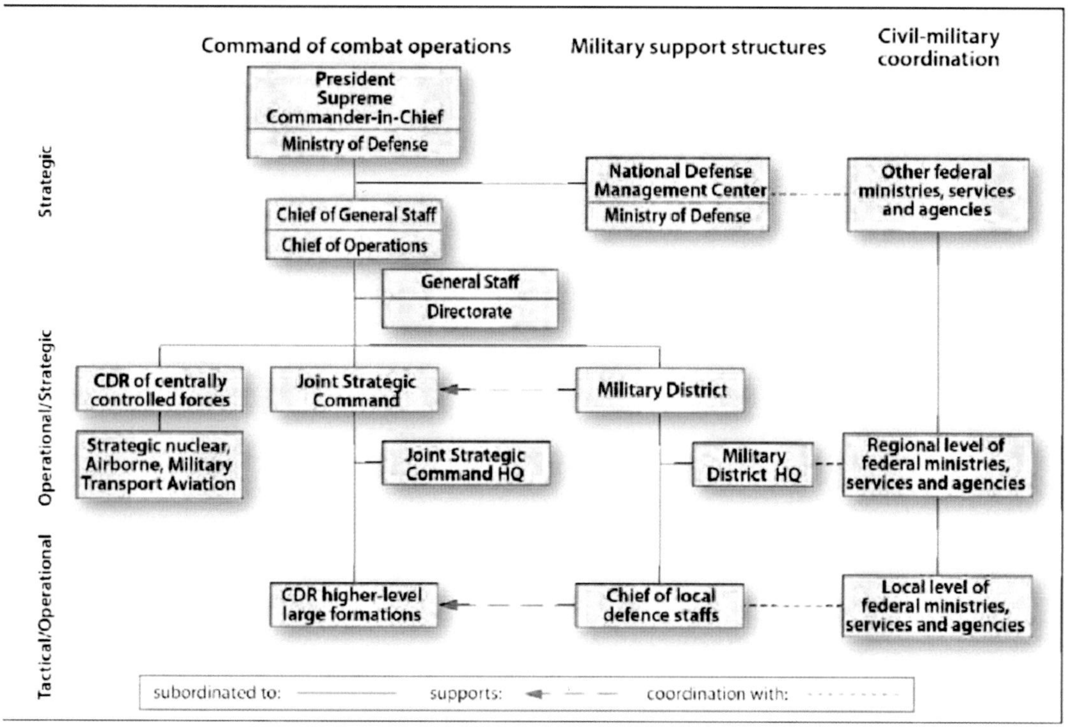

(Above) The above graphic was recreated from "Russian Military Capability in a Ten-Year Perspective – 2016." Of particular note, the graphic does not depict the National Security Council, which consists of various military officers and civilian ministry and agency heads. These members of the National Security Council serve in senior positions at the operational and strategic levels in the boxes shown above.[3]

The Russian Federation recently enacted a major reform of its military forces by establishing a National Guard. This National Guard is in no way similar to the U.S. National Guard, but consists of active duty troops who were already part of Russia's other internally focused security services, reportedly including the Ministry of Internal Affairs-Internal Troops (MVD-VV), Special Rapid-Response Detachment (SOBR), the Special-Purpose Mobile Detachment (OMON), the MVD Prompt-Response and Aviation Forces' Special-Purpose Center, and aviation subunits. Estimates of the total National Guard personnel have varied between 200,000-300,000. For the purposes of clarity, in this book, the term "Armed Forces" will refer specifically to the MoD, while the term "military" will refer to all of Russia's militarized intelligence and security services, including the MoD.[4]

---

[3] "Russian Military Capability in a Ten-Year Perspective – 2016," *Swedish Defence Research Agency,*" 2016, <https://www.foi.se/rapportsammanfattning?reportNo=FOI-R--4326--SE>, accessed 21 December 2016.

[4] Christopher N. Donnelly, *Red Banner: The Soviet Military System in Peace and War*, first edition. (Coulsdon, Surrey: Jane's Information Group, 1988), pp. 47.

Aleksandr Boyko, "Why Russia Needed a National Guard," *Komsomolskaya Pravda* Online, 6 April 2016, <http://www.kp.ru/daily/26510/3382734/>,accessed 15 April 2016.

Charles K. Bartles, "MVD-VV Spetsnaz: The Elite of Russia's Ministry of Interior Troops," *OE Watch* Online, October 2015.

The Assessed Chain of Command for Combat Operations

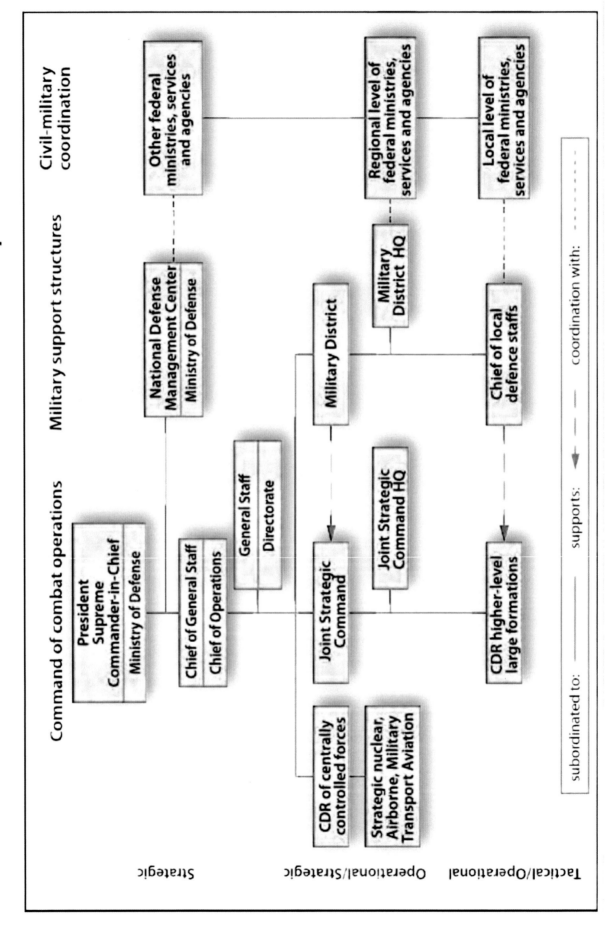

Structure of the Russian Ministry of Defense

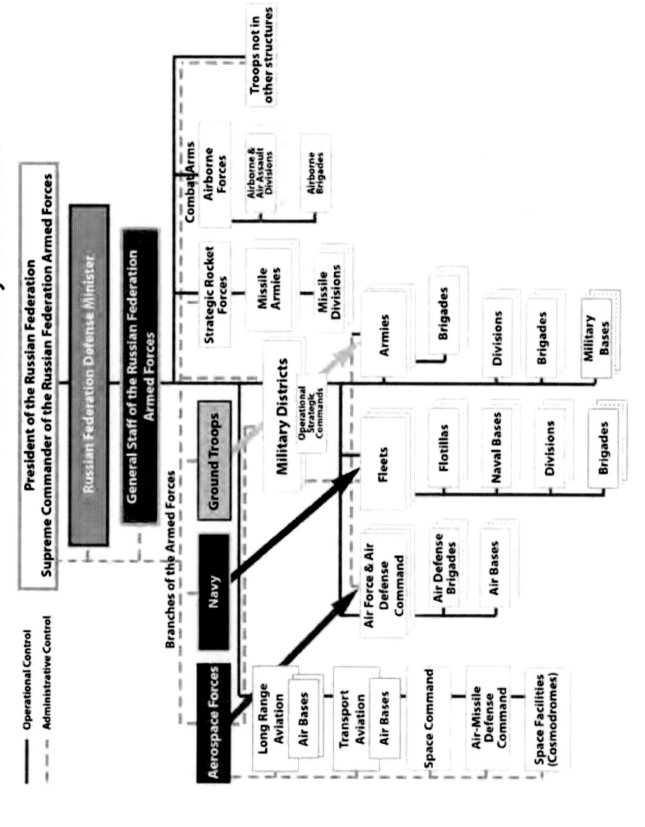

Structure of the Russian Ministry of Defense

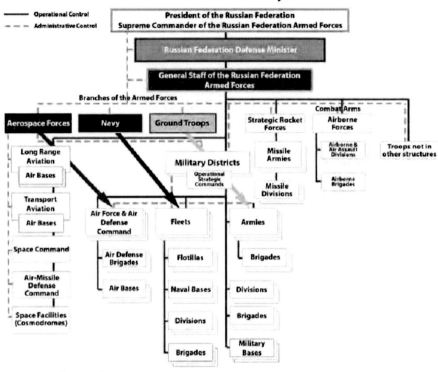

The 2008 "New Look" Reforms

The Russian Federation had great difficulties reforming its Armed Forces after the collapse of the Soviet Union. Russia's civilian leadership's mantra of military reform was modernize, downsize, end conscription, and increase servicemen salaries. Former President Boris Yeltsin made these promises in the early 1990s, with decidedly mixed results. Russia's massive conscript-based army was substantially trimmed down from the Soviet high of 5,000,000 uniformed personnel. Aside from the significant changes that took place immediately after the collapse of the Soviet Union, Russia generally took the "band-aid" approach to military reform by applying superficial fixes instead of serious reforms. The net result of this inaction was that Russia retained a bloated command structure designed for the command and control of literally thousands of divisions, regiments, and battalions. The vast majority of these units were "skeleton units" manned by small cadres who help flesh out the unit with conscripts and reservists in the event of a mass mobilization. In Soviet times, such a system made much sense due to the type of war expected and the economic costs of maintaining large military forces, but in the post-Soviet era such a system seemed unnecessary. Moreover, it hindered the formation of a more modern, and combat-ready force.

Russia's post-Soviet military experiences have occurred on a much smaller scale, which have been ill suited for a mass conscript army. Russia's political leadership appeared to have turned a corner in 2007, when it decided to implement a massive reform of the Russian Armed Forces, which has been described as the greatest reform of the Russian Armed Forces in over one hundred years. This reform was led by a newly appointed Defense Minister, Anatoliy Serdyukov, and is often referred to as the "'New Look" reforms of the Russian Armed Forces.[5]

[5] Charles K. Bartles, "Defense Reforms of Russian Defense Minister Anatolii Serdyukov," *Journal of Slavic Military Studies* 24, no. 1 (2011).

Russian Operational Strategic Commands

Military District System Reform

One of the most high profile "New Look" reforms was that of the Russian military district system. This reform involved not only condensing six military districts into four, but also significantly changed command and control relationships.

In the Soviet system, the military district commander (there were up to 16 military districts in Soviet times) was responsible for garrisoning, training, rear area logistical support, protection of strategically vital areas, and coordination of civil defense. These missions were his primary concern, and fulfilling them involved pre-conscription training, conducting the fall and spring conscription campaigns, operating military state farms, doling out pensions, etc. In wartime, the military district was responsible for conducting mass mobilization, including preparation of units for combat, transportation of units to the front, logistical support, and replenishment. The military district commander was not responsible for operational control of most units in his territory. This responsibility generally lay within the Branches of Arms (Ground Forces, Air Force, Navy, etc.) in peacetime.

Ground Forces Peacetime C2

Before "New Look" Reforms

Ground Forces HQ

Army Group

Division

Regiment

After "New Look" Reforms

Operational Strategic Command

Army Group

Brigade

The 2010 reform gave the military district commander operational control of most military and MoD forces in their respective regions, with the exception of all nuclear and certain

Russian Ground Forces Dispositions

The above graphic annotates approximate locations of Army and Tank Groups, Divisions, and Brigades, where the vast majority of the Ground Forces' 220,000 personnel may be found. Russia is in the midst of a major reorganization of assets in the Western and Southern Operational Strategic Commands (OSKs), so this depiction is speculative at best. The command and control relationship between the Army Groups (Combined Arms Armies and Tank Armies) is not depicted.

strategic assets such as the Strategic Rocket Forces (RVSN), Airborne (VDV), and GRU spetsnaz units. At this time, the military districts were renamed "Operational Strategic Commands" (OSK), although the term "military district" is still used when referring to the organization when it is involved with more mundane rear-services activities. (Due to the periodic mentions of military districts in official pronouncements and the very different missions of the OSKs and military districts, it is possible the military district hierarchies were not completely subsumed by the OSKs. Instead, the military districts still exist, but are collocated at the same headquarters as their respective OSKs and are commanded by one four-star flag level officer who is dual-hatted for both commands.) In 2014, the Russian Federation established the Arctic Operational Strategic Command, based upon the Northern Fleet Headquarters at Severomorsk, due to the size and strategic importance of the Arctic region to Russia. Although the Arctic OSK is considered a Joint Strategic Command, it is apparent that it is not considered as a military district, as are its sister commands (Western, Central, Eastern, Southern), and is essentially "last among equals." In regards to Russian Ground Forces' maneuver brigades, the military districts control most maneuver brigades via Army Groups.[6]

ПУ фронта, рода войск, флота, военного округа, зоны ПВО

КП

Command Post of a Front, Fleet, Branch of Arms (with flag of corresponding branch color), Military District, Air Force Zone, Air Defense Zone, or Air Force and Air Defense Zone

[6] Donnelly, pp. 149–151.
Bartles, "Defense Reforms of Russian Defense Minister Anatolii Serdyukov."
Charles K. Bartles, "Missions and C2 Structure of New Russian 'Northern' Strategic Command Analyzed," *OE Watch*

Proposed Baseline Army Group Structure

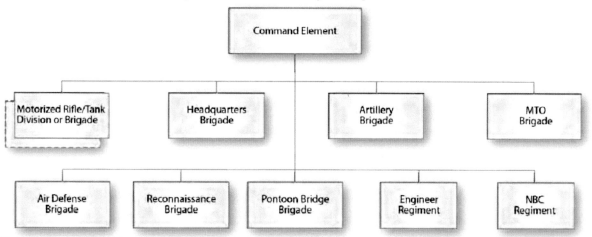

The Role of the Army Group

The intermediate echelon of command between the OSKs and maneuver units is the Army Group (a Combined Arms Army or Tank Army).[7] The Army Group system was developed by the Soviets during the Second World War, when the echelons of corps and armies were merged together. Unlike Russian brigades and divisions, there is no uniform set of capabilities or assets that these Army Groups currently possess; some units do not even have motorized rifle or tank units. This is one area that is undergoing some change, as there appears to be an effort to develop a standard set of capabilities for each Army Group. It is likely that in the future each Army Group will have at least several motorized rifle and tank divisions and brigades; headquarters, artillery, air defense, reconnaissance, and MTO (logistics) brigades; and two regiments, an engineering regiment and a NBC defense regiment. During combat operations the Army Group detaches needed assets to support the various maneuver units. Perhaps the most important assets provided by the Army Group in this endeavor are the MTO brigades, which feed, fuel, supply, and maintain the maneuver brigade(s), and the artillery and/or MLRS artillery brigades, which regularly detach assets to support the formation of the Brigade Artillery Group (BrAG), which will be discussed in depth in the following chapter.[8]

Command Post of a Army, Air Force and Air Defense Army, Flotilla, or Cosmodrome

Command Post of a Corps, Air Defense Corps, Air Force and Air Defense Corps, Squadron, or Naval Base

Online, November 2014.

[7] Russia also has Army Corps which serve a similar function, all Army Corps are currently oriented for coastal defense missions and are assigned to, and collocated with, the naval fleet headquarters. The 22nd Army Corps (Sevastopol/Black Sea Fleet), 11th Army Corps (Kaliningrad/Baltic Sea Fleet), and the 14th Army Corps (Severomorsk/Northern Sea Fleet) provide command and control of mostly Coastal Defense Troop units (Naval Infantry and Coastal Defense Artillery), and also some Ground Forces units.
Aleksey Nikolskiy, "Moscow Moves Staffers Up to the Front Line," *Vedomosti* Online, 12 May 2016, <http://www.vedomosti.ru/politics/articles/2016/05/12/640715-shtabistov-peredovuyu>, accessed 15 June 2016.
[8] "Every Combined Arms Army Will Receive an Engineering Assault Brigade by 2020," *TASS* Online, 2 December 2015, <http://tass.ru/armiya-i-opk/2492454>, accessed 20 June 2016.

Proposed Baseline Army Group Structure

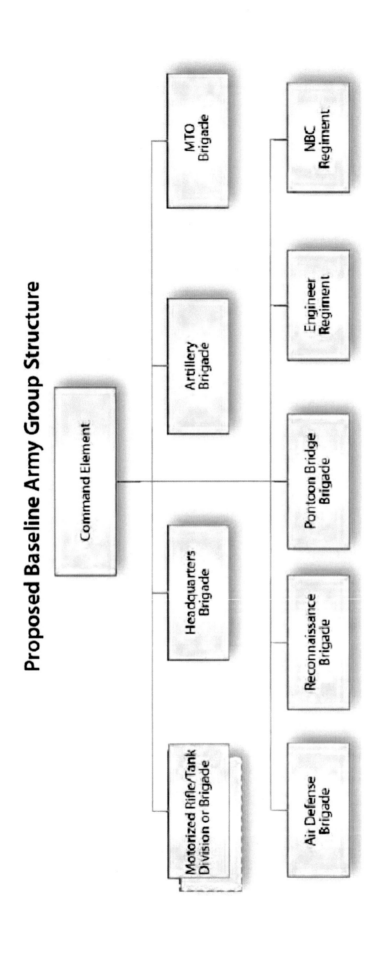

Motorized Rifle Brigade Structure (variant)

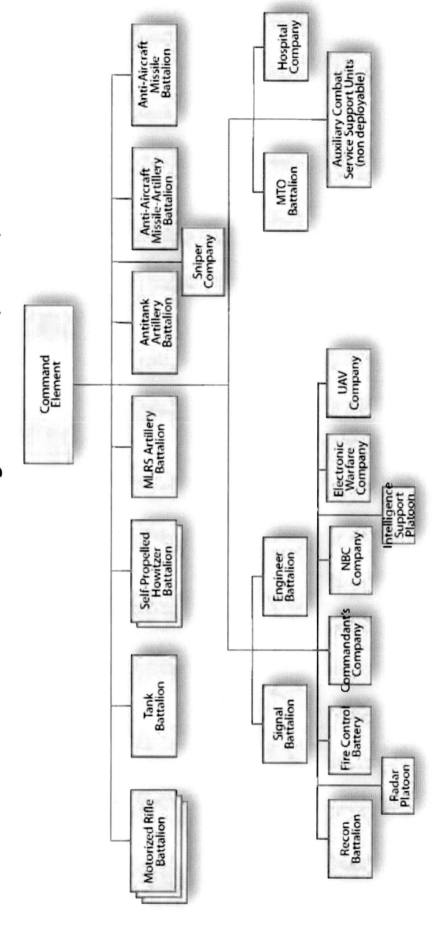

Motorized Rifle Brigade Structure (variant)

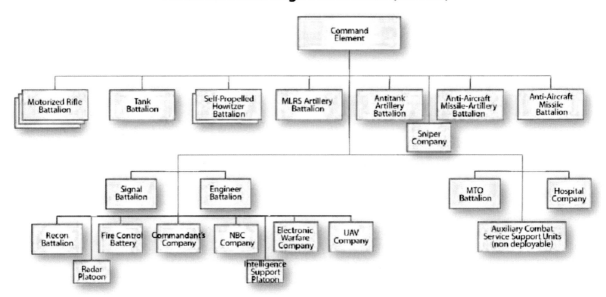

Transition to the Brigade Structure

In terms of brigade-level and below operations, these reforms are significant for several reasons. The first is that they are responsible for consolidating the division/regimental structure into modular maneuver brigades of approximately 3,000-4,500 soldiers, each capable of conducting independent action and providing its own organic support (each brigade is typically also a separate garrison). The transition to the brigade not only reduced a level of management, but was also instrumental in reducing the bloated officer corps. When the Russian Federation converted to the brigade structure, it also designated all units as "permanent readiness units," eliminating all "cadre units" and the positions of the cadre (mostly officers) that manned them. In all, the Russian Armed Forces reputedly downsized from 1,890 to 172 large units.

Command Post of a Brigade, or Fortified Area

In order to understand the impact that this change had on the officer corps, consider that in 2008, the Russian Armed Forces was short some 40,000 officers. By 2010, even after ending the program of conscripting university graduates to serve as officers, the Russian Armed Forces had such an abundance of officers that in some cases lieutenants were placed in NCO positions. The reduction was so extensive that the Russian Federation reduced/consolidated the number of military academies from 65 to 10 to better match officer accession and training needs. In sum, the transition to the brigade structure was the key change needed to downsize a bloated officer corps. The funds freed from this endeavor were put towards the improvement of salaries and the modernization of equipment.[9]

[9] Major-General (retired) Ivan Vorobyev and Colonel Valeriy Kiselev, "Ground Troops Transition to Brigade Structure as a Phase of Improving Their Maneuverability," *Military Thought*, 1-28 February 2010, No. 2, pp 18-24. Igor Ivanov, "Boys with Military Stripes: Where Are the Future Suvorov's and Zhukov's to Be Trained," *Rossiyskaya Gazeta* Online, 1 April 2010, <http://www.rg.ru/2010/04/01/armiya.html>, accessed 1 May 2016. Alexander Golts, "Reform under the 'SECRET' Classification," The New Times Online, 15 December 2008. <http://

Russia has a somewhat sophisticated classification system for determining unit echelon type. There are several caveats and exceptions, but, in general, elements that are incapable of functioning independently over time, such as battalions, companies and below are considered "subunits" [подразделение]. Units that can function independently over time, such as regiments, are considered "units" [часть], while a formation that consist of a collection of units, such as a division, is considered a "soyedineniye" [соединение]. Serdyukov's reforms converted most of the force into independent brigade soyedineniye. The regimental/division structure is still common in the Russian Airborne (VDV), and there are still a few of the Ground Forces divisions, but the vast majority of Russian combat power is now found in independent brigades. Although brigades and divisions coexist, brigades are not subordinated to divisions (unlike the U.S. system), each is considered a soyedineniye. Major military formations such as Corps, Army Groups, Fronts and Strategic High Commands (military districts) are considered "ob'yedineniye"

Approximate Unit Manpower

Unit Type	Personnel
Motorized Rifle Division	8,500
Motorized Rifle Brigade	3,000-4,500
Separate Motorized Rifle Regiment	2,000
Battalion Tactical Group	700-900
Tank Division	6,500
Tank Brigade	3,000
(Iskander) Rocket Brigade	500
Artillery Brigade	1,000
MLRS Brigade	500
Air Assault Division	5,500
Airborne Division	5,500
Naval Infantry Brigade	2,500
GRU Spetsnaz Brigade	1,500
MTO Brigade	2,000

[объединение].[10] In terms of logistics, the difficulties of deploying and supporting a brigade is an order of magnitude easier than that of a division. Russia now has a much easier time projecting combat power by using smaller soyedineniye. This is in large part due to the fact that the Russian Ground Forces (and lesser extent VDV and Naval Infantry) makes extensive use of rail transport, smaller soyedineniye, are easier to deploy and sustain with Russia's rail infrastructure. This discipline is regularly practiced. It is not uncommon for Russian brigades and their equipment to be transported (by ship or rail) thousands of kilometers for training events.[11]

lenta2012.ru/pulsblog/9705_reforma-pod-grifom-sekretno.aspx>, accessed 1 May 2016.
Marina Yeliseyeva, 'On the Level of Training in the New Century,' Krasnaya Zvezda Online, 2 April 2010, <http://old.redstar.ru/2010/04/02_04/2_05.html>, accessed 1 May 2016.
[10] ob'yedineniye [объединение] and soyedineniye [соединение] are often translated as "unit" or "formation," which is technically correct, but loses some meaning in translation.
[11] Aleksey Ramm, "The Ukraine Test: New Image of Armed Forces Spoiled by Field Kitchens," Voyenno-Promyshlennyy Kuryer Online, 29 April 2015, <http://vpk-news.ru/articles/25027>, accessed 1 May 2016.
Andrei Santarovich, "Second Ukrainian Front: Why Putin Is Redeploying Troops to Belarus," Apostrof Online, 24 November 2016, <http://apostrophe.ua/article/world/ex-ussr/2016-11-24/vtoroy-ukrainskiy-front-zachem-putin-perebrasyivaet-voyska-v-belarus/8492>, accessed 22 December 2016.

Reintroduction of the Division?

Although Russia transitioned to a brigade structure in 2009/2010, a few divisions remained in the Ground Forces, but they were definitely the exception and not the rule. Now the Russian Federation is reintroducing the division into its organizational structure in a few key locations, notably on Russia's Western border with Ukraine and NATO (reportedly, these divisions will deter any NATO invasion). There have been few details about these divisions and how they will be structured. They will reportedly resemble Soviet-era divisions, with three motorized rifle regiments and one tank regiment (for a motorized rifle division) or three tank regiments and one motorized rifle regiment (for a tank division) plus supporting units. According to one Russian journalist, these divisions will have fewer than the four maneuver regiments that were customary in Soviet times. Russian tacticians envisage the functioning of brigades and divisions in the same Army Groups.

Anatoliy Serdyukov, Minister of Defense February 2007 to November 2012
Image Courtesy: Russian Ministry of Defense

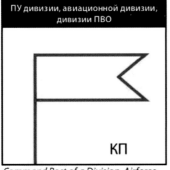

ПУ дивизии, авиационной дивизии, дивизии ПВО

КП

Command Post of a Division, Airforce Division, or Air Defense Division

Prior to 2009/2010 the Russian Ground Forces had never used maneuver brigades as permanent formations. When they were used, it was typically in an ad-hoc manner, being formed for a specific purpose or set period of time. Since these units are now functioning together, there is some thinking about how they would interact in large-scale combined arms warfare. The brigades will use their mobility to function as a combined arms reserve to either repel penetrations of the defense or exploit offensive successes. Unlike the U.S. system, division and brigades will be subordinated directly to a Combined Arms Army or Tank Army; the maneuver brigades will never be subordinated to a division.

One reason that Russia turned away from the regimental/divisional structure was the difficulties with deploying these units. Russia determined it needed a brigade structure to more easily project combat power, as it is much easier to move a brigade than a division. Since these new divisions will be formed just on the western border (near the perceived threat), there is likely little concern about these units' effect on strategic mobility. In sum, current Russian thinking sees value in maintaining both the brigade and divisional structures. The brigades provide needed strategic mobility to rapidly protect the vast borders of the Russian Federation, while the relatively static division provides an abundance of combat power in high risk areas. Although Russia has introduced a few new divisions, the vast majority of the Russian Ground Forces combat power will reside in brigades for the foreseeable future.[12]

[12] Charles K. Bartles, "Fleshing Out the Details of Reintroducing Divisions," *OE Watch* Online, June 2016. Aleksey Ramm, "Russia Is Reviving Divisions," *Izvestiya* Online, 10 May 2016, <http://izvestia.ru/news/612939#ixzz48GcOt8FZ>, accessed 20 May 2016.

Russian Graphic Symbols Depicting Subunits

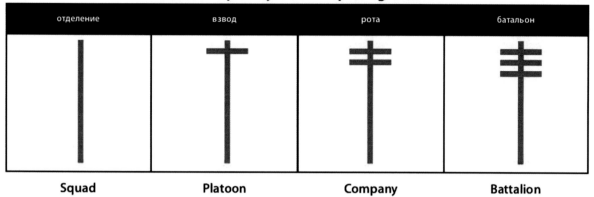

отделение	взвод	рота	батальон
Squad	Platoon	Company	Battalion

Subunit symbols are used in conjunction with vehicle, weapon systems, and other symbols to indicate unit size and type in Russian military graphics.

Building Blocks of the Russian Brigade

Russian maneuver brigades are composed of battalions, companies, platoons, and squads. Unlike U.S. brigades, which typically have only battalions reporting directly to the brigade commander, Russian brigade commanders may also have companies, platoons, and squads reporting to them as well. This number of direct reporting units may seem daunting from a U.S./Western view, but not from a Russian one. Typically, Russian brigade (and to a lesser extent battalion) commanders have several deputy commanders who assist in the command and control of these directly reporting units. In addition, many of the commanders of these subordinate units are also on the commander's staff. For instance, the senior signal officer not only sits on the staff, but also commands the signal unit. The building blocks of a brigades consist of:

- Squad [отделение]- The squad is the smallest troop formation in the Russian Armed Forces. They vary in size, but typically consist of 4-14 personnel. The motorized rifle squad is the basic building block of the motorized rifle battalion, consisting of seven-nine soldiers. Motorized rifle squads are mounted on a combat vehicle, either a BMP, BTR, or MT-LB (the MT-LB is considered a light tracked BTR). Typical personnel include vehicle commander, driver-mechanic, grenadier, assistant grenadier, machine gunner, senior rifleman, and rifleman (in squads mounted on BTRs, a designated marksman).

Мотострелковое отделение (мсо)

The single line representing a squad is often omitted in tactical maps

- Platoon [взвод] - Russian platoons typically consist of two-four squads with 20-45 personnel led by a lieutenant or senior lieutenant with the help of an officer assistant (senior NCO). Most platoons are part of companies, but some platoons report directly to battalion, brigade, or higher echelon units. A motorized rifle platoon based upon BMPs has a command element with three squads. A motorized rifle platoon, based upon three BMPs, has a command element and three squads. The command element consists of a commander, senior sergeant, designated marksman, machine gunner, crewman and medic. The platoon has a total of 32 personnel.

- Company [рота] - Russian companies vary in size, but the majority have two-four platoons with a total of 30-100 personnel. Most companies are part of battalions, but some companies report directly to battalion, brigade, or higher echelon units. The motorized rifle company has three platoons led by a captain with the help of an officer assistant (senior NCO) and a small headquarters element (seven personnel- company commander, deputy commander, senior sergeant, senior mechanic, medic, grenadier, ground radar operator) for a total of approximately 100 soldiers. In motorized rifle companies based on BTRs, there may be an additional antitank squad.

- Battalion [батальон] - Battalions and below are considered "subunits" [подразделение] in the Russian system. Subunits are the basic building blocks of the Russian Armed Forces, creating whole units [войсковая часть] such as regiments and brigades. Battalions that are "separate" [отдельный] are considered "whole" units, and will have larger staffs to support the additional administrative overhead. "Whole" units in the MoD are referred to with five digit numbers, while FSB and MVD units are referred to with four digit numbers. For instance, the 54th Separate Guards Air Assault Battalion is в/ч [войсковая часть] 85954.

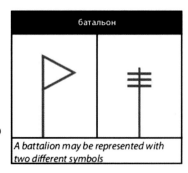

A battalion may be represented with two different symbols

Motorized rifle battalions have very similar structures, whether they are based on MT-LBs, BTRs or BMPs. The subunit typically has three motorized rifle companies, a mortar battery, and reconnaissance, grenade launcher, antitank, signal, engineer, and combat support platoons, for a total of approximately 500 soldiers. Since BTRs have less fire power than BMPs, BTR-mounted battalions may have an additional antitank platoon. If the motorized rifle battalions is acting independently, the unit could have attachments including air defense artillery (missile), reconnaissance, and logistical support subunits as needed. A motorized rifle battalion is usually led by a lieutenant colonel, but a major may also be found in command. His staff typically consists of a senior deputy commander, deputy commander for personnel, deputy commander for logistics and maintenance, and advisor for artillery.

Combined Arms Combat

Horse cavalry with horse-drawn artillery and wagon-mounted machineguns was an important aspect of the Russian Civil War. These mobile forces were able to project power over Russia's vastness, but cavalry clashes were seldom decisive. Sturdy foot-mobile infantry were necessary for decisive battle. World War I proved the effectiveness of combined arms combat and introduced the tank to modern warfare. The Soviet Workers and Peasants Red Army practiced combined arms battle as soon as practical. Artillery was integrated into infantry (later motorized infantry) battalions and tank battalions usually had infantry and artillery attached. Motorized rifle battalions usually had tanks and artillery attached, as well as its own organic artillery. While mortars and infantry direct support artillery batteries remained part of artillery branch, they were easy to integrate into motorized rifle battalions, as they maintained their own training program and used the same vehicles to move their weapons and ammunition. After World War II, the Soviets attempted to form permanent combined arms battalions of organic tank,

Colonel General Oleg Salyukov
Ground Forces Commander-in-Chief
Image Courtesy: Russian Ministry of Defense

motorized rifle and artillery companies/batteries, but the logistics and training frustrated the effort. Instead, the infantry, direct support artillery or mortar battery remained an organic part of motorized rifle and infantry units, while tanks and infantry regularly trained together and developed habitual partnerships.[13]

The Russian Army has realized this long-term goal by regularly using battalion tactical groups incorporating tank and motorized rifle companies and artillery batteries in the same battalion tactical group (BTG).[14] This makes coordination by mission, locale and time for the rapid destruction of the enemy possible and enables the battalion commander to tailor his force optimally for each combat mission. The Russians extend this combined arms combat philosophy throughout the organization of actions by their large strategic formations (ob'yedineniye), operational/tactical formations (soyedineniye) and units (chast') for the fulfillment of their assigned missions.

---

[13] Lester W. Grau, "The Soviet Combined Arms Battalion—Reorganization for Tactical Flexibility," Soviet Army Studies Office, Fort Leavenworth, Kansas, September 1989.

[14] The Russian media has reported that in 2016, that each brigade or regiment (Ground Forces, Airborne, and Naval Infantry) had at least two BTGs in that were completely manned with contract servicemen, and by the end of 2016, the Russian Armed Forces would have 96 BTGs, by the end of 2017- 115 BTGs, and by the end of 2018- 125 BTGs.

"The Armed Forces Will Increase by Twofold the Number of Reinforced Battalions with Contract Servicemen," *RIA Novosti* Online, 14 September 2016, <https://ria.ru/defense_safety/20160914/1476912391.html>, accessed 20 November 2016.

The Role of the Battalion Tactical Group

The Battalion Tactical Group is now a commonly seen ad hoc formation, based upon a motorized rifle or tank battalion with attachments. It has been around in various forms since Soviet times, and is employed by not only the Ground Forces, but also Airborne and Naval Infantry units. The BTG appears to be Russia's instrument of choice in Eastern Ukraine, prompting some analysts to speculate that Russia was fielding BTGs because it was difficult or impossible to field fully functional brigades. Since Russia now regularly transports brigades and their equipment considerable distances for exercises, it is unlikely that Russia is fielding BTGs in Ukraine due to logistic difficulties, but instead because they believe that the BTG is the most effective formation for combat in those circumstances.[15]

It is important to note that the BTG was always intended to be a means of projecting a brigade's combat power, as the idea was discussed in the early years of implementing the brigade system.[16] In 2005, well before the introduction of the brigades, Chief of the General Staff, General Yuri Baluyevskiy said: "events in Chechnya have shown that self-sufficient battalions and tactical groups with self-sufficient means of intelligence, communications and provisions operated more successfully in local conflicts. That is why we are considering the possibility of moving away from a strict organizational staffing structure today."[17] General Baluyevskiy is referencing BTGs.

The combined arms BTG was intended to be used as a detachable instrument of the brigade. One lesson learned from Russia in 2008 was the difficulty in deploying troops far from their garrisons. In order to remedy this problem, Russia now routinely mobilizes brigade and division-size units and transports them and their equipment considerable distances before they begin exercises.[18] The use of detached BTGs in the Ukrainian theater does not mean that the Russians cannot deploy full brigades. The use of BTGs in this manner may be a way that Russia is handling troop rotations through the conflict. It also could mean that the BTG is the best force mix for this particular environment.

Although the BTGs likely have a common training program, there still are problems. Problems with command and control and suitable employment of attached units are subjects that are not highlighted in open Russian military discussion. There are also logistical and maintenance

---

[15] Charles K. Bartles, "The Future is Bright for Battalion Tactical Groups," *OE Watch Online*, April 2016.

[16] Sergey Buntman and Anatoliy Yermolin, "Interview with Colonel Andrey Ivanayev, Commander of the 5th Guards Separate Motorized Rifle Brigade," *Ekho Moskvy* Online, 12 June 2010, <http://echo.msk.ru/programs/voensovet/686657-echo.phtml>, accessed 15 June 2016.

[17] Viktor Mikhaylov, "The Russian Military Brigade Contract" *Nezavisimoye Voyennoye Obozreniye* Online, 22 May 2009, < http://nvo.ng.ru/forces/2009-05-22/1_podryad.html?mthree=3>, accessed 8 May 2015.
Igor Chernyak, "Igor Baluyevskiy: We Do not Intend Waging War with NATO," *Rossiyskaya Gazeta* Online, 1 November 2005, <http://www.rg.ru/2005/11/01/baluevsky.html>, accessed 8 May 2015.

[18] "Information Resistance Has Detected Russian Troops from More Than 10 Brigades in Donets Basin," *Ukrayinska Pravda* Online, 20 April 2015, <http://www.pravda.com.ua/rus/news/2015/04/20/7065276/>, accessed 9 May 2015. The US Army conducts EDREs-Emergency Deployment Readiness Exercises- where combat battalions and larger units are transported over distance, after short notice, to a training site to draw equipment and train.
Aleksey Ramm, "The Ukraine Test: New Image of Armed Forces Spoiled by Field Kitchens," *Voyenno-Promyshlennyy Kuryer* Online, 29 April 2015, <http://vpk-news.ru/articles/25027>, accessed 6 May 2015.

issues, although use of the Armata common chassis will mitigate some of them. One reform that has not been successful was the abolition of some logistics and maintenance units in favor of private contractors. Russia is currently trying to rebuild some of its organic logistics and maintenance units that were disbanded, but the process is slow going.[19] BTGs are not immune to the logistics problems that still plague the Russian military, and BTG commanders still complain about them. There is also reporting that BTGs are augmented by staff at the Army Group and Military District level. Due to the Russian planning process, battalion staffs are quite small by U.S. standards. This augmented staff may substitute for the lack of an on-site higher headquarters (brigade/regiment), but these staff members might also be liaising with the General Staff and advising the unit commander as needed.[20]

The Battalion Tactical Group in Relation to Mission Command
The Russian military views the tactical, operational, and strategic levels of warfare differently from the West. In the West these levels are typically defined by echelon size (battalion, corps, army, theater, task force, etc.), but in the Russian system these levels are more nuanced, defined by the unit's scope of mission. For instance, a division operating under an Army Group would be considered to be acting at a tactical level, but if the same division were detached and operating under a Front-level command, it would be considered to be acting at the operational level. By the same token, a brigade is usually considered as acting at the tactical level, but in a conflict with a much smaller opponent—as in the Russian–Georgian War—a brigade could be a "war winner," and therefore a strategic asset.[21] In the Russian system, a BTG is a tactical entity.

In the U.S. system, if at lower echelons Mission Command is more of a science than art and higher levels more of an art than science, this situation is even more so in the Russian system. The system of tactics lends itself well to mathematical precision and calculation. The science of command involves the commander picking the best option for accomplishing the mission and adjusting variables as needed. This process is assisted by rigid tactics and predictability that allow such practices as utilizing tables that estimate the percentage of an enemy unit that will be destroyed with a given amount of time from a specified unit (artillery firing tables, etc.). In terms of tactics, from a U.S. military decision-making process (MDMP) perspective, Russian military commanders have limited options for developing plans to accomplish given tasks. Commanders pick from the "menu" of known tactics. Although this would irk a U.S. commander, Russian commanders are comfortable with this system because, although tactics are simple, albeit in aggregate, when multiple simple tactics are combined to accomplish a given task, a given maneuver could appear complex. Since these maneuvers are not

[19] One factor complicating the matter is that contract troops are funneled into the combat arms, leaving combat support and combat service support roles being filled by conscripts.
Charles K. Bartles, "Details of Russia's Spring 2015 Conscription Campaign, " *OE Watch Online*, May 2015.
Aleksey Durnovo, "Features of Organizing the Spring 2015 Draft of Citizens for Military Service," *Ekho Moskvy Online*, 4 April 2015, <http://echo.msk.ru/programs/voensovet/1522994-echo/>, accessed 8 May 2015.
[20] Aleksey Ramm, "The Ukraine Test: New Image of Armed Forces Spoiled by Field Kitchens," *Voyenno-Promyshlennyy Kuryer* Online, 29 April 2015, <http://vpk-news.ru/articles/25027>, accessed 6 May 2015.
[21] Charles K. Bartles & Roger N. McDermott, "Russia's Military Operation in Crimea: Road-Testing Rapid Reaction Capabilities," *Problems of Post-Communism*, Vol. 61, No. 6, November–December 2014, 51-52.

developed "on-the-fly" and are instead a collection of simple tasks, the planning process is much less involved than for an equivalent maneuver by a U.S. unit. At the tactical level, this system allows these units to have miniscule staffs in comparison to Western units and do not require extensive operations orders to plan their missions. All that is typically required in a Russian operation order is a map signed by the commander, with a few notes jotted in the margins. Tactics are simple and rigid, but since they are universal, when used in aggregate they can provide great operational flexibility.[22]

The Battalion Tactical Group in Relation to Operational Art
The BTG has no relationship to operational art in a Russian military context. This is because the term "operational art" has a much different meaning for the U.S. than Russia. In a NATO context it is defined as:

> ...the use of creative thinking by commanders and staffs to design strategies, campaigns, and major operations and organize and employ military forces. It is a thought process that uses skill, knowledge, experience, and judgment to overcome the ambiguity and uncertainty of a complex environment and understand the problem at hand. Operational art also promotes unified action by encouraging JFCs and staffs to consider the capabilities, actions, goals, priorities, and operating processes of interorganizational partners, while determining objectives, establishing priorities, and assigning tasks to subordinate forces. It facilitates the coordination, synchronization, and, where appropriate, integration of military operations with those of interorganizational partners, thereby promoting unity of effort.[23]

In practice, this definition has led NATO militaries to think not just about the military aspects of force projection, but also about the coordination of the full gamut of the state's means of leverage to achieve a desired end state. In contrast, the definition of the term in a Soviet/Russian context is much more military oriented:

> Operational art encompasses the theory and practice of preparing for and conducting operations by large units (fronts, armies) of the armed forces. It occupies an intermediate between strategy and tactics. "Stemming from strategic requirements, operational art determines methods of preparing for and conducting to achieve strategic goals." Operational art in turn "establishes the tasks and direction for the development of tactics." Soviet operational art provides a context for studying, understanding, preparing for, and conducting war...[24]

In a Russian context, operational art has typically been thought of in the way that the great Soviet military thinkers (e.g., Tuchachevsky, Svechin, Triandafilov and Isserson) had, focusing mostly on military matters, such as maneuvering of large military formations for optimum effect.[25] Modern war is becoming more unpredictable. General Gerasimov, the Russian Chief of the General Staff stated: "In the 21st century, a tendency toward the elimination of the differences between the states of war and peace is becoming discernible. Wars are now not even declared, but having begun, are not going according to a pattern we are accustomed to."[26] While retaining the ideas of its major military theoreticians, there are some signs that

[22] Ibid.
[23] Joint Publication 3.0, *Joint Operations*, 11 August 2011, <http://www.dtic.mil/doctrine/new_pubs/jp3_0.pdf>, accessed 22 December 2014.
[24] David M. Glantz, *Soviet Military Operational Art: In Pursuit of Deep Battle*. London, England: F. Cass, 1991.
[25] Charles K. Bartles, "Russia's Indirect and Asymmetric Methods as a Response to the New Western Way of War" *Special Operations Journal*, June 2016.
[26] Valeriy Gerasimov, "The Value of Science Is in the Foresight: New Challenges Demand Rethinking the Forms and Methods of Carrying out Combat Operations," *Voyenno-Promyshlennyy Kuryer* Online, 26 February 2013, <http://vpk-news.ru/articles/14632>, accessed 22 December 2014.

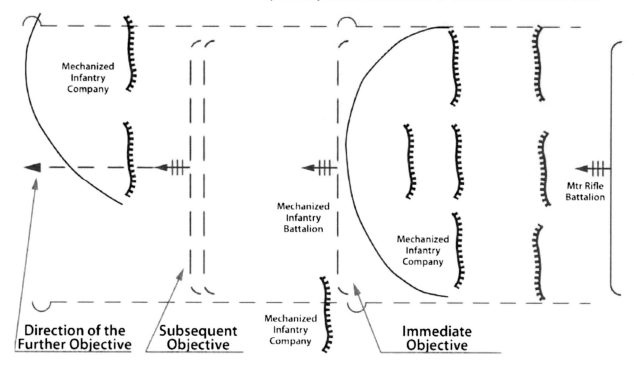

Combat Missions for a Motorized Rifle Battalion in the Offense

Russia may be expanding its definition of operational art to that of a definition more in line with U.S./NATO, due to current interests in new forms, methods, and ways of conducting warfare.[27] Regardless of Russian interests in indirect and asymmetric methods (which the West has dubbed "hybrid warfare" or Russian "New Generation Warfare,") and an increase in the quality of enlisted personnel through a new system of contract manning, in terms of systemic operation little, if anything, has changed at the tactical level for the Russian military. However the self-sufficiency of the BTG does expand the capability of the Russian Army to conduct deep tactical battle and provides a modality for the projection of the brigade or division's combat power.

In short, Russian tactical leadership, especially as practiced at the brigade level and below, does not relate to operational art as defined by the Russian military, and is difficult to understand through a Western notion of the MDMP and a different world view of present and future war. Furthermore, the highly specialized nature of Russian personnel and training practice means that at the tactical level (generally brigade and below) Russian commanders will be primarily focused on the application of combat power (getting steel on target) and will be far less interested in the diplomatic, informational, and economic aspects of war, as are their Western counterparts. In the Russian system, these areas are generally the responsibility of higher echelons, or other branches of the Russian government.

[27] Aleksandr Korabelnikov, "Military-Field Breakdown: Armed Forces Need New Regulation Documents to Further Increase Combat Effectiveness," *Voyenno-Promyshlennyy Kuryer* Online, 19 November 2014, <http://vpk-news.ru/articles/22730>, accessed 16 December 2014.

Elements of Offensive and Defensive Combat
Combat Missions
Soviet and Russian military theorists have long studied the changing nature of warfare. Modern combat will involve greater depth, fluidity and mobility than in the past. Contiguous defensive lines of shoulder-to-shoulder formations will give way to open flanks, meeting battles and the struggle to gain important areas that will undermine the tactical stability of defending forces.[28] While objective lines remain important, linear combat based on linear defensive lines and defensive zones will give way to combat to defeat artillery groupings working in conjunction with maneuver forces. Russian tactical units will be assigned objective limits. Russian maneuver brigades normally are assigned an immediate and subsequent mission, and a mission of the day. The brigade's immediate objective will usually be the rear of the enemy first-echelon battalion's defensive combat formation. The brigade's subsequent objective will usually be the rear of the enemy first-echelon brigade's defensive combat formation. The brigade's mission-of-the-day objective will usually be the rear of the enemy's second echelon brigade's defensive combat formation. The mission of the day is flexible and will change with the brigade's restated mission every 24 hours. A first-echelon brigade's subsequent objective may correspond to the parent army's immediate objective. Battalions are normally assigned immediate objectives and a direction for further attack.

Getting to and Conducting Battle
Maneuver is the organized movement of troops during combat to a more advantageous position to attack or repulse the enemy. Maneuver makes it possible to seize and hold the initiative and prevent enemy success; however, maneuver alone does not accomplish the mission. Fire is an essential partner of maneuver. The long-range fire battle, especially the effective employment of reconnaissance-strike and reconnaissance-fire assets, makes successful maneuver possible. Tank and motorized rifle tactical units and subunits generally use three basic types of formations when conducting movement to and during the attack: march formation, pre-combat formation, and combat formation.[29]

March Formation
For Russia, combined rail and road movement is often the most effective and quickest way to move brigades and other large units. March planning includes priority for movement, march capabilities (so that the forces and heavy equipment on rail arrive together) and march support in the form of air defense, security of bridges and choke points, supply of POL and material reserves, maintenance support, secrecy, assembly areas, dispersion areas, lager sites, rest sites, information operations cover and misdirection.[30]

Marches can be administrative or under threat. Marches under threat have usually been conducted at night for concealment. Depending on the state of electronic combat and air superiority, marches may be conducted during the day under smoke. The Russians use smoke in a variety of circumstances. It is used instead of building expensive counters to top-attack

[28] Lester W. Grau, "Changing Soviet Objective Depths in Future War," *Military Review*, December 1989.
[29] Major General (retired) Ivan Nikolayevich Vorobyov, "Know, Anticipate, Win: Revisiting the Issue of a Commander's Tactical Foresight," *Armeyskiy Sbornik*, June 2006.
[30] Ministry of Defense of the Russian Federation, "March Preparation," [Маршевая Подготовка], *Military Encyclopedia* [Военная Энциклопедия], Volume 5, Moscow: Voyenizdat, 2001, 20-21.

and may be used to screen movement effectively, provided that its particulates serve as a screen against electronic probes. Heavy equipment transports are used to save wear and tear on tanks and artillery pieces. In marches under threat, it is optimal that first echelon brigades have three routes from the final assembly area to commitment. The march column is organized so that the battalions may move directly into combat if needed. March columns must flow smoothly and quickly from the march into battle in combat order determined by the enemy composition and terrain where contact is expected. This provides an advantage in the event of a meeting engagement or overcoming a surprise enemy defense. Marches are usually used in an attack from the depth, meeting engagement or pursuit.

Pre-Combat Formation

The Tsarist and Soviet Army used the pre-battle formation to facilitate rapid and efficient maneuver of their units and subunits from the march to combat formation and back again. The Russian Ground Forces continue to use the pre-combat formation for this purpose. When in pre-combat formation, elements adjust the distance between vehicles and subunits to meet the realities of terrain and enemy forces. A Russian Ground Forces brigade, battalion, company, or platoon can transition from the march to pre-battle formation and back into march formation in a very short period of time. A unit in pre-combat formation is deployed in columns and dispersed laterally with less depth than in the march formation. The pre-battle formation is used when conducting a pursuit or an attack against a defending enemy, if the enemy's defenses are relatively weak or are effectively suppressed.

Combat Formation

Before engaging in battle, whether on the offense or in the defense, a Russian maneuver brigade and its subordinate units will deploy into a combat formation. These elements may deploy into the combat formation from the march or from a pre-combat formation depending on the mission and expected enemy strength. Instead of deploying into a combat formation, a brigade's subunits may deploy into different configurations to support other mission-specific requirements. Maneuver brigades typically have a dedicated reconnaissance element, but since subunits usually do not, they form ad-hoc formations to fulfill these missions. Most units not in combat formation are in configurations for fulfilling reconnaissance and security missions. These configurations include reconnaissance detachments, reconnaissance groups, reconnaissance patrols, forward detachments, advance guard, raiding detachments, combat security outposts, combined arms reserves, antitank reserves, anti-airborne/air assault reserves, armored groups, special reserves, and flank and rear security elements.[31]

Reconnaissance Detachment [разведывательный отряд] - Reconnaissance detachments are typically mounted reinforced companies that are capable of conducting observation, searches, raids, ambushes, installing/removing observation equipment, and, if necessary, engaging the enemy. They move on primary axes in advance of a march, meeting battle or offensive and are normally proceeded by a reconnaissance patrol (platoon). The standard

---

[31] Major General (retired) Ivan Nikolayevich Vorobyov, "Tactics: The Art of the Offense," *Military Thought*, March 2003.

operating range of a Reconnaissance Detachment varies by mission, but an operational depth of 50 kilometers for company-sized units and 80 kilometers for battalion-sized elements is common.[32]

Reconnaissance Group [разведывательная группа] - Reconnaissance groups are typically motorized rifle or spetsnaz squads dispatched to reconnoiter in the enemy rear area to locate nuclear delivery systems, enemy forces, headquarters, airfields, signal sites and other important targets. Reconnaissance groups are capable of conducting observation, raids, ambushes, and installing/removing observation and communication equipment. They may be inserted by helicopter, vehicle or on foot.[33]

Reconnaissance Patrol [разведывательный дозор] - Reconnaissance patrols are typically platoon-sized elements, reinforced with engineers and other specialists, that reconnoiter up to 10 kilometers ahead of the parent unit. Reconnaissance Patrols can be combat, officer reconnaissance, NBC or engineer.[34]

Forward Detachment [передовой отряд] - A forward detachment is a combined arms force normally built around a reinforced maneuver battalion and capable of independent action. When conducting offensive combat, the forward detachment of a brigade moves well ahead of the advanced guard of the lead brigade but behind the brigade's reconnaissance patrols. Its mission is to seize key objectives and water crossings in advance of its parent brigade to facilitate the fastest possible advance and to quickly wedge itself deep into the enemy territory or defenses. Sub-elements of a forward detachment may conduct raids against key targets en route to their objectives. A forward detachment is not assigned a specific march route and will attempt to avoid contact with enemy forces until it reaches its objective. Forward detachments often link up with air-landed forces on their objectives. Water-crossing sites of operational and tactical significance are very important forward detachment objectives. When conducting defensive combat, forward detachments are tasked to establish a series of defensive positions in the brigade's security zone astride main avenues of approach to delay, disrupt, or destroy the advancing enemy. Forward detachments are essential for pursuit operations and will be described in greater detail in the Pursuit section.[35]

Advance Guard [авангард] - Each first-echelon brigade forms an advance guard from a first-echelon maneuver battalion while moving and expecting contact with the enemy. An advance guard ensures the high speed of the brigade in securing the advance of its parent brigade's main body. Unlike forward detachments, advance guards move directly on the brigade's route of advance. It is a security element and does not avoid contact with the enemy; rather, it seeks to defeat all enemy forces encountered. Its goal is to fight through

[32] Ministry of Defense, USSR, *Military Encyclopedic Dictionary* [Военный Энциклопедический Словарь], 2nd Edition, Moscow: Voyenizdat, 1986, 617.

[33] Ministry of Defense of the Russian Federation, *Military Encyclopedic Dictionary* [Военный Энциклопедический Словарь], Volume 2, Moscow: Ripol Klassik, 2001, 438.

[34] Ministry of Defense, USSR, *Military Encyclopedic Dictionary* [Военный Энциклопедический Словарь], 2nd Edition, Moscow: Voyenizdat, 1986, 617.

[35] Ministry of Defense of the Russian Federation, *Military Encyclopedic Dictionary* [Военный Энциклопедический Словарь], Volume 2, Moscow: Ripol Klassik, 2001, 290.

or fix all opposition to free its parent brigade from deploying its main body. It facilitates the movement of the main body while preventing enemy surprise attacks and overcoming the enemy security zone.[36]

Raiding Detachment [рейдовый отряд] - A raiding detachment is a reinforced battalion capable of functioning independently, which is dispatched to destroy important military targets, disrupt command and control, occupy key terrain and block enemy reserves. In this effort, it overlaps the mission of forward detachments; conversely, forward detachments may also conduct raids.[37]

Combat Security Outpost [боевое охранение] - Combat security outposts (CSOs) are security elements formed when a covering zone instead of a security zone is established forward of the main defensive area. CSOs are reinforced platoons deployed from the first-echelon companies of defending first-echelon battalions. They are placed up to 1,000 meters in front of the forward edge of defensive positions. The purpose of a CSO is to conceal the battalion's main defensive position, prevent enemy reconnaissance, provide early warning, engage enemy forces, and slow the enemy's rate of advance. Positions for the CSO are normally chosen by the brigade commander and refined by the battalion commander. These positions will be covered by direct fire from antitank weapons from the first-echelon companies' strong points. CSO positions are improved by engineer obstacles and construction. A CSO is withdrawn only when ordered by the battalion commander with the concurrence of the brigade commander. CSO withdrawal, if ordered, is along predesignated, covered routes that afford whatever cover is available and that do not interfere with the battalion's defensive fire plan.[38]

Combined Arms Reserve [общевойсковой резерв] - When organized as one echelon, brigades and battalions often form a combined arms reserve. This is a small force (about one-ninth of the force: a platoon at battalion and a battalion at brigade) that is directly subordinate to the commander. The combined arms reserve, unlike the second echelon, is not assigned a specific mission. This reserve is a contingency force used to meet any unanticipated requirements. Common contingencies include blocking a breakthrough, counterattacking, providing flank security and covering gaps.[39]

Antitank Reserve [противотанковый резерв] - Antitank elements at the brigade and battalion level form the antitank reserve and are often reinforced with engineer and artillery assets. The antitank reserve is usually employed as a blocking force against an enemy counterattack during the offense, covering threatened areas, open flanks and deployment areas. At the brigade level, it is usually led by the antitank artillery battalion commander.[40]

[36] Ministry of Defense of the Russian Federation, *Military Encyclopedic Dictionary* [Военный Энциклопедический Словарь], Volume 1, Moscow: Ripol Klassik, 2001, 8-9.

[37] Ministry of Defense of the Russian Federation, *Military Encyclopedia* [Военная Энциклопедия], Volume 7, Moscow: Voyenizdat, 2003, 465.

[38] Ministry of Defense of the Russian Federation, *Military Encyclopedic Dictionary* [Военный Энциклопедический Словарь], Volume 1, Moscow: Ripol Klassik, 2001, 196.

[39] Ministry of Defense of the Russian Federation, *Military Encyclopedic Dictionary* [Военный Энциклопедический Словарь], Volume 2, Moscow: Ripol Klassik, 2001, 186.

[40] Ministry of Defense of the Russian Federation, *Military Encyclopedic Dictionary* [Военный Энциклопедический

<u>Anti-Airborne/Air Assault Reserve</u> [противодесантный резерв] - This reserve is a mobile, combined arms force created from second-echelon assets. It was added to Soviet tactical units in the mid-to-late 1980s and has been used by the Russians since that time. This development was due to Soviet fears that NATO could deploy a prodigious "air echelon" that would be able to jump over Soviet defensive positions, wreak havoc in the Soviet rear and threaten the operational stability of the defense. The anti-*desant* reserve is a mobile, combined arms force created from second-echelon assets. It is used in defensive situations where there is a strong possibility that the enemy will air-land forces. If an anti-*desant* reserve is designated, a combined arms reserve usually will not be formed. The formation of an anti-*desant* reserve will depend on the tactical situation. Russian units will only create an anti-*desant* reserve when fighting a highly advanced enemy which has the capability to air-land troops into combat. The anti-*desant* reserve is composed of combined arms subunits drawn from the second echelon-similar to the combined arms reserve.[41]

<u>Bronegruppa (Armored Group)</u> [броннегруппа] - When motorized rifle forces have dismounted from their BMPs, BTRs or MT-LBs, they may remain with their dismounted personnel to provide fire support, or they may be withdrawn to form an armored maneuver reserve with a significant direct-fire capability. This grouping is particularly true when the Russian force is defending, occupying blocking positions or engaged in city fighting. Sometimes tanks augment the armored group. (The terms "*bronegruppa*" and "armored group" can be used interchangeably.) This armored reserve normally is constituted from platoon through brigade. It is particularly common among second echelon subunits. It is often commanded by a deputy commander. This concept was widely practiced during the Soviet-Afghan War and continued in the fighting in Chechnya and Georgia.[42]

<u>Special Reserve</u> [специальный отряд] - Special reserves, such as chemical defense or engineer, may also be formed, depending on the tactical situation. Special reserves are not normally found at battalion level because of their limited organic assets.

<u>Flank and Rear Security Elements</u> [боковое охранение и охрана тыловых районов] - During the march, every maneuver brigade in the first or second echelon provides flank security for itself using assets taken from its main body. Rear security in a brigade march is provided by the second-echelon battalions. Forces operating alone (forward detachments, advanced guards) provide their own rear and flank security. Flank and rear security elements normally operate up to five kilometers from and paralleling or trailing their parent organizations.

<u>Air Assault Detachment</u> [тактический воздушный десант] - This unit is part of a reinforced motorized rifle company trained to air assault into the rear area where an enemy has broken through. The air assault detachment will cooperate with subunits of the brigade's second echelon in the conduct of a containment or counterattack.

Словарь], Volume 2, Moscow: Ripol Klassik, 2001, 409.

[41] Ministry of Defense of the Russian Federation, *Military Encyclopedic Dictionary* [Военный Энциклопедический Словарь], Volume 2, Moscow: Ripol Klassik, 2001, 401.

[42] Lester W. Grau, *The Bear Went Over the Mountain: Soviet Combat Tactics in Afghanistan*, Washington: NDU Press, 1995, 2.

Echelonment of Forces

A Russian maneuver brigade can attack independently, but will most often conduct maneuver combat as part of an army. As part of an army, it may be an enveloping force in a single or double envelopment to encircle an enemy force. It may be part of an army offensive on several axes. It may have a screening mission along a coastline or river. The meeting battle is the preferred form of offensive combat since the enemy has not had time to go to ground and entrench. Attacking an entrenched defending enemy can be costly in time and combat power.

An attack against a defending enemy can be from positions in direct contact with the enemy or from the march. When possible, Russians prefer to attack from the march. Often the first battle will be the covering force battle, where Russian forward detachments push through light enemy defenses and call in air, missile and artillery strikes on them. Air assaults may supplement forward detachment efforts to cut off enemy units in the covering force area.

A breakthrough attack against an entrenched enemy is difficult, and, consequently, it is a carefully choreographed event meshing air and missile strikes, phased artillery strikes, electronic countermeasures (ECM) and obscurants with the deployment of the attacking force from the march to pre-combat to combat formation. It brings the full firepower of the attacker to bear on the defender, either killing or incapacitating him. The attack is designed to rapidly punch through a sector of the defense and widen the gap while pushing follow-on forces through the gap to seize the enemy rear areas and defeat enemy reserve forces in meeting battles.

A Russian maneuver brigade (and subordinate units) will usually form two echelons in both the offense and in the defense. The first echelon typically has one-half to two-thirds of the brigade's combat power, while the second echelon has one-half to one-third. The second echelon is a combined arms force that is assigned a specific mission, and this mission differentiates it from a reserve.

On the offense, the first echelon conducts the main attack. It is charged with achieving the higher headquarters immediate objective and is usually responsible for attaining the subsequent objective. The second echelon is intended to exploit the success of the first echelon, continue the attack, and achieve the subsequent objective of the parent organization. If one sector of the first echelon's attack fails and another succeeds, the second echelon will be committed into only the successful sector. Therefore, the second echelon's attack may be in a different direction than originally planned. The second echelon is committed to combat through gaps between enemy strong points and breaches formed in the enemy's lines as a result of nuclear and conventional fire strikes. Other specific second-echelon missions may be to conduct pursuit, destroy bypassed enemy elements, defeat a counterattack, or replace first-echelon units that are combat ineffective before or during commitment. The Russian defense is designed to defeat or mitigate the effects of enemy nuclear and MLRS strikes, air attacks, tank attacks and air assaults. To do so, it employs the following principles:[43]

[43] The following discussion is based on G. D. Ionin and V.V. Turchenko, *Ministry of Defense of the Russian*

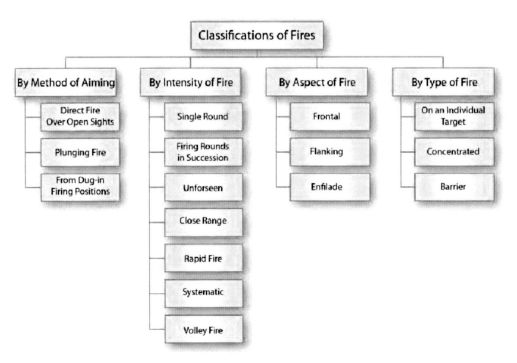

Russian Classifications of Fire Theory

Concentration and Dispersal

Concentration of fire: Fires, not personnel and systems, are massed to achieve effect. Fire planning from squad to brigade designates areas of interlocking fire, massed fire, stopping fire and final protective fire. Artillery planning includes individual targets, concentrations, moving barrages, and standing barrages, as well as offensive fire planning to support counterattacks. It even plans for concentrated direct fires.

Disperse laterally and in depth: Defend in depth, limiting the effects of enemy fire and forcing constant attrition on the advancing enemy. Use a deep security zone where possible to draw out the enemy force, use his supplies, disclose his strength and create an opportunity for deep attack. High ground is often vital, but to sit on vital ground is to attract enemy fire. It may be better to defend the approaches while dominating the ground by fire from flank and rear. If it is necessary to put forces on that ground, minimal forces may hold the ground until enemy preparation artillery fire is concluded; the designated force is then quickly moved into position. The second echelon should be strong and tank-heavy.

Activeness and Maneuver

Pre-empt the enemy: The defender cannot be passive and rely on positional defense. The defender must retain or attain the initiative. An aggressive defense is a stable defense. Destroy the enemy nuclear delivery systems. Alter unfavorable force ratios at the last minute or disrupt enemy timetables. Conduct spoiling attacks to disrupt enemy deployment.

Federation, "Defense," Military Encyclopedia [Военная Энциклопедия], Volume 5, Moscow: Voyenizdat, 2001, 530-534 and long conversations with Charles Dick, Retired Director of the British Combat Studies Research Centre.

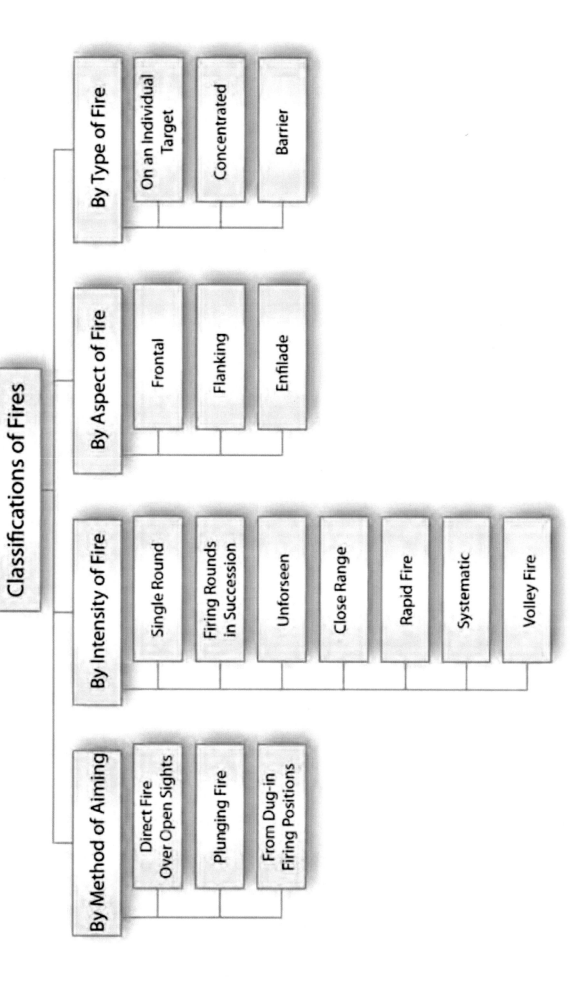

Russian Classifications of Fire Theory

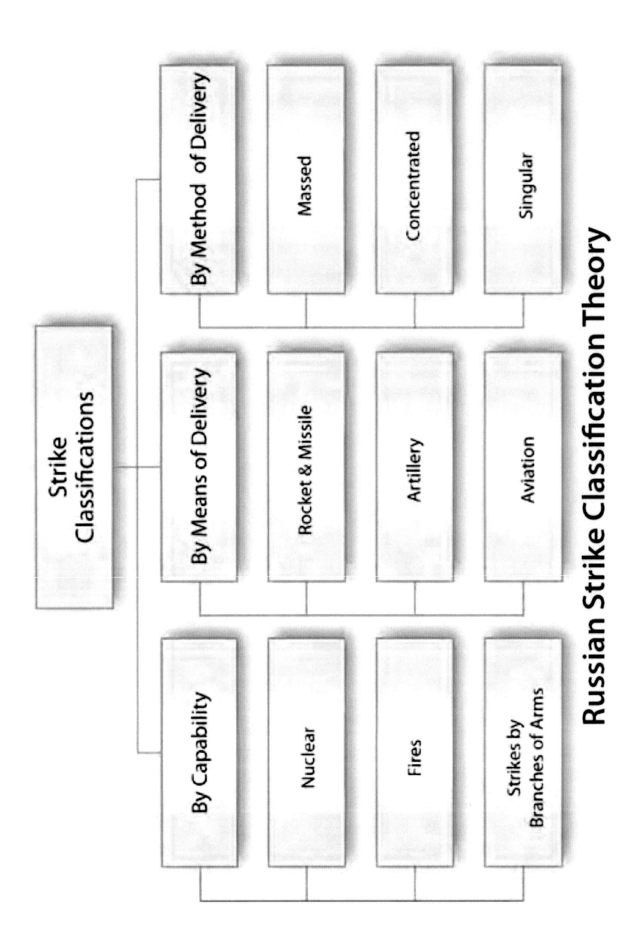

Russian Strike Classification Theory

Maneuver: Maneuver by fire is key. Maneuver of forces is equally vital. Shift forces from quiet sectors or from the depth for counter-penetration or counterattack. Avoid loitering in assembly areas inviting enemy fires. Move counterstroke forces frequently.

Counter-attacks: Counterattack before the enemy commits his immediate reserve to maintain the stability of the defense.

Counterpenetration: Should the enemy disrupt the stability of the defense and penetrate with sufficient combat power, hold and shape the penetration with the second echelon and reserves while reinforcing first echelon forces. Leave the more decisive counterstroke to the senior commander. Do not just stop the enemy, destroy him.

Reconnaissance: Constant, aggressive reconnaissance in the enemy depth must determine the enemy main axes, location of forces and time table to preempt his attack through long-range fires, maneuver and counterattack.

Conduct deep battle: Long-range fires, air strikes and amphibious and air assault landings will disrupt, damage and delay the attacker. Controlled partisan actions may tie down considerable enemy forces.

Steadfastness: Some areas and lines must be held to maintain the stability of the defense, disrupt the enemy and gain time for the use of outside maneuver to rectify the situation. Defending forces do not have the right to withdraw without orders from the senior commander. This is true even when communications are lost and the force is surrounded. It is better to hold and wait for the counterattack than to break out of the encirclement and lose the combat power and effectiveness of the force. An intact force in the enemy depth reduces enemy possibilities. The senior commander will determine which areas will be held steadfastly and which areas are appropriate for maneuver defense.

Engineering Preparation: Forces in positional defense must be well dug in to survive nuclear, precision and concentrated artillery fire. Second echelon and reserve forces will need to be similarly protected, as will assembly areas and deeper defenses. Obstacles are an important part of defense, and minefields are very effective. Minefields that are laid at the last minute in the path of the enemy advance are particularly effective, since the possibility of enemy detection is lessened, preventing him from having breaching equipment at the exact spot needed. Mobile obstacle detachments, working with the antitank reserve are key assets. Mines can also be quickly laid from helicopters or by multiple rocket launchers. These are especially useful in sealing gaps or frustrating the deployment of the enemy reserve during an attack.

Surprise: The side with the initiative has an advantage in achieving surprise; however, the defender can achieve surprise by concealing the defense, deceiving the attacker as to the location and alignment of the defense or by attacking to win the initiative. Techniques to achieve surprise include:

Avoid stereotypes: Published defensive graphics are a guide, not a directive. Lay out the defense to take advantage of the variations in the terrain without being predictable. Adhere to the norms, but use them imaginatively, remembering that they are averages that will vary due to terrain, mission, capabilities and weather.

Conduct counter reconnaissance: Locate, defeat and destroy enemy reconnaissance efforts. Use dummy positions and radio nets, conduct false movements. Camouflage real and dummy positions. Check the effectiveness of camouflage habitually and particularly from the air.

Create a false forward edge of the defense: Where possible, create a false forward edge to draw enemy artillery preparation and premature deployment for attack. If that is not possible, consider withdrawing the bulk of the force secretly before the enemy air and artillery preparations and then reoccupy the fighting positions.

Counterpreparation: Secretly prepare to conduct artillery and airstrikes before the enemy has an opportunity to conduct his planned strikes.

Maneuver: Maneuver is essential for maintaining the stability of the defense, but maneuver must be covert to avoid enemy detection and counterattack or fire strikes. Prepare routes planning the use of concealment, bad weather, smoke and camouflage to cover movement.

Air Defense: Defeat of enemy aviation, missiles and UAVs is essential to deny enemy air reconnaissance, deter enemy air strikes and prevent or interdict enemy air assaults. Air defense should be multilayered, overlapping and redundant. It should involve missiles and guns so that it can function despite electronic jamming and ECM. Consider the use of particulate smoke.

Anti-*desant* Defense: Defend against aerial or amphibious raids and insertions by constituting an anti-desant reserve, constructing anti-landing obstacles, stringing overhead wire, mining landing zones and planning artillery strikes on landing zones. Air defense is an essential component against aerial insertions and direct fire artillery, and deployment of the *bronegruppa* can be an effective addition to the strength of the anti-desant reserve.

Deep battle: Deep battle is the concern of senior commanders using deep targeting, raids, sabotage, air assaults, missile strikes and air interdiction to weaken the attacking enemy.

In the brigade defense, the first echelon occupies the main forward position and is responsible for stopping the enemy's attack in front of or within this position. It will normally have two battalions forward and two battalions in the second echelon. Should it defend with three battalions forward, it may also constitute a combined arms reserve. Where possible, the brigade will establish a security zone which may extend in excess of 20 kilometers in front of the brigade main defense. If it cannot establish a security zone, it will establish a forward position that will mimic the forward line of the defense.

Battalions in the first echelon are intended to:
- Engage the enemy as it deploys and transitions from column movement to attack formation
- Repel assaults by the enemy in order to avoid enemy pockets in the defensive area
- Deny enemy breakthrough into the depths of its defense;
- Destroy enemy subunit pockets at established kill zones and lines.

The second echelon (or reserve) is intended to:
- Deny the enemy's seizure of strong points throughout the depth of the defense
- Prohibit enemy breakthroughs throughout the depth of the defense
- Defeat pockets of the enemy through actions of subunits at designated positions and lines
- Conduct counterattacks
- Reoccupy contested positions at the forward edge of the defense.

The brigade may employ a single echelon if the situation allows or if opposed by a weak enemy. When organized as one echelon, brigades and battalions often form a combined arms reserve. This is a small force (about one-ninth of the force: a platoon at battalion, a company at regiment, and a battalion at brigade) that is directly subordinate to the commander. The combined arms reserve, unlike the second echelon, is not assigned a specific mission. This reserve is a contingency force used to meet any unanticipated requirements. A second echelon battalion does not normally conduct a counterattack. Usually all that is available to counterattack from within the brigade defensive area is the antitank reserve and the combined arms (anti-*desant*) reserve. If the enemy has managed to penetrate through the first-echelon defenses, it is a robust force. The second echelon (or combined arms reserve) needs to stop the

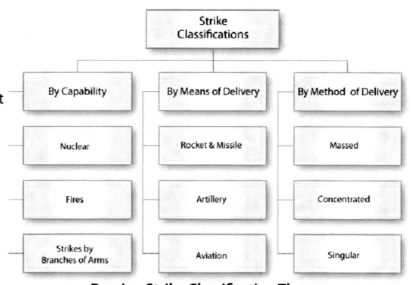

Russian Strike Classification Theory

penetration and hold it in place. Stopping the penetration is first priority, and it is safer to stop it from prepared defensive lines augmented with internal fire lines from the antitank and the combined arms reserves. Once the penetration is stopped, an external counterattack can then eliminate the enemy penetration with a flank attack. Of course, if the enemy penetration has been stopped before it has been fully engaged with the second echelon defense, it may be weakened enough that the two reserves can deal with it. What the Russians do not want is to launch a meeting battle from within the second echelon defenses-and lose the battle. Then, the brigade has been split open with no prepared defenses behind it to stop the enemy advance.

Military Decision Making Process

The contemporary maneuver battlefield, under nuclear-threatened conditions, has changed in terms of tempo, reaction time, battle space and lethality. Once battle is joined, the tempo and sudden changes on the battlefield leaves little time to produce and disseminate intelligence and formulate plans and orders. Cyber-attacks and electronic warfare threaten timely communication. Parallel planning must supplant sequential planning. Battle management needs to be decentralized at the tactical level, but under centralized operational control. Tactical commanders need the authority and initiative to conduct battles in order to meet rapidly developing and changing situations in an effective and timely manner. In practice, battle drills are implemented at the squad through battalion levels. These battle drills, in conjunction with combined arms battalions, quick and effective staff procedures, and improved planning tools, aid rapid decision making and troop leading.

Commander and Staff Roles

The US Army uses a commander-driven decision making process where the staff uses direction and guidance from the commander to study the situation and develop courses of action for the commander's review and approval. The Russian system is different. Although both systems are "commander-driven," the role of the commander in these systems differ substantially. The Russian commander is much more involved with the orders process. In the Russian system, the commander, not the staff, develops the course of action. Upon receipt of orders, the Russian commander makes his decision based on his orders and understanding of the operational environment, and passes his decision to his staff and subordinate commanders for implementation. His decision has at least three elements: the concept of the fight, tactical missions, and coordination. The concept of the fight specifies which enemy elements are to be destroyed by what resources and in what order; the sector of main effort; and the organization for combat and the concept of maneuver. The tactical missions are specified for the first and second echelons, reserves, artillery, air defense and other subunits. Coordination includes objectives, phase lines, targets and times of link-up and achievement.

The commander often outlines his plan on a battle map, selecting from a collection of well-rehearsed tactical battle drills. Following the commander's decision, he and his senior commanders make an on-ground reconnaissance of the area that they intend to fight on. Since the role of the commander is different in the Russian system, so is the structure and role of the staff at tactical levels. The Russian tactical staff is normally smaller than Western counterparts, this is due not only to the more active role of the commander, but also due to the emphasis on battle drills and repetition, which lessens planning duties. In addition, the staff makes extensive use of nomograms to support most aspects of staff planning, especially in the areas of logistics, artillery planning, and determining the correlation of forces.[44] These nomograms are produced at higher levels (possibly at the General Staff, or one of its subordinate organizations) and are presumably updated as needed so they may be used to develop the staff's running estimates.

[44] A nomogram is a diagram representing the relations between three or more variable quantities by means of a number of scales, so arranged that the value of one variable can be found by a simple geometric construction, for example, by drawing a straight line intersecting the other scales at the appropriate values. For examples, see A. Ya. Vayner, *Tactical Calculations* [Тактические расчеты], Moscow: Voyenizdat, 1982. The formulae and nomograms in this book have since been computerized, updated and expanded to further speed up planning.

51

Nomogram Example

Nomogram for the destruction of enemy personnel and weapons with 100mm or 122mm artillery fire or 120mm mortar fire.

Artillery Nomogram Formula (example)

S_i — the target area in hectares (2.471 acres)

$$S_i = \frac{N_i \cdot n_i(t)}{m_i}$$

N_i — the quantity of assigned artillery pieces (mortars) of i caliber

$n_i(t)$ — the sustained rate of fire of one artillery piece (mortar) of i caliber expressed in rounds per minute

m_i — the quantity of rounds required for the destruction of one hectare of the target area expressed in rounds per hectare.

Example: Determine the area of destruction of enemy personnel and weapons by an artillery strike of 18 artillery pieces in the course of 7 minutes, if a single artillery piece can fire 25 rounds per minute, with the required expenditure of rounds per hectare at 80 rounds.

$$S = \frac{18 \text{ artillery pieces} \times 25 \text{ rounds per minute}}{80 \text{ rounds per hectare}} \qquad S \approx 5.6 \text{ hectares}$$

This nomogram is used to determine quickly the planning data for various smaller caliber artillery systems for area fire with mathematical probability of achieving artillery destruction norms.

Example #1: Determine the area of destruction of 12 122mm howitzers against enemy personnel in the open using a 15-minute artillery fire strike. This is shown by the red line.

Begin at the "Duration of Fire" axis and find 15 minutes. Go straight up to find the 122m "Type of Fire" line. Move horizontally left from that point to find the 12 line for the "Quantity of Artillery Pieces (Mortars)". Drop from that point to the 122mm line for "Personnel and Weapons in the Open". From that point, go horizontally to the "Area of Destruction" axis to read the answer-33 hectares. When the red line passed through the "Quantity of Rounds" axis, it showed that it will require 600 rounds.

Example #2: Determine the duration of a fire strike by 12 122mm howitzers to destroy enemy personnel in the open in a target area of 20 hectares. This is shown by the blue line.

Begin at the "Area of Destruction" axis and find 20 hectares. From that point, move horizontally to the 122mm line in "Personnel and Weapons in the Open". From that point,

Artillery Nomogram (example)

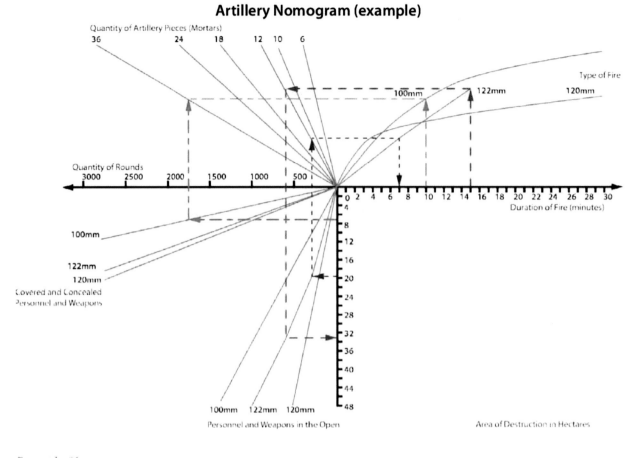

Example #1 – – – – – – – – – – –
Example #2 - - - - - - - - - - - - - - -
Example #3 – — - — - — - — - — -

move vertically to the 12 line in "Quantity of Artillery Pieces (Mortars)". From that point, move horizontally to the 122mm line in "Type of Fire". From that point, drop down to the "Duration of Fire" axis to determine the answer-7 minutes. When the blue line passed through the "Quantity of Rounds" axis, it revealed that the mission will require 300 rounds.

Example #3: Determine how many 100mm cannon and the quantity of rounds needed to destroy dug-in personnel and weapons in a 7.2 hectare target area in a ten-minute artillery strike. This is shown by the green line.

Begin at the "Duration of Fire" axis and find 10 minutes. From that point, move vertically to the 100mm line in "Type of Fire". Mark that point. Next, drop down to the "Area of Destruction" axis and find 7.2 hectares. Move horizontally to the 100mm line in "Covered and Concealed Personnel and Weapons". Move vertically and determine where the second point on the "Type of Fire" line and this line intersect. They intersect at 36 on the "Quantity of Artillery Pieces (Mortars). The green line crossed the "Quantity of Rounds" axis at 1800. Thus, the mission will require 36 100mm cannon and 1800 rounds.

53

Steps of the U.S. Army's Military Decision Making Process

Key Inputs	Steps	Key Outputs
• Higher headquarters' plan or order or a new mission anticipated by the commander	**Step 1: Receipt of Mission**	• Commander's initial guidance • Initial allocation of time
	Warning order	
• Higher headquarters' plan or order • Higher headquarters' knowledge and intelligence products • Knowledge products from other organizations • Army design methodology products	**Step 2: Mission Analysis**	• Problem statement • Mission statement • Initial commander's intent • Initial planning guidance • Initial CCIRs and EEFIs • Updated IPB and running estimates • Assumptions
	Warning order	

• Mission statement
• Initial commander's intent, planning guidance, CCIRs, and EEFIs
• Updated IPB and running estimates
• Assumptions
	Step 3: Course of Action Development	• COA statements and sketches
		  - Tentative task organization
		  Broad concept of operations
		• Revised planning guidance
		• Updated assumptions

• Updated running estimates • Revised planning guidance • COA statements and sketches • Updated assumptions	**Step 4: COA Analysis (War Game)**	• Refined COAs • Potential decision points • War-game results • Initial assessment measures • Updated assumptions
• Updated running estimates • Refined COAs • Evaluation criteria • War-game results • Updated assumptions	**Step 5: COA Comparison**	• Evaluated COAs • Recommended COAs • Updated running estimates • Updated assumptions
• Updated running estimates • Evaluated COAs • Recommended COA • Updated assumptions	**Step 6: COA Approval**	• Commander-selected COA and any modifications • Refined commander's intent, CCIRs, and EEFIs • Updated assumptions
	Warning order	
• Commander-selected COA with any modifications • Refined commander's intent, CCIRs, and EEFIs • Updated assumptions	**Step 7: Orders Production, Dissemination, and Transition**	• Approved operation plan or order • Subordinates understand the plan or order

CCIR	commander's critical information requirement	EEFI	essential element of friendly information
COA	course of action	IPB	intelligence preparation of the battlefield

Another significant difference between the staff systems, are the duties of the staff members. In the Russian system, tactical staff members often command the troops associated with their staff section. (For instance, if the Russian system was implemented in a U.S. maneuver brigade, the brigade S-2 would also be the military intelligence company (MICO) commander.) Russian tactical staffs spend less time planning than their Western counterparts, but are more involved with the implementation of the commander's orders, by directly tasking their subordinates. (This differs substantially from the U.S. system, where the members of the brigade staff typically directly control few personnel.) After the commander issues his initial orders, the staff and subordinate commanders begin their planning. The staff issues necessary warning orders while checking force ratios, requesting additional supplies, and adjusting frontages or dispositions to attain a mathematical probability of success. (In Russian parlance, Correlation of Forces and Means (COFM) analysis and mathematical verification) Fragmentary orders assist and adjust the parallel planning. The chief of staff produces the final battle map, which is the combat order and is signed by both the commander and chief of staff. There may be a small written annex of two to three pages. With the U.S. system, a

Key Inputs	Steps	Key Outputs
• Higher headquarters' plan or order or a new mission anticipated by the commander	**Step 1: Receipt of Mission**	• Commander's initial guidance • Initial allocation of time
	Warning order	
• Higher headquarters' plan or order • Higher headquarters' knowledge and intelligence products • Knowledge products from other organizations • Army design methodology products	**Step 2: Mission Analysis**	• Problem statement • Mission statement • Initial commander's intent • Initial planning guidance • Initial CCIRs and EEFIs • Updated IPB and running estimates • Assumptions
	Warning order	

• Mission statement
• Initial commander's intent, planning guidance, CCIRs, and EEFIs
• Updated IPB and running estimates
• Assumptions
	Step 3: Course of Action Development	• COA statements and sketches
		  - Tentative task organization
		  Broad concept of operations
		• Revised planning guidance
		• Updated assumptions

• Updated running estimates • Revised planning guidance • COA statements and sketches • Updated assumptions	**Step 4: COA Analysis (War Game)**	• Refined COAs • Potential decision points • War-game results • Initial assessment measures • Updated assumptions
• Updated running estimates • Refined COAs • Evaluation criteria • War-game results • Updated assumptions	**Step 5: COA Comparison**	• Evaluated COAs • Recommended COAs • Updated running estimates • Updated assumptions
• Updated running estimates • Evaluated COAs • Recommended COA • Updated assumptions	**Step 6: COA Approval**	• Commander-selected COA and any modifications • Refined commander's intent, CCIRs, and EEFIs • Updated assumptions
	Warning order	
• Commander-selected COA with any modifications • Refined commander's intent, CCIRs, and EEFIs • Updated assumptions	**Step 7: Orders Production, Dissemination, and Transition**	• Approved operation plan or order • Subordinates understand the plan or order

CCIR	commander's critical information requirement	EEFI	essential element of friendly information
COA	course of action	IPB	intelligence preparation of the battlefield

Approximation of the Russian Military Decision Making Process

Key Inputs	Steps	Key Outputs
• Receipt of mission (senior commander's decision) • Intelligence reports • Order allocating additional attached/supporting units	**Step 1:** **Commander's Plan**	• Commander's plan
• Coordinating instructions - attached/supporting artillery - engineer support - logistics	**Step 2:** **Commander's Terrain Reconnaissance** (with key subordinates) [Simultaneous]	• Staff issues warning orders • Updated running estimates
• Correlation of Forces and Means (COFM) analysis from higher headquarters (if provided) • Running estimates • Coordinating instructions - attached/supporting artillery - engineer support - logistics	**Step 3:** **Staff Verification**	• Correlation of Forces and Means (COFM) analysis • Mathematical verification • Back brief to commander of plan viability • Route and area designations
• Correlation of Forces and Means (COFM) analysis • Running estimates	**Step 4:** **Issue Final Plan**	• Final plan in the form of a map possibly with a 2-3 page written annex - signature of the commander - signature of the chief of staff • Subordinate commanders' receipt of mission • Updated running estimates
• Higher level contingency options • Running estimates	**Step 5:** **Preparation for Combat**	• Contingency mission consideration/coordination

Approximation of the Russian Military Decision Making Process

Key Inputs	Steps	Key Outputs
• Receipt of mission (senior commander's decision) • Intelligence reports • Order allocating additional attached/supporting units	**Step 1:** **Commander's** **Plan**	• Commander's plan
• Coordinating instructions - attached/supporting artillery - engineer support logistics	**Step 2:** **Commander's Terrain** **Reconnaissance** (with key subordinates) Simultaneous	• Staff issues warning orders • Updated running estimates
• Correlation of Forces and Means (COFM) analysis from higher headquarters (if provided) • Running estimates • Coordinating instructions - attached/supporting artillery - engineer support logistics	**Step 3:** **Staff Verification**	• Correlation of Forces and Means (COFM) analysis • Mathematical verification • Back brief to commander of plan viability • Route and area designations
• Correlation of Forces and Means (COFM) analysis • Running estimates	**Step 4:** **Issue Final Plan**	• Final plan in the form of a map possibly with a 2-3 page written annex signature of the commander - signature of the chief of staff • Subordinate commanders' receipt of mission • Updated running estimates
• Higher level contingency options • Running estimates	**Step 5:** **Preparation for** **Combat**	• Contingency mission consideration/coordination

(Above) The above graphic is in no way "Russian doctrine" and is only intended to illustrate the authors' understanding of the differences between the Russian decision making process and the U.S. Army process described in Army Doctrine Reference Publication 5-0.

military unit with a weak commander, and a strong staff, could conceivably be successful, as a strong staff may be able to shepherd a weak commander in the right direction. This is not the case with the Russian system, the commander is not just guiding and deciding, but also doing the planning. There is a Russian proverb "as goes the commander, so goes the unit."

Military Decision Making in Relation to War Fighting Functions
Since the Russians use a much different military decision making process than used in the West, applying the Western concept of War Fighting Functions (WFFs) to their tactics and operations should be done with great care. In practice, the Russians do not discuss or even have a concept of WFF (Movement and Maneuver, Fires, Intelligence, Sustainment, Mission Command, Protection) as distinct elements assigned to various members of the staff. Instead, the WFF are always discussed in aggregate. As the commander is much more involved with the mechanics of planning, he is also responsible for the coordination of the WFFs essential for the execution of the mission. One example of how the Russian system is different from the U.S. system is by looking at how the Russians handle Intelligence, Surveillance, and Reconnaissance (ISR). In the U.S. system, ISR falls squarely in the Intelligence WFF, with the intelligence staff bargaining and compromising with the other WFFs for resources and priorities, such as UAVs, which the brigade's intelligence staff typically do not directly control. In the Russian system, the commander is responsible for intelligence, along with the other WFFs, and he decides what does and does not get resourced. All assets that are capable of

performing ISR functions, such as the UAV company's UAVs, the air defense battalions' radars, the electronic warfare company's sensors, and the brigade's reconnaissance battalion and signal intelligence platoon are used as he deems fit, and are networked accordingly. The commander will pull assets as needed to perform other tasks associated with other WFFs, but this is done at his discretion, and never as a compromise among the staff. This system prevents any problems that could arise from a particularly dominant personality on the staff acquiring more resources than would otherwise be allocated. The commander's personal attention to all of these aspects seems daunting to most persons familiar with the Western MDMP, but not unduly so for Russians. Since a Russian commander usually just selects maneuvers from his well-rehearsed tactical battle drills, the details of WFFs only need to be tweaked as necessary to fit the operational environment. The significance of differences between these systems is that a Russian unit in similar circumstances as it its Western counterpart may pursue a radically different "best" course of action due to these differences. In short, a U.S. staff cannot simply "put on their red hats" and reasonably expect to ascertain the decisions of their Russian counterparts, as both are using different systems for military decision making.

Theory of Implementation

The Russian education system continues to emphasize mathematics and science. Consequently, "math anxiety" is not a problem, particularly among military professionals. Mathematical determination articles are a normal part of most Russian professional military journals. Russian officers use mathematical models to aid in their planning. Nomograms and calculations quickly resolve issues such as determining pass times and march durations; duration and density of artillery fire to achieve necessary percentages of kills and equipment destruction in area fire missions; the time and place where the forces will encounter the enemy main force; the optimal march routes; the time required to move from the assembly area and transition from battalion to platoon attack formation; the artillery expenditure required during this transition; or the numbers of trucks and trips required to move tonnages of different cargo. The math does not stop there. A key component of operational and tactical planning is determining the Correlation of Forces and Means (COFM). This methodology is the mathematical determination of the combat power of the opposing sides after making mathematical adjustments for differences in combat systems, quantity and quality of systems, quality and training of the forces, terrain, morale, activity (attacking, defending, withdrawing, flanking, etc.), and combat experience. The Correlation of Forces and Means provides the ability to determine a mathematical probability of success, most advantageous avenues of attack or withdrawal and rate of advance in an operation or battle and can be the decisive determinant in the commander's decision.[45] Determination of the Correlation of Forces and Means used to be a fairly lengthy mathematical drill, but the methodology has been computerized and upgraded. Mathematical models are also widely used for ammunition, fuel and personnel expenditure rates.

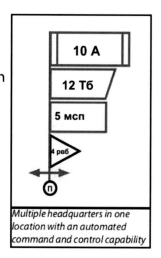

Multiple headquarters in one location with an automated command and control capability

[45] Ministry of Defense of the Russian Federation, "Correlation of Forces and Means" [Соотношение сил и средств], *Military Encyclopedia* [Военная Энциклопедия], Volume 7, Moscow, Voyenizdat, 2003, 583-584.

Correlation of Operational Planning Time

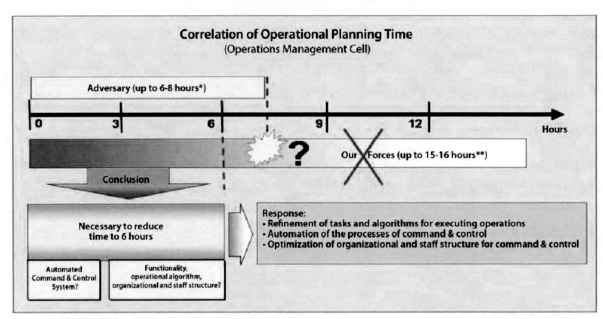

*   Information provided by the Department of Foreign Military Studies of the Combined Arms Academy of the Russian Federation

** In accordance with «Guidelines for the work of the staff and commander in relation to the organization of operations and practical preparations of subordinate commands and troops for combat»

Implementation of the Planning Process

Computerization, automation and stream-lined staff procedures are a priority for Russian staff planners. The motorized rifle brigade has five personnel in its operations section (two officers, two sergeants and one civilian). According to a recent Russian estimate, "typical" brigade-level staff procedures take up 200 man-hours per week. Experience shows that this translates to the requirement to produce 1.5-2 pages of printed text or enter 600-800 tactical symbols and operations notes per hour. Fatigue impacts on this output. For a "typical" brigade battle plan, the operations section spends three hours alone on planning rear services (supply and maintenance) support. Previously, this planning could take up to a day. The Russian goal is not simply to make the planning process faster, the Russian goal is to make the planning process faster than that of the potential adversaries. Current Russian estimates suppose that the most-advanced foreign armies require eight hours to produce a battle plan, the Russian goal is to reduce their planning process for a similiar Russian force to under six hours. In U.S. military speak, the Russians are attempting to gain a decisive Mission Command advantage by using a shorter OODA (Observe, Orient, Decide, Act) loop *vis-à-vis* their adversaries (see image above).

Significance of Automated Command and Control

Perhaps the greatest factor that has caused the development of such a different planning process is Russian thinking on future war. The Russian Armed Forces still believe their first priority is high-speed maneuver warfare, and for this purpose, they believe their system is ideally suited. (The Russian Ground Forces do not see a need to implement a planning system that more easily facilitates counterinsurgency or nation building.) Although the study of

57

battles in the Second World War is rare in the West, these battles are still widely studied in the Russian military at all levels. The Soviet experience in the Second World War has taught generations of Russian officers that high-intensity maneuver warfare is extremely fluid. The best laid plans are quickly overcome by events as the situation rapidly changes. The best way of military decision making (in the Russian view) is not an in-depth staff planning process that requires much coordination and de-confliction, but a system where one person (the commander), who has situational understanding, rapidly issues timely orders to perform standard tactics and/or battle drills (as appropriate) adjusted for the enemy, terrain, etc. (operational environment) to influence the outcome of the battle. While the U.S. and West have made great efforts to incorporate technological developments into modern warfare, there has been relatively little effort to refine the NATO military decision making process. This is not the case for the Russians. They believe that an automated command and control system is a key development for Russian attaining information dominance on the modern battlefield by allowing a Russian commander to more quickly gain situational understanding, draft and transmit plans, and execute operations more quickly than his adversary, (shorter OODA loop). As can be seen by the accompanying graphic, the desired Russian end state is to field a decision making system that cycles faster than the adversary's decision making system.[46] Although automated command and control systems may be fielded (in some form or another) by the U.S. and NATO, these systems will likely have relatively less impact due to some of the automated command and control systems advantages being mitigated by the U.S./NATO military decision making process that requires more human inputs, such as staffing to provide coordination and de-confliction.

The Russian tactical military decision process not only starts with the commander, but is also executed by him as well. This process is facilitated by well-rehearsed battle drills, permanent combined arms subunits, quick and effective staff procedures and improved planning tools. It is a different approach than that of Western armies and does not use their more staff-driven, war-fighting-functions methodology for military decision making. Although the Russian system is substantially less flexible than the U.S./NATO system, it does provide one advantage-speed. (In short, the Russians prefer to sacrifice flexibility for speed in planning and executing operations.) The Russian personnel system was built to support this system, battle drills are emphasized for junior officers and their enlisted soldiers, while more senior officers focus on the study of tactics and their historical employment. The Russians pursue a war fighting philosophy that in high-intensity maneuver warfare, it is far better to execute a satisfactory plan early, than a great plan late. Or more simply stated, a Russian commander prefers to execute a previously rehearsed mission that fulfills the mission requirements adequately, than attempting to plan and execute a custom planned mission that fulfills the mission perfectly.

---

[46] Blog site of Lieutenant General Sergei Skokov, former Chief of Staff of the Russian Ground Forces, "Assessment of the Situation in the Military - Part Two" [Оценка обстановки в военном деле - часть вторая], <http://general-skokov.livejournal.com/2691.html>, accessed 27 November 2016.

Image Courtesy:
Russian Ministry of Defense

Major General (ret.) Ivan Nikolayevich Vorobyov

Doctor of Military Sciences and Hero of the Soviet Union, Major General (retired) Ivan Nikolayevich Vorobyov has a distinguished military and civilian career. Born June 22, 1922, Major General Vorobyov served as an infantry officer in the Great Patriotic War (Second World War) from June 22, 1942 to May 9, 1945 in positions ranging from rifle platoon to battalion commander. He was three times awarded for actions in combat, and is a recipient of the "Order of the Red Banner" award. In 1950, he graduated from the Frunze Combined Arms Academy, earning a prestigious "Gold Medal" for academic excellence. In 1955 he completed a post-graduate program and taught tactics at the academy for the next seventeen years. Later, he served in the Science Division of the Soviet General Staff, retiring from uniformed service in 1987. Major General Vorobyov is a prolific writer, authoring over 200 papers on tactics and operational art. These works have included writings on principles of combined arms combat; the future of warfare; combat actions under special conditions; fighting at night; military-science methodologies; counterterrorism and peacekeeping operations; and interministerial cooperation during combat operations. Major General Vorobyov continues to author articles and still serves on faculty at the Russian Combined Arms Academy.[47] Most of the sources in this, and the following three chapters can be directly or indirectly attributed to his work, as his influence on Soviet, and later Russian, tactics has no Western equivalent. Major General Vorobyov has also written extensively on the importance of the information component of war (including electronic warfare). In the past, Russian military thinkers have thought of combat in terms of space: depth, width and height. Due to Major General Vorobyov's writings, many Russian officers believe that a fourth value – information - is now equally important.

---

[47] Major General Ivan Nikolayevich Vorobyov's biography as found at: <dic.academic.ru/dic.nsf/enc_biography/131179/Воробьев>.

Chapter 3
The Defense

Defensive Theory
The Goals of the Defense
- Deflect attacks by superior enemy forces
- Inflict maximum losses
- Retain important areas, objects, and key terrain
- Create favorable conditions for the conduct of an offensive[1]

Requirements for the Defense
The main requirements for the defense are that it is <u>stable</u> and <u>active</u>. In terms of stability, the defense should be able to withstand any type of enemy assault, including attacks by massed tanks and infantry and airborne/air assault landings. It must protect vital areas and destroy any enemy elements that penetrate the defense. In order to fulfill these requirements, the defense must have:
- In depth echelonment, prepared for an extended defense against an enemy with weapons of mass destruction, precision-guided munitions, and electronic warfare
- Antitank Capabilities
- Air Defense Capabilities
- Anti-Assault Capabilities

Achieving Stability in the Defense
Stability in the Defense is achieved by the accomplishment of a number of objectives:
- It must be able to withstand the effects of nuclear weapons.
- It must have a low vulnerability to enemy precision weapons. In order to protect against precision weapons, forces must be dispersed, covered and concealed. Forces must have means of obscuring their positions from radar and thermal imaging devices, and means of protection from precision weapons using electronic warfare.
- It has to be antitank capable, able to repel assaults by tanks and armored vehicles.
- It must be capable of defending against tactical and operational air strikes.
- It has to be capable of repelling airborne (parachute) and air assault attacks, and handling sabotage and reconnaissance groups.

Characteristics of an Active Defense
The characteristics of an Active Defense:
- Places the enemy under constant fire
- Creates unfavorable conditions for the enemy to conduct battle
- Conducts extensive maneuver of forces and systems in the conduct of fires and assaults
- Conducts decisive counterattacks.

[1] This section, including graphics, has been compiled from many sources to include:
"Requirements for the Defense" [Требования предъявляемые к обороне], as found on *Studiopedia*, <http://studopedia.info/1-67775.html>, accessed on 1 July 2016.
V.N. Zaritski and L.A. Kharkevich, *General Tactics* [Общая Тактика], Tambov: Tambov Government Technical University, 2007.
Field Manual: Preparation and Conduct of Combined Arms Warfare [Боевой Устав: По Подготовке и Ведению Общевойскового Боя], Moscow: Ministry of Defense of the Russian Federation, 2005.
Source material has also been obtained from a variety of training documents produced by Russian military academies and military departments in civilian academic institutions.

Achieving an Active Defense
The Active Defense is achieved by:
- Careful organization of the means of nuclear and conventional fires to destroy the enemy and the skillful implementation of this during combat.
- Timely maneuver of forces and systems, fires and obstacles against a threatened axis.
- Jamming of enemy C2 systems, weapons, and aircraft.

The maneuver of forces and systems involved in the transfer of reinforcements and their deployment on a new axis of advance, line or area is carried out to create a more advantageous grouping of forces to fulfill a military mission. The maneuver of forces and systems in the defense may be carried out along the front line of the defenses, from the rear to the front or from the front to the rear, and includes units and subunits of all branches.

Types of Defense
Positional- This is the primary type of defense that more fully achieves these goals. This defense inflicts maximum losses upon the enemy by stubbornly holding prepared defensive positions.

Maneuver- The purpose of this defense is to inflict losses on the enemy, gain time and preserve one's own force. This defense is conducted by successive defensive battles, planned in advance and echeloned throughout the depth of the defense. Short counterattacks augment the defense of the security zone.

Forms of Maneuver Defense
- The maneuver force has means to prevent attacks in the threatened area in order to prevent an enemy breakthrough on the axis of the main attack, eliminating the threat of being flanked and exploiting an enemy flank or boundary.
- Maneuver of the second echelon (reserve) for employment on a prepared firing lines to close any gaps in the defense resulting from massive air strikes and enemy precision munitions, in order to repel any enemy breakthroughs.
- Maneuver strikes and fires on essential enemy formations.
- Maneuver of antitank artillery and antitank guided missiles subunits, attack helicopters, the antitank reserve, and the mobile obstacle detachment on the axes of deployment in threatened areas to prevent enemy tank breakthroughs.
- Anti-airborne/air assault maneuver by the reserve or an element of the second echelon, as well as attack helicopters with goal of destroying the enemy air assaults.

Motorized Rifle Subunits in the Defense
Motorized rifle battalion- defends a fortified area 3-5 kilometers wide and 2-2.5 kilometers in depth. It is a unified position with the strong points of the battalion's motorized rifle companies, which are prepared for 360° defense. In those areas where the terrain is not all accessible for attacking forces and in a security zone defense or with a forward position, the defense width may increase. The battalion position has three or four trenches, consisting of company strong points and positions for TO&E and attached weapons. These positions are linked by a unitary fire plan, obstacles and communications trenches.

<u>Motorized rifle company</u>- defends a strong point up to 1.5 kilometers wide and one kilometer deep. It consists of two trenches and includes the strong points of the company's motorized rifle platoons and fighting positions for company weapons and attached subunits. These positions are linked by a unitary fire plan, obstacles and communications trenches.

<u>Motorized rifle platoon</u>- defends a strong point up to 400 meters wide and up to 300 meters deep. The strong point consists of squad positions, fighting positions, and firing positions for BMPs or BTRs and attached weapons. The strong point for a tank platoon consists of firing positions for the tanks and attached weapons.

Conditions for the Transition to the Defense
In the absence of contact with the enemy (in advance), forces may transition to the defense for the following reasons and/or under the following conditions:
- To protect the state border
- On an axis where one's offensive forces are not engaging, but where enemy forces may attack
- On the coastal areas where there is a threat of enemy landings
- When assigned to the second echelon (reserve)
- On an axis required to transition to the offensive.

In direct contact with the enemy (forced), forces may transition to the defense for the following reasons and/or under the following conditions :
- To repel counterattacks
- To secure and retain captured defensive lines
- To cover the flanks of an advancing force on a threatened direction
- Due to the results of an unsuccessful meeting engagement
- During an offensive when the force has suffered heavy losses.

Preparation of the Defense
Preparation of the defense begins with receipt of orders from the senior commander. It includes:
- Organizing for combat
- Decision making
- Giving the orders to subordinate units
- Reconnaissance
- Organization of cooperation and an integrated system of fires, comprehensive logistic support and C2
- Development of diagrams for the battalion's area of defense, company strong points
- Preparation to carry out combat missions
- Conduct of the defense, creation of combat orders and systems of fires
- Engineering support in the area of defense (strong point)
- Organization and conduct of morale and psychological work
- Practical work of the commander, his deputies, the battalion staff with the subordinate subunits, and other activities.

The Defense in Special Conditions

Defense in a City (Village)

A battalion in a city (village) usually defends one or more blocks, a company a quarter or more of the buildings (defended by the battalion), and the platoon - one or two buildings. Every populated area and separate building held by a battalion (company) must be turned into an impregnable fortress with all-around defense, that can hold on, even when fully surrounded by the enemy.

Defense in the Mountains

Defense in the mountains, as a rule, is built on a broad front, intercepting the most accessible areas of enemy action, plateaus, and valleys, as in normal conditions. The main efforts are concentrated on the defense of the commanding heights, passes, road junctions and other important terrain. Strong points are prepared for a circular (360°) defense. Reconnaissance, patrols and ambushes and obstacles cover the areas between them.

Defense in the Forest

Defense in the forest is based on company and platoon strong points, prepared for a circular (360°) defense and on road intersections, clearings, and gorges between lakes and swamps. Reconnaissance, patrols and ambushes and obstacles cover the areas between them.

Defense in the Desert

Defense in the desert is established on the most probable direction of enemy advance. It is based on a well-organized system of fire and maneuver and a wide second echelon (reserve). Availability of rugged terrain with dunes and salt flats allows the battalion to build defenses on a broad front in one echelon with more gaps between strong points than usual.

Defense in the Northern Regions and Winter

Defense in northern regions is organized on a broad front on the axes available for an enemy attack. The defense usually consists of company and platoon strong points that are prepared for a circular (360°) defense. Efforts are focused upon securing roads and adjacent heights, settlements, gorges, crossings over water barriers and other important objects.

Squad in the Defense

A motorized rifle squad in the defense works, as a rule, as part of a platoon, and can also be assigned as an ambush party. A BMP without dismounts can conduct a fire ambush, serve as a roving firing platform, and be part of a group of BMPs or part of the *bronegruppa* of a battalion or company. A squad defends a fighting position with up to a 100-meter frontage. A defense requires a combat formation, system of strong points and firing positions, and an integrated fire plan.[2]

Elements of the Combat Formation

The combat formation includes:
- Maneuver group
- Fire group
- BMP or BTR

System of Strong Points and Firing Positions

A motorized rifle squad consists of primary and alternate (temporary) firing positions for BMPs (BTRs), machine guns, grenade launchers and locations for rifle firing, in conjunction with adjacent squads destroying the enemy in front and on the flanks of the platoon's strong point. The distance between the main and reserve positions for machine guns and rocket-propelled grenade launchers (sometimes riflemen) must be at least five meters. The fighting position of the squad may be co-located with weapons controlled by the senior commander. If time permits, the BMP (BTR), should be dug in.

Integrated Fire Plan

A system of fire for a motorized rifle squad includes a zone of fire for the duty weapons, a zone of continuous multilayered squad fire to the front and on the flanks and planned maneuver fire on threatened axis of advance. The squad commander commands by radio, voice, signals, and personal example. The squad leader is positioned where he can best ensure effective fires.

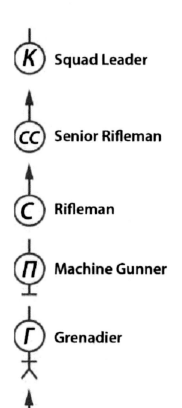

K Squad Leader

CC Senior Rifleman

C Rifleman

П Machine Gunner

Г Grenadier

ПГ Assistant Grenadier

Composition of Dismounted Squad (variant)

---

[2] This section, including graphics, has been compiled from many sources to include:

"Squad in the Defense" [Отделение в обороне], as found on *Studiopedia*, <http://studopedia.info/1-67776. html>, accessed on 1 July 2016.

V.N. Zaritski and L.A. Kharkevich, *General Tactics* [Общая Тактика], Tambov: Tambov Government Technical University, 2007.

Field Manual: Preparation and Conduct of Combined Arms Warfare [Боевой Устав: По Подготовке и Ведению Общевойскового Боя], Moscow: Ministry of Defense of the Russian Federation, 2005.

Source material has also been obtained from a variety of training documents produced by Russian military academies and military departments in civilian academic institutions.

Aspects of Fire for a Motorized Rifle Squad

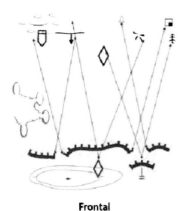

Frontal

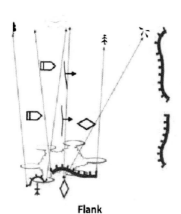

Flank

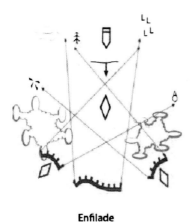

Enfilade

(Left) The defending motorized rifle squad conducts frontal, flanking and enfilade fire. In the frontal example, the squad is the center squad of a platoon defending on line. It is supported by a tank and a medium machine gun from the platoon or company. Each has its limits of fire and these limits overlap with those of the flanking squads. In the flanking example, a motorized rifle squad, a tank and an AGS-17 automatic grenade launcher crew have dug in at a position flanking an expected enemy axis of attack. As the enemy attacks the main defensive position, the defending flanking force takes the enemy under fire. In the enfilade example, the defending motorized rifle squad holds against a frontal attack while two tanks open enfilade fire from dug-in positions.

The graphic on the facing page depicts the 1st Motorized Rifle Squad's range card which the squad leader prepares and uses to ensure that there are no gaps or unintentional overlapping fields of fire. He is defending as part of a platoon and company defense, so necessary details from his neighboring squads and the company fire plan are included. The squad defends in the middle of the platoon defensive position. It is deployed in a fighting trench with an antipersonnel and antitank minefield and barbed wire to its front. It's RPG and squad machine gun have their primary positions in the trench line and their alternate positions dug in against a rear or flanking attack. The squad BMP is dug in about 200 meters behind the trench. It has three alternate prepared fighting positions. Two are located just behind the trench on the left and right flanks of the squad. The third is located to the rear as part of a 360° defense. There are also prepared primary and alternate fighting positions for a tank on the squad's right flank. The squad's sector of fire is marked by landmark limits—the right limit is Target 4, the left limit is some trees. Crew-served weapons (RPG, machine gun and BMP) are assigned sectors of fire based on landmarks with a right and left limit. The squad and its crew served weapons may extend their sectors of fire on order. The new limits are drawn with dashed lines. Limit stakes, or the machine gun's T&E mechanism, mark the sector limits for night firing or when firing through smoke. Part of the preparation includes walking the area forward of the trench to determine dead space that should be covered by rifle or hand grenades. The platoon leader has determined two concentrated fire areas in his sector. These areas are designed to stop an enemy advance on a likely axis of advance by focusing the entire platoon's direct fire power on a line approximately 400 meters long. The first squad fires into box one. The company commander has also determined a company concentrated fire area for his company. Each platoon fires into its designated box.

Motorized Rifle Squad Range Card

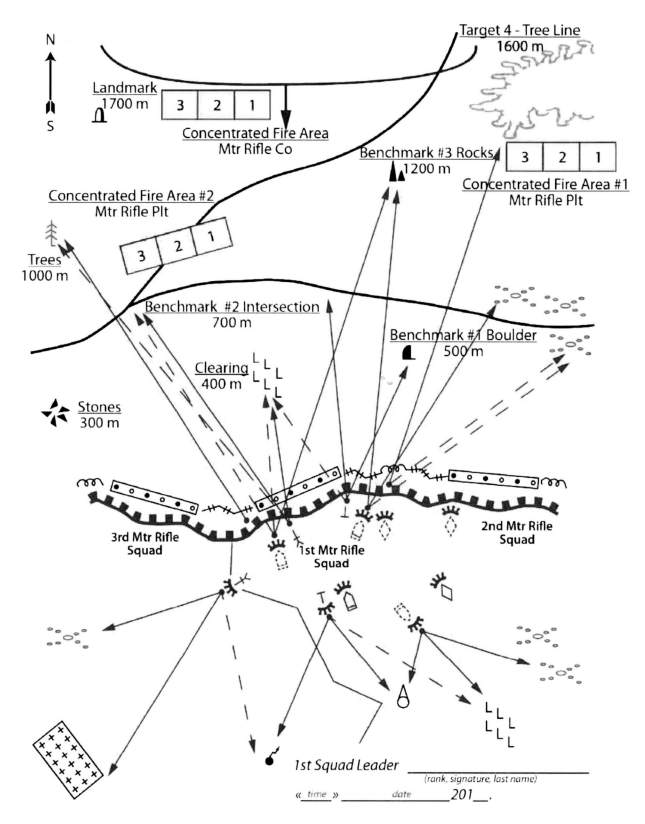

Target 4 - Tree Line
1600 m

Landmark
1700 m

3	2	1

Concentrated Fire Area
Mtr Rifle Co

Benchmark #3 Rocks
1200 m

3	2	1

Concentrated Fire Area #1
Mtr Rifle Plt

Concentrated Fire Area #2
Mtr Rifle Plt

3	2	1

Trees
1000 m

Benchmark #2 Intersection
700 m

Benchmark #1 Boulder
500 m

Clearing
400 m

Stones
300 m

3rd Mtr Rifle
Squad

1st Mtr Rifle
Squad

2nd Mtr Rifle
Squad

1st Squad Leader _____
                    (rank, signature, last name)

«___time___» _____ date _____ 201___.

Platoon in the Defense

A motorized rifle or tank platoon can occupy the defense in a first- or second-echelon company, be part of a combined arms reserve of a battalion or company, be in a combat

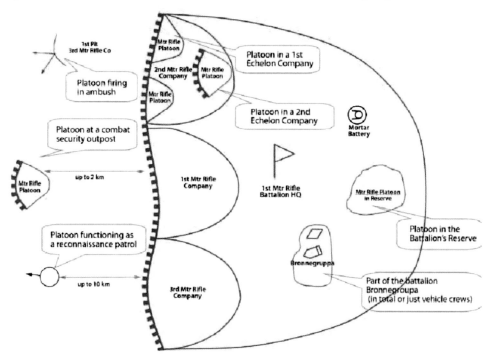

Positions for a Motorized Rifle Platoon in the Defense

security outpost, be a combat reconnaissance patrol and conduct ambush by fire, or be in a battalion or company *bronegruppa*. The defense must support the repulse of the enemy's attack, and destruction of the enemy's tanks and personnel on the forward edge of the defensive area, on the flanks, and throughout the depths of the defense. A motorized rifle or tank platoon is assigned to a strong point with a field of fire, a supplemental field of fire and one or two areas of concentrated fire. The platoon, when part of a battalion combined arms reserve, may have an additional one or two firing lines and routes of travel to them. A motorized rifle (tank) platoon defends a strong point up to 400 meters wide and 300 meters deep. A defense includes a platoon combat formation, system of strong points and firing positions, and integrated fire plan.[3]

---

[3] This section, including graphics, has been compiled from many sources to include:
"Platoon in the Defense" [Взвод в обороне], as found on *Studiopedia*, <http://studopedia.info/1-67777.html>, accessed on 1 July 2016.
V.N. Zaritski and L.A. Kharkevich, *General Tactics* [Общая Тактика], Tambov: Tambov Government Technical University, 2007.
Field Manual: Preparation and Conduct of Combined Arms Warfare [Боевой Устав: По Подготовке и Ведению Общевойскового Боя], Moscow: Ministry of Defense of the Russian Federation, 2005.
Source material has also been obtained from a variety of training documents produced by Russian military academies and military departments in civilian academic institutions.

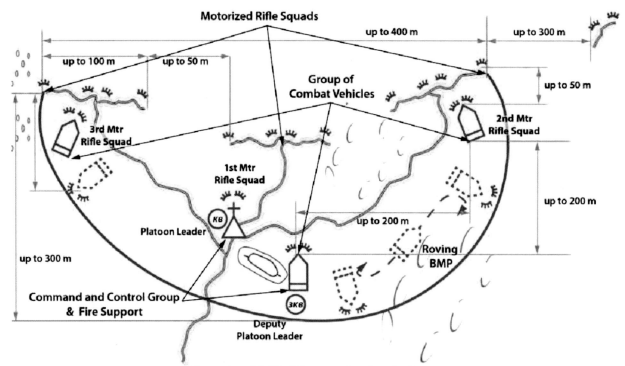

Motorized Rifle Platoon in the Defense

(Above) The motorized rifle platoon defends with two or three squads forward, and usually creates alternate positions for a 360° defense. The BMPs or BTRs have primary and alternate fighting positions, or may be withdrawn into a company bronegrupa (mobile armored reserve). In this case, the platoon defends with three squads forward. The BMPs of the 2nd and 3rd squads have fighting positions directly behind their squads, while the BMP of the 1st squad backs up the 1st squad and has a contingency mission to rove from position to position, securing the right rear of the platoon position. The 3rd squad BMP has an alternate position securing the left rear of the platoon position. The first squad BMP serves as an alternate platoon CP. The main platoon CP is located by the juncture of the communications trenches from the squads and leading to the company CP.

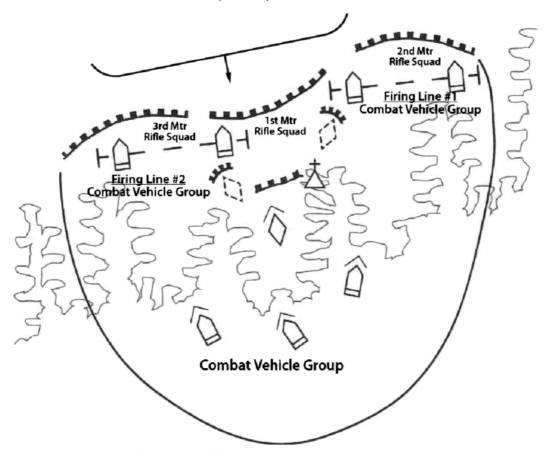

Motorized Rifle Platoon in the Defense

(Above) This graphic shows a motorized rifle platoon defending along a wood line. There is a tank dug in supporting the platoon. The tank has two alternate fighting positions. The BMPs are dug in back in the woods, but the intent is not to fight them from three individual positions. Rather the BMPs will be committed behind the 2nd or 3rd squad in a firing line. The tank has three prepared fighting positions. (Described in more detail on page 72.)

The graphics on the facing page depict three variants of a platoon defense. The first has three squads forward. The second has two squads forward and one back. The third has three squads forward with the right flank refused. All have a 360° defense and the second and third examples are reinforced with a medium machine gun and an AGS-17 automatic grenade launcher squad.

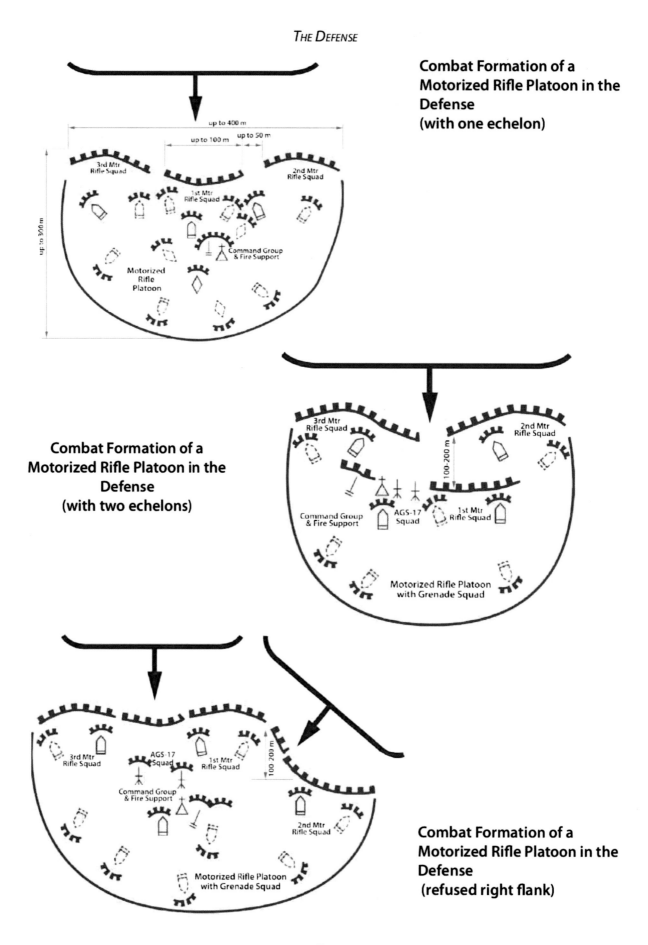

Combat Formation of a Motorized Rifle Platoon in the Defense (with one echelon)

up to 400 m

up to 100 m

up to 50 m

up to 300 m

3rd Mtr Rifle Squad

1st Mtr Rifle Squad

2nd Mtr Rifle Squad

Command Group & Fire Support

Motorized Rifle Platoon

Combat Formation of a Motorized Rifle Platoon in the Defense (with two echelons)

3rd Mtr Rifle Squad

2nd Mtr Rifle Squad

100-200 m

Command Group & Fire Support

AGS-17 Squad

1st Mtr Rifle Squad

Motorized Rifle Platoon with Grenade Squad

3rd Mtr Rifle Squad

AGS-17 Squad

1st Mtr Rifle Squad

100-200 m

Command Group & Fire Support

2nd Mtr Rifle Squad

Motorized Rifle Platoon with Grenade Squad

Combat Formation of a Motorized Rifle Platoon in the Defense (refused right flank)

Elements of the Combat Formation
- Squads in position
- BMPs (BTRs) in firing position
- Weapons fire controlled by the platoon leader

In addition, the platoon can constitute a grouping of military vehicles. Motorized rifle squads are usually located in a single trench in a line. In order to reinforce the stability of the defense, one of the squads of the platoon may be set back within the strong point and fight from a 100-200-meter trench. If there is a threat of attack from the flanks, the combat formation can be laid out as an echelon right or echelon left. The command and control element and fire support is designed to control subunits and fire support during the battle, as well as to address a requirement for rapid response fires. It consists of weapons and firepower directly subordinate to the platoon commander and attached firepower. A group of combat vehicles is used to improve the stability and provide an active defense and support motorized rifle subunits on their firing line from previously selected positions. The group is located in a designated locale (back in the forest, on the heights of the opposite slope). On the command of the platoon commander, the group goes forward to a designated firing line and from that line defeats the enemy and returns to its original position, and is once again ready to act when needed. Every combat vehicle has a prepared fighting position in the designated firing lines. The group is controlled by the platoon commander's deputy. (Graphic on page 70)

System of Strong Points and Firing Positions
The platoon's strong point includes the platoon's squad firing positions, the platoon command-observation post, the platoon's organic and attached weapons and a deployment area for the group of combat vehicles. The gap between platoon strong points can be up to 300 meters and up to 50 meters between the squad positions. A continuous trench may be dug across the front of the platoon strong point, which joins the squad fighting positions. Communications trenches [not shown] join the fighting trench with the vehicle fighting positions and extend into the depth of the defense to the next trench line. The trenches provide communication and move personnel to protected areas, fighting bunkers, squad sheltered quarters, ditches and dugouts for ammunition and rocket storage. The platoon commander controls his subordinates from the command-observation post, which is dug into the trench network communications (located either in a squad fighting position or deeper within the strong point). The commander of a tank platoon commands from inside his tank.

Scheme of Fire for a Platoon in the Defense

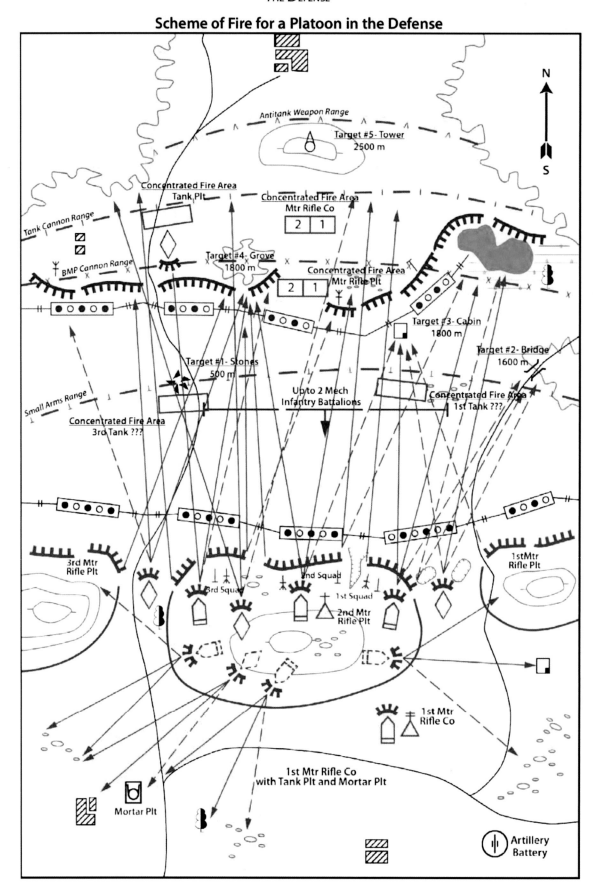

Integrated Fire Plan
- Participation in concentrated fire along the forward edge of the defense
- Zones of antitank fires conducted by BMPs (tanks) and continuous multilayered fires by other platoons' weapons along the forward edge of the battle area, in the gaps, on the flanks, and throughout the depth of the defense
- Prepared maneuver fire by BMPs, tanks and other weapons systems on threatened axes.

The system of fire for a motorized rifle (tank) platoon is an integral part of the system of fire for its company (battalion) and includes preparatory fires by duty weapons,[4] antitank and platoon multilayered continuous fire zones, concentrated fire sectors, and planned maneuver by fire. The system of fire is organized to take into consideration the combat potential of all the weapons of the platoon, attached weapons and integrated fires of neighboring units, all tied into engineer and naturally occurring obstacles. The system of fire should ensure the defeat of the enemy, particularly its tanks and other armored vehicles, on the approaches to the defense, on the forward edge of the defense, between squad fighting positions, and on the flanks of the platoon's strong point throughout the depth of the defense, with the potential of conducting effective fire to the front, flank and overlapping fires. An all-round defense of the strong point is also conducted. The readiness of the system of fire is determined when the BMPs, tanks, crew–served weapons and other weapons are in their prepared firing positions, range cards and firing data are prepared and verified,[5] and ammunition and rocket round supply points are dug in. Infantry fighting vehicles and tanks are located along the front and in the depth of the platoon fighting position, with at least a 200-meter interval between each other. Fields of fire for platoons and squads are determined by left and right boundaries. Each boundary is specified by two points (benchmarks). BMPs, tanks, antitank missile systems, grenade launchers, flamethrowers and machine guns have specified primary and secondary sectors of fire, and their firing positions have ranges and type of fire coverage indicated. These fields of fire should overlap.

Means of Reinforcement
Common Attachments for a Motorized Rifle Platoon
- A Tank
- Antitank subunit
- AGS-17 subunit
- Flamethrower subunit
- Anti-aircraft subunit
- NBC Recon personnel

---

[4] Duty weapons are weapons deployed out of their primary firing positions for the purpose of drawing enemy fire and engaging enemy targets before the main battle is joined. Russian troops are trained to not respond to enemy probing fires or the appearance of enemy vehicles, since the enemy is hoping to determine the location and outline of the defense, location of crew-served weapons and vehicles, and the type and readiness of the defending unit. Duty weapons will fire from a temporary position and then move to another temporary position. On order, the duty weapons will reoccupy their primary fighting positions.

[5] Range cards are prepared for each primary and alternate firing position. Ranges are walked to identify dead space and other areas where the enemy may escape detection and destruction. Tranverse and elevating mechanisms are used on machine guns, particularly at night, to prevent weapons from being fired over the heads of the advancing enemy.

Sequence of Work after Receipt of Mission
In the absence of direct contact with the enemy, the platoon leader receives an order and does the following:
- Makes his decision and draws his plan of defense on his map
- Briefs his squad leaders
- Guides the platoon to its specified strong point or from concealed places on the approaches to the platoon position and covertly organizes its security
- Together with the squad and attached forces leaders, conducts on-site reconnaissance
- Gives his combat order
- Organizes his system of integrated fires, support and C2
- Organizes the occupation of the strong point
- Sites in positions of the combat formation and checks range cards and integration of fires
- Organizes observation and engineer field fortification of his platoon strong point.

Having received the orders to transition to the defense while in direct contact with the enemy, a platoon commander must:
- Quickly make his decision for the conduct of the defense
- Give his orders to his squads to occupy the positions in the designated platoon strong point
- Organize surveillance to the front and on the flanks of the platoon's strong point
- Coordinate platoon interaction and the platoon system of integrated fires, as well as logistic support, C2 and engineer field fortification of his platoon strong point
- Subsequently study the terrain, clarify squad missions and platoon layout, coordinate platoon interaction and if necessary, deal with other matters.

Considerations of the Platoon Leader
- Missions of subordinate squads, their positions, fields of fire and additional sectors of fire
- Main and reserve (temporary) firing positions of BMPs (BTRs), their primary and secondary sectors of fire from each position
- Platoon zones of concentrated fire and each squad's portion of the zone where it must fire (similar to final protective fire)
- Missions of attached weapons, their primary and reserve firing positions, and their primary and supplementary sectors of fire for every position
- Designated marksman missions, their primary and alternate firing positions, and sequence of observation and fire
- Missions for the combat medic and the sequence for the provision of medical assistance to the wounded
- Which weapons will cover gaps with their neighboring units and secure flanks.
  The platoon commander's orders specify the time to occupy the defense, prepare a system of fires, and the sequence and timing of engineering support.

Company in the Defense

A motorized rifle (tank) company may be part of a first or second echelon battalion in the defense, be in the security zone, occupy a forward position, or be a combined arms reserve or antilanding reserve. When breaking contact and withdrawing, a company may be designated as a point security march detachment, rear guard security detachment or flanking march security detachment. A motorized rifle (tank) company in the defense can occupy strong points up to 1.5 kilometers wide and 1 kilometer deep. Platoons in company strong points may be angled backwards, allowing them to be echeloned in various locations. A defense includes a combat formation, system of strong points and firing positions, integrated fire plan, and engineer obstacle system.[6]

Elements of the Combat Formation

The elements of the combat formation are structured as follows:
- The first echelon consists of two platoons
- A second echelon or reserve consists of one platoon
- An artillery subunit (artillery battery or mortar platoon, attached company) remains subordinate to the company commander and is used to support the first-echelon motorized rifle platoons
- Subunits and weapons (ordnance) subordinate directly to the company commander.

Depending on the situation, a *bronegruppa* or ambush team may be formed. The combat formation of companies in the defense usually consists of two echelons. In some cases, the combat formation can consist of just one echelon, with a combined arms reserve.

System of Strong Points and Firing Positions

The system of strong points and firing positions are created to support the defense mission of the company in accordance with the commander's decision, the combat capabilities of subunits, the time available and the nature of the terrain. They include:
- Combat security positions
- Firing positions for tanks, BMPs, BTRs, antitank missiles, TO&E and attached weapons
- Trenches and communications trenches
- Platoon and company strong points united in the battalion defensive area.

A company strong point has two trenches and consists of strong points of the company's subordinate platoons, firing positions for the company weapons and those of attached subunits, and a *bronegruppa* staging area. In addition, it is equipped with a command-observation post.

---

[6] This section, including graphics, has been compiled from many sources to include:
"Company in the Defense" [Рота в обороне], as found on *Studiopedia*, <http://studopedia.info/1-67778.html>, accessed on 1 July 2016.
V.N. Zaritski and L.A. Kharkevich, *General Tactics* [Общая Тактика], Tambov: Tambov Government Technical University, 2007.
Field Manual: Preparation and Conduct of Combined Arms Warfare [Боевой Устав: По Подготовке и Ведению Общевойскового Боя], Moscow: Ministry of Defense of the Russian Federation, 2005.
Source material has also been obtained from a variety of training documents produced by Russian military academies and military departments in civilian academic institutions.

Combat Formation of a Motorized Rifle Company in the Defense (in the first echelon)

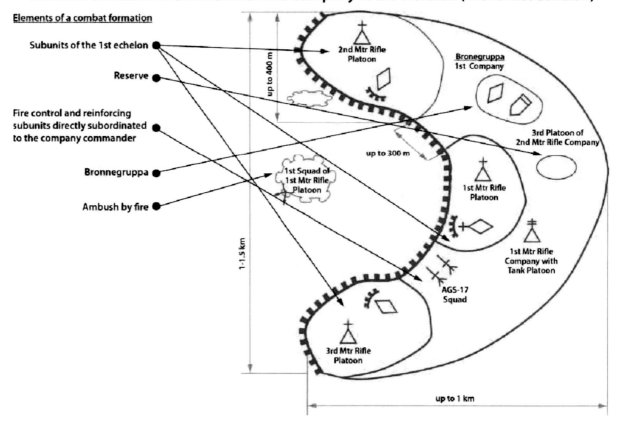

Elements of a combat formation

Subunits of the 1st echelon ●

Reserve ●

Fire control and reinforcing
subunits directly subordinated
to the company commander ●

Bronnegruppa ●

Ambush by fire ●

2nd Mtr Rifle
Platoon

Bronegruppa
1st Company

3rd Platoon of
2nd Mtr Rifle Company

up to 300 m

1st Squad of
1st Mtr Rifle
Platoon

1st Mtr Rifle
Platoon

1st Mtr Rifle
Company with
Tank Platoon

AGS-17
Squad

3rd Mtr Rifle
Platoon

up to 400 m

1-1.5 km

up to 1 km

(Above) This graphic depicts a typical layout of a defending first echelon motorized rifle company with an attached tank platoon. The commander defends with three motorized rifle platoons on line, but has refused the center to create a fire sac. A lone squad is positioned within the sac to deceive the enemy as to the defense's forward edge and the presence of the fire sac. The plan is to pull the enemy attack within the sac where it will be decimated by enfilade fire. The company has two reserves-a motorized rifle platoon from another company and the company bronegruppa which is a mobile maneuver reserve.

The gaps between the platoon strongpoints are up to 300 meters. The platoon strong points are placed on the most probable axes of enemy advance in order to intercept the enemy.

The first trench is the front edge of the defense. In front of the trench are mines and obstacles. The first trench is selected with consideration of the presence of natural antitank obstacles, ability to provide good observation of the enemy, and the best position to lay all types of continuous fire at the forward edge of the defense, the flanks, and in the gaps throughout the depth of defense.

The second trench is placed at a distance of 400-600 meters from the first trench, with an expectation that defending units can support subunits in the first trench, lay fire onto the approaches to the forward edge of the defense and provide covering fires onto the forward obstacles.

Positions for a Motorized Rifle Company in the Battalion Defense

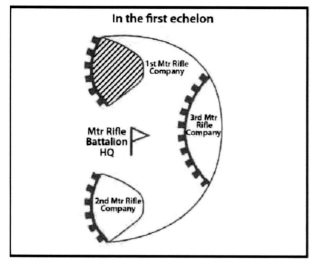

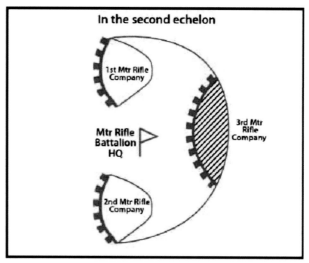

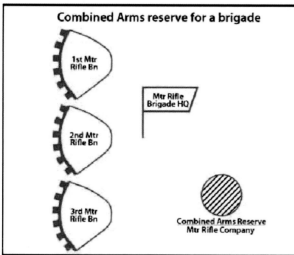

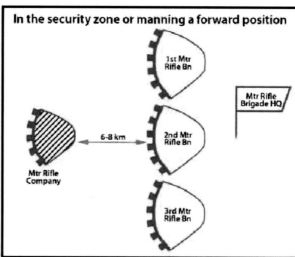

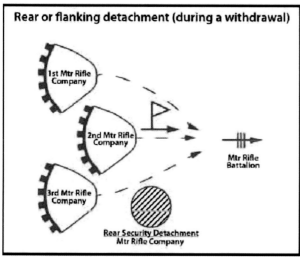

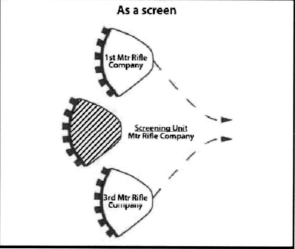

(Above)The motorized rifle company can be positioned in a variety of locations in the defense. The rear or flanking detachment is used during a fighting withdrawal while the screening detachment is used during a break in contact.

The command-observation post of the company is placed in the depth of the defense up to 800 meters from the forward edge of the defense, where the terrain is best for observation and command and control.

Integrated Fire Plan

The system of fire of a company consists of the massing the various weapons' fires by the senior commander to destroy the enemy. The system of fire must be carefully integrated with the obstacle system. It includes:

- Zones of concentrated fire and lines of antiaircraft gun fire on the approaches to the defense, in front of the forward edge of the defense, on the flanks and throughout the depth of the defense
- Antitank zones of fire and continuous multilayered fire by all types of weapons before the forward edge of the battle area, in the gaps, on the flanks and throughout the depths of the defense to destroy the first wave of tanks and other armored vehicles of the enemy
- Prepared maneuver fire.

Motorized Rifle Company in the Defense (in the second echelon)

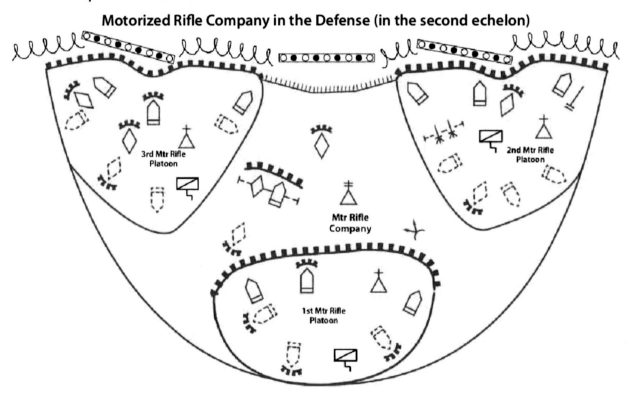

(Above) This graphic shows a second echelon motorized company with an attached tank platoon defending in the second echelon of a battalion defense. It has incorporated a fire sac in its defense that is initially held by a tank. There is a fall-back position where a dug-in firing line of tanks and BMPs (a company bronegruppa) and an ambush prevent breakthrough.

The system of fire is formed by taking into account the following:
- The firing capabilities of all the types of weapons involved
- Their close integration of these weapons
- Their effect of these weapons when combined with the engineering obstacles and natural barriers.

Readiness of the system of fire is determined by:
- Manning of the firing positions
- Prepared range cards and firing data
- The presence of missiles and ammunition.

Means of Reinforcement

The following are common attachments for a motorized rifle company:
- Tank platoon
- Artillery battery/platoon
- Antitank platoon (crew)
- Anti-aircraft squad
- Engineer squad.

A company defending on a main avenue of approach may be reinforced with attached artillery units (mortar platoon or artillery battery), an AGS-17 grenade launcher and antitank subunits. A motorized rifle company may have an attached tank platoon, while a tank company may have an attached motorized rifle platoon.

Sequence of Work after Receipt of Mission

In the absence of direct contact with the enemy, the commander of a company:
- Makes his plan of defense
- Briefs his deputies and subordinate commanders
- Conducts reconnaissance during which he refines his decision
- Gives his combat order
- Organizes cooperation and an integrated system of fires, support, and C2
- Guides the company onto a specified area of defense (strong point) and organizes its engineer support.

After receiving an order to transition to the defense, while in direct contact with the enemy, the commander of the company:
- Organizes the seizure and fortification of designated (advantageous) lines
- In the course of fortifying the lines, makes his decision on the plan of defense
- Gives his combat order to his subordinate units
- Organizes cooperation and an integrated system of fires, NBC defense, and countermeasures against enemy precision weapons
- Gives orders on the basic issues of comprehensive combat support
- Organizes engineering support in the area of defense (strong point)
- Conducts reconnaissance, in course of which, he refines the subunit's order, the order of cooperation and, if necessary, other matters.

System of Fires for a Motorized Rifle Company

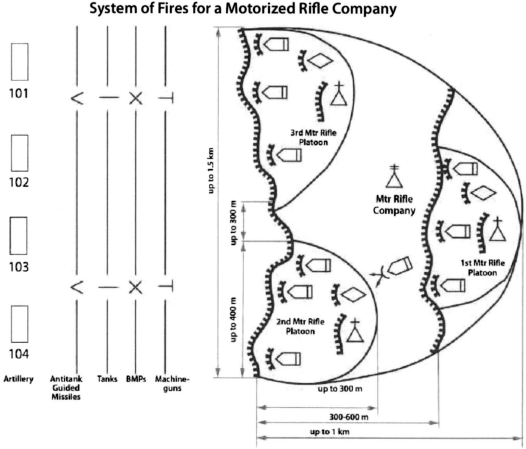

(Above) This graphic shows typical distances for laying out a company defense, but they will be modified to fit the demands of the situation, forces available, threat and terrain. The engagement lines for various firing systems is based on the location of the weapons systems closest to the front line and indicates the point where various weapons systems will begin engaging the advancing enemy. Individual range cards will be modified for those weapons positioned further back

Considerations of the company commander:

- Platoons of the first echelon – reinforcements; strong points and direction on which to concentrate the main effort; tasks to repulse the offensive and destroy the enemy which has penetrated into one's defenses; the number of trenches (including their physical location and layout); fields of fire, additional sectors of fire and zones of concentrated fire; what forces and means are needed to secure the flanks, joints, and gaps, and who is responsible for them; who provides support;
- Platoon of the second echelon - the same duties as that of their platoons of the first echelon, plus, for companies, their lines of deployment for counterattack; for tank companies and motorized rifle companies with BMPs, their firing lines;
- Reserve - assembly area (strong point), on-order missions to prepare for; additionally, for tank companies and motorized rifle companies with BMPs, their firing lines;
- *Bronegruppa*- composition, assembly area and time to occupy it, firing lines and on-order missions to prepare for;
- Ambush – composition, place, mission for engaging an advancing enemy and sequence of withdrawal;

- Attached artillery and mortar battery support – sequence of supporting fire for the security zone; fire missions during enemy movement to the forward edge of the defense and deployment and transition to the attack; fire against enemy stuck into the defense; support of the counterattack of the second echelon, main, alternate and temporary firing positions;
- Grenade launcher (AGS-17) - missions supporting companies of the first echelon and repelling enemy infantry assaults; main and reserve positions; belts of fire; additional sectors of fire; zones of concentrated fire; lines of barrier fire.
- Antitank subunits - the place in the defense and the direction of the enemy advance; the line of deployment; the sequence for occupying positions and on-order missions to prepare for; the signal for opening and ceasing fire; actions after mission accomplishment;
- Anti-aircraft units - launch (firing) positions; sectors of reconnaissance to detect enemy aircraft; time and degrees of readiness; sequence of conduct of fire;
- Security subunits forward of the defense – position; mission; weapons designated for support; sequence of calls for fire; sequence of withdrawal - Concluding the order- the time to be ready to fulfill the order, the time to occupy the defense, the time for readiness of the scheme of integrated fire and time for engineering obstacle work to be completed, the order and sequence for camouflage and field fortification of the area of defense (strong point).

(Right) The graphic on the facing page shows the scheme of fire for a company strong point defense. It is defending with two platoons forward and one back and is configured for a 360° defense. There are an additional tank platoon and two flame projectors (the RPO shoulder-fired rocket launcher has the RPO-Z flame round, RPO-A thermobaric round and the RPO-D smoke screen round). There is the company medical point and feeding point in the second echelon platoon. The company commander has determined sectors of fire and marked the platoon and company areas of concentrated fire on the map. He has drawn the lines where ATGMs, tank main guns, BMPs and small arms and machine guns may open fire. As before, landmarks and benchmarks play a prominent role in laying out the range card.

Motorized Rifle Company in the Defense

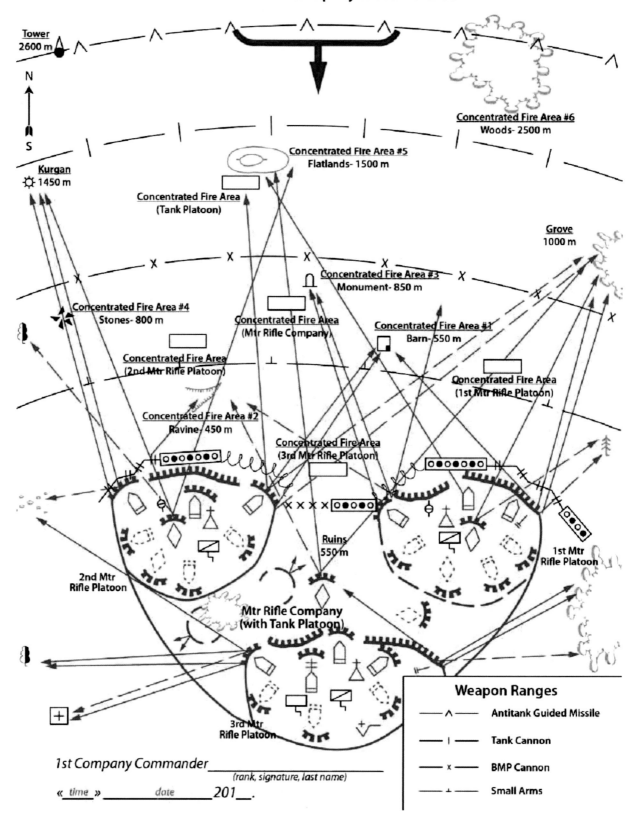

Battalion in the Defense

A motorized rifle or tank battalion can serve in either the first or second echelons of the brigade, in the security zone, in a forward position or as part of the combined arms reserve. A battalion of the first echelon prepares and occupies the first defensive position. The battalion is assigned a defensive region. The width of the battalion defensive area is up to five kilometers and the depth of the defensive area is up to three kilometers. A battalion of the second echelon prepares and occupies the second defensive position. The mortar battery and AGS-17 grenade launcher platoon are, as a rule, directly subordinate to the battalion commander and remain intact to support the defending subunits. A defense includes a combat formation, system of strong points and firing positions, integrated fire plan, and engineer obstacle system.[7]

Elements of the Combat Formation
- 1st echelon motorized rifle companies with reinforcements
- A second echelon motorized rifle company or reserve platoon
- Weapons fire controlled by the battalion commander (artillery battalion, mortar battery, antitank platoon, AGS-17 platoon, air defense platoon)
- *Bronegruppa* (Armored Group)
- Ambush team

The motorized rifle or tank battalion in the defense, as a rule, consists of two echelons, but sometimes one echelon, and has a combined arms reserve of at least one motorized rifle platoon. The combat formation consists of a first echelon comprising two-three motorized rifle companies. The second echelon consists of a motorized rifle company or combined arms reserve of at least one motorized rifle platoon. Artillery subunits include the mortar battery (an artillery battalion may be attached to a maneuver battalion). Subunits that are directly subordinate to the battalion commander include the: AGS-17 grenade launcher platoon, antitank platoon, and attached flamethrower company. Depending on the situation, the formation may include a *bronegruppa* and/or an ambush team. A *bronegruppa* is a mobile reserve that is formed primarily from the infantry fighting vehicles after the motorized rifle soldiers have dismounted from them. It occupies an assembly area and has designated firing lines and blocking positions within the defense.

A first echelon battalion is designed to:
- Defeat the enemy during his deployment and transition to the attack
- Repel the offensive
- Prevent the breakthrough of the forward defense
- Retain strong points
- Prevent an enemy breakthrough into the depths of the battalion defensive region.

[7] This section, including graphics, has been compiled from many sources to include:
"Battalion in the Defense" [Батальон в обороне], as found on *Studiopedia*, <http://studopedia.info/1-67779.html>, accessed on 1 July 2016.
V.N. Zaritski and L.A. Kharkevich, *General Tactics* [Общая Тактика], Tambov: Tambov Government Technical University, 2007.
Field Manual: Preparation and Conduct of Combined Arms Warfare [Боевой Устав: По Подготовке и Ведению Общевойскового Боя], Moscow: Ministry of Defense of the Russian Federation, 2005.
Source material has also been obtained from a variety of training documents produced by Russian military academies and military departments in civilian academic institutions.

A second echelon battalion is designed to:
- Prevent an enemy breakthrough of the first position.
- Destroy or counterattack an enemy breakthrough across the forward edge of the defense.

A motorized rifle company of the second echelon prepares strong points at full speed at the third trench, and then the fourth trench.

The combined arms reserve of a motorized rifle battalion occupies a staging area behind the subunits of the first echelon, prepares a strong point, and prepares to carry out sudden developing missions.

The artillery subunits of a motorized rifle battalion remain intact and are used to support the companies in the first echelon. A battery from an artillery battalion may be attached to a motorized rifle company.

The grenade launcher (AGS-17) subunit, flamethrower subunit, and different means of fires remain subordinate to the battalion commander, occupy positions in the company strong points or between them, and remain intact to concentrate on the direction of the main enemy effort to cover flanks and support counterattacks.

The antitank reserve consists of the antitank platoon. It is designed to destroy tanks and other armored vehicles that penetrate into the depth of the defense and cover tank avenues of approach and the flanks.

The *bronegruppa* is established for the purpose of closing gaps that formed due to enemy fire strikes, as well as other tasks. It consists of tanks, BMPs, and BTRs from first- and second-echelon units and defends against the main avenues of approach. It is commanded by the commander of a platoon of a first-echelon company.

An ambush team attempts to inflict maximum destruction by sudden direct fire and use of minefields. It may consist of a motorized rifle platoon or squad reinforced by flamethrowers and sapper subunits. The firing positions for the fire ambush are put in fortified positions on tank avenues of approach, on the flanks, and on the outskirts of populated areas.

System of Strong Points and Firing Positions
The system of strong points and firing positions of the battalion includes:
- The strong points of companies, connected to each other along the front and throughout the depth, with an integrated system of fires and obstacles
- Primary, alternate and temporary positions for artillery, tanks, infantry fighting vehicles, and other organic and attached firepower
- The positions of combat security outposts.

The battalion defensive area is based on its defensive positions. It has three or four trenches and consists of company strong points, firing positions for artillery subunits, firing positions for other weapons which remain under the direct command of the battalion commander, the assembly area and the firing line for the *bronegruppa*. The gaps between the company strongpoints are up to 1000 meters, and between platoon strong points are up to 300 meters.

The first trench is on the forward edge of the defense. The second trench is 400-600 meters from the first trench, the third trench is 600-1000 meters from the second, and the fourth is 400-600 meters from the third trench.

Positions for a Motorized Rifle Battalion in the Brigade Defense

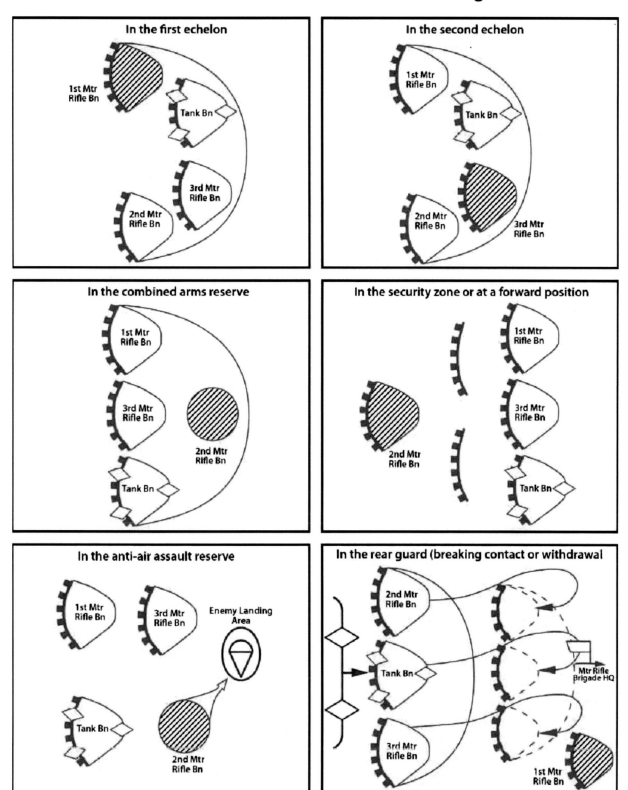

(Above) This graphic shows the possible locations and missions for a motorized rifle battalion in the defense.

Motorized Rifle Battalion in the Defense

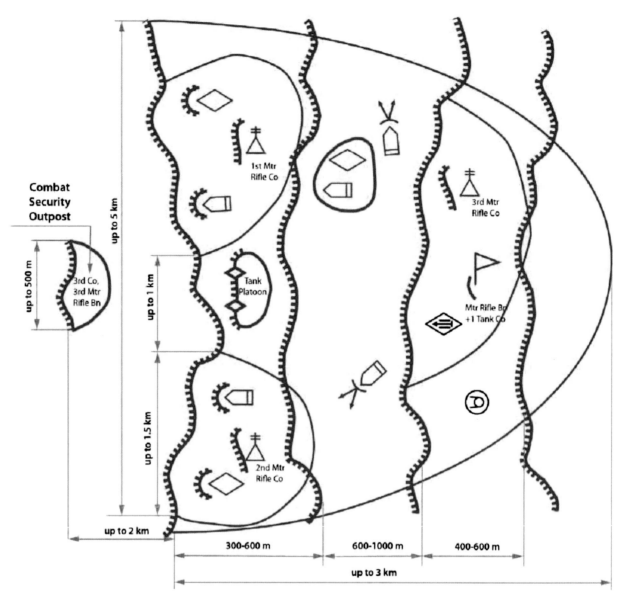

(Above) This graphic gives a range of distances involved in a defense by motorized rifle battalion with an attached tank company. This battalion is defending in two echelons and incorporates a fire sac. It has constituted a bronegruppa with the tanks and BMPs of the second echelon company and has positioned the primary firing positions for its mortar battery fairly deep. A battery of 2S6 Tugunska self-propelled anti-aircraft gun and missile systems are deployed in the rear company. The location of systems and distances will be adjusted to fit the demands of the situation, threat, forces available and terrain.

Integrated Fire Plan

The system of fire of a battalion consists of the massing the various weapons' fires by the senior commander to destroy the enemy. The system of fire must be carefully integrated with the obstacle system. It includes:

- Zones of concentrated fire and lines of antiaircraft gun fire on the approaches to the defense, in front of the forward edge of the defense, on the flanks and throughout the depth of the defense
- Antitank zones of fire and continuous multilayered fire by all types of weapons before the forward edge of the battle area, in the gaps, on the flanks and throughout the depth of the defense to destroy the first wave of tanks and other armored vehicles of the enemy
- Prepared maneuver fire.

The system of fire is formed by taking into account:

- The firing capabilities of all the types of weapons involved
- Their close integration
- Their effect when combined with the engineering obstacles and natural barriers.

Readiness of the system of fire is determined by:

- Manning of the firing positions
- Prepared range cards and firing data
- The presence of missiles and ammunition.

Battalion command-observation posts are usually dug-in within the area of the first echelon companies or in the vicinity of the second echelon (reserve) company strong points two kilometers from the forward edge of the battalion's defenses.

Engineer Obstacle System

Obstacles are objects prepared for on-order destruction (mining). They are emplaced in front of combat security outposts; on the forward edge of the battle area; in gaps between subunits; and on the flanks of the battalion (company) throughout the entire depth of the battalion defensive area in accordance with the planned system of fires and natural obstacles, and after considering the maneuver of subunits and neighboring units.

The system of engineer obstacles includes:

- Minefields
- Mine clusters
- Choke point obstacles
- Locally fabricated obstacles
- Different types of antitank and antipersonnel obstacles.

Means of Reinforcement

The following are common attachments for a motorized rifle battalion:

- Tank company
- Artillery battalion/battery
- Anti-aircraft battery
- Engineer platoon
- NBC reconnaissance subunit.

Sequence of Work after Receipt of Mission

In the absence of direct contact with the enemy, the commander of a battalion:

- Makes his decision of the plan of defense
- Briefs his deputies and subordinate commanders
- Conducts reconnaissance, during which he refines his decision
- Gives his combat order
- Organizes cooperation and an integrated system of fires, support, and C2
- Guides the battalion (company) onto a specified area of defense (strong point) and organizes its engineer support.

After receiving an order to transition to the defense, while in direct contact with the enemy, the commander of the battalion:

- Organizes the seizure and fortification of designated (advantageous) lines
- In the course of fortifying the lines, makes his decision on the plan of defense
- Gives his combat order to his subordinate units
- Organizes cooperation and an integrated system of fires, NBC defense, and countermeasures against enemy precision weapons
- Gives orders on the basic issues of comprehensive combat support
- Organizes engineering support in the area of defense (strong point)
- Conducts reconnaissance, in course of which he refines the subunit's order, the order of cooperation and, if necessary, other matters.

Considerations of the battalion commander:

- Companies of the first echelon – reinforcements; strong points and direction on which to concentrate the main effort; tasks to repulse the offensive and destroy an enemy which has penetrated into one's defenses; the number of trenches and their trace; fields of fire, additional sectors of fire and zones of concentrated fire; what forces and means are needed to secure the flanks, joints, and gaps, and who is responsible for them; who provides support;
- Company of the second echelon - the same duties as that of the companies (platoons) of the first echelon, plus, for companies, their lines of deployment for counterattack; for tank companies and motorized rifle companies with BMPs, their firing lines;
- Reserve - assembly area (strong point); on-order missions to prepare for; additionally for tank companies and motorized rifle companies with BMPs, their firing lines;
- *Bronegruppa* - composition; assembly area and time to occupy it; firing lines; on-order missions to prepare for;
- Ambush team – composition; place; mission for engaging an advancing enemy; sequence of withdrawal;
- Attached artillery and mortar battery support – sequence of supporting fire for the security zone; fire missions during enemy movement to the forward edge of the defense; deployment and transition to the attack; fire against enemy wedged into the defense; support of the counterattack of the second echelon; main, alternate and temporary firing positions;
- Grenade launcher (AGS-17) - missions supporting companies of the first echelon and repelling enemy infantry assaults; main and reserve positions; belts of fire; additional

sectors of fire; zones of concentrated fire; lines of barrier fire;
- Antitank subunits - the place in the defense; the direction of the enemy advance; the line of deployment; the sequence for occupying positions and on-order missions to prepare for; the signal for opening and ceasing fire; actions after mission accomplishment;
- Anti-aircraft units - launch (firing) positions; sectors of reconnaissance to detect enemy aircraft; time and degrees of readiness; sequence of conduct of fire;
- Security subunits forward of the defense – position; mission; weapons designated for support; sequence of calls for fire; sequence of withdrawal;
- Concluding the order-the time to be ready to fulfill the order, the time to occupy the defense, the time for readiness of the scheme of integrated fire and time for engineering obstacle work to be completed, the order and sequence for camouflage and field fortification of the area of defense (strong point).

Brigade in the Defense

A motorized rifle (or tank) brigade defends in either the first or second echelon of an Army Group, or Army Corps. (A Russian Army Group has approximately the same combat power as a small U.S. Army Corps.) It can also serve as a reserve or defend a separate axis. A first-echelon brigade defends on the first defensive axis, where it occupies two to three defensive positions. A motorized rifle brigade defending in the first echelon of the Army Group on the enemy main axis of attack may be reinforced with two or more artillery battalions, antitank subunits and subunits of rocket-propelled flamethrowers. If the brigade is part of an army, it constitutes a defensive belt. If it is serving independently on a separate avenue of approach or in a separate armed conflict, the brigade constitutes a zone of responsibility. The defensive belt or the zone of responsibility are assigned based upon the range of the reconnaissance systems and the flanks and rear of the boundary line that separates the brigade from neighboring units. The assigned size of the zone and area of defense must facilitate the counteraction against the attacking enemy and tactical cooperation between the combat elements of the brigade, and allow adequate space for the freedom of maneuver and dispersion of subunits.[8]

A motorized rifle or tank brigade in the defense includes:
- Brigade combat formation
- Integrated defensive positions, areas and lines
- "Kill zones" for destruction of the enemy
- Integrated air defense
- Integrated antitank defense
- Integrated obstacles
- Integrated air assault/air drop defense
- Integrated command and control.

Elements of the Combat Formation

Depending on the situation, the brigade combat formation in the defense can consist of one or two echelons. A combined arms reserve of at least a motorized rifle company should be constituted from one of these echelons.

The brigade combat formation in the defense includes:
- The first echelon (two or three motorized rifle battalions)
- The second echelon (or combined arms reserve) - one or two battalions, including a tank battalion. The anti-assault reserve is at least a motorized rifle or tank company
- Brigade artillery group
- Air defense subunits
- Antitank reserve
- Obstacle construction detachment
- Anti-air assault subunits.

The combat formation can include a forward detachment, tactical air assault units, and electronic warfare subunits, depending on the situation.

---

[8] "Composition of a Brigade in the Defense" [Построение обороны мотострелковой], as found on *Studiopedia*, <http://studopedia.info/1-67780.htm>, accessed on 1 July 2016.

Battalions in the first echelon are intended to:
- Engage the enemy as it deploys and transitions from column movement to attack formation
- Repel assaults by the enemy in order to avoid enemy pockets in the defensive area
- Deny enemy breakthrough into the depths of its defense
- Destroy enemy subunit pockets at established kill zones and lines.

The second echelon (or reserve) is intended to:
- Deny the enemy's seizure of strong points throughout the depth of the defense
- Prohibit enemy breakthroughs throughout the depth of the defense
- Defeat pockets of the enemy through actions of subunits at designated positions and lines, conduct counterattacks, and reoccupy contested positions at the forward edge of the defense.

The combined arms reserve of the brigade is intended to:
- Deal with unexpected problems
- Reconstitute first echelon units in the event of their loss of combat effectiveness.

Artillery- A motorized rifle or tank brigade in the defense will be supported by a Brigade Artillery Group (BrAG). The BrAG is usually composed of the maneuver brigade's organic two self-propelled artillery battalions and one MLRS battalion. It is intended to defeat the enemy in the approach march, on the line of deployment, in the attack staging area, or, should the enemy penetrate the first defense positions, defeat them from temporary firing positions. The artillery primary fire positions are usually located 2-4 kilometers from the forward edge of the defensive and occupy an area of 3-5 kilometers wide and 1-2 kilometers in depth.

Air Defense- A defending brigade will be supported by its organic anti-aircraft and missile systems. These air defenses are designed to protect the brigade from air strikes and cruise missiles. The air defense missile battalion will provide zonal coverage to protect the brigade's subunits and command post from air strikes. A battery of "Tunguska" rocket artillery protects the first-echelon forces. Two platoons of the "Strela-10" missile battery protect the BrAG. Two platoons equipped with "Igla" MANPADS cover the first echelon, while the third platoon in the "Igla" company protects the brigade command post.

Antitank Reserves- The antitank reserve is designed to destroy tanks and other armored vehicles that breach the defense, and cover other hazardous areas on the flanks. The basis of the antitank reserve is the brigade's organic antitank artillery battalion.

Mobile Obstacle Detachment – The mobile obstacle detachment weakens the enemy by the emplacement of minefields. It works in conjunction with the antitank reserve. It is constituted from the brigade's organic engineer company, particularly incorporating its mobile mine-layers.

Anti-Assault Reserve- The anti-assault reserve is designed to destroy enemy assaults in areas where sabotage and reconnaissance activities are expected. It usually consists of a motorized rifle company from the second echelon.

Motorized Rifle Brigade in the Defense

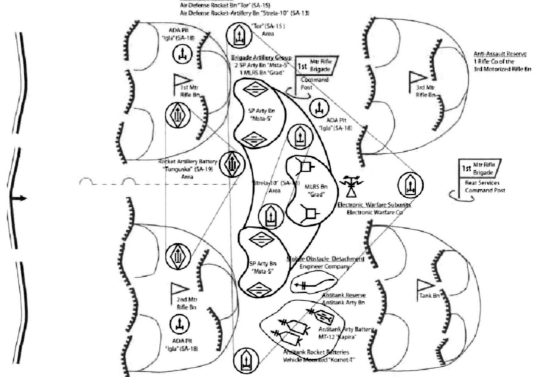

(Above) This graphic shows a notional laydown of additional forces, including the antitank reserve, the mobile obstacle detachment, the anti-assault reserve, the electronic warfare subunits and air defense subunits.

<u>Forward Detachment in the Security Zone</u>- This subunit delays the arrival of the enemy or makes him deploy and attack prematurely in an unfavorable direction for him. The forward detachment is constituted using subunits from a motorized rifle battalion in the second echelon.

<u>Air Assault Detachment</u>- This unit is part of a reinforced motorized rifle company designed to conduct an air assault into the rear area where an enemy has broken through. The air assault detachment will cooperate with subunits of the brigade's second echelon in the conduct of a counterattack.

<u>Electronic Warfare Subunits</u>- These subunits are intended to suppress enemy radios and electronics and protect the brigade subunits from electronic proximity fuses and other signal-detonated munitions.

Integrated Defensive Positions, Areas and Lines
The system of defensive positions, areas and lines include:
- Forward security zone
- Forward security outpost position
- Two to three defensive positions
- Alternative positions
- Separate areas and centers of resistance
- Areas for the firing positions of the BrAG and other artillery and initial positions for anti-aircraft assets.
- Second echelon (reserves) assembly areas
- Firing lines for tanks and BMPs (infantry fighting vehicles)
- Counterattack deployment lines
- Antitank reserve deployment lines
- Mobile obstacle detachment deployment lines
- Anti-assault reserve assembly area
- Places for the construction of fire sacs
- Landing zones and ambush sites for combat helicopters
- Locations for troop control points
- False and reserve defensive areas (strong points, positions).

The security zone is created at a depth of up to 40 kilometers in front of the forward edge of the defense, when the defending force is not in immediate contact with the enemy. Within the security zone there are 5-6 positions, 6-8 kilometers from each other. Separate company (platoon) strong points designed to hold important areas are constructed and fortified with engineering obstacles in the defensive area.

When there is no combat security zone, a motorized rifle or tank brigade will establish a forward position 6-8 kilometers in front of the forward edge of the defense to deceive the enemy as to the location of the forward edge of the defense, to repulse sudden attacks on the first-echelon subunits, and to cause the enemy to prematurely deploy the main body of his force. Reinforced companies are dispatched from the first-echelon motorized rifle battalions to defend the forward positions by creating separate company and platoon strong points.

The combat security zone is created at a distance of up to two kilometers from the forward edge of the defense on those approaches where there are no forward positions and where there is no contact with the enemy, with the goal of preventing a surprise attack and preventing enemy ground reconnaissance of the first-echelon motorized rifle battalions. In the event of no direct enemy contact, the mission of the combat security zone is accomplished by subunits from the first positions of the first trench. The combat security zone will be formed by reinforced motorized rifle platoons dispatched by the brigade's subordinate battalions.

The main defensive position consists of combined company strong points joined within the battalion defense area. The depth of these defensive positions will be up to 3 kilometers. They will be established within 3-4 trenches.

Relative Positions of a Motorized Rifle Brigade in the Defense

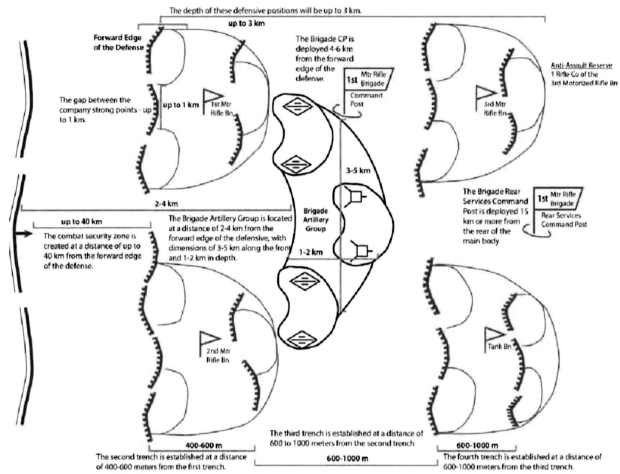

This graphic shows the considerations and relative positioning of a brigade defending in two echelons with two battalions forward and two back. The location of forces, systems and distances will be adjusted to fit the demands of the situation, threat, forces available and terrain.

The First Trench- The first trench is located in the first defensive position on the forward edge of the defense, the trace of which is determined by the brigade commander. The exact location of this position is determined by the battalion commander and is defended by platoons of the first echelon. Mines are emplaced in front of this first trench.

The Second Trench- The second trench is established 400-600 meters from the first trench. The positions of subunits occupying the first trench are covered by fire from the second trench. The second echelon subunits also cover the approaches to the forward edge of the defense and the obstacles arrayed in front of it.

The Third Trench-The third trench is established 600-1000 meters from the second trench and is situated so its subunits can conduct direct fire on the zone between the second and third trenches, on separate sections and in front of the forward edge of the defense. The third trench can also be used as a starting position for maneuver against threatened areas in the event of an enemy counterattack.

<u>The Fourth Trench</u>- The fourth trench is established 600-1000 meters from the third trench. The positions of subunits occupying the third trench are covered by fires from the fourth trench, and the fourth trench also covers the approaches to the forward edge of the defense and the obstacles arrayed in front of it.

The first position in the brigade defensive belt is the most important. It is defined by the brigade's first-echelon battalions. The second brigade position is defended by the brigades' second-echelon battalions. The defensive positions of the brigade are the battalions' areas of defense. The battalion areas consist of company strong points connected from the front to the depth by interlocking fires, obstacles, trenches and connecting passageways for the conduct of 360° defense. The gap between the company strong points is up to 1 kilometer.

Channeling and blocking positions are spread throughout the depth of the defense to deter enemy maneuver toward the flanks and drive them onto obstacles and blocking positions. These may be lines for commitment of a counterattack, as well as firing lines for tank units (subunits) located in the second echelon. These consist of 1-2 trenches and connecting communications trenches linking the front to the rear.

Individual areas of defense (intersections) are created for the protection and support of intrapositioning stretches between road intersections, built-up areas, crossings and other important objectives for an air assault.

The BrAG's firing positions are assigned to those axes that could be threatened by enemy tanks (a Russian artillery mission is direct lay fire against armor). For the BrAG of an army's first-echelon brigade, the firing positions are located between the first and second positions. The BrAG's firing positions are selected based on the range of its artillery systems, 2-6 kilometers from the forward edge of the defense. Reserve and temporary firing positions and routes to them are prepared for the BrAG's artillery.

A defending brigade will also be supported by its organic anti-aircraft systems. The Strela-10 (SA-13) and Tor-M1 (SA-15) air defense missile systems are deployed in initial firing positions three-four kilometers along the front and in depth. The distances between the air defense batteries are eight kilometers or more. The initial positions of the Tor-M1 systems assigned to the first position are sited 5-10 kilometers from the forward edge of the defense, and the separation between them along the front and in depth are from 5-10 kilometers. Initial positions of a first-echelon motorized rifle or tank brigade's anti-aircraft missile batteries and anti-aircraft artillery batteries are established at 0.5-1.5 kilometers from the forward edge of the defense.

The reserve assembly area is held in pre-combat order as it prepares the second (and sometimes third) brigade defensive belt.

The firing lines of tanks, BMPs, and BTRs of the second echelon (combined arms reserve) are focused on areas where precision weapon or massed tank assaults are expected. Tank battalions (or motorized rifle companies on BMPs) of the second echelon have one or two firing lines immediately behind the first strong point, and then between the first and second strong points.

A tank company (or motorized rifle companies on BMPs) is deployed on firing areas at the front, with 1-1.5 kilometer intervals between companies, with the total length of the firing line extending up to five kilometers. The firing line may coincide with the commitment line for the conduct of counterattacks.

To carry out counterattacks in the defense, the second echelon battalions plan one or two areas for a counterattack on the probable axes of enemy attack. On each avenue of approach the counterattack has a main and back-up line of deployment for counterattack, with 2-3 kilometers between them.

Lines of deployment of the antitank reserve are assigned against probable areas where enemy precision weapons and large tank attacks will occur. In the defense, the antitank reserve is located in an assembly area. The brigade antitank reserve assembly area is located on an armor avenue of approach between the second and third positions or within the second position.

The antitank reserve may be assigned 3-5 deployment lines or more between the first and second positions. An antitank guided missile (ATGM) battery is deployed up to 2 kilometers from the front, the antitank battalion - up to 5 kilometers. The mobile obstacle detachment must protect the line of deployment of the antitank reserve. It is located in reserve close to the antitank assembly area and sometimes in it.

Designated equipment is prepared to ambush by fire on the enemy unit's flanks throughout the depth of the defense to limit the enemy's ability to maneuver. The most appropriate places for these ambushes are the reverse slopes of hills, outskirts of populated areas, the forest edge, and at road junctions.

The anti-assault reserve assembly areas should provide rapid access to those objectives most likely to be assaulted by air. The brigade anti-assault reserve is located within the boundaries of the second (or third) position.

Designated control points (primary and reserve) are selected throughout the depth of defense in areas where tank assaults are difficult, away from the direction of the enemy main attack.

The brigade command post- is deployed 4-6 kilometers from the forward edge of the defense. From this point the commander can view the most likely enemy avenues of approach, 1-3 kilometers from his forces.

The brigade rear services command post is deployed 15 kilometers and sometimes more from the forward edge of the defense. It is located with the brigade trains (maintenance and logistics elements).

The <u>command-observation post</u> for the motorized rifle battalion is located behind the first-echelon motorized rifle companies or in the vicinity of the battalion's second-echelon company, which is approximately two kilometers from the forward edge of the defense.

False strong points and false firing positions are constructed throughout the defense in between the defending units, on the flanks, and in unoccupied areas.

Fire Support
Fire support includes:
- Aviation strikes
- Direct and indirect fires from the BrAG
- Integrated fires from the maneuver battalions.

Air Defense
The air defense system is created throughout the entire defense, and includes:
- An integrated system of radar reconnaissance and early warning
- An integrated system of anti-aircraft missile and anti-aircraft artillery cover
- An integrated command and control system for air defense units.
The integrated reconnaissance of the aerial enemy is based on army radar sites. They are supplemented by the reconnaissance of the radar control posts of the brigade air defense subunits. The integration of missile and antiaircraft coverage includes the combat formation of brigade air defense forces and their integrated fires, coordinated by direction, height, lines, points to be protected, types of targets and time.

The system of command and control unites the command posts, communication systems and computers with the air defense units and subunits to support the control of units and subunits and to direct their fires.

Integrated Antitank Defense
Integrated antitank defense includes:
- Artillery fire against tanks and other armored vehicles from concealed locations;
- Integrated antitank fires (planned fires of antitank weapons, tanks and BMPs in direct lay) by subunits on armor avenues of approach.
The antitank reserve and mobile obstacle detachment prepare an assembly area and lines to mine plus lines of deployment during combat, starting at the security zone and forward position, to defeat a massed tank attack and destroy it as it attempts to wedge into the defense.

Integrated Engineer Obstacles
Obstacles can be made from anything that hinders movement (mines, electrified fences, etc.) to protect company strong points, areas between them, artillery emplacements, command posts, unit boundaries, and other points. These obstacles can be employed in conjunction with direct and indirect fires, as well as with naturally occurring obstacles.

Integrated Air Assault Defense
The air assault defense force prevents enemy air assaults and destroys enemy forces before they land, during their landing and after they land, as well as countering airborne and airmobile sabotage and reconnaissance efforts. The integrated air assault defense includes:
- Anti-air assault defense reserve
- Subunits of the second echelon (reserve)
- Air strikes and air defense weapons fire
- Integrated direct and indirect fires, and anti-landing obstacles in potential landing zones.

Fire Destruction of the Enemy by the Defense
Fire destruction of the enemy is the coordinated fires directed on the enemy by the designated forces and means of destruction using ordinary and incendiary ammunition to fulfill the tactical mission and achieve the aims of the battle. The goal of fire destruction is to diminish the combat potential of enemy subunits to the degree that it will guarantee that friendly subunits achieve their assigned missions without losing their combat capability. Fire destruction is organized by the senior commander with the agreement of the subunits that will carry it out during the period of fire destruction:
- Fire preparation to repel the advancing enemy
- Fire preparation to support the defending force

Fire preparation to repel the advancing enemy is conducted with the goal of disrupting his advance, deployment and transition to attack in order to inflict destruction on his first-echelon units and subunits. This phase continues until the enemy transitions to the attack. Fire preparation to support the defending force is conducted with the goal of inflicting maximum damage on the enemy and preventing his breakthrough into the depths of the defense. This phase continues throughout the entire defensive combat by friendly subunits.

During the conduct of counterattack, fire destruction of the enemy is accomplished in the periods of fire preparation for a counterattack and fire support of the counterattacking force. In order to achieve the effective destruction of the enemy by fire in battle, the brigade, battalions and companies create a system of fire which the senior commander uses as the basis for his unit's system of fire destruction of the enemy. It includes the fires of artillery, tanks, BMPs, BTRs, antitank missiles, grenade launchers, and small arms, and also the use of flame and incendiary weapons [thermobaric]. The system of fire for the brigade (battalion) must include aviation strikes within the range of designated aviation resources.

The brigade's (battalions', companies') integrated fires are organized as a strong response, using integrated fire destruction planned by the senior commander, with coordination with radio-electronic destruction and integrated engineer obstacles. The mission is to destroy enemy artillery subunits, command and control elements, troop control, the forces and weapons of the mechanized infantry and tank subunits of the first echelon and other enemy targets. For a discussion of artillery types of fire, see the artillery section in Chapter six.

Commentary on Brigade in Defense

The motorized rifle brigade may defend with two or three motorized rifle battalions forward, depending on the situation. Its tank battalion may have platoons forward, but is usually located in the second echelon or reserve in the defense. When possible, the brigade creates a security zone. When it is not in direct contact with the enemy, this may be as deep as 40 kilometers with five or six fallback positions. As a minimum, the brigade will man a forward position 6-8 kilometers in front of the main defense. The reason for the security zone or forward position is to deceive the enemy as to the location of the main defenses, slow and disrupt the enemy approach and make the enemy disclose his force disposition and strength. If the security zone or forward position actions can cause the enemy to deploy early (especially his artillery), it is well worth the effort.

Depending on the time available to prepare the defense, much of the brigade defense will be dug in. The work of trenching machines and bulldozers will be supplemented with old-fashioned shovels to provide protection for men and equipment. Land mines and other obstacles will protect the forward edge of the defense and canalize the enemy into fire sacs within the defense. Priority of effort will be to the first-echelon defenses and BrAG. Work on the defenses will continue throughout their existence. The emphasis on going underground is based on the requirement that coherent portions of the defense will survive a tactical nuclear strike.

The BrAG consists of, at a minimum, the brigade's organic two howitzer battalions and multiple rocket launcher battalion. Other nonorganic artillery battalions may be attached as necessary and other artillery battalions may provide support to the BrAG if in range. The organic antitank artillery battalion is normally not part of the BrAG, but serves in the brigade antitank reserve. The battalion mortars normally remain with the motorized rifle battalions in direct support of them, but are hooked into the brigade fire control net.

The brigade has the 2S-19 "Msta-S" howitzer (named after the Russian Msta River). It is a 152mm self-propelled howitzer that entered the inventory in 1989, just before the Soviet Union collapsed. It is based on the T-80 tank chassis, but uses the T-72 tank diesel engine. It has a semi-automatic laying system, automatic loader, NBC protection system, wading kit, dozer blade, smoke generator and 81mm smoke launchers. It has an elevation of -4° to +68° and can traverse 360°. It fires 6-8 rounds per minute and can fire HE, HEAT, smoke, chemical, illumination, precision-guided and, theoretically, tactical nuclear rounds. It has a 29-kilometer range with base-bleed ammunition and 36 kilometers with a RAP round. It carries 50 rounds on board and has a five-man crew. There are 18 howitzers per battalion, and 36 per brigade.

The brigade also has a battalion of 18 BM-21 "Grad" multiple rocket launchers (*grad* is Russian for hail). The BM-21 has been around since 1963. It is basically a truck with 40 launch tubes that fire 122mm rockets. The system may be old, but the rockets are new and can project a 20-kilogram warhead out to 45 kilometers. The warheads are HE, FRAG, chemical, smoke, antitank mines, antipersonnel mines and incendiary. It has a three-man crew and there are 18 BM-21 Grads in the battalion. A launcher vehicle can clear the rack of all 40 rounds in 20 seconds, and the battalion can fire a 720-round volley in close to the same time.

The antitank artillery battalion has an antitank artillery battery of six MT-12 "Rapira" antitank guns. The towed MT-12 antitank gun fields a 100mm smoothbore gun and has a six-man crew (commander, driver of the towing vehicle, gun layer, loader, and two ammunition handlers). When the MT-LB is used as the tow vehicle, 20 rounds are typically carried (10 APFSDS, 4 HE-Frag, 6 HEAT). The standard equipment consists of the panoramic PG-1M sight for indirect fire and an OP4M-40U telescope for direct fire. The APN-5-40 or APN-6-40 night sight is used for direct fire. The gun can be fitted with the LO-7 ski gear for travel across snow or swampy ground.

The brigade antitank battalion also has two batteries of 9P162 Kornet-T self-propelled heavy antitank guided missile vehicles (*kornet* means cornet in Russian). The Kornet missile entered the Russian inventory in 1994, and the 9P162 Kornet-T is on a BMP-3 chassis. It has two launchers and an autoloader and carries 16 missiles. The two launchers can engage the same target or two targets simultaneously. It is a fire-and-forget laser-guided missile with a range of 100-5,500 meters. It has tandem HEAT and thermobaric warheads. It has a two-man crew. There are six 9P162 Kornet-T in a battery, and 12 in the brigade.

Russia has fielded the most modern integrated ground-based tactical air defense system on the planet. There are two air defense battalions in the brigade. The schematic shows a missile battery of "Tunguska" protecting the first-echelon battalions. Two platoons of the "Strela-10" rocket battery protect the BrAG. Two platoons equipped with "Igla" MANPADS also cover the first-echelon battalions, while the third platoon in the "Igla" company protects the brigade command post. The "Tor-M1" anti-aircraft missile battalion provides zonal cover for the brigade to defend it from air strikes. The intent of this dense air defense is to deny the enemy use of helicopter gunships, fighter bombers, cruise missiles and unmanned aerial systems. Missiles are being upgraded to compensate for the increased range of some aerial ordnance.

This motorized rifle brigade defense has a stationary and a mobile component. It provides strong points designed to stop and destroy an enemy attack. Should the enemy break through, there are a series of fire sacs, canalizing obstacles, firing lines, counterattacks, and reserves. Some of the graphics and concepts for employing the Russian maneuver brigade are familiar to those students of the Soviet Army, but much is new. Fully integrated combined arms organization is becoming the standard at the battalion level. The brigade has four maneuver battalions, four artillery battalions, two air defense battalions and a more robust combat support and combat service support package. Equipment upgrades are evident throughout the brigade. Officer and NCO training has improved, with single-tracked officers who are commanders or chiefs of staff throughout their career. NCOs now attend a formal academy, which may take three years to complete. The force still has short-term conscripts, but the jobs requiring more skill and training are held by long-term contract soldiers. Brigade annual training usually requires a long-distance move by ship or rail, testing the unit's ability to deploy on short notice.

Chapter 4
The Offense

Offensive Theory

The <u>attack</u> is a rapid and non-stop movement of armored and motorized rifle sub-units in a combat formation using the integrated intense fire from tanks and BMPs (BTRs) in order to close with the enemy. Fire is conducted with various weapon systems with the aim of destroying the enemy.

The attack is the main type of combat action. It is carried out in order to defeat the opposing enemy, to occupy a designated area (line), or to create the conditions for the conduct of the follow-on attack. It includes the destruction of the enemy using all available means, decisive attack, the rapid advance of forces into the depth of the defense, the destruction and/or capture of personnel and the capture of weapons, equipment, and various facilities and designated areas (lines). Depending on the situation and mission, the offensive may be carried out against a defending, advancing or withdrawing enemy. The offensive against enemy-occupied prepared defenses is carried out while in direct contact with the enemy, and having quickly overcome the defense, moving throughout the depth of his defense. The attack on an advancing enemy is conducted with a meeting engagement, while a retreating enemy is dealt with by a pursuit.

An advance against an enemy in a prepared defense most often begins with a breakthrough, which, as a rule, is carried out while in direct contact with him. During an offensive, there is the possibility of taking advantage of breaks, gaps and open flanks in the enemy defenses.[1]
Considerations for the attack include:
The Goals of the Attack
     - Defeat the enemy
     - Seize important areas (objects) sites
Implied Goals and Tasks
     - Decisive attack
     - Rapid advance of subunits into the depths of the defense
     - Defeat of the enemy by all means available
     - Destruction and capture of personnel and seizure of weapons, combat equipment, and designated areas (lines) of terrain
Types of Attack
     - Attack on a defending enemy
     - Attack on a retreating enemy
     - Attack on an advancing enemy (meeting engagement)

---

[1] This section, including graphics, has been compiled from many sources to include:
"Fundamentals of the Offense" [Основы наступления], as found on *Studiopedia*, <http://studopedia.info/1-67784.html>, accessed on 1 July 2016.
V.N. Zaritski and L.A. Kharkevich, *General Tactics* [Общая Тактика], Tambov: Tambov Government Technical University, 2007.
Field Manual: Preparation and Conduct of Combined Arms Warfare [Боевой Устав: По Подготовке и Ведению Общевойскового Боя], Moscow: Ministry of Defense of the Russian Federation, 2005.
Source material has also been obtained from a variety of training documents produced by Russian military academies and military departments in civilian academic institutions.

Methods of Transitioning to the Offense

<u>From positions in direct contact with the enemy</u>: This method is initiated in accordance with the concept of the commander of the combat formation. The starting position for the attack depends on the size of the subunit (a motorized rifle battalion occupies an assembly area, a motorized rifle company occupies an assembly position, a motorized rifle platoon occupies part of the company assembly position). The attack occurs either after the necessary regrouping from within the defense or with the simultaneous attack by subunits from their defensive positions.

<u>From the March</u>: This method is initiated from an assembly area, usually selected at some distance from the forward edge of the enemy defense, which will prevent destruction of the subunit by long-range artillery fire and supports the concealment of ground forces from radio-electronic reconnaissance.

Fundamentals for Subunits Conducting an Offensive

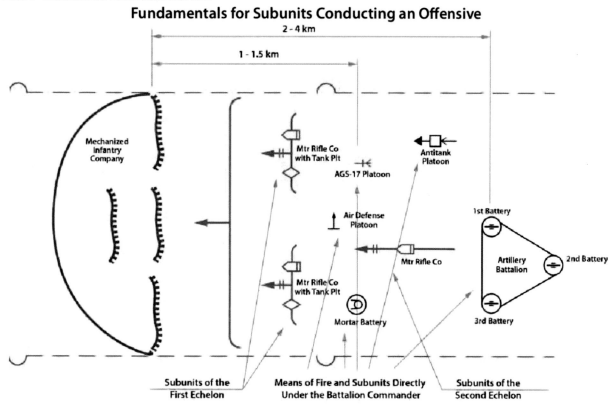

(Above) This graphic portrays the span of distances and locations of elements of an attacking motorized rifle battalion with an attached tank company. The battalion objective is an enemy defending company and the width of the attack may be the width of the defending company or only a portion of it. The location of systems and distances will be adjusted to fit the demands of the situation, threat, forces available and terrain. The preferred method of attack is from the march where the attack originates from an assembly area. The battalion moves from its assembly area in march column and, during the march, deploys into company and platoon columns and then goes into platoon attack line. Forward of this, the line may slow to dismount squads who will form their own line of attack supported by fire from their carriers. If the situation warrants, the squads may stay mounted during the attack. The location of systems and distances will be adjusted to fit the demands of the situation, threat, forces available and terrain.

Methods of Attacking the Forward Edge of the Defense

Determining the layout of enemy defenses, the degree of destruction inflicted by one's nuclear and conventional weapons, enemy unit equipment, and the nature of the terrain, an attack of the forward edge of the defense can be made as follows:

On BMPs (BTRs)
- Combat Formation – assault line
- Rate of Assault – 8 -12 kilometers/hour

Dismounted
- Combat Formation – infantry assault line

Motorized Rifle Battalion in the Offense

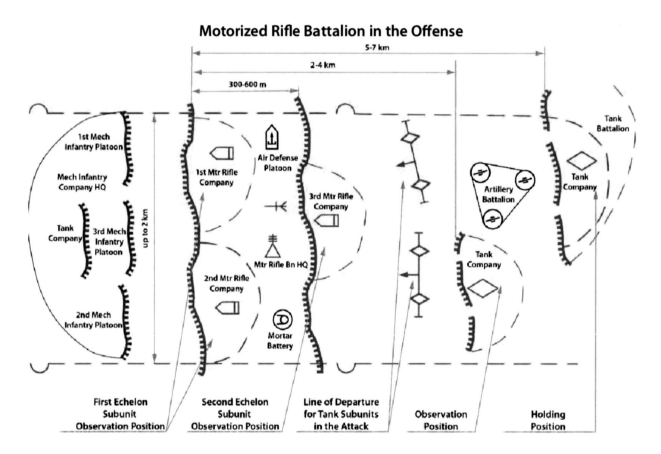

(Above) This graphic lays out typical distances for a motorized rifle battalion conducting an attack from positions in direct contact.

Deployment Lines for Subunits in an Attack From The March

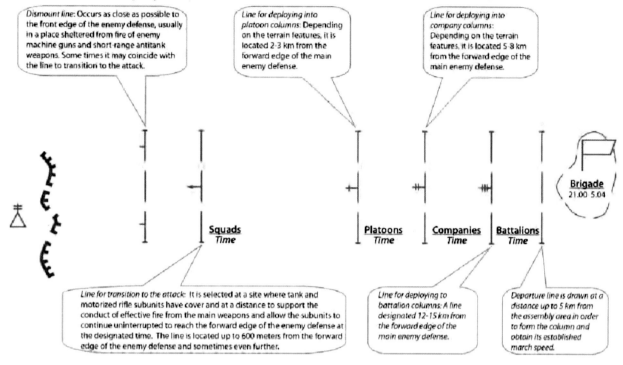

Dismount line: Occurs as close as possible to the front edge of the enemy defense, usually in a place sheltered from fire of enemy machine guns and short-range antitank weapons. Some times it may coincide with the line to transition to the attack.

Line for deploying into platoon columns: Depending on the terrain features, it is located 2-3 km from the forward edge of the main enemy defense.

Line for deploying into company columns: Depending on the terrain features, it is located 5-8 km from the forward edge of the main enemy defense.

Squads
Time

Platoons
Time

Companies
Time

Battalions
Time

Brigade
21.00 5.04

Line for transition to the attack: It is selected at a site where tank and motorized rifle subunits have cover and at a distance to support the conduct of effective fire from the main weapons and allow the subunits to continue uninterrupted to reach the forward edge of the enemy defense at the designated time. The line is located up to 600 meters from the forward edge of the enemy defense and sometimes even further.

Line for deploying to battalion columns: A line designated 12-15 km from the forward edge of the main enemy defense.

Departure line is drawn at a distance up to 5 km from the assembly area in order to form the column and obtain its established march speed.

(Above) This graphic portrays the deployment lines for subunits to break into multiple columns, go on line and dismount. Artillery is well forward in the march order. Depending on the situation, the artillery may be positioned before the attack.

Preparation for the offensive begins immediately after receipt of the order and includes:
- Organization for Combat:
- Making the decision
- Reconnaissance
- Tasking subordinate units
- Coordination
- Defeating enemy fires
- Combat Support
- Command and Control
- Preparation of the battalion (company, platoon) to carry out missions
- Preparation in the assembly area
- Organization and conduct of training
- Practical work of the battalion (company) commander, his deputies, the battalion headquarters, and subordinate units
- Other tasks.

An attack from positions in direct contact with the enemy begins with a deployed combat formation moving from starting positions into the offense. The starting positions for the troops conducting the offensive are occupied after the necessary regrouping within the defensive positions or with the simultaneous replacement of defending forces. This regrouping is carried out in order to create an offensive combat formation under the guise of reinforcing the defense. It is done quickly, and usually done the night before the offensive. The occupation of the starting positions for the offensive, when conducted while conducting a relief in place of defending forces, is done during the course of one-two nights prior to the offensive in accordance with the plan for the relief in place. During the relief in place of subunits of the first echelon, their BMP and attached tank subunits occupy the assembly area. The starting position for a brigade within the army's first echelon is located within the first and second positions; the first-echelon battalions within the first position; the second-echelon battalions in the second position. Motorized rifle subunits occupy the starting position on the night before the offensive, and simultaneously artillery, guns and tanks designated for direct fire support occupy their positions.

An attack from the depth is conducted from assembly areas for the offensive, from permanent garrison deployment points, from alert assembly regions and from marches. An attack from the depth is usually conducted from an assembly area for the attack from where the units and subunits deploy into pre-combat and combat formation for the attack. The assembly area designated for the attack is 20-40 kilometers from the forward edge of the enemy's main defenses. In order to ensure an organized attack, with all units and subunits attacking at the same time, the following are designated:
- Starting line
- Lines of deployment into battalion, company, and platoon columns
- Transition to the attack line
- Dismount line.

The Offense in Special Conditions
The Offense in Urban Areas
During an offensive in a city (settlement) a special role is played by small units functioning separately on squad missions. The offensive is determined by the density of buildings and availability of space, parks, underground utilities, etc. The offensive is carried out along the streets. A successful attack can only be achieved by close cooperation of motorized rifle (tank) platoons (companies, battalions) with other kinds of troops, supported by artillery and aviation.

Offensive in the Mountains
Significant factors in this type of terrain are:
- steep terrain
- "dead" spaces and closed approaches
- rapidly flowing rivers
- mountains blocking vision
- a poor road net-work (or lack thereof)
- rocky soil that complicates engineering works
- other factors.
The attack is carried out along the roads and mountain ranges, on the slopes of heights and in other possible directions, with a wide possibility of flanking attacks and bypassing forces using concealed exits to hit the flanks and rear of the enemy.

Offensive in the Forest
The factors for the conduct of the offense in forests are:
- closed areas with wetlands
- a limited number of roads
- forest debris
- fire (combined with minefields).

Observation is restricted, hindering target designation, adjustment of fire, and command and control. The attack is carried out primarily along roads and glades, using flanking and bypassing small subunits moving by compass azimuth.

Offensive in the Desert
The factors for the offense in the desert are:
- open terrain
- the almost complete absence of human settlements
- the almost complete absence of distinct landmarks
- poor road networks
- extremely poor vegetation
- sandy, rocky and saline soils
- an acute shortage or complete absence of water and building materials
- an arid climate
- abrupt temperature fluctuations.

Daytime temperature may reach 50° C (122° F) and inside a tank 70° C (158°F). Therefore, it is better to attack at night. The offense is usually conducted on a broad front, off-road, in certain areas due to the need to capture vital areas, oases, and water sources. The open terrain is conducive to a wide variety of maneuver.

Defense in the Northern Regions and in Winter
The factors for the offense in the northern regions and winter are:
- vast areas of tundra
- boggy tundra
- forest areas
- possibly large numbers of lakes
- boulders and rocky areas
- a limited number of roads
- difficulties for engineering fortification of an area, concealment, and orientation
- harsh climates
- polar nights lasting three to four months
- frequent snowfalls, snowstorms and blizzards
- deep snow (over 50 centimeters/19 inches) that severely limits the maneuverability of units
- bad weather
- ionospheric and geomagnetic disturbances that disrupt radios and compasses (the error can be up to 15°).

The offensive is usually conducted from positions prepared for advancing or deploying subunits or from the march. The attack is conducted mainly along roads, rivers and other accessible areas.

This Page Intentionally Left Blank

Squad in the Offense

The motorized rifle squad attacks as part of a motorized rifle platoon or can be attached to a tank platoon. When dismounted, the motorized rifle squad attacks on a frontage of up to 50 meters.[2]

The Combat Formation of a Motorized Rifle Squad on Foot

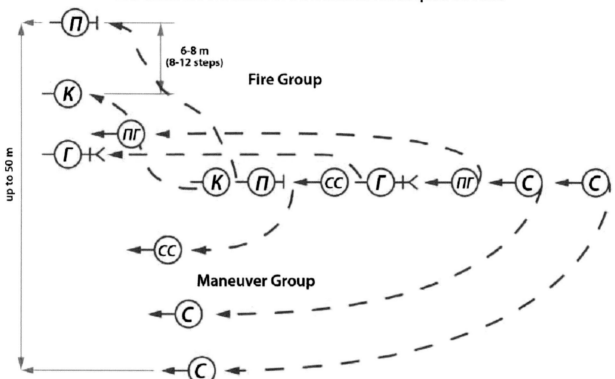

(Above) When dismounted, a motorized rifle squad moves in a column and fights in a line. The squad is split into a fire group and a maneuver group. The soldiers in both groups are dispersed within the squad column so that both groups go on line simultaneously. The squad leader leads the squad column and is followed by his machine gunner. The senior rifleman follows the machine gunner. When the squad column deploys on line, the squad leader controls the fire group and the senior rifleman controls the maneuver group.

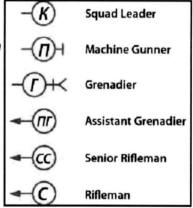

K	Squad Leader
П	Machine Gunner
Г	Grenadier
ПГ	Assistant Grenadier
СС	Senior Rifleman
С	Rifleman

---

[2] This section, including graphics, has been compiled from many sources to include:
"Squad in the Offense" [Отделение в наступлении], as found on *Studiopedia*, <http://studopedia.info/1-67785.html>, accessed on 1 July 2016.
V.N. Zaritski and L.A. Kharkevich, *General Tactics* [Общая Тактика], Tambov: Tambov Government Technical University, 2007.
Field Manual: Preparation and Conduct of Combined Arms Warfare [Боевой Устав: По Подготовке и Ведению Общевойскового Боя], Moscow: Ministry of Defense of the Russian Federation, 2005.
Source material has also been obtained from a variety of training documents produced by Russian military academies and military departments in civilian academic institutions.

Squad Formation for Overcoming Mine Obstacle (maneuver group)

Squad Formation for Overcoming Mine Obstacle (fire group)

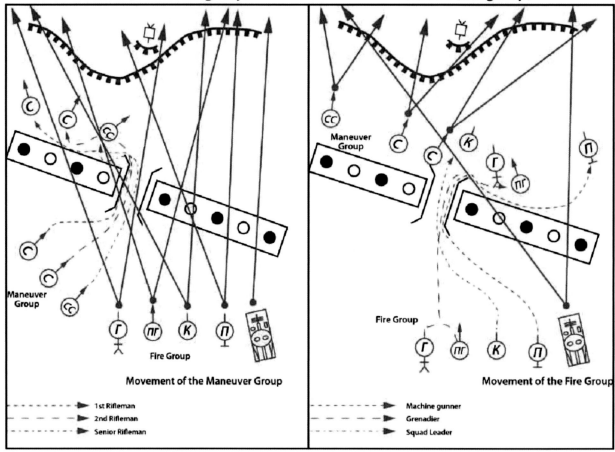

(Above-Left) This graphic shows the first stage of a squad moving through a minefield breach. The fire group and BMP provide suppressive fire on the enemy position as the maneuver group moves through the breach and takes up fire-in-support positions.

(Above-Right) The maneuver group join the BMP in laying down suppressive fire while the fire group moves through the breach and takes up fire-in support positions. Then, the fire group will join the BMP in laying down suppressive fire while the maneuver group assaults the enemy position. The squad leader is responsible for controlling fires to keep the enemy's head down while not killing his own soldiers.

Combat Tasks

The motorized rifle squad in the attack is given an immediate objective and a direction of subsequent advance. The objectives of the attacks are usually enemy personnel in trenches, tanks, guns, antitank missiles, machine guns and other weapons located in the first trench and the near depth of the enemy defense. The direction of further advance will support achieving the immediate objective of the platoon.

Elements of the Combat Formation
The combat formation of a motorized rifle squad, may assault on foot or be part of a maneuver group or fire group mounted on a combat vehicle.

System of Fire and Command and Control
Depending on the combat mission and situation, a combat group may attack on line, echelon left or echelon right with an interval between the soldiers in the group of 6-8 meters (8-12 steps). To facilitate firing and for the best use of terrain, the soldiers may move in a file or

Deployment of the Motorized Rifle Squad from Behind a Vehicle (variant)

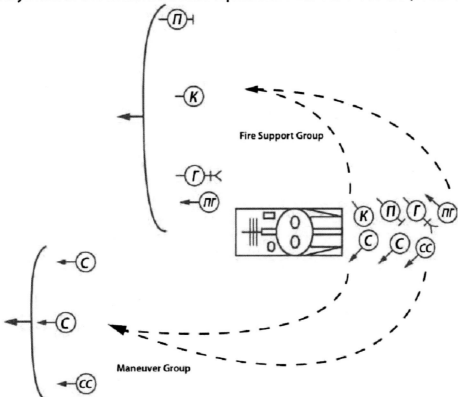

(Above) The motorized rifle squad moves in a BMP, BTR or MT-LB and provides fire on the move. When the vehicle stops, the squad dismounts and goes on line. The fire group sits on one side of the vehicle and the maneuver group on the other. The first out are the assistant machine gunner and the senior rifleman. The squad leader is the last out, since he sits forward where he can communicate with the driver and vehicle commander. The squad leader is positioned where he can readily control the fires of the machine gunner and grenadier.

a line with several soldiers behind and others forward. This should not limit the width or firepower of the squad attack line nor hinder the movement of neighboring units. The BMP (BTR) of the combat group may move on one of the flanks of the squad or in the middle of the squad line. When the attack is dismounted, the squad leader commands by radio, voice, signals, and personal example. The position of the squad commander ensures the effective fires. Targeting is done with tracer bullets (projectiles) and signal devices, using known landmarks, along the axis of movement (attack).

Platoon in the Offense

A motorized rifle (tank) platoon may attack as part of a of a motorized rifle company, constitute the combined arms reserve of a battalion (company), operate as a combat-reconnaissance patrol, and provide the bulk of an assault group. A tank platoon, motorized rifle platoon on BMPs in full, or by individual machines can be allocated for the destruction of the enemy by direct-fire weapons in preparation for the offensive. A platoon occupies a frontage of up to 300 meters in the attack. An offensive includes a platoon combat formation, system of fire, and system of command and control.[3]

Combat Formation of a Motorized Rifle Squad in the Offense (variant)

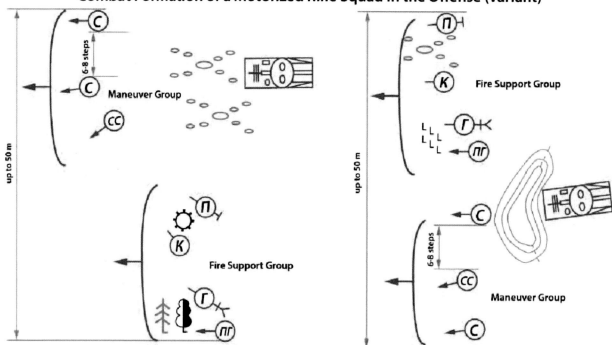

(Above) The infantry fighting vehicle or personnel carrier is an important component of the infantry squad, both for its transport capacity and its heavy machine gun and antitank missile support. When possible, the squad in the attack hopes to provide some cover or concealment for its vehicle and some cover for its fire group. The maneuver group normally gets the open ground. The left hand example shows the squad BMP partially concealed by brush and firing over the heads of the maneuver group. The fire group is concealed partially by some woods and sawmill. The right hand example shows the BMP in hull defilade behind a hillock providing supporting fire while the fire group supports from the brush and the remnants of a timber-cleared copse of trees.

[3] This section, including graphics, has been compiled from many sources to include:
"Platoon in the Offense" [Взвод в наступлении], as found on *Studiopedia*, <http://studopedia.info/1-67786. html>, accessed on 1 July 2016.
V.N. Zaritski and L.A. Kharkevich, *General Tactics* [Общая Тактика], Tambov: Tambov Government Technical University, 2007.
Field Manual: Preparation and Conduct of Combined Arms Warfare [Боевой Устав: По Подготовке и Ведению Общевойскового Боя], Moscow: Ministry of Defense of the Russian Federation, 2005.
Source material has also been obtained from a variety of training documents produced by Russian military academies and military departments in civilian academic institutions.

Combat Tasks

In the attack, a motorized rifle (tank) platoon has an objective and a direction of further advance. A platoon, functioning as a combined arms reserve for a battalion (company) is given a direction or a march route, a position in the march column, and possible missions which it might have to accomplish. The objectives of a platoon attack may be enemy personnel detected in the trenches, tanks, guns, antitank missiles, machine guns and other enemy weapons located in the first trench and throughout the depth of the enemy's defense. The direction of further advance will support achieving the immediate objective of the company.

Combat Formation and Missions of a Motorized Rifle Platoon in the Offensive

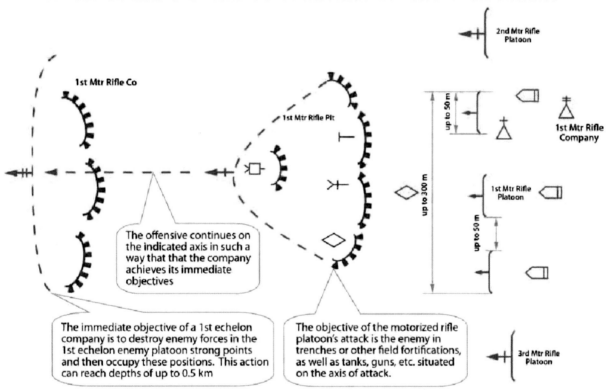

(Above) A motorized rifle platoon in the offensive has an immediate objective and a direction of further movement.

Elements of the Combat Formation

A motorized rifle platoon combat formation typically includes:
- Motorized rifle squads
- Command and control
- Fire support

In addition, the platoon can have a group of combat vehicles.

Depending on the mission and situation, motorized rifle squads attack in squad line, wedge, reverse wedge, echelon right or echelon left. The interval between squads on line or in depth is up to 50 meters.

System of Fire and Command and Control

The command and control and fire support group is assigned to control the attacking subunits and fire support. In the course of the offensive, the command and control and fire support group maintains a distance of up to 50 meters from the combat formation or is part of it. The combat formation of a motorized rifle platoon attacking mounted on BMPs (tank platoon) moves in a vehicle line, wedge, reverse wedge, echelon right or echelon left. The interval between combat vehicles (tanks) can be up to 100 meters. The motorized rifle platoon may attack dismounted, on BMPs, or riding on tanks. A motorized rifle (tank) platoon may constitute a combined arms reserve for a battalion (company); it advances 1.5-2 kilometers behind the first-echelon company and is prepared to fulfill any unexpected mission that arises.

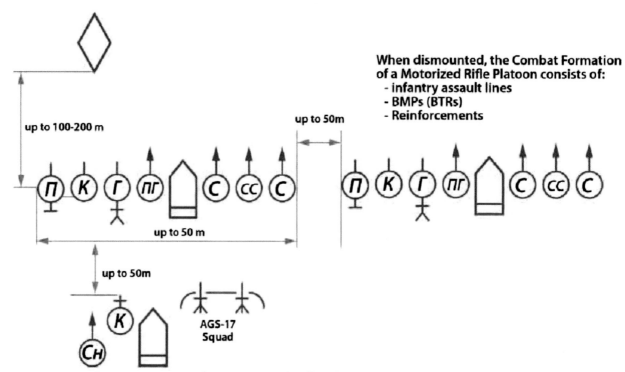

When dismounted, the Combat Formation of a Motorized Rifle Platoon consists of:
- infantry assault lines
- BMPs (BTRs)
- Reinforcements

Combat Formation of a Motorized Rifle Platoon in the Offense (dismounted)

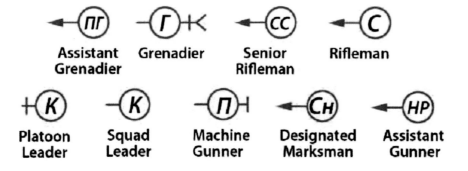

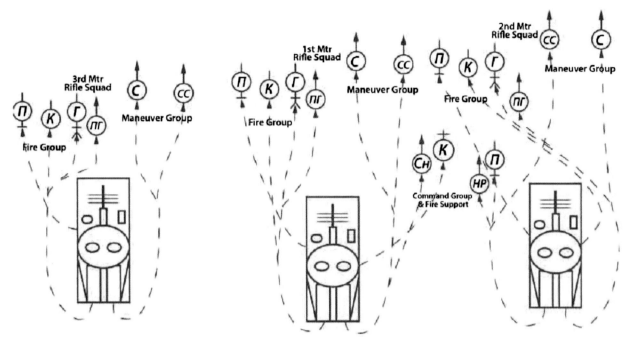

Dismount and Deployment of a Motorized Rifle Platoon into a Combat Formation (variant)

(Above) This graphic shows a motorized rifle platoon mounted on BMPs coming on line and dismounting with the squads then moving ahead of the BMPS. These are eight man squads (four in the fire group, two in the maneuver group and two vehicle crew).

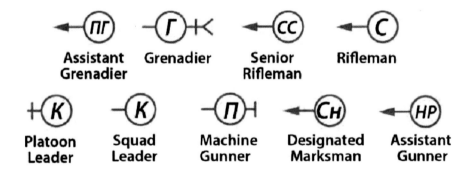

Roles of a Motorized Rifle Platoon in the Attack

As part of a another unit
      - As part of a company
      - In the battalion's reserve

As a stand-alone unit
      - In an assault group
      - As an advance party for an air assault
      - As a reconnaissance patrol

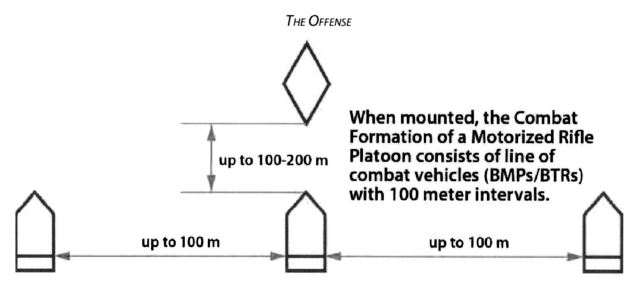

When mounted, the Combat Formation of a Motorized Rifle Platoon consists of line of combat vehicles (BMPs/BTRs) with 100 meter intervals.

up to 100-200 m

up to 100 m   up to 100 m

Combat Formation of a Motorized Rifle Platoon in the Offense (mounted)

(Above) This graphic shows a motorized rifle platoon in the mounted attack. The platoon is on line following a tank. A mounted attack, when possible, is quicker and the on onboard squad can assist by firing through vehicle firing ports.

Means of Reinforcement
The following are means to reinforce a motorized rifle platoon
- Automatic grenade launcher
- Antitank subunit
- Flamethrower subunit
- Air defense subunit
- Engineer subunit
- A tank
- NBC subunits

Depending on the situation and mission, grenade launcher, antitank and flamethrower subunits and weapons may be attached to a platoon, and when performing independent tasks – an engineer subunit.

117

Combat Formation for a Motorized Rifle Platoon Breaching a Minefield

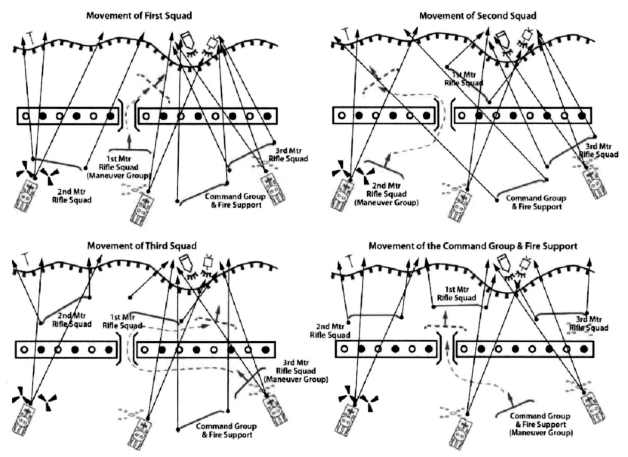

(Above) The graphic shows the four steps involved in a motorized rifle platoon crossing a minefield breach under fire. The platoon pulls up on line and dismounts while the BMPs provide suppressive fire. The maneuver group of the first squad crosses the breach first and established a support by fire position. The fire group of the first squad follows and joins the maneuver group in its support by fire position. Then the maneuver group of the second squad crosses the breach first and establishes another support by fire position. The fire group of the second squad follows and joins its maneuver group in its support by fire position. The third squad then follows the same procedure. Finally the platoon leader, platoon sergeant, designated marksman and any attached weapons (flame projectors, AGS-17 automatic grenade launchers) cross the breach and launch an attack on the enemy.

Sequence of Work after Receipt of Mission

After receipt of the order, the platoon commander states:

- The objective of the attack, the direction of the follow-on attack and line of transition to the attack. If it is a dismounted attack, the dismount point
- Tasks for his deputy.
- The order in which the BMPs or BTRs will fire
- Combat formations of the platoon and subordinate attachments

Company in the Offense

A motorized rifle (tank) company can advance in the battalion first echelon or constitute the second echelon or reserve. It can serve as a forward detachment, a flanking detachment or a special purpose detachment. A first-echelon motorized rifle (tank) company's attack frontage extends up to one kilometer and narrows to 500 meters at the breakthrough sector. An offensive includes a company combat formation, system of fires, and system of command and control.[4]

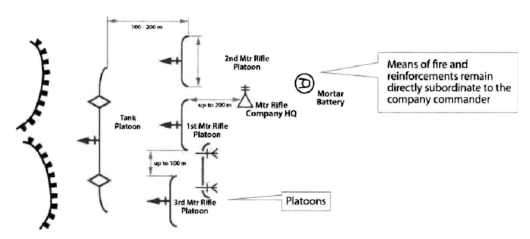

Composition of a Motorized Rifle Company in the Offensive

(Above) This graphic portrays the spacing in a motorized rifle company attack. The location of systems and distances will be adjusted to fit the demands of the situation, threat, forces available and terrain.

Combat Tasks

In the offensive, a first-echelon company has an immediate objective and a direction of further advance. Its immediate objective is to destroy the enemy in his first-echelon platoon strong points, and then control these positions. The direction of further advance will support achieving the immediate objective of the battalion. A second echelon company has an immediate objective upon being committed to combat and a direction of further advance.

The immediate objective of a second-echelon company upon being committed to combat is to complete of the destruction of the enemy together with the companies of the first echelon in the enemy strong points throughout the depth of his defense and controlling his forward positions. The direction of further advance of second-echelon companies will support

[4] This section, including graphics, has been compiled from many sources to include:
"Motorized Rifle (Tank) Companies in the Offense" [мотострелковой (танковой) роты в наступлении], as found on *Studiopedia*, <http://studopedia.info/1-67787.html>, accessed on 1 July 2016.
V.N. Zaritski and L.A. Kharkevich, *General Tactics* [Общая Тактика], Tambov: Tambov Government Technical University, 2007.
Field Manual: Preparation and Conduct of Combined Arms Warfare [Боевой Устав: По Подготовке и Ведению Общевойскового Боя], Moscow: Ministry of Defense of the Russian Federation, 2005.
Source material has also been obtained from a variety of training documents produced by Russian military academies and military departments in civilian academic institutions.

achieving the subsequent objective of the brigade. An offensive requires a combat formation, system of fires and system of command and control.

Elements of the Combat Formation

An attacking company's combat formation usually consists of one echelon. Depending on the combat mission and the situation, the combat formation can be a company in one echelon with a combined arms reserve of up to a platoon. A combat formation consists of:
- A first echelon
- A combined arms reserve
- Attached artillery subunits
- Weapons directly controlled by the company commander

During the offensive, the platoons of the company are deployed in line, wedge, reverse wedge, echelon right or echelon left formation. The first echelon is tasked with defeating the opposing enemy, achieving the immediate objective and developing the offensive with the combined arms reserve throughout the depth of the combat mission. It consists of 2-3 platoons with reinforcements. The combined arms reserve is tasked with handling unforeseen problems, replacing depleted first-echelon subunits, and other tasks. It consists of one platoon. During the offensive, it is 1.5-2 kilometers behind the units of the first echelon. Attached artillery subunits and weapons support the platoons of the first echelon and their attachments.

Pre-Combat and Combat Formation

A company moves into pre-combat formation 1-3 kilometers from the enemy's positions when its platoons deploy from the company march column into platoon columns. Platoon columns are usually separated by 150-300 meters. The company pre-combat formation provides a combination of speed, dispersion, flexibility, and firepower. As with the battalion, a company takes different formations, depending on the tactical situation. Company pre-combat formations are flexible and will change rapidly to facilitate movement through restrictive terrain or in response to enemy actions.

A company is considered to be in combat formation when its subordinate platoons have deployed their individual combat vehicles on line. A company can assume a combat formation 800-1000 meters forward of enemy defensive positions. The combat formation maximizes the unit's firepower by deploying its weapons systems forward. When the terrain is unfavorable for vehicular movement or when enemy antitank defenses are too strong, the motorized rifle squads will dismount and advance on line. The dismount line is no more than one kilometer from the forward line of enemy troops. Normally, the dismount line is some 400 meters from the enemy and will be as close as concealing terrain allows. If dismounted, the motorized rifle squads follow close behind the supporting tanks and receive supporting fire from their BMPs or BTRs. These combat vehicles move up to 400 meters behind, on the flank of, or within the assault line of the advancing force, depending on terrain and enemy fire. The vehicles may also move by bounds from one firing position to another, supporting the attack by fire.

System of Fire & Command and Control
The system of fire is based on the fires of motorized rifle and tank platoons and includes attached weapons, supporting artillery, and attached company weapons. To ensure adequate command and control, the commander of the company is in a BMP while his company is in its combat (pre-combat) formation. During a dismounted assault, the company commander usually dismounts.

Roles of a Motorized Rifle Company in the Attack
In the attack the motorized rifle company fulfills the following functions:
- As part of a motorized rifle brigade
    - In a combined arms reserve of the brigade
- As part of a motorized rifle battalion
    - In the first or second echelon
- As part of a tank company (in special conditions, the MRC can be supported by an artillery {mortar} battery and be integrated into a tank company)
- As a stand-alone unit
    - As a forward detachment
    - As a flanking and special detachment
    - The main component of an assault group
    - As part of an air assault

Means of Reinforcement
Common attachments for a motorized rifle company are:
- Mortar (artillery) battery or platoon.
- Automatic grenade launcher, antitank, flamethrower, and engineer squads
- Tank platoon
It can be supported by an artillery (mortar) battery and be integrated into a tank company.

Company reinforcements depend on the situation and the assigned mission. Reinforcements may include artillery and flamethrower subunits, and engineer subunits. A first-echelon motorized rifle (tank) company will have a reinforcing tank (motorized rifle) subunit and be supported by the bulk of the senior commander's artillery subunits.

Sequence of Work after Receipt of Mission

<u>Decisions about the offense</u>: The commander of the motorized rifle company personally makes the decision based on his understanding of the mission and determination the situation.

1. Concept of Battle
   - The direction and concentration of the main efforts
   - How to defeat the enemy
   - Combat formation of the company (platoon)

Depending on the conditions when transitioning to the attack, he determines
   - The assembly and holding areas
   - The starting line
   - The deployment lines and their safe distances from enemy attack
   - The line for transitioning to the attack and march routes

2. Tasks of subordinate units
3. Main questions of coordination
4. Command and control and combat support

Considerations of the Company Commander
   - Motorized rifle platoon:
        - reinforcements, objective of the attack
        - direction of the follow-on attack
        - assembly position
   - Attached artillery subunits;
        - fire missions
        - time and manner of their implementation
        - firing positions
        - order of displacement
   - Anti-tank squads and attached weapons;
        - their targets for engagement during the attack on the forward edge of the enemy defense
        - their position in the combat formation
        - their order of displacement.

For an attack from the march, the company commander also directs the march for the company, the lines to deploy into company and platoon columns, the places where infantry will mount and dismount tanks (should this be part of the attack), the line of safety from enemy fire, the line to dismount motorized rifle company and platoon personnel when attacking dismounted and the line to transition to the attack.

Battalion in the Offense

A motorized rifle or tank battalion can advance in the first echelon of a brigade, constitute the brigade's second echelon or combined arms reserve, act as an advance guard, forward detachment, raiding detachment, special purpose detachment, flanking detachment, and tactical air (sea) landing detachment, and also form the base of an assault detachment. A

Combat Formation of a Motorized Rifle Battalion in the Offense

(Above) This graphic shows the usual distances involved with an attacking motorized rifle battalion

motorized rifle or tank battalion's mortar battery and grenade launcher platoon are directly subordinate to the commander of the battalion, and remain intact to support the attacking subunits on the axis of the main attack. In some situations, the mortar battery provides a platoon and the grenade launcher platoon provides a squad to the first-echelon companies. A first-echelon motorized rifle (tank) battalion advances on a front of up to two kilometers, with a depth of up to one kilometer. An offensive includes a battalion combat formation, system of fires and system of command and control.[5]

Composition of a Motorized Rifle Battalion in the Offensive

First echelon company with reinforcements

2nd Echelon or Reserve

Means of fire and reinforcements remain directly subordinate to the battalion commander

(Above) This graphic shows the usual layout of a motorized rifle battalion in the offensive

Combat Tasks
A battalion advancing in the first echelon is assigned an:
- Immediate objective
- Subsequent objective
- A direction of further advance.

The immediate objective of a first-echelon battalion usually includes defeating the enemy in his first-echelon company strong point, which is contained within the width of the battalion attack sector, and controlling that area. A subsequent objective may be to continue the offensive, to defeat the enemy within the depth of the defense or to hold the enemy's first position. The direction of further advance will support achieving the brigade's subsequent objective.

---

[5] This section, including graphics, has been compiled from many sources to include:
"Motorized Rifle (Tank) Battalions in the Offense" [мотострелкового (танкового) батальона в наступлении], as found on *Studiopedia*, <http://studopedia.info/1-67788.html>, accessed on 1 July 2016.
V.N. Zaritski and L.A. Kharkevich, *General Tactics* [Общая Тактика], Tambov: Tambov Government Technical University, 2007.
Field Manual: Preparation and Conduct of Combined Arms Warfare [Боевой Устав: По Подготовке и Ведению Общевойскового Боя], Moscow: Ministry of Defense of the Russian Federation, 2005.
Source material has also been obtained from a variety of training documents produced by Russian military academies and military departments in civilian academic institutions.

Areas, Positions and Lines for an Attack From Positions in Direct Contact with the Enemy

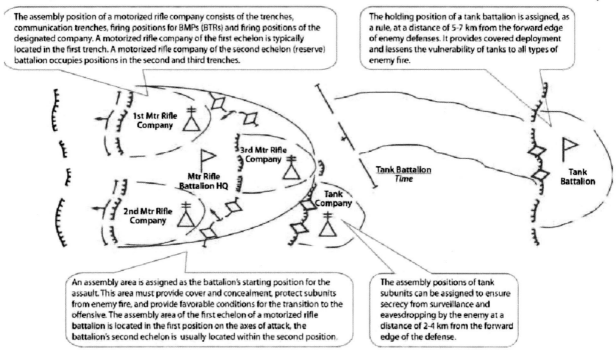

The assembly position of a motorized rifle company consists of the trenches, communication trenches, firing positions for BMPs (BTRs) and firing positions of the designated company. A motorized rifle company of the first echelon is typically located in the first trench. A motorized rifle company of the second echelon (reserve) battalion occupies positions in the second and third trenches.

The holding position of a tank battalion is assigned, as a rule, at a distance of 5-7 km from the forward edge of enemy defenses. It provides covered deployment and lessens the vulnerability of tanks to all types of enemy fire.

An assembly area is assigned as the battalion's starting position for the assault. This area must provide cover and concealment, protect subunits from enemy fire, and provide favorable conditions for the transition to the offensive. The assembly area of the first echelon of a motorized rifle battalion is located in the first position on the axes of attack, the battalion's second echelon is usually located within the second position.

The assembly positions of tank subunits can be assigned to ensure secrecy from surveillance and eavesdropping by the enemy at a distance of 2-4 km from the forward edge of the defense.

(Above) An attack from positions in direct contact with the enemy will preferably be from the march by a battalion moving from an assembly area through the friendly defensive area. The defending battalion will usually follow directly behind the attacking battalion. Usually the defending battalion will attack dismounted with its carriers following in a fire support mission or as a separate bronegruppa.

A battalion attacking in the second echelon is assigned an:
- Immediate objective
- A direction of further advance

The immediate objective of a second echelon battalion may be to continue the offensive, to defeat the enemy brigade or regimental reserves in conjunction with the first-echelon battalion or to control the enemy rear boundary. The direction of further advance of a second-echelon battalion will support achieving the brigade's subsequent objective.

(Right) This graphic on the facing page depicts two battalion attacks from the march. The top is a mounted attack by a tank battalion with an attached motorized rifle company and engineer platoon. The battalion has left its assembly area, deployed from battalion to company to platoon column and then into platoon line. The third tank company is trailing in reserve in platoon columns. There is no artillery depicted, although an artillery battalion in support of a maneuver battalion is common. For the amount of enemy depicted, two artillery battalions may well be in support. The enemy in sector is a defending mechanized infantry company plus two platoons of another mechanized infantry company reinforced with a tank platoon and two antitank platoons. The battalion immediate objective is the rear of the first echelon mechanized infantry company and the subsequent objective is beyond the enemy battalion CP. It has a direction of further advance. It anticipates a counterattack by up to a tank battalion reinforced with a mechanized infantry company.

The bottom graphic depicts a dismounted attack by a motorized rifle battalion with an attached tank company. The tanks and two motorized rifle companies are fully deployed and advancing on line with the third motorized rifle in reserve in company column. Again, there is no artillery depicted, only the battalion mortar battery. The enemy defense is robust and includes most of a mechanized infantry company reinforced with several tanks. The immediate objective is the rear of the mechanized infantry company and the subsequent objective breaks into the enemy battalion rear area. The battalion commander anticipates a counterattack from higher ground of up to a reinforced mechanized infantry battalion strength. The battalion has a direction of further attack.

Combat Formation and Missions of Subunits in the Attack (mounted and dismounted)

Elements of the Combat Formation

The combat formation of a motorized rifle or tank battalion consists of one or two echelons. The battalion usually consists of two echelons for the breakthrough of an enemy defense. In the event of an attack using only one echelon, the formation will have a company-sized reserve.

Elements of the combat formation include:
- First echelon
- Second echelon (or combined arms reserve)
- Artillery subunits
- Subunits and weapons, which remain directly subordinate to the battalion commander.

The first echelon is designed to defeat the opposing enemy, carry out the immediate objective and continue the offensive together with the second echelon (or combined arms reserve) throughout the entire depth of the combat mission. This element consists of two or three companies and attachments. The second echelon exploits the successes of the first echelon, assists the first echelon in fulfilling its immediate and subsequent objectives, replaces or reinforces depleted first-echelon subunits, repels counterattacks, defeats enemy reserves, destroys any enemy on the flanks or in the rear of the first echelon, secures seized objective lines and performs other tasks as needed. It consists of up to a company. The combined arms reserve deals with unforeseen problems, replaces depleted first echelon units, repels counterattacks, destroys any enemy on the flanks or in the rear, performs other tasks assigned to the second echelon. It consists of up to a company. The second echelon (combined arms reserve) of the motorized rifle battalion stays 1.5-2 kilometers behind the companies of the first echelon while they deploy line by line. At the line for deployment into platoon columns, the second echelon remains in pre-combat formation or platoon columns. The mortar battery artillery subunit supports first-echelon units. It deploys to firing positions 500 meters behind the first-echelon companies.

The following are subunits and weapons directly subordinate to the motorized rifle battalion commander:
- Grenade Launcher Subunit (the AGS-17 Grenade Launcher Platoon), which attacks enemy personnel and lightly-armored objects, covers the flanks, and juncture points with adjacent friendly units. It occupies firing positions 300 meters behind companies in the first echelon to protect the gaps between company strong points and the flanks;
- Flamethrower subunits, which defeat the enemy using thermobaric and flame rockets;
- Antitank platoon, which engages tanks and other armored vehicles.

Pre-Combat and Combat Formation
The battalion assumes a pre-combat formation 4-6 kilometers from the enemy's forward positions, when its companies deploy from the battalion march column into company columns. Company columns usually are separated by 500-800 meters. However, depending on the tactical situation, this distance may vary. A battalion can assume different formations as it moves forward. The deployment of the battalion in combat is determined by combat power, readiness of enemy and friendly forces, terrain, time, and weather. Because of these factors, a battalion's pre-combat formation will change as it moves forward. A Russian commander will vary his formations to suit the situation and his concept of the operation. Because of these variables, there is no templated deployment scheme.

A battalion is in combat formation when its first-echelon companies are in columns. Depending on the tactical situation, a battalion's second-echelon companies can be in either march or column formation.

System of Fire and Command and Control
The system of fire includes the systems of fire of the motorized rifle and tank companies, organic assets, attached and supporting artillery, the battalion's direct-fire assets, the grenade launcher platoon, and attached antitank and flamethrower units. To ensure command and control, a command-observation post is deployed forward at a position that provides the best view of the terrain and the enemy. The position provides for continuous battlefield management and allows coordination with adjacent units. The position is placed up to 300 meters from the front line.

Roles of a Motorized Rifle Battalion in the Attack
In the attack the motorized rifle battalion fulfills the following functions:
- As part of a motorized rifle brigade
    - In the first or second echelon
    - In a combined arms reserve
- As a stand-alone unit
    - As an advanced guard
    - As a forward, flanking, raiding, assault or special detachment
    - Conducting amphibious and tactical air assaults

Means of Reinforcement
Common attachments for a motorized rifle battalion include:
- 1-2 tank companies
- Artillery battalion or battery
- Engineer platoon, mine clearance means, scissor bridge and engineer route clearance vehicle
- Antitank subunits and means of repelling airborne assaults
- NBC units.

A tank company is normally attached to a motorized rifle battalion, while a tank battalion normally has a motorized rifle company attached. An attached artillery battalion takes up firing positions 2-4 kilometers from the troops on the forward edge. In addition, the

129

motorized rifle battalion is supported by artillery battalion fire, direct support and brigade level air defense systems and sometimes by helicopter gunships.

Sequence of Work after Receipt of Mission

<u>Decisions about the Offense</u>: The commander of the motorized rifle battalion personally makes the decision based on his understanding of the mission and determination of the situation.

1. Concept of Battle
    - The direction and concentration of the main efforts
    - How to defeat the enemy
    - Combat formation of the battalion (company, platoon)

Depending on the conditions when transitioning to the attack, he determines
    - The assembly and holding areas
    - The starting line
    - The deployment lines and their safe distances from enemy attack
    - The line for transitioning to the attack and march routes
2. Tasks of subordinate units
3. Main questions of coordination
4. Command and control and combat support

After receipt of the order, the battalion commander states:
    - For the <u>first-echelon companies, including an attached tank company</u> - means of reinforcement, immediate objective and direction of the subsequent attack, the assembly positions and the time of their occupation, and who provides support
    - For the <u>second-echelon company</u> - the assembly (waiting) area and time of its occupation, possible lines for commitment to battle, immediate objective and direction of the follow-on attack, reinforcements when entering into battle.
    - For the <u>reserve</u> – assembly position, direction and order of displacement during the offensive, and missions to prepare for
    - For <u>attached subunits of artillery and mortar batteries</u> - targets designated for destruction during the fire preparation of the attack and who directs them, firing positions, march routes and the order of movement, time to be ready to fire and order of displacement
    - For <u>dedicated direct fire (guns and tanks)</u> - targets designated for destruction during the fire preparation of the attack and who destroys them, firing positions and the time of their employment, actions after carrying out their missions
    - For <u>automatic grenade launcher subunits</u> - targets designated for destruction during the fire preparation of the attack, firing positions, place in the combat formation, routes, etc.
    - For <u>antitank subunits</u> - targets designated for destruction during the preparatory attack by fires, firing position, place in the combat formation, route, etc.
    - For <u>air defense subunits</u> - direction in which to search for enemy aircraft, place in the combat formation, etc.
    - For <u>engineer subunits</u> - place and time for breaching minefields and obstacles and method and marking of crossings through them.

For an attack from the march, the battalion commander also directs the march for the battalion, the lines for deployment into company and platoon columns, the places where infantry will mount and dismount tanks (should this be part of the attack), the line of safety from enemy fire, the line to dismount motorized rifle company and platoon personnel when attacking dismounted and the line to transition to the attack.

Motorized Rifle Battalion Assembly Area

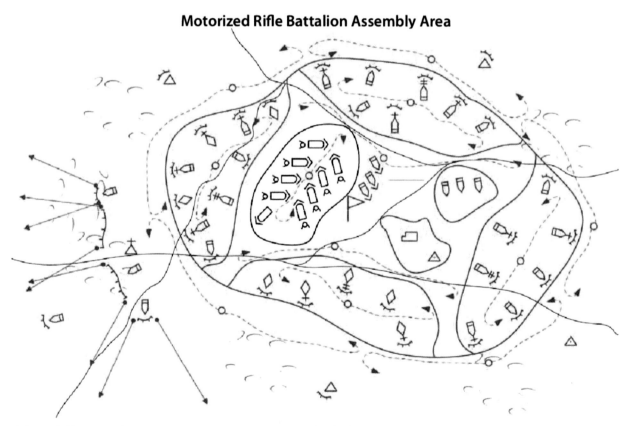

(Above) This graphic is a representative motorized rifle battalion assembly area. It is designed for 360° defense with the mortar battery, battalion CP and trains in the center. Companies are located in separate areas and in order of their expected order of march. Vehicles are dug in and camouflaged. A BMP platoon is dug in on the likely avenue of approach. Other outposts screen the perimeter. Foot patrols cover the perimeter and interior of the assembly area.

(Right) The graphic on the facing page depicts the lines of deployment for an attacking motorized rifle battalion. The artillery will begin the fire preparation phase before the battalion leaves the assembly area. This phase can last 40-50 minutes, although all weapons will not be firing continuously. The preparation covers the attacking movement while attempting to gain fire superiority by suppressing enemy artillery and strongpoints and disrupting command and control. The artillery preparation concentrates on the enemy forward positions from the time when the brigade goes into battalion columns until it hits the line to deploy into platoon columns. The fires begin to lift and shift into the depth of enemy defenses. When the platoons have moved into squad columns and into attack line, all the fires have shifted to form a line of fire slowly advancing through the enemy first echelon defense (forward enemy platoon-battalion immediate objective). This is the beginning of the fire support phase. The artillery fires on the enemy immediately in front of and on the flanks of the attacking force. Successive fire concentrations and rolling barrages are employed during this phase. Artillery battalions or batteries may be attached to attacking companies during this phase. As the attack continues to the depth of the enemy company in the sector of attack (battalion subsequent objective), artillery begins displacing forward as the artillery accompaniment of the attack phase begins. Artillery supports the attack into the enemy positions, concentrating on newly discovered targets, antitank weapons, mortars and artillery.

Fundamentals for Conducting an Offensive by Combined Arms Subunits

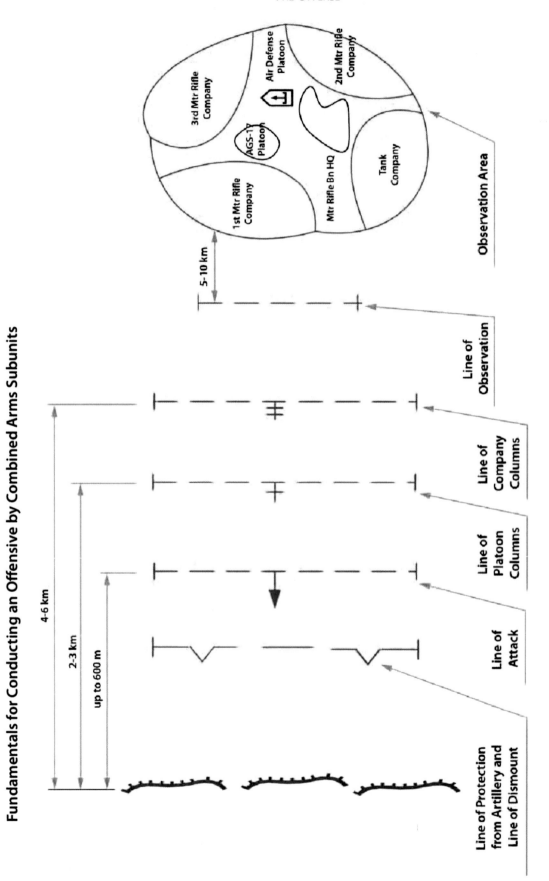

(Right) The graphic on the facing page shows a motorized rifle battalion and two companies of the tank battalion attacking in the south (notionally the brigade main attack), while the northern attack consists of a motorized rifle battalion and a tank company. The third motorized rifle company is moving to reinforce success with two companies. Its third company constitutes the anti-assault reserve. Normally the main attack sector will be narrower than the supporting attack sector. On a Russian military map, Russian maneuver unit positions, boundary lines, axes, deployment lines, command posts and equipment are drawn in red. Artillery boundaries, firing positions, planned fires, and equipment are drawn in black, as are air defense boundaries and equipment, electronic warfare units and equipment and the antitank units and equipment.

Inserting Additional Armor for an Attack in Direct Contact

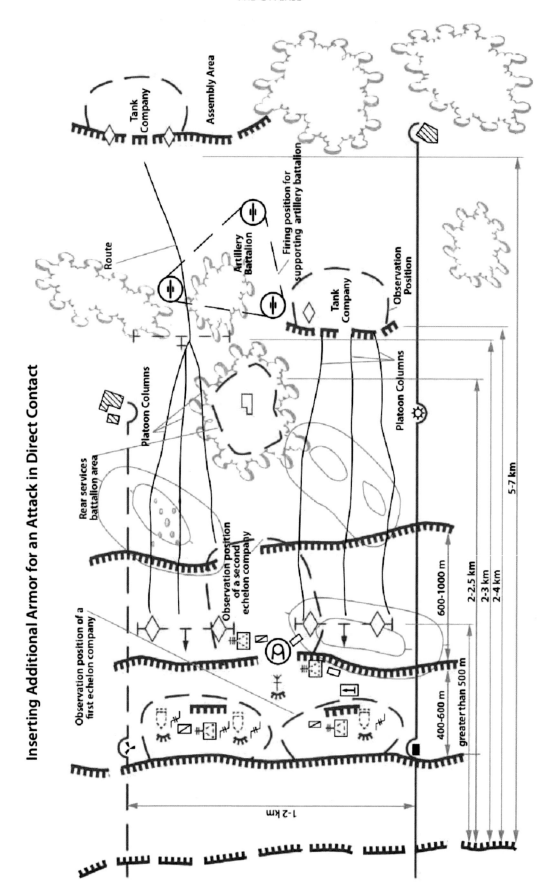

(Right) The graphic facing page depicts an attack from a position in direct contact with the enemy [наступление из положения непосредственного соприкосновения с противником] which is mounted from an established defense or when an attack from the march has failed. In either event, Russian subunits will remain in contact with the enemy. The attack can be launched by the forces already in contact with the enemy or by conducting an attack from the march through the Russian's own forward defending forces. In either event, control of forces and movement will be a challenge. Artillery preparation will be intense since it will be difficult to attain operational surprise.

This graphic shows the defending 1st Motorized Rifle Battalion with an attached tank company and artillery battalion. It defends in two echelons with its 1st and 2nd MRC forward and its 3rd MRC in the second echelon. It is opposed by a dug-in mechanized infantry company with an attached tank platoon. The attack will be reinforced by two tank companies from the parent battalion of the attached tank battalion and the 4th MRC from the 2nd Motorized Rifle Battalion of the parent Motorized Rifle Brigade.

The first task is to concentrate forces for the attack. Forces will move under the cover of night, stormy weather, smoke, artillery fire or other obscurant. Ground guides and one-sided reflective trail markers will move forces into position. The 1st MRC will retain the northern part and second echelon position of its present position. The 4th MRC will move into the southern part of the 1st MRC position and form a single echelon line. The 2nd MRC will concentrate its force in the southern part of its position in a single echelon. The 3rd MRC will move from its second echelon position into the northern part of the 2nd MRC position in a single echelon line. Battalion headquarters and the air defense battery will move forward behind the new 2nd MRC position. The mortar battery, AGS-17 platoon and antitank reserve will stay in position.

The battalion will attack with three motorized rifle companies abreast and the tank battalion in the second echelon. If the first echelon fails to complete the breakthrough, the second echelon may have to complete it. The 1st MRC moves as a reserve. The attack will be preceded by a short artillery preparation (10-25 minutes). Supporting artillery from brigade will add its fires. The attack will have an immediate objective (the depth of the defending enemy company) and a subsequent direction of attack. Should the attack succeed, the commander will attempt to maintain the momentum. After destroying the enemy, the battalions will usually form into pre-combat or march order and move without delay. Should the attack fail, the commander may attempt to bypass the enemy or resume the defense and prepare to try again.

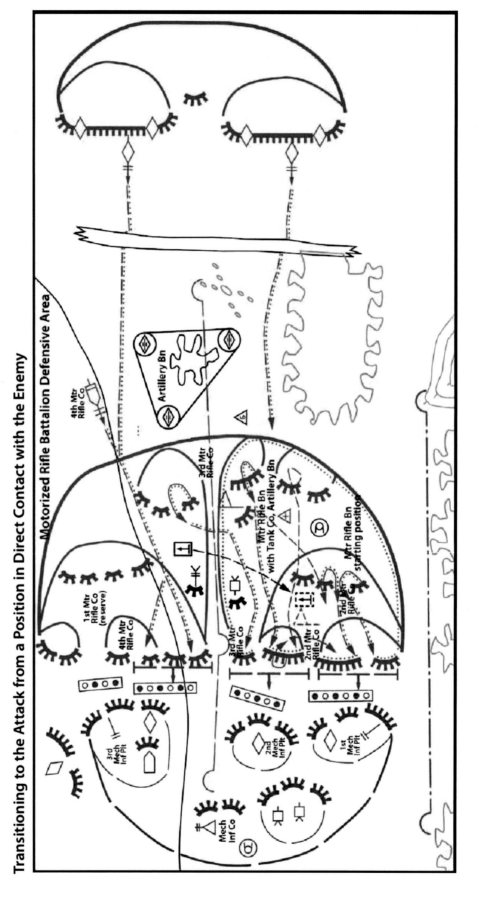

Transitioning to the Attack from a Position in Direct Contact with the Enemy

Motorized Rifle Battalion Defensive Area

4th Mtr Rifle Co

Artillery Bn

3rd Mtr Rifle Co

Mtr Rifle Bn with Tank Co, Artillery Bn

Mtr Rifle Bn starting position

1st Mtr Rifle Co (reserve)

4th Mtr Rifle Co

3rd Mtr Rifle Co

2nd Mtr Rifle Co

2nd Mtr Rifle Co

3rd Mech Inf Plt

2nd Mech Inf Plt

1st Mech Inf Plt

Mech Inf Co

Brigade in the Offense

The motorized rifle or tank brigade may be found in the first echelon, second echelon, or combined arms reserve of an Army Group or Army Corps. As a rule, a tank brigade is usually the main effort to defeat the main enemy force. The brigade is assigned an attack zone of up to 6 kilometers wide in the section of the breakthrough. Its zone of attack is up to 2 kilometers. The depth of the brigade's composition in the attack is 10-15 kilometers. For conducting the offensive, a motorized rifle or tank brigade will create a combat formation and determines tactics for the destruction of the enemy by fires, air defense, and air assault defense.[6]

Combat Tasks

A motorized rifle or tank brigade, advancing in the first echelon has the following combat tasks:

- <u>Immediate objective</u> – defeat the first echelon (brigade/regiment) of the enemy defense and occupy its position. The depth of the immediate objective is up to 5 kilometers;
- <u>Intermediate objective</u> – further develop the offensive by defeating the first echelon's reserve. The depth of the intermediate objective is up to 15 kilometers;
- <u>Further objective</u>- advance farther and defeat the Army Group's divisional reserves, which is the task of the army (corps) on the first day of the offensive. The depth of the further objective is 20-30 kilometers.

Elements of the Combat Formation

A two echelon system is used to defeat an enemy in a prepared defense. The following are the elements of the combat formation:

- The first echelon
- The second echelon
- Combined arms reserve
- Brigade Artillery Group (BrAG);
- Air defense subunits
- Antitank reserve
- Mobile obstacle construction detachments
- Counterair assault reserve.

Depending on the situation, the elements of the combat formation of the motorized rifle or tank brigade can be a forward detachment, an advance guard, special detachment, raiding detachment, helicopter subunit, tactical air assault subunit, electronic warfare subunit, or strike detachment.

The <u>first echelon</u> is designed to defeat the first echelon of the enemy defense within the breakthrough sector of the brigade and then, together with the second echelon, continue the offensive until it extends throughout the entire depth of the defense. It consists of 2-3 battalions with reinforcements.

[6] "Motorized Rifle (Tank) Brigades in the Offense" [мотострелковой (танковой) бригады в наступлении], as found on *Studiopedia*, <http://studopedia.info/1-67789.html>, accessed on 1 July 2016.

Motorized Rifle Brigade in the Offense

(Above) This graphic shows some of the considerations for a brigade in the attack. The brigade attacks from the march with two reinforced motorized rifle battalions and the tank battalion minus abreast. The attack is weighted with two battalions in the south. Air defenses are well forward and on the flanks. Three artillery battalions are in the brigade artillery group (BrAG). The antitank artillery battalion and engineer company are following the main attack. The third motorized rifle battalion is following in battalion column and can be committed to the northern or southern attack. The anti-assault reserve is protecting the brigade from aerial insertion or flank attack. The electronic warfare company is jamming enemy communications, precision-guided weapons and computer systems. While not depicted, smoke is frequently used to conceal artillery, command posts, flanks and minefield or water obstacle crossings.

The <u>second echelon</u> is intended to exploit the success of the first echelon, complete the immediate and intermediate missions, reconstitute first echelon units, repel counterattacks, defeat enemy reserves, etc. During the offensive, the second-echelon battalions move behind the lines of the first-echelon battalions at a distance of 6-8 kilometers.

The <u>combined arms reserve</u> is designed to address unexpected problems, reconstitute units from the first or second echelon, defeat enemy airborne/air assault forces, defeat enemy elements at the rear or flanks, etc.

Pre-Combat and Combat Formation

The brigade does not have a pre-combat formation. It is in its combat formation when its organic battalions have deployed out of the brigade march formation and into battalion columns. A brigade in a combat formation will usually occupy a sector 5-8 kilometers wide. However, depending on the tactical situation, these widths may vary. The number of battalion columns and the type of formation will vary. The brigade will split into battalion columns about 12 to 15 kilometers from the enemy's forward defensive positions. A brigade is in combat formation when its first-echelon battalions have deployed into columns. The brigade's second-echelon battalions normally remain in column formation.

Elements of the Offensive (organic and attached)

Combat Reserve – emplaced into position before employment. It is situated approximately 6-8 kilometers from the first echelon, and moves with the second echelon.

Brigade Artillery Group (BrAG) – conducts destruction by fire missions and supports the first-echelon maneuver battalions. It consists of organic and attached artillery assets of at least one MLRS and two howitzer battalions. The artillery firing positions are usually located in an area that is 3-5 kilometers wide, 1-2 kilometers in depth, at a distance of 2-4 kilometers from the forward edge of one's own forces.

Air Defense assets - cover the main forces of the brigade from enemy air attacks. They consist of two air defense battalions- an anti-aircraft missile-artillery battalion and an anti-aircraft missile battalion. A Tunguska missile battery protects the first-echelon battalions. Two Strela-10 missile battery platoons protect the BrAG. Two platoons equipped with Igla MANPADS cover the first-echelon battalions, while the third platoon in the Igla company protects the brigade command post. The Tor-M1 anti-aircraft missile battalion provides zonal cover of the brigade to defend it from air strikes.

Antitank Reserve- destroys tanks and other armored vehicles, protects the flanks and seams in the defense, and covers enemy avenues of approach. In motorized rifle brigades the antitank reserve consists of an antitank artillery battalion. In tank brigades, it is 1-2 tank companies. During the battle the antitank reserve moves with the first echelon, focusing on armor-hazardous areas, road junctions and flanks. It works in conjunction with mobile obstacle detachments.

Mobile Obstacle Detachment - places mines on likely enemy counterattack avenues of approach, covers the offensive's flanks, and protects gaps. It is the brigade's organic engineer company with mine-laying vehicles.

Anti-Assault Reserve - destroys enemy assaults independently or in conjunction with the second echelon. The anti-assault reserve usually is a motorized rifle company from a second-echelon battalion.

Forward Detachment - breaches the enemy's security zone, captures and holds crossings and accomplishes other tasks. It is a reinforced battalion.

Assault Detachment - destroys enemy troop concentrations, critical facilities, and strong points during the breakthrough of the offensive. It is a reinforced battalion or company.

Detachment for the Destruction of High-Threat Systems - destroys the enemy's tactical nuclear systems, elements of his precision fire systems and reconnaissance strike complexes before they can be employed against the offensive. It is a reinforced battalion or company. (This detachment will probably not be constituted if the enemy lacks these capabilities.)

Raiding Detachment- disrupts C2 and communications systems, destroys air defense units, blocks the employment of enemy reserves, destroys rear area support units, blocks the employment of enemy reserves, blocks withdrawal routes and destroys communications. It is a reinforced battalion or company.

Tactical Air Assault element- designated to cooperate with the brigade's subunits to achieve a high tempo in the advance and to seize designated regions. It will destroy enemy command and control systems, forces and weapons, and disrupt enemy rear area support. It is a reinforced battalion or company and can be organic or attached.

Electronic Warfare subunit- jams enemy radios and electronics, and protects the unit from radio-proximity-fused munitions. It is the brigade's organic electronic warfare company.

Helicopter subunit- destroys enemy tanks, armored vehicles, antitank weapons, artillery, helicopters, enemy air assault forces, C2, reconnaissance assets and air assault landing zones. It also delivers supplies, evacuates wounded, and performs other tasks. It is an attached helicopter subunit.

The system of destructive fires for a motorized rifle or tank brigade includes:
- Preparatory air strikes by supporting and assigned aviation
- Indirect fires from organic, attached, and supporting artillery
- Direct fires
- Fires from specialized troops (fuel-air explosives, flame projectors, chemical (including smoke)
- A system of fire control for the battalions.

To ensure adequate C2 in the offensive, the command posts are deployed behind the forward edge of brigade troops:
- Command post – 3-5 kilometers
- Forward command post (element of the command post) - one kilometer
- Rear services command post - 15+ kilometers.

Lines of Deployment
The starting line is designated for the on-time start of movement out of the assembly area. Its distance from the forward perimeter of the assembly area must allow the full deployment of a battalion march column, achieving and maintaining the prescribed rate of march, and may be established 5-10 kilometers from the assembly area.

Lines of deployment into battalion columns: Deployments into battalion columns are conducted out of range of enemy artillery fire, usually at a distance of 12-15 kilometers from the forward edge of the enemy's defenses.

Lines of deployment into company columns: Deployments into company columns are conducted out of range of enemy direct-fire guns, tanks and ATGMs, at a distance of 4-6 kilometers from the forward edge of the enemy's defenses.

Lines of deployment into platoon columns: Deployments into platoon columns are conducted out of the range of hand-held antitank weapons and small arms fire at a distance of 2-3 kilometers from the forward edge of the enemy's defenses.

At the lines for deployment into battalion, company, and platoon columns, the subunits each begin to move on their own separate axes.

<u>Lines of deployment into the attack</u>: are designated at a distance out of the range of main weapons types and allow the subunit to reach the forward edge by "H-hour." The line for deployment into the attack is 600 meters (sometimes more) from the forward edge of the enemy's defenses. During an attack from positions in direct contact with the enemy, the line of deployment into the attack is the first trench.

<u>Line of dismount</u>: When conducting a dismounted attack, motorized riflemen dismount as close as possible to the forward edge of the enemy's defenses in areas sheltered from machine guns, antitank weapons and close combat fire. Sometimes this line coincides with the line of deployment into the attack.

In order to coordinate the actions of the motorized rifle and tank subunits with artillery, which is firing from concealed firing positions, a "danger close" line is designated to protect friendly forces from the detonations of one's own artillery rounds:

- For dismounted motorized riflemen - 400 meters
- For BMPs - 300 meters
- For tanks - 200 meters

Means of Reinforcement

A motorized rifle or tank brigade in the offense will form a BrAG, which is usually composed of the maneuver brigade's two organic self-propelled artillery battalions and one MLRS battalion. The brigade may gain 2-4 additional artillery battalions from the army artillery group (AAG) to support the offensive, in addition to other forces.

Commentary on Brigade in Offense

A motorized rifle brigade can act in the offensive in a variety of circumstances:

- Meeting engagement, where two moving opposing forces encounter each other with little or no warning;
- Attack from the march against an enemy who has gone into a hasty defense or one that is in a well prepared defense;
- Attack against a withdrawing enemy who is fighting on successive lines or employing a rear guard;
- Attack from positions in contact;
- Attack through a defending friendly unit;
- Pursuit against a disciplined or broken enemy.

The Russian Army is an artillery army with a lot of combat vehicles. While Western Armies have gravitated to precision fires delivered by fewer systems, the Russians maintain a large artillery park and employ mass fires to destroy hectares of enemy-occupied territory. Precision-fire systems are met with massed fires and electronic and masking countermeasures (as well as with Russian precision fires systems). The BrAG shown has the brigade's two organic 152mm howitzer battalions and organic 122mm multiple rocket launcher battalion in position. More artillery battalions from outside the brigade can be added to the BrAG. The forward-most howitzer firing positions are 1-4 kilometers from the forward edge of one's own troops to provide maximum depth in support of the attack. Howitzers usually have a main and two or more alternate firing positions within firing platoon positions. Weapons and platoons are usually shifted between firing missions. Artillery also has deception firing positions to mask the real positions with harassment and interdiction (H&I) fires and "duty" positions for "duty" weapons. Duty weapons provide artillery support in advance of the attack, but return to the main firing position as part of unit fire missions in support of the attack. During the attack the artillery will displace forward to provide fire into the depths. It may displace by battery or battalion, the key factor being the maintenance of fire support throughout the entire attack.

The Russian Army has a robust, modern air defense system that employs missiles and guns on mobile platforms to provide protection against enemy helicopters, jet aircraft and unmanned aerial systems. It consists of an air defense artillery and an air defense missile (rocket-artillery) battalion. Should jamming and/or EMP degrade missile effectiveness, the brigade still has rapid-fire anti-aircraft artillery. The graphic shows a Tunguska missile battery protecting the first-echelon battalions. Two Strela-10 rocket battery platoons protect the BrAG. Two platoons equipped with Igla MANPADS also cover the first-echelon battalions, while the third platoon in the Igla company protects the brigade command post. The Tor-M1 anti-aircraft missile battalion provides zonal cover to the brigade to defend it from air strikes.

The brigade's fourth artillery battalion is the antitank artillery battalion which has guns and missiles to engage enemy armor. It is deployed as the antitank reserve and works closely with the mobile obstacle detachment from the engineer company. It lays antitank mines where directed.

When the brigade attacks from the march, its total march column can extend over 30 kilometers. Its zone of attack is 4-8 kilometers wide (6 kilometers is standard), which is concentrated in a 2-4 kilometer frontage (2 kilometers is standard). There are 5-15 kilometers between echelons. The first echelon is probably three kilometers deep and the forward area, including the BrAG is probably five kilometers deep. The brigade area, including trains, is 15 kilometers deep. When possible, the brigade moves on two or more axes. A brigade attacking mounted out of an assembly area on a single axis would require 20 kilometers to deploy from column to line, with battalions deploying 8-12 kilometers from the enemy front lines, company columns deploying 4-6 kilometers from the enemy and platoon columns deploying 1-4 kilometers from the enemy. A normal battalion attack frontage is 1-2 kilometers within a 2-5 kilometer attack zone. The movement to contact is choreographed with the artillery fire of the BrAG. It begins with preparation fire to find and destroy enemy artillery and then shifts to destroy the enemy in forward positions. As the motorized riflemen dismount and move into assault lines, the fire is shifted back through the forward enemy defenses to keep a wall of fire in front of the attacking infantry. As the brigade fights through the enemy's first-echelon defense, supporting fires maintain fire superiority and ease the advance of maneuver subunits. As the attack continues, artillery displaces forward in accompaniment to provide responsive artillery support to the brigade.

(Right) This notional laydown does not provide the circumstances of the enemy defense. All we know is that it is not a meeting engagement or a pursuit and that there is a Russian brigade on either flank. The attacking brigade has an immediate and subsequent objective and either an objective of the day or a direction of further advance. Depending on the enemy strength and preparedness, a brigade's immediate objective against a prepared defense in depth might be to breakthrough a defending enemy battalion's forward defending companies, and the subsequent objective would be to push through to the rear of the enemy battalion defenses, with an objective of the day being the defeat of the defending enemy's tactical reserve. The immediate and subsequent objectives on the graphic are not to scale, as the attack is expected to penetrate much deeper.

Motorized Rifle Brigade in the Offense

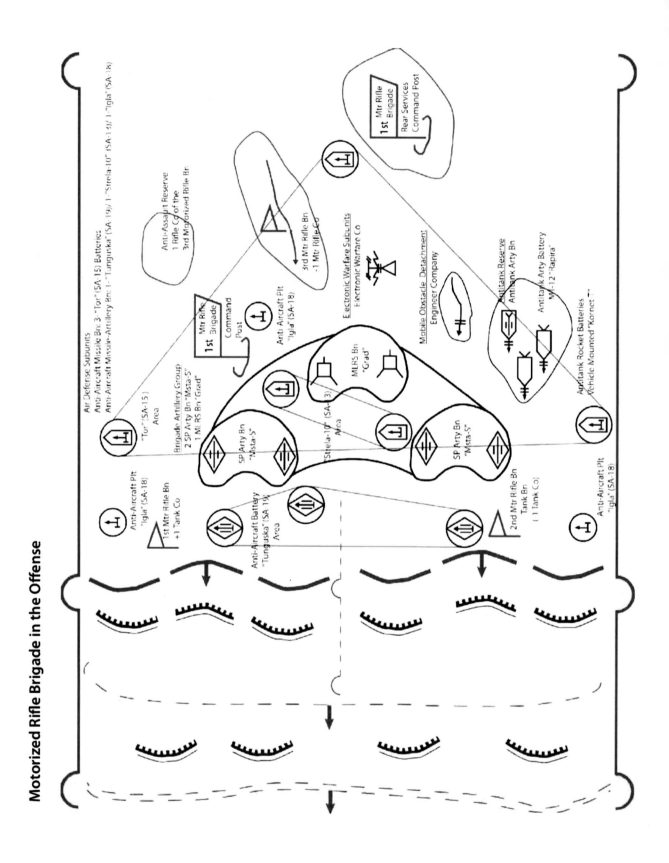

Chapter 5
Tactical Maneuver

The March

Russia covers more land mass than any other country. Its population density of 8.4 people per square kilometer make it one of the most sparsely populated countries on the planet. Russia's ground forces have to be mobile and skilled in long-range deployment in order to deploy to threatened areas. Brigades deploy annually over a thousand kilometers to unfamiliar training areas. Emergency Readiness Deployment Exercises also move troop units over long distances to determine their ability to get to the fight efficiently and effectively. Brigade officers are skilled in conducting road, rail, boat/ship and aviation unit movements. The Soviet Army's entrance into Afghanistan and its later withdrawal were excellently executed. When the Russian Army hit rock bottom just before the 1994 incursion into Chechnya, it still did an impressive job of quickly pulling together pieces of its shattered army from all over the country.

Initial operations shape the course of a war and which side is first to mobilize its forces, concentrate them at the contested area and deploy them for combat has a distinct, if not decisive advantage since that side has the initiative to establish a strong defense or to forestall the other side from creating prepared defenses and thus preempt costly breakthrough operations. For Russia, combined rail and road movement is often the most effective and quickest way to move brigades. March planning includes priority for movement, march capabilities (so that the forces and heavy equipment on rail arrive together) and march support in the form of air defense, security of bridges and choke points, supply of POL and material reserves, maintenance support, secrecy, assembly areas, dispersion areas, lager sites, rest sites and information operations cover, and misdirection.[1]

Marches can be administrative or under threat. Marches under threat have usually been conducted at night for concealment. Depending on the state of electronic combat and air superiority, marches may be conducted during the day under smoke. The Russians use smoke in a variety of circumstances. Instead of building expensive counters to top-attack, the Russians use smoke. Smoke may be used to screen movement effectively provided that its particulates serve as a screen against electronic probes. HETs are used to save wear and tear on tanks and artillery pieces. It is optimal that first echelon brigades have three routes from the final assembly area to commitment. The march column is organized so that the battalions may move directly into combat if needed. March columns must flow smoothly and quickly from the march into battle in combat order determined by the enemy composition and terrain where contact is expected. This provides an advantage in the event of a meeting engagement or overcoming a surprised enemy defense. March columns are normally headed by a reconnaissance detachment some 60 kilometers in front of the main body. A forward security element follows some 15 minutes behind. An advance guard battalion follows another fifteen minutes behind. Movement support detachments move behind the advance detachment, prepared to assist, repair or move stalled vehicles off the route. The main body moves behind the advanced guard with the headquarters and artillery usually in the forward portion of the main body. The march column has flank and rear security elements deployed during movement.

[1] Ministry of Defense of the Russian Federation, "March Preparation" [Маршевая Подготовка], *Military Encyclopedia* [Военная Энциклопедия], Volume 5, Moscow: Voyenizdat, 2001, 20-21.

Battalion Tactical Group on the March (variant)

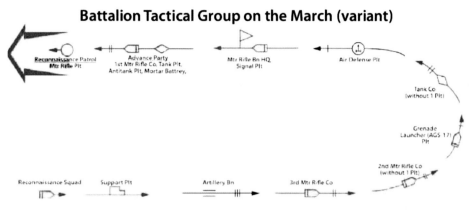

(Right) The graphic on the facing page shows the maintenance and combat service support provided to a tank battalion on the march.[2] The graphic depicts logistics and maintenance support to a tank battalion on a march moving from an assembly area in the upper right corner to a day or night lager site. The graphic is not to scale, since a normal 10-12 hour road march by a mixed march column of tanks and wheeled vehicles would stretch 200-350 kilometers on paved roads, 120-240 kilometers on dry dirt roads and 80-140 kilometers on muddy, hilly or urban roads. In the assembly area are three tank companies; the battalion headquarters; armored, tracked recovery vehicles; a maintenance support element; the battalion support platoon and the medical platoon. A motorized rifle company (MRC) mounted on BMPs or BTRs could be attached to the battalion. A field kitchen is set up to provide hot food. During the 12-14 hours in the assembly area, drivers and mechanics are required to spend 2-3 hours maintaining their tracked and wheeled vehicles. The assembly area is set up for 360° defense, and fighting positions are prepared and vehicles are camouflaged.

The battalion departs the assembly area in column formation stretching over eight kilometers, with some five kilometers between it and another battalion. The combat support and combat service support trucks, including tow trucks, bring up the rear. After the first two hours, the column enters into a rest area for a half-hour halt. The first rest area on this graphic is a maintenance and control center, where drivers and mechanics spend 15-30 minutes in maintenance. Resuming the march, the column reaches a river, which is manned by traffic control personnel (traffic control point #1) to maintain intervals and loads on the crossing bridge. Air defense assets (not shown) will cover the bridge. Maintenance assets (in this case, tank recovery vehicles) are on hand to keep traffic moving and the bridge cleared.

Two-three hours after leaving the first rest area, the battalion closes into a second rest area for another break, while the drivers and mechanics spend another 15-30 minutes on maintenance. The battalion is fed another hot meal at this rest area and the vehicles are refueled. The graphic shows two methods of refueling. The top left box shows 32 tanks parked in 4 rows so that fuel trucks can drive between them and refuel 4 tanks simultaneously. The bottom right box shows a field pumping station that can refuel 20 tanks simultaneously. The march continues and the battalion reaches traffic control point #2. The battalion moves into its day or night lager, takes up defensive positions, and camouflages vehicles, and the drivers and mechanics settle in to another 2-3 hours of maintenance. Vehicles are refueled and a hot meal is served. Personnel get some sleep before the next march (or attack).

[2] Ministry of Defense of the Soviet Union, *Tactics (company, battalion)* [Тактика (рота, батальон)], Second volume, Moscow: Voyenizdat, 1991, plate 28.

Rear Service Support for a Tank Battalion on the March

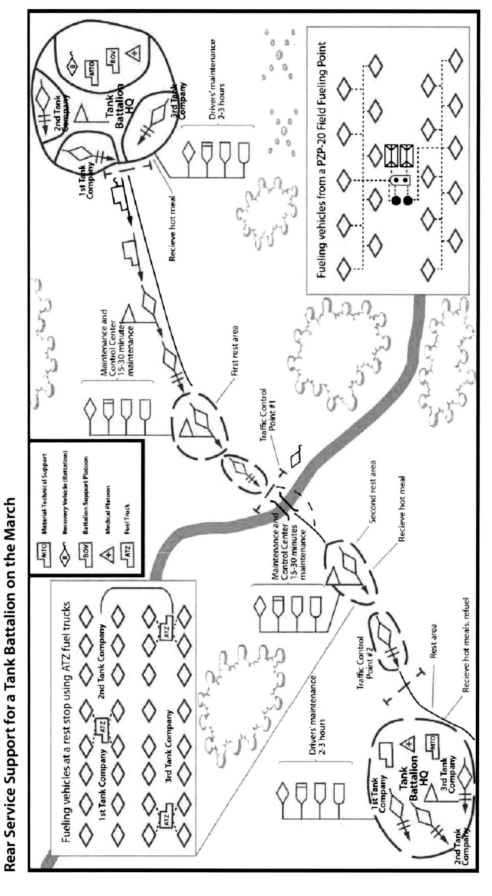

Transportation of Troops by Rail

(Above) The above graphic depicts a rail march where the unit waits in a concealed waiting area some 3-5 kilometers from the railhead. The unit occupies the waiting area in tactical readiness and patrols the perimeter. There is a reserve concealed waiting area in case it is needed. Vehicles are maintained, troops are fed and rested in the area. The unit moves from the waiting area and loads onto train flat cars and box cars and boards personnel. When the trains arrive at the receiving railhead, the unit unloads and occupies another assembly area. Security is maintained while vehicles are topped off, equipment is sorted out and personnel are fed and rested. Once the unit is ready, it conducts a motor march to its next destination.

(Right) The graphic on the facing page shows ways to conduct marches. Each of the examples includes a long, white, jagged-ended belt snaking across the travel routes. This belt simply marks a long span of distance and time during which travel is conducted but the mapping of this area is not included. The top left example shows a subunit march combining a motor march and a foot march. The unit starts in an assembly area on the right, moves on vehicles to a dismount area and continues on foot. The top middle example shows a sequential combination march where a unit moves from an assembly area by river transport to a disembarkation point, where it boards railroad transport and continues to a detraining point and moves into a new assembly area. The top right example shows a combination march where part of the unit is moved by air transport and part by railroad simultaneously. The bottom left example shows a sequential combination march where a unit embarks on maritime transport, disembarks men and equipment, then moves to a road where it continues its march on vehicles. The last example is a combined simultaneous march where a unit conducts a road march while its heavy equipment (usually tracked vehicles) is moved by rail to meet up at a new assembly area. This last example is quite common as the Russian ground forces do not want to expend track and motor life unnecessarily for tanks, self-propelled artillery, and the like.

The Combined Movement of Troops

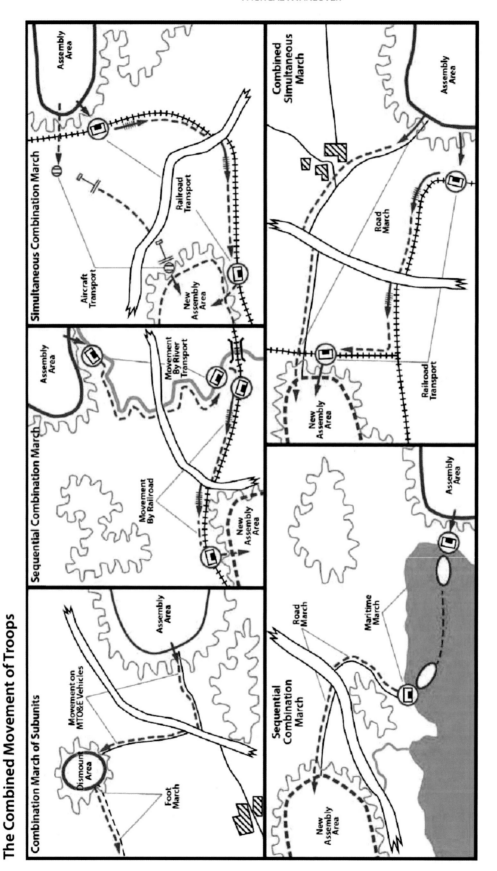

Combination March of Subunits

Movement on MTO&E Vehicles

Foot March

Dismount Area

Assembly Area

Sequential Combination March

Assembly Area

Movement By River Transport

Movement By Railroad

New Assembly Area

Simultaneous Combination March

Assembly Area

Aircraft Transport

Railroad Transport

New Assembly Area

Sequential Combination March

Road March

Maritime March

Assembly Area

New Assembly Area

Combined Simultaneous March

Assembly Area

Road March

Railroad Transport

New Assembly Area

Convoy Operations

Image Courtesy: Russian Ministry of Defense

(Right) The graphic on the facing page depicts a hard-luck unit on a road march. Starting at the bottom right hand corner, the unit departs from its waiting area only to be met by enemy aircraft which attack the column and destroy a bridge crossing. The unit deploys its air defense assets while vehicles respond with on-board machine guns and defeat the air attack. The unit diverts to a river fording site and crosses the river successfully. After some time, the enemy hits the column with a nuclear weapon. The combat capable subunits withdraw from the strike zone on the upwind side. The units take measures (decontaminating men and equipment) to restore combat capability to the stricken units. The unit takes necessary measures to mitigate the effects of the strike in the area (road repair, fire control) and the subunits (including the restored units) resume their march. The determined unit drives on and, after a good while is attacked by enemy FASCAM. The intrepid unit conducts a reconnaissance to determine the extent of the mine field and employs its UR-77 or UR-83 line charge mine clearing systems to clear paths through the minefield. The trapped vehicles exit the minefield. The unit continues its march by either creating a bypass around the stricken area or clearing the route through the minefield.

Our hard-luck unit pushes on, but the enemy is determined to stop it. After driving further, the column encounters an air assault unit. The unit immediately puts artillery fire on the enemy and deploys tanks and motorized rifle subunits to deal with it. The attackers split the air assault unit into pieces and defeat it in detail. In the meantime, the main body of the unit column bypasses the fighting and continues the march. Trouble awaits and the column is now hit with an enemy chemical strike. The part of the column in the contaminated zone quickly exits the zone at maximum speed and spreads out the distance between vehicles. The stricken vehicles are decontaminated by the chemical defense subunit and medical personnel see to the personnel. The main body of the unit column bypasses the stricken area. Further, down the road, the forward detachment encounters the enemy and, in concert with the advance guard, conduct a meeting battle. This is joined by units and subunits of the main body which are in the proximity of the fight. The main body bypasses the fight and continues the march. Finally, the unit reaches its new assembly areas and deploys tactically into it. It's time to maintain and fuel vehicles, clean weapons, feed the troops and get some rest.

A Rough March

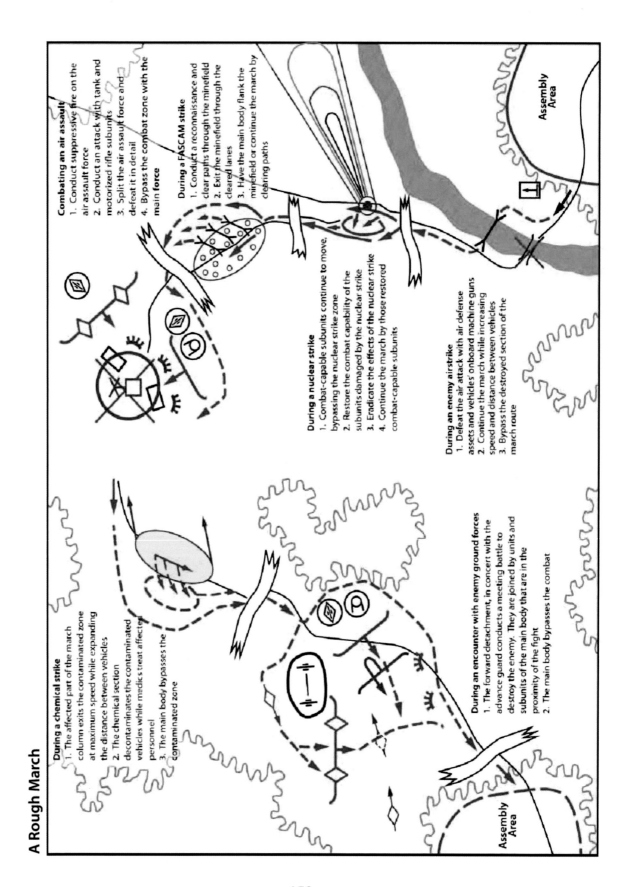

During a chemical strike

1. The affected part of the march column exits the contaminated zone at maximum speed while expanding the distance between vehicles
2. The chemical section decontaminates the contaminated vehicles while medics treat affected personnel
3. The main body bypasses the contaminated zone

During an encounter with enemy ground forces

1. The forward detachment, in concert with the advance guard conducts a meeting battle to destroy the enemy. They are joined by units and subunits of the main body that are in the proximity of the fight
2. The main body bypasses the combat

Combating an air assault

1. Conduct suppressive fire on the air assault force
2. Conduct an attack with tank and motorized rifle subunits
3. Split the air assault force and defeat it in detail
4. Bypass the combat zone with the main force

During a FASCAM strike

1. Conduct a reconnaissance and clear paths through the minefield
2. Exit the minefield through the cleared lanes
3. Have the main body flank the minefield or continue the march by clearing paths

During a nuclear strike

1. Combat-capable subunits continue to move, bypassing the nuclear strike zone
2. Restore the combat capability of the subunits damaged by the nuclear strike
3. Eradicate the effects of the nuclear strike
4. Continue the march by those restored combat-capable subunits

During an enemy airstrike

1. Defeat the air attack with air defense assets and vehicles' onboard machine guns
2. Continue the march while increasing speed and distance between vehicles
3. Bypass the destroyed section of the march route

Assembly Area

Assembly Area

Meeting Battle (Engagement)

The meeting battle (engagement) is a variation of offensive combat where both sides strive to carry out an attack simultaneously, with the goal of destroying the other quickly, seizing the initiative and creating the conditions for further action.[3] A meeting battle may arise while in a march column, particularly in the initial period of the war, when the enemy is surprised while deploying. A meeting battle may also occur while counterattacking from within the defense.[4]

Company Meeting Battle

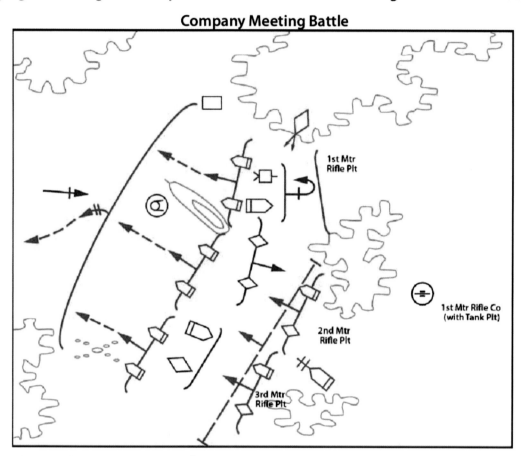

(Above) This graphic shows a motorized rifle company with attached tank and artillery platoon engaging an enemy tank and mechanized infantry platoon. The Russian force detects the enemy force and immediately forms a two-platoon and two tank firing line. The first platoon goes into a hasty defense with a tank setting up a flanking ambush. The enemy force moves onto the open ground and is taken under fire. It drops off a mortar and deploys into assault line under fire incurring losses. The Russian force then counterattacks on line through the enemy force. The artillery platoon plans fire on the northern flank in the event of an enemy counterattack.

Some argue that the meeting battle is no longer possible where satellite and other high technology sensors will produce 100% battlefield clarity. This argument is made despite the recent wars in Iraq and Afghanistan, where coalition forces could not gain 20% battlefield

---

[3] The term "meeting battle" typically refers to tactical situations, while "meeting engagement" refers to operational situations.

[4] V. F. Mozolev, Ministry of Defense of the Russian Federation, "Meeting Battle" [Встречный бой], *Military Encyclopedia* [Военная Энциклопедия], Volume 2, Moscow: Voyenizdat, 1994, 305-306.

clarity against an enemy who had no electronic countermeasures and satellite jammers or other high-tech counters. The Russians have extensive experience with all this technology and a history of employing smoke to mask their own movements and to protect against top-attack munitions.

The meeting battle is the preferred tactic when compared to a breakthrough attack and,

Battalion Meeting Battle

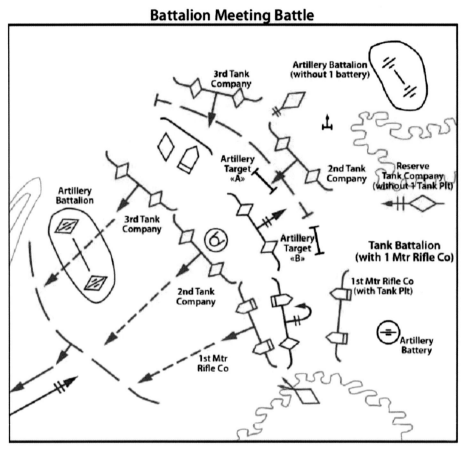

(Above) This graphic shows a battalion meeting battle. A tank battalion with attached motorized rifle company, artillery battalion and air defense platoon encounter an enemy tank battalion with attached mechanized infantry company and artillery battalion. Two tank companies and the motorized rifle company go on line with a tank company (minus) in reserve. One tank platoon establishes a flanking ambush while a howitzer battery moves into direct lay positions behind the motorized rifle company. The artillery battalion (minus) lays down two barrier fire lines in support of the Russian lines. After causing enemy losses, the Russians attack on line through the remnants of the enemy tanks and infantry fighting vehicles, the enemy mortar position and artillery battalion. The reserve tank company follows to deal with pockets of enemy.

often, to being on the defense. The Russians prefer having freedom of maneuver, and the meeting battle is an optimum tactic for achieving that freedom. Naturally, achieving the operational mission without a meeting battle or other fighting is even better. The Russian Army fights to be able to move, not moves in order to fight.

The meeting battle is characterized by changing circumstances and short-term combat; the rapid closure of forces and commitment into combat from the march; the fight to win time to gain and maintain the initiative and fire superiority over the enemy; the discovery of the gap in the enemy combat formation; and the use of maneuver to penetrate his flank and rear.[5] Since both sides are advancing, there will be little time once the presence of the other side is discovered. The situation will usually be obscure, as reconnaissance strives to uncover the rapidly changing situation when aggressive forces move where there is no continuous front. Units may be committed into combat directly from the march. The battlefield is fluid, where open flanks and gaps between units are common and decisive defeat or victory is the probable outcome. Well-rehearsed battle drills provide a marked edge in this type of combat, since they can be executed rapidly on the move without extensive orders and planning.

Success in a meeting battle depends on constant, aggressive reconnaissance to determine enemy size, composition, order of march, and speed and deployment, and the location of nuclear and precision weapons. Pre-emption through air and artillery strikes and force deployment is key to seizing the initiative. Since there will be no time to regroup prior to a meeting battle, the order of march is the order of deployment and commitment. The commander's decision and orders must be prompt, and the consequent maneuver must deny the enemy the advantage of terrain while finding gaps and opening up the enemy flanks. The march column must employ flank detachments and reserves to prevent the main body from being diverted from its primary mission.[6]

The motorized rifle or tank battalion or battalion tactical group will, most likely, be the first combined arms force committed in a meeting battle or meeting engagement, and its meeting battle will often be conducted as an independent action. The maneuver battalion that constitutes a covering force or is the brigade forward detachment, advanced guard or flanking detachment is most likely to meet an advancing enemy. A battalion from the main body may also conduct a meeting battle.[7]

In a meeting battle, the battalion will have an immediate objective and a direction of further advance. If the battalion is serving as a forward detachment, the immediate objective is to seize and hold a designated line and to take the enemy lead elements under fire while supporting the movement and deployment of the main force of the senior commander. There are several possible immediate objectives for an advance guard battalion: destroy the enemy forward security element; decisively attack to break through to the enemy main body; and hold the enemy in place from the front while assisting the deployment and advance into combat of the senior commander's main force. The immediate objective of a maneuver battalion in the main body may include destroying that part of a first-echelon enemy battalion that is within its sector of advance; destroying or capturing the enemy artillery and securing a line; or taking advantage of favorable conditions to destroy the enemy reserve and continue the advance. A maneuver battalion in a meeting battle usually attacks in a single

[5] Ibid, 305.

[6] Conversations with Charles Dick, former director of the Combat Studies Research Centre in the United Kingdom.

[7] David A. Dragunskiy, *Motorized Rifle (Tank) Battalion in Combat* [Мотострелковый (Танковый) батальон в бою], Moscow: Voyenizdat, 1986, 156.

echelon with a designated reserve. This allows it to concentrate the maximum quantity of fire and systems forward in a maximum strength preemptive strike, envelop open enemy flanks or conduct a withdrawal, with the goal of inflicting maximum damage on the enemy while covering friendly flanks.[8]

In the graphic on the following page, an enemy force broke through Russian defenses west of Zaprudnoe and committed its reserve, which began advancing east at dawn on 15 June. It is expected to follow the route which will take it through Zaprudnoe and Vlasovo. The 3rd Motorized Rifle Battalion (MRB) is serving as advance guard for a march column moving west. The march route goes through Vlasovo, Bessonovka, Zaprudnoe and Mukhino. The battalion's mission is to reach the line Mukhino-Peschanka by 1000 hours, 15 June and support the approach and deployment of the brigade main body. The battalion is reinforced with the 3rd tank company, the 1/9 Artillery Battalion (minus one battery), an antitank platoon, an air defense missile platoon, an air defense gun platoon, an engineer platoon, an NBC defense platoon and an armored launch bridge.

The commander formed his march column into a combat reconnaissance patrol (1st platoon, 9th MRC); forward security element (7th MRC with a tank platoon, an artillery battery, the antitank platoon, the air defense missile platoon and an engineer squad); the main body (headquarters, engineer platoon, NBC defense platoon, the tank company minus, the air defense gun platoon, the 8th MRC with the mortar battery and AGS-17 platoon, the 9th MRC minus a platoon, the artillery battalion minus a battery, and the supply, maintenance, medical and other support elements). The unit is at 90% strength and is topped off and fully equipped. The march column's next rest area is 50 kilometers east of Vlasovo.

At 0830, when the battalion main body is southeast of Vlasovo, the forward security element (FSE) reports, "Have reached eastern slope of elevation 97.4 and am engaging enemy mechanized infantry force up to platoon-sized. Can observe up to a company of mechanized infantry and an artillery battery deploying south of Zhigarevo."

The combat reconnaissance patrol (CRP) reports, "Located in the brush 500 meters north of Mukhino. Have observed the passage of a column of armored personnel carriers (APC), tanks, artillery to the west of the outskirts of Kruzhilino (two kilometers west of Mukhino and not on this graphic)."

The brigade commander radios, "Up to two mechanized infantry battalions with tanks in march column are moving on the axis Kruzhilino-Mukhino-Zaprudnoe. Your battalion will seize the line Zhigarevo-Hill 99.6 and support the deployment of the main body on the line Krugloe Lake-Tugarovo for a strike in the direction of Osinki, Zaprudnoe, Mukhino." As the brigade transitions to the attack, the battalion will continue its advance in the direction of height 94.6, Mukhino. At 0850, airstrikes will attack the moving enemy.

The 3rd Battalion commander orders his FSE, "Seize height 97.4 and support the deployment of the battalion main body."

[8] Ibid, 158-159.

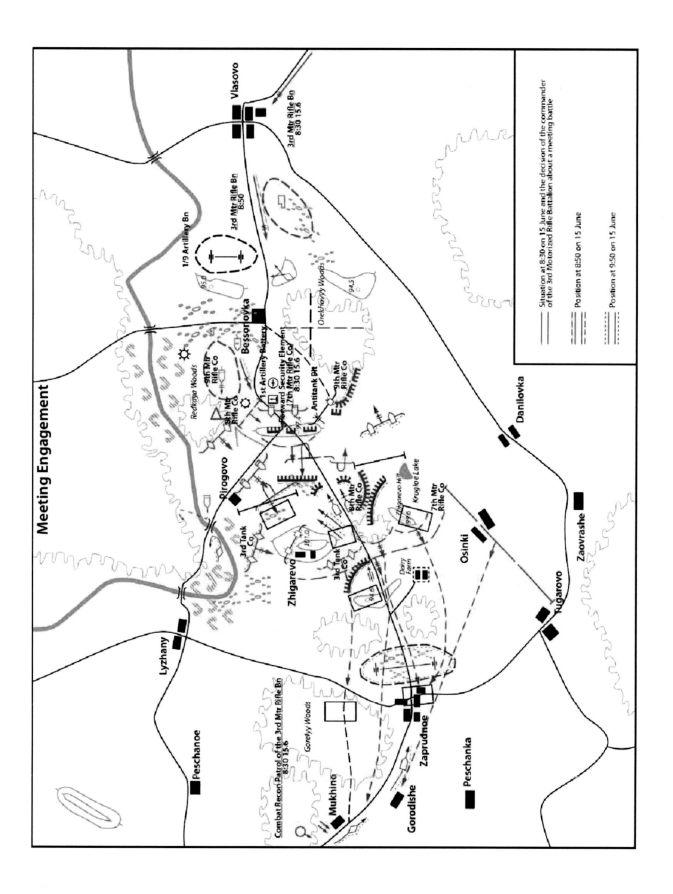

The graphic displays how the FSE seized height 97.4, defeating a defending enemy element, and how the battalion deployed on both sides of it. The solid red and blue lines show the situation at 0830 and the initial positions the battalion seized. The battalion's northern flank is covered by the river and a patrol squad from the 9th MRC while the antitank reserve moves to the south of the FSE to cover the southern flank. The broken red lines show the initial assembly areas for the trail units - the 9th MRC (-) and the rear services, while the broken black lines show the artillery battalion position. The broken red lines also show the planned line that the battalion will seize and the disposition of the battalion in the attack. The battalion will attack in a single echelon with the 9th MRC (minus the platoon serving as the CRP) as the reserve. The tanks will be concentrated in the north as the 3rd Tank Company (now complete, as the FSE has relinquished its tank platoon), the 8th MRC and the 7th MRC make the battalion attack, supported by the antitank platoon. The artillery has established two standing barrage lines on the approach to the Zhigarevo-Hill 99.6 line and plotted concentration areas on high ground, attack axes, a traffic congestion point and a possible assembly area.

The situation at 0850 hours is shown by red and blue lines that are backed with thinner broken lines of the same color. The antitank platoon reports destroying two enemy APCs attempting to enter the "Orekhovyy" woods. A mechanized infantry company is deploying into combat formation opposite the FSE and an enemy artillery battery located south of Zhigarevo is firing on the FSE. An enemy fighter bomber has attacked the artillery battalion and the air defense gun platoon has returned fire. The CRP reports that a column of enemy APCs and artillery is moving from Mukhino to the outskirts of Zaprudnoe. The 3rd MRB commander orders the artillery battalion to take the column under fire. The 9th Tank Company and 8th MRC advance to the top of Hill 101 and its southern slope, but are pushed back by an enemy counterattack.

The battalion attacks at 0950. The situation is shown by red and blue lines backed by a dotted line of the same color. The 3rd Tank Company advances through Pirogovo and meets no resistance. While attacking the northern slope of hill 101, it comes under antitank fire and loses two tanks. An enemy mechanized infantry company holds the heights of hill 101. The tank company commander calls in artillery fire on hilltop 101. Meanwhile the 8th MRC, mounted on BMPs, advances to the southeast of Pirogovo, advancing toward Zhigarevo. It encounters an enemy mechanized infantry platoon that is withdrawing in small groups. The 7th MRC attacks dismounted, its right flank constricted by the enemy along the road. Its left-flank platoon moves around the battalion antitank platoon position to make its advance. In front of the 7th MRC are two mechanized infantry platoons. Up to a company of mechanized infantry on APCs bypasses the left flank of the 7th MRC. The antitank platoon engages the APCs and enemy artillery answers their fire. Two of the ATGM launchers are knocked out.

The battalion commander observes the enemy deploying on the southeast slope of hill 101 and from the east. In Zaprudnoe, up to a battalion of enemy artillery is firing on the 3rd MRB. Further, the CRP reports the passage of a column of tanks, which is approaching the outskirts of Gorodishche. The squad leader of the 9th MRC patrol on the battalion's northern flank reports that as he approached the bridge, two enemy light tanks fired at him from the woods. The tanks are located about 700 meters from Pirogovo and 1.5 kilometers southeast of Lyzhany. The artillery battalion commander reports that his three batteries (which are not masked by smoke) are being fired on from the high ground 800 meters southeast of Bessonovka. The brigade commander informs the battalion that at 0955, an airstrike will target the moving enemy force. The brigade is approaching its deployment line to move into combat formation.

The battalion commander orders the 1/9 Artillery Battalion to conduct a ten-minute fire strike on Hill 101 to suppress the enemy antitank and mechanized infantry defenders. He commits his reserve, ordering the 9th MRC (-) to form a firing line between the barn and Orekhoviy Woods, where, in conjunction with the antitank platoon, they will repulse the enemy advance from Hill 99.6 to Bessonovka. The 3rd Tank Company and 8th MRC will resume their attack to regain Hill 101 and constitute the line Zhigarevo-Hill 99.6 as ordered by the brigade commander. The 7th MRC will join the attack to constitute the line Zhigarevo-Hill 99.6, but will leave part of its force in place to assist the reserve and antitank platoon in containing the enemy advance from Hill 99.6 to Bessonovka. The engineer platoon will move forward to place antitank mines in front of the antitank platoon and reserve.

By 1030, the 3rd MRB secured the line Zhigarevo-Hill 99.6 and continued to fight the enemy from this firing line, supporting the deployment of the brigade main body on the line Krugloe Lake-Tugarovo and attacking in the direction of Osinki, Zaprudnoe, Mukhino.

The above vignette portrays the fast-moving situation that accompanies a meeting battle. The value of quick, accurate spot reports, radio discipline, responsive fires and well rehearsed battle drills are evident throughout the example.

To smoke or not to smoke is an irrevocable decision in a meeting battle. The artillery can fire and maintain smoke screens, but this may detract from its ability to conduct other fire missions. Russian vehicles are capable of creating their own smoke screens, and smoke pots are standard issue for mobile forces. In this vignette, the artillery was very busy and had not laid its own smoke screen before it came under direct fire. It probably responded by using on-board smoke generation and pots while it continued its mission.

Flanking Detachment

Where possible, it is usually better hitting an enemy on the flank or rear than running into his prepared defense with a frontal attack. In wars with contiguous lines, the frontal attack is often the only option, but once the enemy defense is penetrated, the opportunities for flanking attacks open up.

Modern maneuver warfare may not have contiguous lines like World Wars I and II. The recent fighting in the Donbass region involved companies and battalions fighting with open flanks, and flanking detachments were frequently employed on the plains of Eastern Ukraine. Plains are not the only terrain feature where flanking detachments can be deployed. Russian military history shows the wide use of flanking detachments in desert, deep forest, marshland and urban combat. During the Soviet-Afghan War, the Soviets used flanking detachments to trap Mujahideen guerrillas in their mountain sanctuaries. Lester Grau published the following as "A Flanking Detachment in the Mountains" in the May-August 2010 issue of *Infantry* magazine:

Defending mountain terrain has its own challenges. While mountains offer good observation, they also block it, particularly close up. Mountains offer good long-range fields of fire, but they are also full of dead space and concealment. Mountain defenses are not continuous, but are normally separate outposts and fighting positions which may be mutually supporting, but usually are not. They are often not even in the same plane. Mountain fighting positions are difficult to construct and maintain. Mountain fighting positions can be stockpiled with ammunition, but food and water quickly run out at these positions. The latter two are normally supplied in the villages and hamlets down in the mountain valleys and canyons. Consequently, in Afghanistan, the Mujahideen usually congregated in the valley, except when they felt threatened. Some security was maintained at the fighting positions, but this was usually slack, without indications or intelligence of enemy actions.

Attacking in the mountains has its own set of problems. First, the enemy holds the high ground and, if he has occupied the area for any time, he has had time to establish fighting positions and emplace long-range crew-served weapons, such as mortars, heavy machine guns, recoilless rifles and even direct-lay artillery. He has had time to reinforce the defenses with mines and other obstacles. Entries into the mountain valley or canyon are limited and liable to interdiction by a skilled defender.

Still, the irregular mountain terrain offers distinct advantages to the attacker. The enemy is seldom able to mass fires, and the terrain offers numerous concealed attack approaches to defending positions. Enemy withdrawal will be by small groups, often forced to abandon heavy weapons, ammunition stockpiles and wounded.

Too often during the Soviet-Afghan War, Soviet attacks in the mountains were frontal attacks. The Mujahideen response was to kick out a rear guard and exfiltrate. After much effort and the expenditure of much artillery fire and aerial ordnance, the Soviets found themselves somewhat in control of a mountain that they had no intention of garrisoning. The Mujahideen had lived to fight another day. The following article describes the Soviet use of a flanking detachment to seize high ground within the depths of a Mujahideen defense located in the mountains. The attacking troops were paratroopers, trained and equipped to fight as both mechanized infantry and light airborne or air-assault infantry. Each regiment had its compliment of armored personnel carriers, assault guns or tanks, artillery and sappers.

Flanking Detachment- Vignette
A FRONTAL ATTACK...IS NOT RECOMMENDED
by Major V. A. Selivanov[9]

In April 1985, according to intelligence reports, there was a significant grouping of the armed opposition concentrated in the Mazlirud and Kakh Canyons. Their number was estimated at 1,200. Besides assault rifles, this group had 35-40 DShK heavy machine guns and up to 15 ZU anti-aircraft machine guns, as well as mortars, recoilless rifles and rockets.[10] The main body of the enemy (400-600 men) was located in the village of Malakhairu. The general situation was complicated by the fact that earlier large-scale operations in the area showed that surprise was not possible and that, other than the casualties inflicted, the results were insignificant. The main body of the enemy, as a rule, managed to withdraw from the canyon before our troops arrived. The enemy had managed to establish a significant, well constructed system of observation and early warning. Further, this region was particularly unsuited for air assaults, and military vehicles could enter the canyon only on one road, which ran through Mazilishakhr, Zagan and Malakhairu. (See the map).

Considering the peculiarities of the region, during planning, our battalion commander determined to carry out the mission in the following fashion. We were briefed at an officers call that at 1330 hours on 9 April, the bronegruppa of the main body would move from its base camp along the road from the south, with the mission of closing in to the village of Mazlishakhr by 1800 hours.[11] My parachute company was ordered to support the departure and movement of the march column. Then, after the column had passed, my company was to return to garrison to carry out guard duty. The combat action to destroy the enemy grouping was planned for 10 and 11 April by moving the bronegruppa to link up with its paratroopers who would move from the west into the valley.

However, at noon on 7 April, my regimental commander, without any witnesses, gave me an order for a totally different plan.[12] The new mission was a follows: At 1600 hours on 8 April, my parachute company would serve as a flanking detachment, and, without attracting any attention, would secretly move to the region of Khakfakhai village in order to conduct a route reconnaissance for movement through the Afedshakh Pass. With the advent of darkness, I would leave my combat vehicles on the road, go on foot through the pass, enter into the Mazirrud Valley

[9] Major V. A. Selivanov, "A Frontal Aattack...Is not Recommend," *Armeykiy Sbornik*, October 2009, 21-22.
[10] The ZU is an anti-aircraft 23mm machine gun which comes in a single- and dual-barrel model (the ZU-23-1 and ZU-23-2).
[11] The *bronegruppa* (armored group) consists of a unit's tanks and personnel carriers which, after the infantry has dismounted the carriers, are used as a separate reserve. It is usually commanded by the unit's first deputy. In this case, it has the BMPs of two companies (22 vehicles), probably at least 2 tank platoons (6 tanks) and 12 self-propelled howitzers plus other vehicles supporting the mortar platoon, signal platoon and so on.
[12] The Soviets always insured that orders and plans were witnessed and approved so that if things went wrong, the blame might be assigned or shifted. The regimental commander is undertaking a risky ploy, so he issues the order without any witnesses. Apparently, even the battalion commander does not know that one of his subordinate units has this mission. The company commander is on his own if things go wrong.

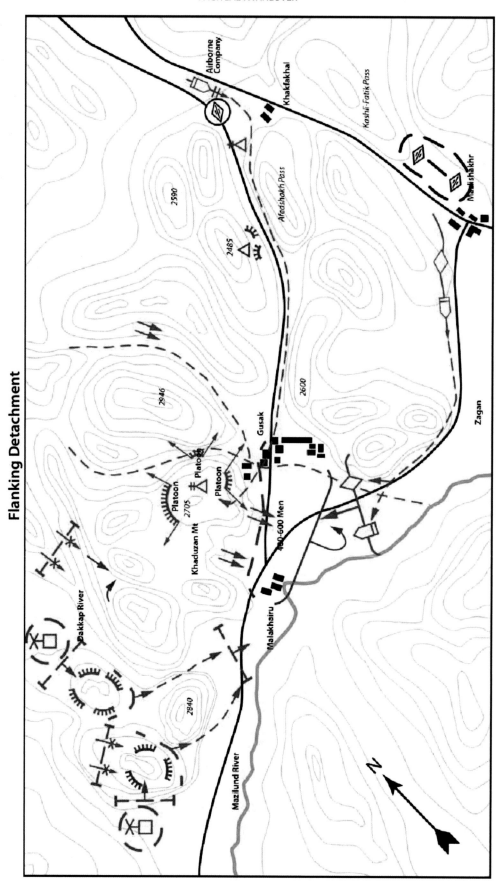

and, by dawn, occupy positions on Khaduzan Mountain. At dawn on 9 April, I would be in position to adjust artillery fire and direct close air support, with the goal of creating panic among the assembled Mujahideen and not allowing them to exit the canyon before the main body struck them. While carrying out this mission, very strict attention had to be paid to the secret movement and independent actions, since it would be impossible to support my detachment in case we were discovered.

At 1800 hours on 8 April, my company was assembled in the designated area near Khakfakhai village. Soon, our observation disclosed that groups of armed men periodically moved on the path through the Afedshakh Pass. There was also a group of eight Mujahideen located in a guard post on that very same pass. Everything appeared calm in the target area. Everyone discussed it and agreed that the "ghosts" [Mujahideen] were not expecting our force. With the onset of darkness, we conducted a radio check with our armored vehicles and our higher headquarters, and then I gave the order to begin movement.

We crossed through the pass by 2200 hours, bypassing the guard post to the south without drawing the attention of the Mujahideen. During nighttime, this post was a main [security] link. They were tied in with other posts using a complex system of varying signals. Even though these "stinkers" were one of the [security] links, we bypassed them literally in 15 minutes.

Just as we began to descend into the canyon, we lost radio contact with our company bronegruppa and with our higher headquarters. By all rules of military science, I must immediately either restore communications or return.[13] But then our company's combat mission would not be accomplished. Therefore, I made a decision to continue to move and to restore communications once we reached high ground. I had to make this decision because I knew that if the Mujahideen discovered our company at night, we could only count on ourselves for help.

From the depths of the canyon, we heard the noise of night firing. We were convinced that the Mujahideen were not expecting the appearance of our force and had occupied their fighting positions to sort things out [conducted an alert]. At midnight, we entered the hamlet of Gusak. This is where I, the company commander, made a mistake that might have compromised all our measures for secrecy. Despite the ample number of night-vision devices that we had, we discovered too late that there were two Mujahideen patrols that we barely avoided running into. Taking necessary precautions, we lost about two hours before we exited the village. At 0300 hours, the company assembled at the foot of Khaduzan Mountain.

The heavens were clear and things were now visible thanks to the appearance of the moon. This additional lighting "worked" to the enemy's advantage and forced us to hurry up. The first platoon, commanded by Senior Lieutenant A. Mikenin, climbed the mountain. After an hour, he reported that his platoon had occupied positions on the heights. I placed two platoons, under the command of Senior Lieutenant V. Plotnikov, in an ambush directed against the hamlet of Gusak, and I followed the path of the first platoon to the top. We established our primary observation post on height 2705.0. I placed Lieutenant Mikenin's platoon on the northern slope and I placed the other two platoons on the southern slope. From these positions, they could also interdict paths on the eastern

---

[13] The commander is already out there on his own without support and loses communication. By Soviet regulations, he is required to reestablish communications or abort the mission. This is a very risky decision.

side and partially on the western side, while blocking enemy bands located in the hamlet of Gusak.

At 0500 hours, we were prepared to carry out our mission. At that time we were able to reestablish radio contact. An under-strength paratrooper company had secretly crossed 12 kilometers of enemy-controlled territory, assembled in the rear of a strong enemy force and taken the commanding heights. It should be noted that the secret movement of the company was key to the success of the action and the complete lack of company casualties.

On the morning of 9 April, the bronnegrupa of the main body of the battalion inconspicuously passed through the village of Mazilishakhr and began to enter the canyon. Instantly, the signal (three individual shots) repeatedly rang from the mountain slopes from the north to the south and even the west. It announced the arrival of our force. Some 15-20 minutes after the signal, a band of 120-200 men emerged from the hamlet of Gusak and began to advance on my company. When the Mujahideen were close to our second and third platoon positions, my paratroopers opened up on them with deadly fire. It caught the Mujahideen completely by surprise and inflicted such heavy casualties on them, that they were unable to offer resistance. The "ghosts" panicked and ran back into the hamlet.

At this point, I should note that the sun was in our eyes and it was hard to find the enemy. After five minutes, the Mujahideen suddenly launched an attempt to break out of the canyon to the northeast. I called artillery fire on them. Again, after a half hour, they attempted to bypass the company to the north and up the southern slope of height 2946.6, but they came under the fire of Senior Lieutenant A. Mikenin's platoon.

From 1400-1500, we conducted two tactical air assaults [with the remaining two companies of paratroopers] on the western side of the canyon. The [bronegruppa of the] main force, by this time, had already pushed through the hamlet of Gusak. The company's mission was over.

Thinking over our combat action as a flanking detachment in the mountains of Afghanistan, I have arrived at several conclusions. First, in order to conduct combat in similar circumstances, it is necessary to plan to assign an element of the combat formation to be a flanking detachment. It will be able to secretly enter the flank or rear of the enemy without engaging in combat with small subunits and guard posts. It will be able to prevent the enemy withdrawal and hit him with a surprise attack to destroy him and his capabilities in order to facilitate the successful mission accomplishment of the main force.

The experience of conducting such operations shows that most successful flanking detachments are company-sized. Well trained subunits and personnel should be used in forming the detachment.

Second, the nature of mountainous terrain prevents small subunits from carrying heavy weapons and ammunition. At the same time, it is necessary to have sufficient fire power to conduct effective fires at various ranges. Besides our assault rifles and sniper rifles, my company carried one AGS-17 and a heavy machine gun.[14] In every squad, we had one AKM assault rifle with the under-barrel

---

[14] The AGS-17 is a tripod-mounted 30mm automatic grenade launcher which fires rounds out to 1,700 meters. The machine gun was probably the 7.62mm PKM machine gun.

grenade launcher.[15] Our ammunition load was 600-700 rounds per assault rifle and 1200 rounds for the machine gun. Our special gear included some night-vision devices.

*The successful actions of a flanking detachment in the mountains is dependent on close, well planned coordination with the forces and resources of the senior commander. **Of primary importance is the support of artillery and aviation as well as agreement on the action with the main force before it departs to carry out its mission. Thus, in the course of combat it is impossible to fulfill the mission without reliable uninterrupted communications. Experience shows that in order to guarantee communications, it is better to establish retransmission stations or simply to use aircraft that are equipped for retransmission** [emphasis is in the original].*

In conclusion, selection of company-grade officers for assignment to a flanking detachment requires care. You know that they will be required to make independent mission decisions while separated from the main body on unfamiliar territory that is controlled by the enemy. This requires detailed planning and thorough preparation, as well as a high degree of individual training. In part, it is absolutely necessary that the commander has concrete experience working with maps and can quickly detect objectives in the mountains, determine the necessary data for their destruction, precisely direct the fires of his subordinate units, and skillfully use all possibilities for secret and sudden actions.

Analysis of the Vignette

In this article, the Soviets conducted the apparent main attack with their armored vehicles moving into the canyon on the only road. This attack included the personnel carriers of two paratroop companies, attached tanks, and an attached battalion of self-propelled artillery. There was little infantry in this attack. The two airborne companies that the armored vehicles belonged to conducted an air assault approximately six hours after the beginning of the supposed main attack to eliminate Mujahideen positions in the west and then moved into the canyon to link up with their vehicles. Helicopter gunships provided close air support to the air assault. The flanking detachment, which had inserted itself into the depths of the enemy position, was particularly useful in calling in artillery strikes and defeating the enemy advance and his withdrawal attempt. Although the article provides no casualty figures, the flanking detachment suffered none, while the Mujahideen did.

There are some interesting aspects to this attack. The flanking detachment left its armored personnel carriers (bronegruppa) at the dismount point. It was responsible for its own security and served as a mobile reserve in the event that the flanking detachment got into trouble. Once the flanking detachment was deep into enemy territory, however, the reserve role was problematic. A self-propelled artillery battery joined the bronegrupa for the attack the following morning. The Soviets had entered this war with a limited ability to conduct split-fire direction center operations. By 1986, this capability was well developed. Soviet artillery usually accompanied the ground attack, since it was more accurate than jet aircraft in support in the mountains. Further, the artillery was often used in direct-lay against a

[15] The GP-25 sub-barrel grenade launcher fires a 40mm grenade out to 100 meters. These paratroopers preferred the older AKM Kalashnikov, with its 7.62mm round, over the newly issued AK-74 with its 5.45mm round. Combat in the mountains is long-range and requires a subsonic medium-weight bullet. The AK-74 was designed for close combat and has less range and punch over distance.

stubborn enemy.

The flanking detachment was not part of the original battalion planning and was controlled by regiment. In the interests of operational security, the company's role and presence were not disclosed to the rest of the battalion. The company, except for on-call artillery and close air support, was basically on its own for at least 15 hours. Both require communications and were iffy at night.

Communications were a problem and remain such in the mountains, despite modern technology. Mountains absorb radio waves and distort GPS signals.[16] Satellite communications are spotty and a savvy opponent could jam the GPS and satellite telephone receivers in the mountains. Ground retransmission units are hard to move, emplace and defend, and retransmission aircraft are few and seem to go down for maintenance at critical points.

The infantryman's load remains a problem, and in Afghanistan, where the bulk of engagements are beyond 500 meters, small-caliber supersonic bullets fired from short-barreled carbines are ineffective. The fight devolves to the machine gunners while the rest of the platoon tries to get involved. The Soviets issued the AK-74 with the thought that the infantryman could now carry more ammunition. Where possible, units such as this airborne unit went back to the longer-range, medium weight 7.62 cartridge. Still, the weapons that the airborne carried did not give it an advantage over its opponent. The paratrooper's position on commanding terrain did.

Going into the mountains is critical to gaining the initiative and bringing the fight to the enemy's sanctuary. Still, bulling into the mountain valleys and canyons without securing high ground or establishing a blocking force is futile. The lightly equipped enemy will withdraw over familiar territory, leaving his burdened attacker behind. Flanking detachments are an excellent way to shape the battlefield and hold the enemy in place for punishment.

---

[16] In the mountains, GPS accuracy can slip from a 5-meter diameter circle to a 500-meter diameter circle or more.

Relief in Place

A relief in place is the organized reception and dispatch of subunits, units and large units occupying positions, lines, sectors and belts during combat. It is conducted in the defense, in the course of regrouping for deployment into another area, when placing forces in their positions for an offensive or counteroffensive, while in direct contact with the enemy and under other circumstances.[17] It is often used to replace subunits that have lost their combat potential through casualties.[18] It is normally conducted at night or during periods of limited visibility. It demands thorough preparation, quick and secret conduct, and strict observance of the schedule and orders of the conducting force.

A relief in place is one of the more difficult measurements of the readiness of subunits to conduct defensive and offensive combat. It is executed under conditions where the enemy has effective reconnaissance systems and fire delivery systems. Since the relief in place is usually conducted at night or under conditions of limited visibility, it is necessary to consider that people hear better at night than during the day since sound travels farther at night.[19]

Range that Sound Travels at Night When the Wind is not Blowing

Person's quiet footsteps	40 meters
Single person's speech	50 meters
Sound of a breaking branch	80 meters
Conversation of several people	100 meters
Sound of a weapon bolt closing	300 meters
Sound of a falling tree	300 meters
Strike of a hammer, cross-cut saw	300-400 meters
Troops moving on a country road	300 meters
Troops moving on a hard-surface road	600 meters
Loading a machine gun	500 meters
Hammering in a stake	700 meters
Truck movement on a hard-surface road	800 meters
Truck movement on a country road	1000 meters
Tank moving on a country road	1200 meters
Tank moving on a hard-surface road	3000-4000 meters

Observation at night is affected by the degree of darkness present at different times of night. Modern sensors are able to detect movement through heat, movement, signals traffic, night vision devices and radar imaging. Relief in place may take place in daylight, but requires the cover of airstrikes, artillery strikes, flat trajectory weapons fire, air defenses, particulate smoke screens and radio-electronic suppression or destruction of the enemy command and control system. It is best to conduct the relief in place at night.[20]

---

[17] Ministry of Defense of the Russian Federation, "Relief in place" [Смена войск], *Military Encyclopedia* [Военная Энциклопедня], Volume 7, Moscow: Voyenizdat, 2003, 522.

[18] A. V. Vlasov, "When subunits are no longer combat-ready, conduct a relief in place" [Когда подразделенния уже не боеспособны, то происходит смена войск], *Army Digest* [Армейский Сборник], December 2010, 23.

[19] Vlasov, 23.

[20] Ibid.

Night Observation Conditions

<u>Very dark night</u>: The eyes are unable to see much except nearby movement against the backdrop of an open horizon. Noise carries far, particularly when there is no wind. Use of night vision devices provides excellent results.

<u>Moderately dark night</u>: The eyes can detect the movement of personnel and equipment on open country (100-150 meters). Various sounds carry as well as on a very dark night.

<u>Moonlit night</u>: Vision is notably improved. Excellent results can be achieved with high-resolution binoculars. The eyes can readily determine what objects are and all contours are sharply delineated. Night vision devices are usable.

<u>Stormy night</u>: Hearing is difficult, making it easier to move closer to the enemy. Night vision devices may be used, but the field of vision is strained.

<u>Rainy night</u>: Observation is difficult and hearing is poor. Instead it produces a sound which resonates off of raincoats, tents and feet splashing through puddles and mud. Night vision devices are not effective.

<u>Frozen winter night without snow</u>: Demands the adoption of special measures to prevent the sound of footsteps and the possibility of slipping. Night vision devices produce excellent results.

<u>Snowy winter night</u>: Improved visibility. If snow is not falling, then sound transmission is greatly improved over greater distances. Dark items appear distinctly against a white field of vision. Night vision devices do not work.

<u>Foggy night</u>: Everything is indiscernible and vague. Night vision devices do not work.

Preparations for a relief in place begin during the day. Rendezvous areas are designated for the departing force and assembly areas for the relief force. Any indications of the location of these areas must be concealed from ground and air observation, protected from air strikes and the approach and withdrawal routes must be hidden. The rendezvous and assembly areas may coincide. The areas for the first echelon battalions may be located between the first and second defensive positions (3-5 kilometers from the forward edge of the defense). The areas for the second echelon battalions or combined arms reserve and the remaining units would be behind the defensive area involved in the relief in place.[21]

The commander begins his work in the rendezvous area or assembly area, where he will organize a defense or an attack from positions in direct contact with the enemy in conjunction with the relief in place of a defending combined arms unit. The senior commander will determine the combat formation and the time to conduct the relief in place. The plan will be issued on a map sheet which the relief subunit commanders must verify and refine onsite. They do so during a commanders' reconnaissance along with the full assistance of the commanders that they will relieve to occupy defensive positions, strong points fighting positions or the assembly area for an attack. In the course of the reconnaissance, the relieving commander must determine the enemy situation; the dispositions of the subunit; the handover of the defense and the schedule for its conduct; the organization of the system of fire; the air defense layout; the engineering improvements to the defense; the strong points, fighting positions and obstacles; and the NBC situation. Further, it is necessary to coordinate with the commanders being relieved as to the defensive area (strong points and

[21] Ibid, 24.

fighting positions); or the attack assembly area; the rendezvous area for the relieved force; the assembly area for the relieving force; the approach routes used to accomplish the relief; the place to meet the guides from the force being relieved; and the exit routes for the relieved force from the various positions. The commanders must also determine where the enemy positions are; the areas susceptible to fire and radio-electronic attack; and the lines where smoke screens may be laid to cover the relief in place.[22]

The commanders of the subunits being relieved must handover their detailed maps and sketches showing their defenses, strong points, fighting positions and firing data as well as details as to enemy firing positions, weapons and obstacles. Considering the complex circumstances involved with a relief in place, the commanders' reconnaissance must include not only the subordinate commanders, but also the drivers and vehicle commanders. Experience has shown that having the vehicle crews study the approach route, the vehicle destination position, the order of march and the route markers is necessary as is repeated training in night movement behind a ground guide.[23]

During the coordination among the subunit commanders, the following must be agreed on: the actions of subunits during the period of movement from the assembly area through the period of the relief in place, which will include whether to conduct a fire strike on the enemy with all weapons; whether to conduct remote mining on enemy routes using engineer assets; whether to employ smoke to cover the movement and relief; whether to conduct artillery and radio-electronic strikes during the relief; actions of air defense assets; the recognition signals between the guides and the relief force commanders; the timing and requirements for signal communications between the forces during relief; and who will command during the entire relief and from where. During the organization of fire support, determine how to attack the enemy to destroy him during a possible counterattack and to forestall enemy actions during the relief in place.[24]

During the relief in place, the defense must remain stable while replacing departing elements with arriving elements and retaining a combat formation for upcoming missions. The reconnaissance subunits are the first to arrive and move into position. The artillery subunits are next. They must be in position and ready to fire before the combined arms subunits begin their relief. It may happen that the relieving subunits may not be immediately ready for combat, so, in order to maintain the stability of the defense at this time, the artillery subunits assume their firing positions on the order of the senior artillery commander or his deputy. An attached artillery subunit assumes its firing positions upon the command of the commander of the combined arms subunit. A motorized rifle battalion mortar battery assumes its firing position upon the command of the motorized rifle battalion commander. Only after this, do the waiting motorized rifle and tank subunits begin the relief in place, occupying the defensive region, strong points and fighting positions while organizing their system of fire and command and control. Artillery battalions or batteries supporting the subunits defending the forward position (the position in front of the main defense) are the last

---

[22] Ibid.
[23] Ibid.
[24] Ibid, 25.

relieved. Should the senior artillery commander decide to conduct a fire strike on the enemy, the relief artillery units will occupy their primary firing positions after the mission is fired.[25]

Simultaneously with the relieving artillery subunits taking up positions to repel an enemy attack, the brigade conducts expedient planning for the movement of antitank subunits to defeat enemy armor. At this point, the relieving motorized rifle subunits and their equipment move forward. In the interests of security, the approach movement to the forward defenses is on foot. The BMPs, BTRs and other tracked vehicles will move when the tank subunits move. The subunits move quickly into position and, by dawn, are completely camouflaged. The distance between the assembly and/or rendezvous areas and the front line is no closer than 5-7 kilometers. If the relief in place is being conducted during a transition to a defense under the cover of supporting fires, the distance may be shortened to 2-4 kilometers.[26]

After the relieving motorized rifle subunits complete their hike and meet with their guides, they move into the forward defensive area to a forward withdrawal area. There they meet other guides from the company, platoons and squads being relieved who bring the relief force to their new area, strong points or fighting positions which they occupy. During the movement to the forward edge of the defense, haste and fuss are inadmissible. It is necessary to consider that all movement at night takes longer than during the day and guiding in every individual is of vital consequence. It follows that if the entire subunit does well, but one scatter-brain makes a serious mistake (for example, an accidental discharge of a weapon or the non-observance of night discipline) everyone could get killed. In this manner, night movement demands not only excellent training of the subunit, but also strict training of every soldier. [27]

During the relief in place of the motorized rifle subunits, the danger of weakening the first echelon or sometimes a sector of the defense arises, which the enemy could take advantage of. To eliminate this problem, use different variants of the relief in place. If there is sufficient time, move a relieving company from the second echelon in the battalion defense forward, a platoon at a time, to occupy the front line and ward off an enemy attack. If there is insufficient time, move all the platoons of a relieving company simultaneously forward. However, this requires taking measures to cover a potential weak area with fire from all means deployed at this time. The relieving units assume the defensive mission, organize a system of fire and observation and fine tune plans to defeat a possible enemy attack. Subunits deployed in the forward position or in combat security are relieved after the main defense has been relieved.[28]

A more difficult problem is the relief of combat vehicles, particularly those located in firing positions on the forward edge of the battlefield or close behind. The first approach is to exchange a large part of the vehicles already deployed forward with relief force vehicles in the rear by the order of the senior commander. Second is to camouflage the shape and muffle the sound and use firepower during a simultaneous movement of vehicles, hopefully lessening

[25] Ibid.
[26] Ibid.
[27] Ibid.
[28] Ibid, 26.

the possibility of their destruction. The third approach is move the armored vehicles during an artillery fire destruction of the enemy mission while simultaneously moving the vehicles. This could result in the loss of a large part of the relieving and relieved vehicles. A consideration is that when combat vehicles are damaged and evacuation machines tow them off, it is difficult to differentiate between a vehicle moving under its own power or being towed away or merely starting up its engine or giving another vehicle a push. Besides which, combat vehicles in a defending subunit are used differently than during normal combat. The crews carefully study the location of the enemy weapons when digging in with the result that the enemy efforts to pinpoint their position is very difficult and practically useless.[29]

The motorized rifle combat vehicles that are already positioned in the defense are sited for one purpose-to defeat an enemy attack. It is ineffective to use those vehicles in an attack during the artillery fire preparation of the attack and the fire support of the attack, since these vehicles are in the wrong positions. Consequently, the senior commander may decide to exchange a number of the combat vehicles of the relief force with the relieving force.[30]

If the relief in place is done during the day time, the relieving and relieved combat machines may occupy the same firing position simultaneously. However, this requires reliable covering fire from aviation, artillery fire, flat-trajectory fire, air defense systems and an aerosol curtain of particulate smoke and radio-electronic warfare conducted against the enemy communications and command and control systems of missile forces, artillery, helicopter and fixed-wing aviation, combined arms subunits, reconnaissance subunits and electronic warfare units.[31]

Relieving tank subunits move into their designated positions or assembly areas: as the relieved force transitions to the attack-particularly during the artillery fire preparation phase; and during the transition to the defense, particularly at the beginning of the artillery destruction of an attacking enemy phase. If subunits are exchanged during these firing phases, an assembly area should be set up beforehand as the place to meet subunit representatives who will serve as guides. The remaining subunits and elements of the combat formation meet their guides and move to their positions and areas. Air defense subunits conduct their movement under the cover of the other subunits.[32]

During the relief in place, the commanders of the subunit being relieved remain at their COPs for the area, position or strong point. During this time, command and control of the subunits is conducted over landline, which is normally stays in place. The relieving subunit supplies an identical set of wire communications gear to the departing subunit.[33]

Covering the relief in place is the responsibility of the subunits being relieved. Should the enemy attack during the relief in place, all the subunits will defeat the attack. The departing commander is in charge of the fight and will command his and the relieving subunits. After

[29] Ibid.
[30] Ibid.
[31] Ibid.
[32] Ibid.
[33] Ibid.

the attack is defeated, the relief in place will resume. An officer and several sergeants from the relieved subunit, who know the area and the enemy dispositions well may remain with the relief force to assist in studying the area and enemy until the subunit transitions to the attack or initiates defensive combat. The commander of the relief subunit submits a report on the completion of the relief in place in two copies promptly.[34]

The relief in place is difficult and begins with the reconnaissance and artillery. Motorized rifle subunits follow. It is difficult to move BMPs or BTRs from forward firing positions. Brigades and subunits that constitute bronegruppa should not have difficulty, but it is often better to swap forward vehicles rather than try to move them back and forward at night. Wire communication is almost always swapped. Tanks move once the motorized rifle units are in place and defending. The final relief is of the subunits positioned in the forward position or security zone. Remote mining by engineer vehicles or MLRS is possible, but hard to conceal.

[34] Ibid.

Breaking Contact and Withdrawal

Withdrawal is either premeditated or from necessity. A force leaves an occupied line or region and withdraws for the purpose of avoiding the strike of a superior enemy force and occupying a more advantageous position for subsequent action. A premeditated withdrawal is usually connected with a deteriorating situation on a neighboring sector of the front or in the rear. A forced withdrawal normally arises when a neighboring unit's strength is such that they are unable to continue occupying the line or region and it follows that enemy military action must result in the destruction of the defending force.

In either circumstance, the withdrawal is conducted only by the order of or permission from the senior leader, it is organized in secret with the goal of conducting a timely, withdrawal of forces in combat-capable condition. The withdrawal begins with forces breaking contact with the enemy. Brigades and units will designate a line or a withdrawal march route with a start and finish line and the order for their occupation, the location of areas for rocket units and artillery firing positions, the site for deployment and the control points. Further, the brigade or unit commander focuses on the characteristics of the follow-on military action after the withdrawal. During the withdrawal, the combat formation usually includes units or subunits designated to cover the break in contact, the main body and the rear services. The rear service units and subunits withdraw in the first march order. Breaking contact begins after the rearguard brigade or unit occupies the start line and continues until after the entire main body has crossed the start line. In order to conceal the activities of the force as it breaks contact and moves away from the enemy, it is conducted at night and during other periods of limited visibility and is supplemented with a variety of camouflage and concealment measures. If the enemy is not particularly active (aggressive), the second echelon and reserve withdraw in the first march order. The entire first echelon of the brigade or regiment (in a division) moves simultaneously to a rear defensive line that is not in direct contact with the enemy. This movement is covered by subunits left on the front line trace.

After breaking contact, the main body assembles into march column and, not delaying at intermittent lines, withdraws under the cover of the rear guard to its designated area. Units or subunits designated as a covering force, maintain the previous pattern of military activities and do not allow the enemy to transition to an organized pursuit. The covering forces withdrawal begins, as a rule, after the main force has all passed the start line and the rear guard has occupied the start line. The covering force withdraws quickly and usually simultaneously. With the goal of preventing the enemy from seizing gorges, bridges, crossings, road intersections and other important points on the withdrawal routes, subunits (or units) are designated to cover these obstacles to movement and hold them until the main body has withdrawn and the rear guard has taken over.[35]

The rear guard occupies a rear line and actively and decisively contains the enemy advance and secures the uninterrupted withdrawal of the main body. It maneuvers from one line to the next, in accordance with the orders of its commander and is conducted in sequence. The rear guard uses ambushes, obstacles and controlled destruction extensively during

[35] Ministry of Defense of the Russian Federation, "Withdrawal" [Отход], *Military Encyclopedia* [Военная Энциклопедия], Volume 6, Moscow: Voyenizdat, 2002, 201-202.

its maneuver, particularly at the lines of withdrawal and on the flanks. Depending on the situation, the main body, or units from it, may deploy back into battle along an intermittent line, should the rear guard and march security elements be unable to contain the enemy pursuit or an attack on the march route. Depending on the situation, at the last designated position or region, the rear guard withdraws as a group.[36]

The rear guard is usually a tank or motorized rifle brigade or battalion that is capable of independent action and is supported by long-range artillery and army aviation. It may be reinforced with self-propelled artillery, subunits of other branches and specialized troops. Its mission is to occupy a designated position or line and to hold it for the required time and then withdraw when ordered to the next position or line. The withdrawal can be simultaneous or by leapfrogging. When the withdrawal is simultaneous, a company per battalion will first withdraw to the next line and occupy a broad front. The company will then cover the withdrawal of the remaining rear guard force. When the withdrawal is by leapfrogging, the rear guard occupies two successive lines in the depth simultaneously. When the first line withdraws, it withdraws past the second line and occupies a third. When the second line withdraws, it passes through the third line and occupies a fourth. This may continue until the end of the rear guard mission. A rear guard may be designated during the entire march from the front to the rear. The rear guard will constantly conduct reconnaissance for the purpose of determining the enemy composition, groupings and direction of advance.[37]

The more roads that are available for a withdrawal, the better. A brigade prefers that each maneuver battalion, the artillery and the trains each have their own routes. Often, subunits will have to share routes and the challenge is not to have traffic bunched up on them. Cross traffic must be avoided or tightly controlled. Vehicle spacing, evacuation vehicles and engineer road repair and constructions assets are key. Reserve roads, unused up until the withdrawal, are ideal for withdrawals. The engineer battalion will employ corner reflectors, laser deflectors, false radar signals and physical masking to cover movement. Mining the withdrawal routes can aid the withdrawal provided that it does not interfere with the rear guard. Night, rain and particulate smoke help the effort and supplement ECM efforts. Historically, if wind and weather conditions permit, grass and forest fires can aid a withdrawal. Air defense of bridging and fording sites are critical, and engineer crossing assets need to be available to assist water crossings.

[36] Ibid.
[37] Institute of Military History of the Ministry of Defense of the USSR, "Rear Guard" [Арьергард], *Soviet Military Encyclopedia* [Советская Военная Энциклопедия], Volume 1, Moscow: Voyenizdat, 1990, 247.

Theory of the Withdrawal

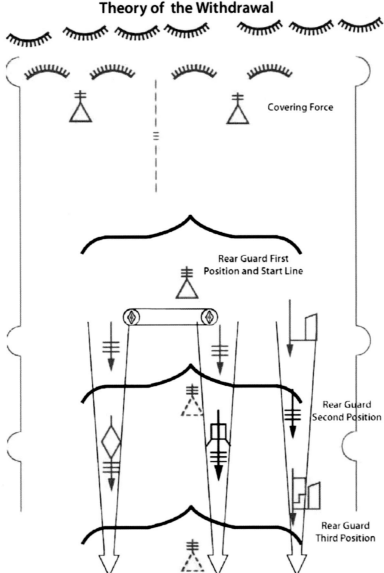

(Above) The above graphic depicts a notional motorized rifle brigade withdrawal. The forward two motorized rifle battalions each leave a company covering force as they secretly withdraw. The enemy is not too active at this time, so the brigade commander has decided to withdraw the trains and second echelon first. A second echelon motorized rifle battalion assumes the rear guard mission. It is reinforced with an artillery battalion as well as tanks, engineer mining assets and air defense assets. This brigade withdraws on three primary routes. The trains, an artillery battalion and brigade forces withdraw on one route. The MLRS battalion and a motorized rifle battalion withdraw on a second route, while the tank battalion and a first echelon motorized rifle battalion withdraw on the third route. Determination of the start line and the sequential positions for the rear guard are a function of terrain, weather, enemy activity, subsequent mission and hours of darkness available. The start line and first position of the rear guard do not have to be the same. Which units travel on what routes is a function of which are the safest and more exposed routes, expected enemy actions, using more trafficable routes for heavy equipment, water crossings enroute and potential traffic problems (built up areas, road intersections, mud, blown bridges and the like).

The covering force is usually withdrawn after the main body has passed the start line. It withdraws through the rear guard and follows the route taken by its parent battalion. In this example, the rear guard will withdraw simultaneously from position line to position line instead of leapfrogging back.

Withdrawal under heavy enemy pressure may devolve into a series of hard-fought engagements while attempting to preserve as much combat power as possible on a more advantageous line. Historically, the Russian soldier is a stubborn defender. During the Second World War, Stalin's famous order 227 issued on 28 July 1942 "Not one step backward" [Ни щагу назад], caused a lot of units to die in place, rather than withdrawing. When ordered, the Russian soldier will stand his ground tenaciously.

Withdrawal in Practice

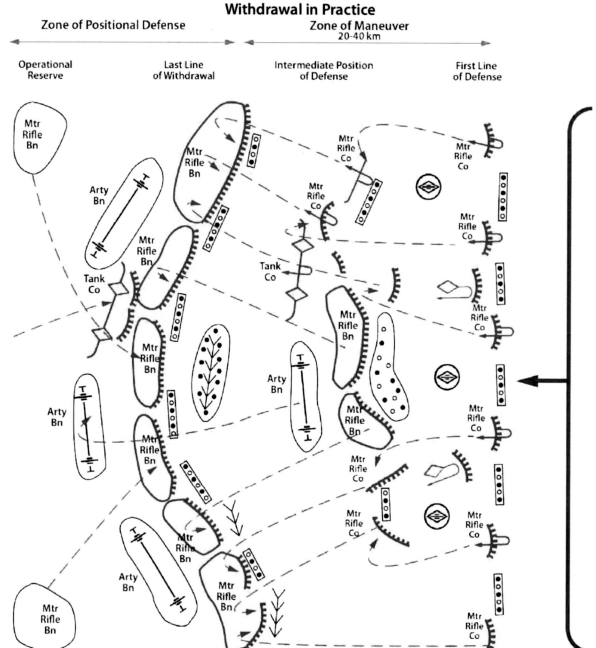

Zone of Positional Defense · Zone of Maneuver 20-40 km

Operational Reserve · Last Line of Withdrawal · Intermediate Position of Defense · First Line of Defense

(Right) The graphic on facing page depicts a withdrawal under pressure by a defending motorized rifle battalion with an attached tank company. It is defending with two companies forward and one back. There are two east-west roads through the battalion defense that meet behind the battalion defense. Since the enemy is attacking, the battalion must conduct a fighting withdrawal. The northern company is defending in two echelons with a tank platoon and the 1st MRP in the north on higher ground. The 2nd platoon defends the main road. In the south, the 2nd MRC defends in two echelons with the 1st MRP and a tank platoon on higher ground. The 3rd MRC defends in a single echelon in the battalion rear.

The withdrawal begins with a feint attack by the 2nd platoon of the 1st MRC which then withdraws into a temporary assembly area in a covered patch of woods behind their position. After assembly, the platoon withdraws to a company assembly area behind the battalion defensive position. The 3rd platoon withdraws directly to the company assembly area. Simultaneously with the feint attack, the 2nd and 3rd platoons of the 2nd MRC, the entire 3rd MRC (with attached tank platoon) and the mortar battery withdraw to company assembly areas behind the battalion defenses. The mortar battery moves to the 3rd MRC assembly area.

Upon a signal from battalion, 1st platoon of the 1st MRC and 1st platoon of the 2nd MRC withdraw, along with their attached tank platoons, to the vacated positions of their 3rd platoons and defend. The 3rd MRC and mortar battery move to the battalion assembly area in the vicinity of the road junction, followed by the two platoons of the 1st and 2nd MRCs. As the enemy pressure mounts, the embattled 1st platoons with their attached tank platoons withdraw again and take up a defense in the vacated positions of the 3rd MRC. Finally, upon signal from battalion, the battered 1st platoons and tank platoons move quickly into their company areas for a quick nose count and then move to the battalion assembly area. The battalion has probably begun its march and the battered platoons join the march column, with luck, not as the rear guard.

The battalion marches a distance to its new positions and assumes a single echelon defense. The battalion commander's intent was to preserve as much combat power as possible, while banking on two motorized rifle and two tank platoons to conduct a determined fighting withdrawal from three prepared fighting positions. His feint created a diversion under which the withdrawal began. He took advantage of high ground defenses while leaving the road approaches subject to flanking fire in a variant of the fire sac. He will have available artillery fire planned on the roads.

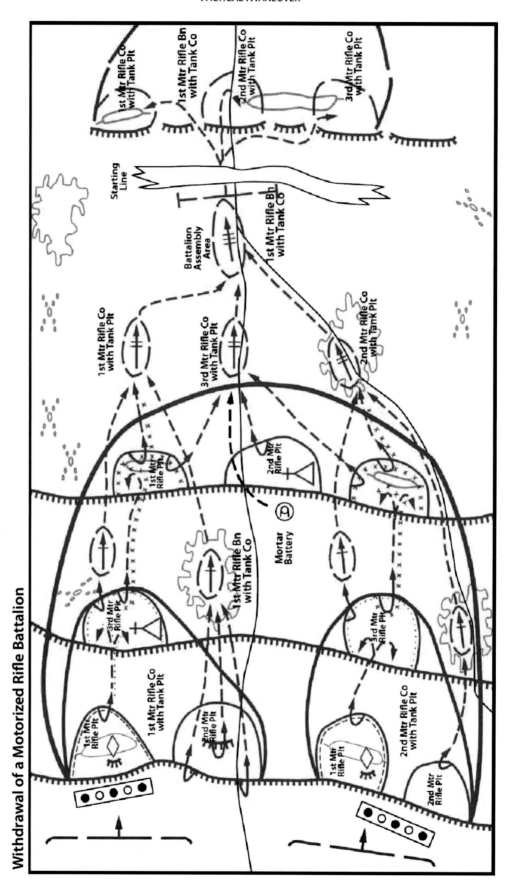

Withdrawal of a Motorized Rifle Battalion

Fighting in an Encirclement and Breakout

The rolling plains, forests and marshlands of Western Russia and Eastern Europe invite the use of combined arms battalion and brigade maneuver. The nature of the terrain and the tempo of the maneuver can readily allow open flanks, gaps and bypassed forces. The probability of conducting or falling into an encirclement multiplies in this terrain. For the Soviet Union, the opening weeks of the Second World War (the Great Patriotic War in Russian parlance) resulted in massive operational-level encirclements of Soviet forces with chilling losses. As the war progressed, the Soviets were gradually able to turn the tables and conducted twelve of their own operational-level encirclements of German forces and their allies.[38] The operational encirclement differs from the tactical encirclement in terms of scope, duration and response. During the Great Patriotic War, the Soviets employed an inner encirclement line and an outer encirclement line against the Germans. The purpose of the inner encirclement line was to prevent the trapped enemy from breaking out. The purpose of the outer encirclement line was to prevent a rescue force from breaking in and expanding the encircled area into a bulge in the defensive line or extracting the entrapped force. Operational encirclements were designed to destroy the combat effectiveness of the entrapped major force and to capture equipment and units. The encirclements could be porous, allowing individuals to escape individually or in small groups with their rifles, but little else. The idea was to destroy the combat potential or capture the encircled units and equipment, but not become overly concerned with individuals. In the Soviet-Afghan War, the porous nature of the Soviet encirclements worked to the Mujahideen advantage, but the Mujahideen usually lost their trucks and heavy weapons when encircled.[39]

Often, when combating an enemy, it is more advantageous to isolate a dangerous force and let artillery weaken that force before committing to a decisive attack. When conducting an encirclement, the encircling force will take advantage of the terrain to isolate the enemy force rapidly and seize road intersections, escape routes and approach routes for an enemy relief force. The outer encirclement line may be fragmented and the outer encirclement force will first seize the key routes to prevent the enemy from escaping while preventing the external enemy force from approaching the inner encirclement force. An encirclement is normally reduced by sectors, rather than simultaneously. The reserve of the outer encirclement force is frequently used in sector reduction.[40]

Based on their Great Patriotic War experience, the Soviets and Russians studied and have developed operational and tactical techniques for conducting encirclements and fighting when encircled. Larger-scale encirclements are likely to occur during the initial period of a war or when forces are pinned against a natural obstacle such as a seacoast or major river or are within a city.[41] Since an advance guard mission, meeting battle, forward position

[38] Ministry of Defense of the Russian Federation, "Encirclement" [Окружение], *Military Encyclopedia* [Военная Энциклопедия], Volume 6, Moscow; Voyenizdat, 2002, 43-45.
[39] Ali A. Jalali and Lester W. Grau, *The Other Side of the Mountain: Mujahideen Tactics in the Soviet-Afghan War*, Quantico: US Marine Corps Study DM-980701, 1998, 241-266.
[40] Ministry of Defense of the Russian Federation, "Encirclement" [Окружение], *Military Encyclopedia* [Военная Энциклопедия], Volume 6, Moscow; Voyenizdat, 2002, 43-45.
[41] I. N. Manzhurin, "Actions of forces in an encirclement," [Действия войск в окружени], *Military Thought* [Военная мысль], February 1990, 14-21.

in a security zone, failed counter-attack or inability to retreat pose the greatest danger of encirclement for a battalion, battalion-level fighting in encirclement and breakout training exercises have been conducted. [42] These exercises involved a combined arms battalion or task-organized motorized rifle battalion with tanks, BMPs and artillery. The best way to break out of a tactical encirclement is not to be encircled in the first place. The battalion commander does so by additional reconnaissance, placing ambush sites on the flanks and boundaries with adjacent subunits, concentrating fires (especially antitank fires) on threatened avenues of approach, and grouping forces and means to conduct a counterattack. Should the battalion find itself in the rear of an advancing enemy, it must actively and decisively commit its maximum strength to retain the most tactically significant feature of the area or the area which will support its breakout of encirclement. [43]

Tactical Considerations

Experience shows that being encircled is not necessarily a catastrophe that leads to death or captivity, but it is a serious situation. It is a situation where one is fully or partially cut off from his own force; fighting a superior force simultaneously to the front, flanks and rear; fighting under conditions where maneuver is limited, resupply is difficult, and casualties to men and material mount to a significant level. An encirclement may involve a single or double pincer movement designed to cut off a unit from its neighboring and second echelon units, disrupt its ability to receive supplies and assistance and establish an unbroken containment area. The encircled force must break out to restore its freedom of maneuver. [44]

Primary tactical missions required for forces fighting in an encirclement:
- prepare a defense and construct strong points or a defensive area;
- ward off aerial attacks;
- repulse enemy ground attacks and retain established firing lines, positions and areas;
- prevent the enemy from breaking through into the depths of the defense;
- destroy enemy forces wedged into the defense;
- restore the situation on the primary axes;
- eliminate enemy assault forces, sabotage and diversionary groups acting in the rear area and irregular armed formations. [45]

The requirements for fighting in an encirclement require that the commander and staff:
- seize and retain the most important tactical position in the path of the enemy;
- constitute a strong, mobile antitank reserve and deploy it on the most-threatened axes;

[42] N. Vinokur, "Combat in an encirclement" [Бой в окружении], *Military Herald* [Военный Вестник], December 1979, 38-40.
E. Denizhkin, "In extreme situations (Motorized rifle battalion combat in an encirclement and breakthrough from it)" [В экстремальных услонях (Бой мотострелкового батальона в окржении и вызход из него)], *Military Herald* [Военный Вестник], September 1990. Although these are Soviet examples, the theory is still quite relevant, particularly on a fluid, maneuver battlefield.
[43] Denizhkin, 40.
[44] A. P. Kozachenko, "From combat-out of encirclement: Algorithms for commander and staff work" [С боем-из окружения: Алгоритм работы командир и штаба], *Army Digest* [Армейский Сборник], April 2011, 8.
[45] Ibid.

- position part of the artillery so that it can conduct direct fire to defeat an enemy tank attack;
- prepare to mass fire and maneuver artillery on the most-threatened axes;
- order the combat engineers to mine the most-probable enemy approach;
- maintain uninterrupted communications with the senior commander and, most importantly, with neighboring units in order to combine efforts to thwart enemy intentions.[46]

Combat in an encirclement requires active and decisive actions to pin down a larger force and to be prepared to fight for an extended period of time. Offset insufficient forces and means with active combat, skilled maneuver and military cunning. Subunits must staunchly defend their strong points and areas, not allow the fragmentation of the encirclement, not lose close contact with the enemy, and not allow their own forces to bunch up in a small space where they can be destroyed by all types of fire. The commander must establish a coherent perimeter defense; secure the junctures between subunits; assume command of all forces in the encirclement and assign them missions; maintain a high fighting spirit, while organizing and maintaining combat readiness; establish and maintain coordination with forces fighting outside of the encirclement; and at all times know the situation in each of his subunits.[47]

Further, the commander must employ aviation, all means of fire, surprise and courageous counterattacks to evict enemy wedged into his defenses; quickly and secretly maneuver subunits, fires and particularly tanks and BMPs against a threatened axis; reconstitute the reserve; support helicopter landings and position them; receive and collect cargo dropped from aircraft; institute strict rationing of rockets, ammunition, food and fuel.[48]

The basic tactical missions for fighting in an encirclement include:
- seizing a region that provides freedom of internal maneuver;
- block enemy attacks, direct and deploy our forces and destroy any enemy wedged into our defenses;
- preserve command and control and maintain combat readiness during the breakout from encirclement;
- prevent forces from crowding into a small area that can be attacked by enemy artillery;
- establish a group of forces and weapons to break through the encirclement.[49]

Tactical missions for a breakout of an encirclement include:
- regrouping forces and resources and creating an attack combat formation;
- retaining the perimeter with a covering force while breaking out and withdrawing;
- breaking out through the encircling enemy defense with the main force and withdrawing from the encirclement;
- breaking contact and withdrawing the covering force from the encirclement.[50]

[46] Ibid, 8-9.
[47] Ibid, 9.
[48] Ibid.
[49] Ibid.
[50] Ibid, 10-11.

The breakout sector of the encircled force should line up with the breakthrough sector of the external force. The combat formation for the breakout is usually the breakout force, the support force and the reserve. There will be a requirement to assemble and direct these elements in the direction of the breakthrough. The initial withdrawing force will normally include no less than half the force and the bulk of tanks and artillery. The flanks of the breakthrough must be held against enemy counter attack. Normally one-third to one-fourth of the force will perform this mission. The commander will specify each subunits mission, the time and method of the breakthrough and the order of withdrawal from the encirclement.[51]

The commander's concept must include:
- the sector, direction and time for the breakout, if these are not included in the senior commander's orders, and the sectors for diversionary actions;
- the method and sequencing of the breakout and withdrawal from the encirclement;
- the order of withdrawal of subunits holding the encirclement perimeter and the flanks of the breakthrough sector;
- the sequencing of destruction of the enemy by fire;
- the follow-up mission of the withdrawing breakthrough subunits and the order of their readiness;
- the formation of the combat formation (forces and means assigned to the breakthrough, diversionary actions, flank security and perimeter security);
- provision for secrecy during preparations and for fulfilling the assigned missions.[52]

The designation of the breakout, diversionary, flank security and perimeter defense forces and systems and their actions during each phase of the breakthrough and withdrawal, plus their missions upon reaching friendly positions, is critical. The flank security subunits are the last to withdraw and will withdraw on the order of the commander by lines, each of which they will defend. They may have to conduct a limited counterattack to check an enemy pursuit and gain time for the withdrawing subunits. The withdrawal should conduct a determined and crippling blow to the enemy on the chosen axis. The breakout of small groups from the encirclement is forbidden. A night breakout of force and tanks requires tight discipline and order, surprise, and an attack on enemy forces astride the selected axis. A daytime breakout requires a short, but intense, artillery preparation and, if possible, air strikes.[53]

After the breakthrough, the organized withdrawal is quickly conducted. The maintenance and supply subunits move with the breakout force. The sick and wounded are moved on available transport. If necessary, vehicle cargo may have to be unloaded in a heap to make room. Destroy the heap.[54]

When the commander receives the order to break out of an encirclement, he must concentrate his forces and means into a mighty fist for the breakthrough. A determined and energetic effort is necessary to conduct this mission. Active reconnaissance, a sober assessment of the situation, a clear decision, precise coordination between forces, strict

[51] Ibid, 11.
[52] Ibid.
[53] Ibid.
[54] Ibid.

command and control and courage will not only result in the breakthrough and withdrawal from an encirclement, but destroy a significant group of the enemy in the process.[55]

Encirclement Training Example
The following deals with the tactical fighting within an encirclement and breakout by a motorized rifle battalion. It is taken from a battalion exercise conducted shortly before the collapse of the Soviet Union, so the battalion is part of a regiment, but is fighting combined arms and the principles covered are still valid and instructive.

In this exercise scenario, the enemy has broken into a defense and encircled a motorized rifle battalion. The 1st Motorized Rifle Battalion is mounted on BMPs and has a tank company, an air defense missile platoon and a self-propelled howitzer battalion. It is joined by another tank company and the 9th Motorized Rifle Company that have been isolated as well. At 1500 hours, the battalion commander received his orders: "Assume command of the encircled subunits and constitute an unbroken defensive perimeter. Your mission: Firmly retain the area within the limits delineated by Clear Pond-height 178.6-the irregular grove, prevent the enemy from weakening the combat power of the battalion, pin down those enemy subunits not in direct contact through combat, and hinder their maneuver in the direction of the dairy farm to the village of Sentsovo." The battalion commander also learned that the enemy reserve might commit a tank battalion against his encirclement. The enemy battalion could cross the departure line, dairy-farm to long woods, in one to 1.5 hours.[56]

The battalion commander considered his situation. He had an extensive perimeter of up to 10 kilometers to hold, there were several threatening avenues of approach on different sides of his perimeter and there were insufficient forces and means. In order to allow his subunits to inflict significant casualties required the ability to concentrate his force quickly against any avenue of approach. Therefore, he decided to conduct a single-echelon defense with a strong reserve located near the command post. The commander considered the northern enemy avenue of approach as the most likely and dangerous. He positioned his 2nd Motorized Rifle Company on it with a recessed fire sac. Two tank ambushes secured its flanks and another tank platoon had a firing line directly behind its position. The battalion reserve was the 9th Motorized Rifle Company and a tank company (minus one platoon). The artillery battalion was located in the center of the defense, where it could fire in any direction. The battalion's mortar battery was attached to the 3rd Motorized Rifle Company.[57]

The commander paid close attention to maintaining the steadfastness and activeness of his defense, and to the tactical and fire coordination among subunits, their tenacity and their protection from high precision fires, aerial attack and artillery fire. The company and platoon positions were prepared in order to provide a zone of unbroken defensive fire to the front and flanks, guaranteed to break up an armored and/or infantry attack on the various approaches. The company defensive areas occupied 1500 meters of frontage and 500 meters of depth with gaps of up to 1,500 meters between them. Platoon strong points occupied 300-400 meters of frontage and 200 meters of depth with gaps of 300 meters between them.[58]

[55] Ibid.
[56] Denizhkin, 40.
[57] Ibid, 40-41.
[58] Ibid, 41.

Fighting in an Encirclement

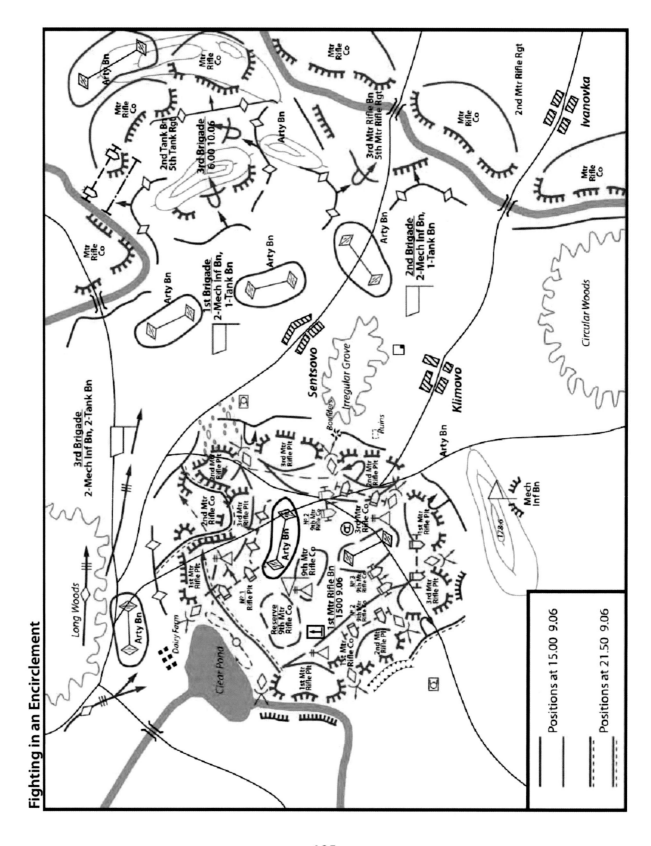

The battalion commander was concerned with organizing his system of fire. The basis of this is concentrated barriers of artillery and mortar fire before the forward edge and in the depth of his defense, combined with the antitank fires of the tanks, BMPs, ATGMs, ordnance, grenade launchers and other means. The positioning of machine guns and small arms completed turning the encirclement front into a solid multi-trajectory fire zone with frontal, flanking, interlocking and close combat fires. The battalion commander also planned for the maneuver of artillery, tanks, BMPs and the reserve from unthreatened sectors. This included planning for alternate firing positions, firing lines and assembly areas.[59]

The battalion commander assigned missions to his air defense missile platoon to protect his subunits, the command post and his helicopter landing zone. He had to consider the strict rationing of ammunition, fuel and other supplies and take the necessary steps to receive cargo delivered by helicopter or parachute. His staff established radio contact and coordinated with those subunits that were outside the encirclement. The battalion used landline communications primarily within the defense. Wire was laid and buried in the trenches and in the communications trenches as a protection from artillery fire.[60]

The enemy attacked the 2nd Motorized Rifle Company positions at 2130 hours. Two tank companies and some mechanized infantry managed to wedge some 400 meters into the fire sac and overrun part of the 1st and 2nd platoon positions. The battalion commander focused the fire of his artillery battalion on the enemy self-propelled artillery positioned south of long woods. He committed his antitank reserve to firing line #1 to combat the enemy incursion. While the 2nd MRC fought to retain the second and third trenches, they were supported by fires from the mortar battery. The battalion commander attached a motorized rifle platoon from the quiet sectors of the 1st and 3rd Motorized Rifle Companies to the 2nd MRC as reinforcements in the fight. These measures enabled the company to stop the enemy and reoccupy some lost positions. A similar attempt by the enemy to penetrate the 1st MRC position near the ravine was also unsuccessful.[61]

Taking advantage of the situation, the battalion commander ordered his reserve, in coordination with the tank platoons and the 2nd MRC, to destroy the enemy within the 2MRC area and restore the 2MRC original defensive front line. They secretly approached the jump-off line and launched a counterattack. The determined night attack regained more of the company positions and inflicted heavy losses on the enemy.[62]

Breakout Training Example
The next mission was the breakout from encirclement at 0300 hours the next morning. The battalion commander's decision had to determine the breakout sector and the diversionary action; the direction and time of the breakout; what forces and means to commit to the breakout, covering force and flank security (blocking force); the missions of each; as well as the withdrawal mission and the time required to carry it out. The commander planned the order of withdrawal from the encirclement, the withdrawal of the covering force and flank security, and coordination with the

---

[59] Ibid.
[60] Ibid.
[61] Ibid, 42.
[62] Ibid.

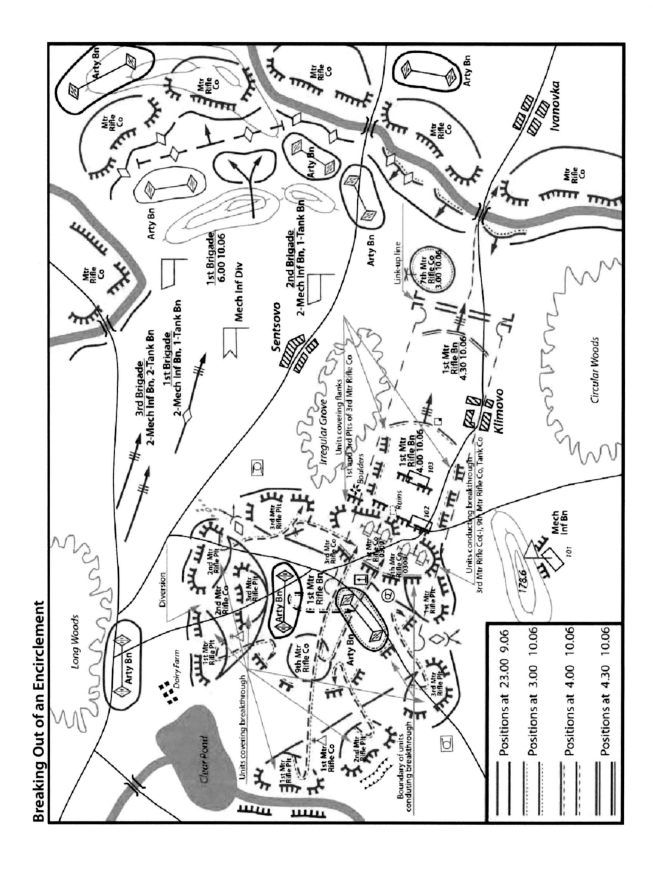

Breaking Out of an Encirclement

linkup forces outside the encirclement.[63]

The commander decided to have the 2MRC conduct the diversionary action in the area where the enemy was still wedged into part of the 2MRC forward defenses. He calculated that the enemy might think that action in this area indicated an attempt to restore the positions and undo his successful breakthrough attack [in the north]. In reality, the breakout axis would follow the ruins, the individual house and the village of Ivanovka.[64]

The battalion commander began the covert repositioning of the 3rd MRC, the 9th MRC along with the tanks and self-propelled artillery battalion to break through the encirclement. The breakout would be assisted by the 2nd Motorized Rifle Regiment, whose commander planned to conduct an air assault at 0300 hours in a counterattack in the direction Ivanovka-Klimovo. The rest of the perimeter would be held by the 1MRC and 2MRC covering force.[65]

At 0045 hours, the battalion commander gathered his company commanders and other subunit commanders and briefed them on his decision: The main force will concentrate on the direction ruins-single house-Ivanovka. The 3MRC, 9MRC and the tanks will conduct a night attack to break through the enemy defenses in the region of the barn, Kilmovo, the boulder, the southern edge of the "irregular" bushes. Destroy the enemy in the region of the barn, single house and boulder. By 0400 hours 10 June, seize the line between the western limits of Klimovo and the southern edge of the "irregular" bushes.

Continue the attack in the direction of the single house-Ivanovka, and in cooperation with the air assault forces, destroy the enemy and by 0430, link up with the subunits of the 2nd Motorized Rifle Regiment who will meet you.

The fires of the artillery battalion, mortar battery and tanks will destroy the enemy in the two platoon strong points and the command post of the mechanized battalion and provide support to the covering force and flank security force.

At 0200, the 2MRC will conduct a phony attack as a diversionary action in the sector between the brush and "Clear" Lake. The perimeter will be held by the covering force-1MRC and 2MRC. The flanks in the vicinity of the breakthrough will be held by two platoons of the 3MRC who will hold positions and assist in the orderly evacuation of subunits from the encirclement.

Combat formation is a single echelon: breakthrough subunits-3MRC, 9MRC, tank company; covering force: 1 MRC and 2MRC; flank force-1st and 3rd Platoons, 3MRC after the breakthrough. Reserve-2nd Platoon, 3MRC.[66]

An hour before the breakthrough, the 2MRC launched a diversionary attack to cover the concentration of the breakthrough force. At 0300, following a short but powerful fire strike, the battalion commander signaled the start of the attack. The attack met its immediate objective and

[63] Ibid.
[64] Ibid.
[65] Ibid, 42-43.
[66] Ibid. 43.

continued the advance. Two platoons from the 3MRC moved to the flanks and took up firing positions. Their action prevented the enemy from sealing the breach and supported the withdrawal from the encirclement-first the artillery and reserve and then the covering force.[67]

In one-and-a-half hours of night combat, the battalion defeated the enemy opposite the breakthrough sector, moved over five kilometers and at 0430 hours, east of Kilmovo, linked up with subunits of the 2nd Motorized Rifle Regiment.[68]

[67] Ibid.
[68] Ibid.

Maneuver Defense

Russia's long borders, smaller army and evolving mobilization system, coupled with the presence of enemy electronic reconnaissance systems and precision weaponry dictate that tied-in Russian defensive lines stretching for hundreds of kilometers will not exist, at least during the initial period of war. Aleksandr A. Svechin (1878-1938), who is now considered the preeminent Russian strategist, argued before the Second World War that the best strategy for the USSR would be the conduct of a protracted defense during the initial period of war. The enemy would be drawn into Russia's vastness where his strength would be weakened and his supply lines over-extended. Once the enemy drive had culminated, the Red Army would counterstrike and destroy the aggressor. The Soviet leadership did not heed his attrition strategy and the debacle of 1941 was the result.[69] Svechin's ideas are now well regarded in the Russian General Staff.

Much of Russia is ideal for Svechin's strategy (the exemption being the 84 miles between the Estonian border and large, urban Saint Petersburg). Most major cities are well-removed from the border areas, industry is well-distributed over the country and rail is the primary method of transport. The river network, snow, the spring thaw and fall flooding limit outside aggressors' mobility. Russian military equipment is designed for this terrain. The best option for Russia is to establish a maneuver defense that eventually leads to a positional defense where the enemy will finally be defeated.

Maneuver defense is a form of defense whose purpose is to inflict enemy casualties, gain time, and preserve one's own force while risking the loss of territory. As a rule, it is conducted when the defending force has insufficient personnel and weapons to conduct a positional defense.[70] However, the impact of new technology has changed warfare and the basic relationship between the offense and defense. Many of the advantages of the offensive are negated by the new technology. The initiative can be seized while on the offense or defense. Just before the collapse of the Soviet Union, leading military theoreticians were looking to the strength of the defense against the new technology.

Today, battle may be initiated by a bitterly contested, long-range engagement, well before the combatants come into contact. Under these circumstances, defending forces in prepared positions, which are deployed with fewer forces and combat power than the attack, may obtain a definitive superiority. This is done by the more effective protection of personnel and weapons systems during the massive fire strikes and the preservation of the combat potential of one's own armies and divisions.[71]

Defense may be conducted in direct contact with the enemy and out of direct contact with enemy forces. Establishing coordinated defenses when not in direct contact with the enemy

[69] A. A. Kokoshin and V. V. Larionov, Introductory Essay to English translation of Alexander A. Svechin's 1927 *Strategy* [Стратегия], Minneapolis: East View Publications, 1992, 7.
[70] Ministry of Defense of the Russian Federation, "Maneuver Defense" [Манёвренная Оборона], *Military Encyclopedia* [Военная Энциклопедия], Volume 4, Moscow: Voyenizdat, 1999, 554.
[71] I. N. Manzhurin, "Some questions on the preparation and conduct of the counterstrike during defensive operations" [Некоторый вопросы подготовки и нанесения контраударнов в оборонителъных операцыях], *Military Thought* [Военная Мысль], January, 1989, 14.

is common just prior to the initiation of hostilities. It is also encountered when preparing to meet counterattacks, when regrouping and refitting during an offensive, when preparing to absorb an enemy offensive strike prior to a counteroffensive or when conducting an economy-of-force mission in support of an offensive.[72]

Security Zone

Positions in front of the main defense are outposts, forward positions and security zone/ maneuver defense consecutive positions. A company or platoon establishes outposts, a battalion establishes a forward position, a brigade establishes a maneuver defense and an army or military district establishes a security zone. The purpose of combat outposts is early warning and concealment of the main defense. The purpose of the forward position is early warning, concealment of the trace of the main defense, forcing the enemy to deploy early and attrition of the attacking force. The purpose of the security zone is to provide early warning, mislead the attacker as to the location, configuration and actual composition of the defense and gain time for the construction of the main defense. The security zone determines the composition of the enemy forces, intentions and axes of advance. It provides adequate reaction time to the defender and forces the attacker to deploy early. It may force the enemy to attack in a disadvantageous direction and weakens the enemy force well before it closes with the main defense. It does such through the conduct of maneuver defense. The security zone is normally established when preparing defenses that are not in direct contact with the enemy. The depth of a security zone may extend 40 kilometers in front of the main defense.[73] There are indications that in some cases, it may extend out as far as 90 kilometers.

The depth of a security zone depends on the mission and conduct of the operation, the terrain and the time required to establish the defense. It includes several battle positions, strong points and obstacle networks. If it is located close to an international border, it might be defended by forward detachments and border guard units. These forces will fight from a series of positions prepared in depth and tied in with mine fields, ambushes and prepared demolitions.[74]

Security zone defensive positions are established on important axes of advance into the main defensive area to increase the tactical depth of the defense. The depth of the security zone prevents the enemy from rapidly reaching the main defensive zone, provides for the support of the forward combined arms combat force with its main force and establishes adequate maneuver room for the forward combat force. Defensive positions and obstacles are situated where they cannot be bypassed and are strong enough to make it difficult for the enemy to overcome without significant expenditure of forces, resources and time. Tank-heavy forces and the preponderance of obstacles are positioned on the armor axes of advance. Reinforced motorized rifle battalions usually defend secondary axes. Forces and resources in a security zone include reconnaissance, combined arms forces, long-range attack systems, command and control elements, ambush forces, engineers, forward position forces and helicopter

[72] Lester W. Grau, "Absorbing the Initial Attack: The Security Zone in the Contemporary Russian view of Defense", *Red Thrust Star*, October 1992, 4.
[73] Ministry of Defense of the Russian Federation, "Security Zone" [Полоса Обеспечения], *Military Encyclopedia* [Военная Энциклопедия], Volume 6, Moscow: Voyenizdat, 2002, 493-494.
[74] Ibid.

gunships.[75]

A battalion defending in the security zone normally deploys in a single echelon (seven to ten kilometers width) with a reinforced platoon as a reserve. The battalion does not wish to become decisively engaged and holds a wider frontage than usual (normally three to five kilometers width). Companies and platoons defend their normal strongpoint frontages. Gaps are allowed depending on the terrain and obstacles. The reserve normally occupies a blocking position on the most dangerous approach and two-three kilometers back of the battalion's front line. The reserve adds depth to the battalion defense and prevents the enemy from reaching the battalion's flanks and rear. The reserve holds its position while the battalion disengages. The reserve seldom counterattacks.[76]

Positions in the Security Zone

The number of consecutive prepared positions in a security zone depends on the terrain, the existence of naturally defensible lines and the depth of the zone. The first position (closest to the enemy) should be along a favorable, naturally defensible line at a depth from which main force artillery can support from temporary firing positions. The next (second) position should also be along a naturally defensible line and at a distance from the first position that would require the enemy to displace his artillery and mortars forward in order to shift fires. The positions are dug in and provided with obstacles to the extent possible in the time available. Up to two companies of engineers are assigned to a maneuver battalion to provide obstacles and positions. Companies and platoons are sited in order to provide coordinated, interlocking fields of fire. Additional positions (third, fourth and so on) are constructed depending on time, resources and the depth of the security zone. The final position is closest to the main defensive line and could be a forward position (Передовая позиция) located three to five kilometers from the main defensive line. Companies and battalions from the depths of the main defense will hold the critical forward positions, while the forward detachment battalions, which have fought the mobile defense and expended resources and taken casualties, will occupy the forward positions on secondary approaches.[77]

The forward detachment's artillery, mortars and air defense weapons will have primary, alternate and reserve firing positions throughout the depth of the security zone. Maneuver and withdrawal routes will be reconnoitered, prepared, marked and maintained. Deployment firing lines for tanks, BMPs and the antitank reserve will cover armor avenues of approach. Deployment counterattack lines will be selected as well as direct fire positions for select artillery. Camouflage discipline will be enforced. Obstacles will usually be placed in front of security zone fighting positions and in gaps between strongpoints. Bridges and key sites will be prepared for demolition. Should the enemy attempt to bypass obstacles, the bypass will lead to other obstacles or exposure to flanking fire.[78]

---

[75] Ibid.
[76] Grau, 5.
[77] Ibid, 6.
[78] Ibid, 7.

Artillery Planning for the Security Zone

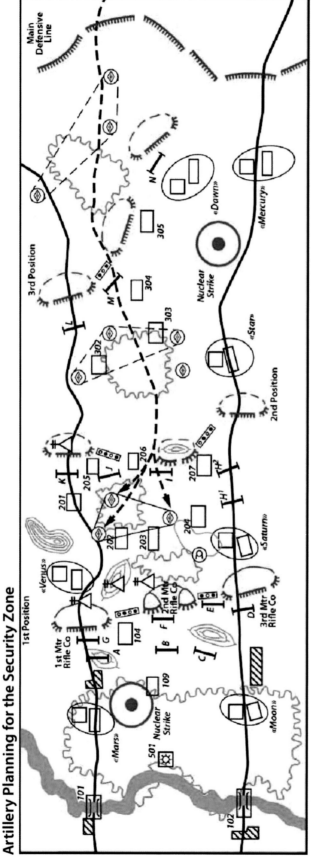

(Above) The accompanying graphic is an example of a fire plan for a security zone employing three positions in a 42-kilometer depth. Standing barrage lines, MLRS concentrations and massed fire concentrations and planned nuclear strikes are depicted. Whereas the motorized rifle or tank subunits in the security zone fight consecutively from one position to the next, artillery subunits normally leapfrog back so that artillery support is constant and uninterrupted. Fixed-wing aviation and helicopter gunships may also provide fire support to the maneuver battle.

(Right) The graphic on the facing page illustrates a security zone with a series of four prepared positions and a main defensive line. The northern-most company (3rd Motorized Rifle Company) fights its way back from the first and second positions to the third position, as does its southern neighbors. Unlike the 1st and 2nd Motorized Rifle Companies, the 3rd Motorized Rifle Company does not fall back and defend the forward position in front of the main line of defense. Instead, it moves from the third position directly back into the main defense. A fresh company (coincidently also the 3rd) from a first-echelon battalion in the main defense defends the northern forward position on the main axis of enemy advance. The 1st and 2nd Motorized Rifle Companies of the forward detachment occupy forward positions astride secondary avenues of advance. The Russians forecast that the forward detachment will be too weakened, too rushed and in need of refitting at this point in the battle to handle the enemy main attack adequately.[79]

One or two artillery battalions are normally attached to the forward detachment in the security zone. Additional supporting artillery (normally MLRS) is also positioned in the security zone and controlled by the army or district commander who constituted the security zone. Artillery positions are selected to interdict major axes of advance and sited so that the guns may deliver effective indirect and direct fire. Direct fire antitank killing zones are tied in with tank ambushes and engineer obstacles, often as part of a fire sac. Fire planning covers probable enemy avenues of advance, probable firing locations of enemy artillery and movement routes. Planned mortar and artillery fires cover gaps between platoon and company strongpoints, the area forward of engineer obstacles and critical points in the defense.

---

[79] Ibid.

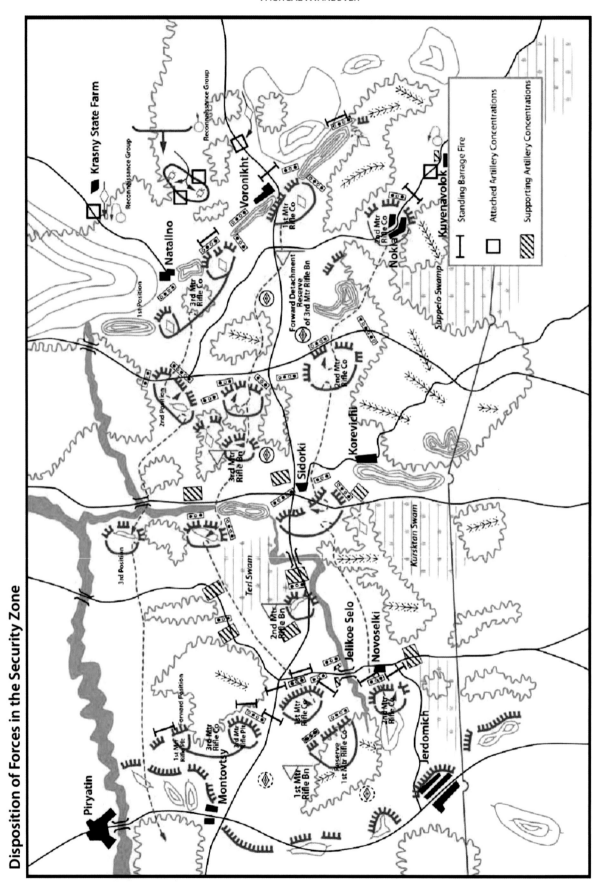

Disposition of Forces in the Security Zone

The Brigade and Maneuver Defense

Maneuver defense [маневренная оборона][80] is a fundamental form of defense for a motorized rifle battalion within a maneuver brigade. The maneuver defense is used on those axes where the enemy has a significant strength advantage and is facing an area that the Russian forces are allowed to withdraw from temporarily. In this situation, a maneuver defense may gain time and allow an advantageous regrouping of forces for the decisive destruction of the enemy. The battalion commander singles out those forward and consecutive defensive positions that his motorized rifle battalion will hold until the last minute against impending enemy breakthrough, while inflicting maximum casualties. Therefore the main mission of the battalion commander is to coordinate the fires of all systems against the advancing enemy while abandoning positions consecutively. Then the battalion commander supports his subunits' withdrawal to their next positions while preserving their combat strength.[81]

The motorized rifle battalion conducting the maneuver defense may be drawn from the brigade first or second echelon. The battalion will resume its defensive positions in the main defense at the conclusion of the maneuver defense. Fires of the various systems are planned for engaging the enemy at a distance, while moving, deploying and just forward of the front line. Forces, systems and fires maneuver and counterattacks are launched when circumstances are favorable. Counterattacks are usually conducted by the reserve or second echelon against the enemy flank and rear. Fire sacs, which are shaped by mine fields and obstacles, are effective tools in maneuver defense. Covert, surprise and quick maneuver allows subunits to move to advantageous positions with respect to the enemy. There, the subunits can inflict casualties or even destroy the enemy. Maneuver defense concludes with the uninterrupted destruction of the enemy using all means to frustrate his will and force him into a disadvantageous position for continuing the attack. Maneuver by fire is widely employed during all stages of the battle.[82]

The accompanying graphic shows one of the consecutive positions occupied by a motorized rifle battalion in the maneuver defense of a brigade.[83] This maneuver defense employs a motorized rifle battalion with an attached howitzer battalion, a tank company, an antitank battery, and an air defense SA-18 or SA-25 battery. Other artillery and engineer units provide support as required. The battalion frontage may be a bit wider than a usual defense and extend 5-10 kilometers. The graphic shows the battalion astride an east-west road that forks behind the battalion defensive line. The terrain is fairly flat and partially wooded with a lake

---

[80] Maneuver defense should not be confused with the Western term-active defense or the shared historic term-covering force. An active defense is the "employment of limited offensive action and counterattacks to deny a contested area or position to the enemy." A covering force is a "force operating apart from the main force for the purpose of intercepting, engaging, delaying, disorganizing, and deceiving the enemy before the enemy can attack the force covered." It can also be any "body or detachment of troops which provides security for a larger force by observation, reconnaissance, attack, or defense, or by any combination of these methods." The Russians use a different terminology for active defense [активная оборона] and covering force [заслон].

[81] D. Kalachev, "Defense is also maneuver-The motorized rifle battalion and maneuver defense" [Оборона-тоже маневр: Мотострелковый батальон и маневренная оборона], *Army Digest* [Армейскнй сборник], October 2016, 27.

[82] Ibid, 28-29.

[83] Ibid, 30.

Combat Formation of a Motorized Rifle Battalion in the Maneuver Defense

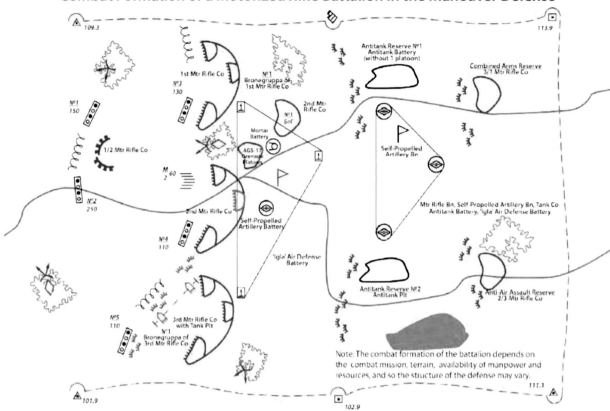

in the southeastern portion of the position. The first platoon of the 2nd MRC holds an outpost position protected by two mixed mine fields of 150 and 250 meters length and a barbed wire entanglement. A squad ambush and a tank ambush flank the outpost. The main defensive line has the battalion's three companies deployed in a defensive line. The 1st MRC holds its forward positions with its 1st and 2nd platoons. The 3rd platoon is the battalion combined arms reserve, and is positioned in the battalion northeast rear covering the anticipated main enemy axis of advance. The 1st MRC *bronnegruppa* holds the 3rd platoon's usual rearward platoon position. The company is protected by a barbed wire entanglement and a 130-meter-long mixed minefield. Its southern flank is protected by a tank in ambush. The 2nd MRC straddles the road and deploys its 2nd and 3rd platoons forward. The 1st platoon is deployed in the battalion outpost position. The 1st platoon's normal place is held by a dummy platoon position. The enemy is expected to make its main attack along the road and into the 2nd MRC position. The 2nd MRC is protected by a 60-meter long two-row antitank obstacle of sunk heavy metal stakes and a 110-meter-long mixed minefield. The 3rd MRC is angled forward to give flanking shots on the main road. Its 1st and 3rd platoon defend forward. Its 2nd platoon is to the southeast of the battalion position serving as the anti-air assault reserve. A tank platoon occupies the rearward platoon position in the 3rd MRC company defense. The 3rd MRC company *bronnegruppa* initially defends forward of the 3rd MRC position. The 3rd MRC is protected by a barbed wire entanglement and an 80-meter-long mixed minefield while an ambush position protects its southern flank.

Supporting subunits back the three defending motorized rifle companies. The SA-18 or SA-25 MANPADS battery establishes mutually supporting air defense positions. The battalion *bronnegruppa*, automatic grenade launcher platoon, mortar battery and battalion headquarters are located where they can stop an attack through the 2nd MRC position. A 152mm howitzer battery has located forward and deployed in direct lay positions backing the 2nd MRC. Further back, the antitank reserve is split into two locations covering the anticipated primary and secondary enemy avenues of approach. The artillery battalion covers the area between the two antitank reserve positions where it can cover both enemy avenues of advance by direct fire if necessary.

The battalion normally defends in a wide single echelon, prepared to flow back intact to its subsequent positions. Its' reserve(s) is/are positioned to react in a variety of directions to transition to a defense, occupy a firing line or conduct a counterattack. In order to support the necessary independence of the subunits, most of the artillery and other firing systems are attached to companies. The firing systems are positioned where they can conduct the bulk of their fires to the front, beginning at their maximum range limits. Their positions fill the gaps between the neighboring company strong points, where, if necessary they can cover the withdrawal of first echelon companies, covering force subunits and others earlier located within the forward subunits. Artillery, tank, BMP, grenade launcher and other fires are planned on likely enemy avenues of approach, on gaps and on the flanks of the strongpoints and are organized into fire ambushes anchored on engineer obstacles and demolished points. The battalion commander may establish security in front of his forward position. This may include a reconnaissance patrol, engineer obstacles on likely avenues of advance and ambushes.[84]

The brigade may be part of a security zone. Then, the maneuver of the battalion to a new position may be on the command of the brigade commander or the battalion commander, his battalion now designated as a forward detachment in the security zone. If the brigade is part of a security zone, engineering obstacles will usually be sited on tank avenues of approach forward of platoon and company strong points. Mine fields are sited on regions of probable enemy deployment and on roads which are not covered by friendly fire. Road and railroad bridges are prepared for demolition. Artillery subunits may occupy temporary firing positions in the security zone or behind the forward position and as part of the main defensive belt. The security zone battle will unfold as discussed earlier in this article.[85]

Military exercises in the Central Military District in 2014 and the Far East Military District in 2015 highlighted the following key issues for motorized rifle battalion commanders conducting a maneuver defense: sequencing the destruction of the enemy starting from maximum range and preventing the enemy from rapidly transitioning to the attack; the possible direction of maneuver by fire and forces to prevent the enemy from flanking the battalion defensive area; sequencing breaking contact and withdrawal (including composition of the covering force and its subsequent withdrawal); the order in which to conduct the withdrawal of the maneuver subunits during the withdrawal to its subsequent

[84] Ibid, 30-31.
[85] Ibid, 31.

position; and the places to constitute fire sacs, lay obstacles and conduct demolitions.[86]

Maneuver Defense Conclusion

Ever since the Gulf War, ground forces have realized that unprotected maneuver in the open may lead to decimation. Less-modern ground forces have attempted to negate this by moving the fight to terrain that defeats or degrades high-precision systems-mountains, jungle, extensive forest, swamps and cities while conducting a long-term war of attrition to sap the political will of the enemy. This difficult terrain will be a valuable ally in future conventional maneuver war as will camouflage, electronic and aerial masking, effective air defense systems and secure messaging. Maneuver defense will clearly be a feature of future conventional maneuver war. One thing that may change dramatically is the fundamental concept of the main, linear, positional defense that the maneuver defense leads to. Perhaps the main linear defense will be anchored in difficult terrain. Perhaps the main defense will more closely resemble the security zone maneuver defense. The main defense may become an expanded security zone containing counterstrike/counterattack forces and a concentration of high-precision weapons systems. Open flanks may be covered by maneuvering artillery fires and positional forces not under duress. The Russian concept of maneuver by fire may dominate the battlefield as it alone may enable maneuver.

The linear battle field may be replaced by the fragmented [очаговый] battlefield where brigades maneuver like naval fleets, deploying maneuver and fire subunits over large areas, protected by air defense systems, electronic warfare and particulate smoke. Strong points will be established and abandoned, artillery fires will maneuver and difficult terrain will become the future fortresses and redoubts. The First World War in the West was a positional fight where artillery, field fortifications and interlocking machinegun fire prevented maneuver. The First World War in the East, however, was not positional, but fluid. The antithesis to the stalemate in the West was the tank. Yet the tank did not spell the end of the linear defense. During the Second World War, the tank enabled maneuver in some places, but in other places, difficult terrain and integrated defenses prevented maneuver and fires prevailed. The Korean War was about fires and not much maneuver. Vietnam was about the maneuver of the helicopter, but difficult terrain dominated the battlefield. The antitank guided missile and precision guided munitions currently threaten maneuver. Still, advances in fires, ECM, robotics and air defense may enable maneuver. The Serbian Army proved quite adept at hiding and surviving in difficult terrain during the 78-day Kosovo air war. What they lacked was a ground force to combat at the termination of the bombing.

The fragmented battlefield has become common following the Gulf War. The Soviet-Afghan War, the Angolan Civil War, the Chadian-Libyan Conflicts, the Battle of Mogadishu, Operation Enduring Freedom, most of Operation Iraqi Freedom, the Libyan Civil War, the Sudan conflicts, the Saudi Arabian-Yemen conflict—all have involved fragmented battlefields. How do peer forces fight conventional maneuver war on a fragmented battlefield? Permanent combined arms battalions appear to be an important component. For decades, the Soviets and Russians have struggled with fielding, training supporting and fighting a combined arms battalion with its own tanks, motorized rifle, artillery, antitank, and support subunits capable of fighting

---

[86] Ibid.

and sustaining independently over a large area. The Russian maneuver brigades now have one or two battalion tactical groups and are working to achieve four.[87] The Russians have a long history of conducting a fragmented defense on a fragmented battlefield. The Russian Civil War is replete with such examples.[88] During the Second World War, the Soviets fielded the largest Partisan Army in history. It conducted a fragmented offense and defense against a linear German force.[89] As Mark Twain noted, "history may not repeat itself, but it does rhyme."

[87] See Lester W. Grau, "Restructuring the Tactical Russian Army for Unconventional War", *Red Diamond*, February 2014.

[88] Ministry of Defense of the Russian Federation, "Очаговая Оборона" [Fragmented Defense], *Military Encyclopedia* [Военная Энциклопедия], Volume 6, Moscow: Voyenizdat, 2002, 214.

[89] Recommend *The Red Army Do-It-Yourself Nazi-Bashing Guerrilla Warfare Manual (The Partisan's Companion)*, Lester W. Grau and Michael Gress (editors), translation and commentary of the 1943 Soviet edition of the manual used to train Partisans to fight the Nazis. Philadelphia: Casemate, 2010.

Soviet/Russian Tactical Nuclear Planning and Future War

The Soviet Union tested its first atomic bomb on 29 August 1949. It was a 22 kiloton blast (the first US atomic bomb test on 16 July 1945, near Alamogordo, was a 20 kiloton blast). The next two Soviet atomic bomb tests were in September and October of 1951 and had blasts of 38.3 and 41.2 kilotons. In December 1953, the Soviets tested a 400 kiloton atomic bomb and a 1.7 megaton atomic bomb in November 1955. The nuclear race escalated into thermonuclear weapons and hydrogen bombs.[90] The initial weapons were strategic weapons developed for delivery by long-range bombers. However, over time, nuclear weapons designers were able to build smaller nuclear weapons that could be delivered by fighter-bombers, rockets and tube artillery. The Soviets built nuclear weapons of varying yields and classified them by yield.[91]

Russian Nuclear Yield Classifications

Very small	Up to one kiloton
Small	One to ten kilotons
Medium	Ten to one hundred kilotons
Powerful	One hundred kilotons to one megaton
Very Powerful	Over one megaton

According to training material, a nuclear shock wave travels 1000 meters in two seconds, 2000 meters in five seconds and 3000 meters in eight seconds. Its thermal radiation travels at 300,000 kilometers an hour and the time of exposure is dependent on the nuclear round's yield.[92]

The Effective Time of Exposure to Thermal Radiation by Weapon's Yield

Very small	Approximately 0.2 seconds
Small	One to two seconds
Medium	Two to five seconds
Powerful	Five to ten seconds
Very Powerful	Twenty to forty seconds

Tactical and operational-level nuclear munitions were introduced into the Soviet ground forces and Army Air Forces. They were delivered by aviation bombs, rockets (and later missiles) and tube artillery. The primary question was where these weapons can be used most effectively. At the tactical level, the primary concern was breaking through a prepared enemy defense.

The initial planning for tactical use of nuclear weapons involved their mass use to create a gap in the defense. Tank battalions and motorized rifle forces would then conduct a mounted attack through the gap and drive deep to exploit the strike. In effect, the nuclear strike was

[90] V. M. Temnov, Ministry of Defense of the Russian Federation, "Nuclear Weapons" [Ядерное Оружие], *Military Encyclopedia* [Военная Энциклопедня], Moscow: Voyenizdat, 2004, 548.
[91] B. A. Konyakhin and A. A. Nezhaiko, Ministry of Defense of the Russian Federation, "Nuclear Munitions" [Ядерные Боеприпасы], *Military Encyclopedia* [Военная Энциклопедня], Moscow: Voyenizdat, 2004, 550.
[92] Yu. A. Haumenko, "Preparation for Reserve Officers of the Ground Forces" [Подготовка Офицеров Запаса Сухопутных Войск], Moscow: Voyenizdat, 1989, 356-357.

the main attack. The graphic to the right is from the 1966 tactics manual. It shows a tank attack through a gap created by a belt of small nuclear weapons, followed by a belt of medium nuclear weapons and capped by a powerful nuclear weapon.[93] The T-54 and T-55 tanks of that day were fitted with a lead interior lining to mitigate somewhat the intense radiation this nuclear pounding would create. The infantry personnel carriers and trucks that would follow the tanks were not similarly shielded.

There was a problem. This many nuclear rounds would clearly create a hole in the defense, but getting through that hole could be a problem even for tracked vehicles. Fire, torn-up terrain, cratering, blowdown, rubble and airborne dust would complicate crossing the area with any kind of speed or formation and would greatly reduce visibility. Residual radiation would drastically shorten the combat life of the soldiers-particularly those following in personnel carriers and trucks. By 1984, the expected expenditure of nuclear rounds for blowing a hole in the enemy tactical main defense was reduced to one per breakthrough sector.[94]

Early Tactical Nuclear Employment

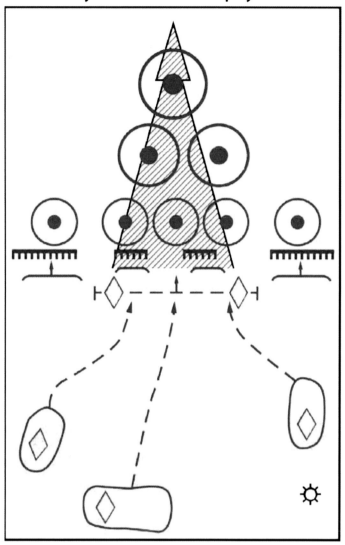

There is still a problem here. (facing page) The battalion is attacking on line through the blast area with dismounted troops. By 1988, the expected tactical use of nuclear rounds was against the second echelon or reserve. Conventional artillery would blow the hole through the main defense.[95] Of interest is that the Chernobyl disaster preceded this text by two years. The lesson is not to dismount and advance through a radiated blast area.

[93] V. G. Reznicheko, *Tactics* [Тактика], Officer's Library Series, Moscow: Voyenizdat, 1966, 79.
[94] V. G. Reznicheko, *Tactics* [Тактика], Officer's Library Series, Moscow: Voyenizdat, 1984, 273.
[95] N. P. Moiseenko, "The Motorized Rifle (Tank) Company in Combat: Training Textbook" [Мотострелковая (Танковая) Рота в Бою: Учебное Пособие], Moscow: Voyenizdat, 1988, 277.

Tactical Nuclear in Support of a Battalion in the Offense (1984)

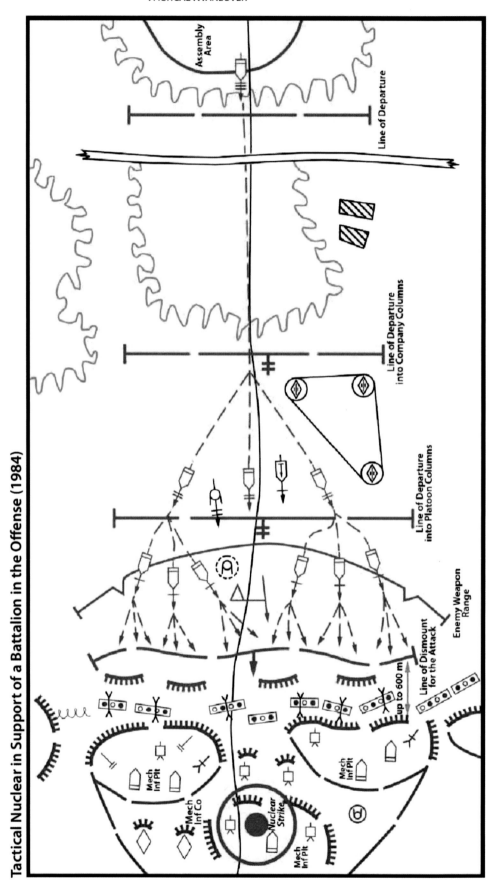

(Right) The graphic on the facing page depicts a nuclear round being used against the reserve of a defending mechanized infantry company. The tank battalion with an attached motorized rifle company on the attack is part of a larger offensive. The neighboring attacking battalion to the south is not shown completely, since the text focuses on the actions of the tank battalion. The battalion's subordinate companies are attacking mounted and skirting the blast area of the nuclear blast.

The Nuclear Dilemma

Early in the nuclear period, the assumption was that nuclear weapons would greatly increase operational tempo and that the conflict would soon be over as mechanized columns would rapidly advance through enemy defenses and seize capitals, economic areas, ports and harbors. However, the reality was somewhat different. In the European theater, the Soviets planned to use thousands of nuclear weapons to blast NATO forces as Warsaw Pact columns snaked their way to the English Channel.[96] The problem with this massive use of powerful nuclear weapons was that it would retard movement more than it would assist it. Forest fires, flooding, radiated zones, rubble and destroyed infrastructure could actually make a nuclear war advance much slower than a conventional fight. There had to be a better approach than laying waste to Europe, particularly since the prevailing winds blow back toward the Soviet bloc. The major problems encountered in mitigating the Chernobyl disaster in April 1986 added to the planners' dilemma. Nuclear weapons have a deterrent value as well as a fall back value when the fortunes of war are decidedly hostile.

Future War

How do nuclear weapons fit in with future war with peer competitors? Before the collapse of the Soviet Union, the General Staff's view of future war envisioned dynamic, high-tempo, high-intensity land-air operation that would extend over vast expanses and include new realms such as space. Tactical combat would be even more destructive than in the past and would be characterized by fragmented or non-linear combat. The front line would disappear and terms such as "zones of combat" would replace terms like FEBA and FLOT. No safe havens or "deep rear" would exist. Nuclear war must be avoided as it could lead to strategic exchange. The Soviets announced a "defensive orientation" during the initial period of war-a way to inflict severe losses on the enemy with fewer forces and create the conditions necessary for a counteroffensive. Qualitative improvements in firepower and mobility, coupled with operational surprise would allow a combatant to insert forces rapidly inside his opponents' territory while covering his own flanks with long-range fires. Aviation and long-range fires would attack reserves and support bases. High-precision weapons systems would take the place of nuclear systems.[97]

This view of future war was put on hold following the collapse of the Soviet Union and a weakened Russia renounced the "no first use of nuclear weapons" proviso in Russian defense. Nuclear weapons figured prominently in Russia exercises. However, Russian conventional military power is clearly now in ascendency in Eurasia and Russia is considering how to fight

[96] When the Soviets pulled out of East Germany, they left a lot of equipment and ammunition behind. They also left nuclear planning documents for possible war against NATO which depicted thousands of nuclear rounds expended in a two-phase operational nuclear strike.

[97] Lester W. Grau, "Soviet Nonlinear Combat in Future Conflict", *Military Review*, December 1990, 16-17.

Tactical Nuclear Strike on the Reserve (1988)

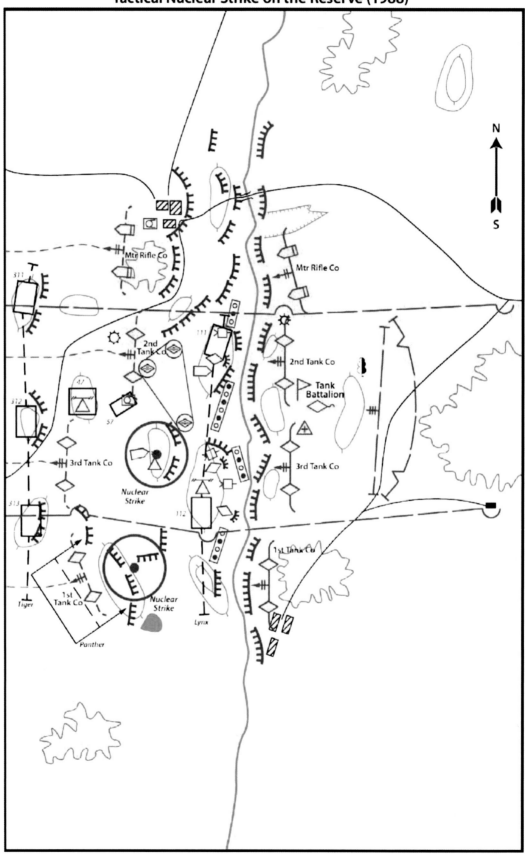

under nuclear-threatened conditions and win. Advances in technology, modernization of the force and a more mobile ground force support this effort. Russian nonlinear battle apparently sees separate tactically-independent battalions and brigades fighting meeting battles while covering their flanks with obstacles, long-range fires and tempo. There are no safe areas and combatants will suffer heavy attrition. Armies may influence the battle through employment of their reserves and long-range attack systems, but the outcome will be decided by the actions of battalion tactical groups and brigades fighting separately on multiple axes in support of a common plan and objective. Attacks against prepared defenses are undesirable and neither side will be able to tie in their flanks or prepare defenses in depth.[98] The new brigade and battalion tactical group structure fits this role.

The initial period of war is crucial in future war as initial actions can disrupt enemy attempts to establish a cohesive, coordinated defense and drive forces deep into enemy territory to conduct fragmented, nonlinear

Motorized Rifle Battalion Attacking in One Echelon

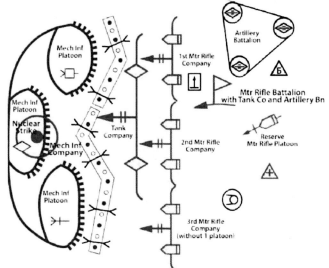

Motorized Rifle Battalion Attacking in Two Echelons

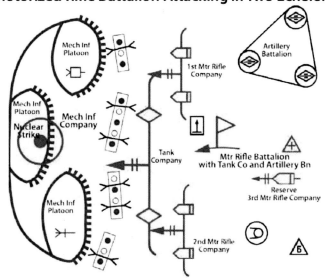

maneuver war. Defensive war may be part of future war and the Russians plan to conduct this with a combination of maneuver defense and positional defense. Maneuver defense is designed to trade space for time and weaken the enemy force while pulling it deep into the expanse of Mother Russia. As the enemy supply lines are overextended and the enemy momentum is slowed, the Russians plan to conduct a counterstroke to destroy the enemy within the depths of the country and then rapidly advance through the shattered enemy force into the enemy rear area. Multiple attacks on multiple axes will frustrate enemy attempts to stem the advance. Before an attack on one axis has culminated, the Russians plan to launch an attack on a different axis to wrong-foot the operational reserve.

Still, Russian force modernization includes a rigorous program to modernize and improve tactical, operational and strategic nuclear weapons. Clearly, the Russians see a need to retain

98 Ibid, 17.

an up-to-date nuclear force for an uncertain world. The Russians also see a need to train for nuclear war. NBC defense units are well-equipped and an integral part of maneuver brigades. Russian wargames and major field exercises frequently include nuclear strikes and their aftermath. Most US and NATO wargames and major field exercises terminate when nuclear strikes are introduced.

The Russians would prefer to fight under nuclear-threatened conditions, but not go nuclear due to the threat of escalation to strategic exchange. The Russians see two serious challenges to the current status quo and nuclear balance. The first is ballistic missile defense. In late 2001, the United States withdrew from the 1972 Anti-Ballistic Missile Treaty, stating that it needed to protect the US from nations that were developing long-range missiles and weapons of mass destruction (i.e. Iran). In 2007, as plans to install portions of the system in Europe were being discussed, Russia offered to cooperate by letting the US use its Gabala Radar Tracking Station in Azerbaijan. The US insisted that, due to technical and operational concerns, the best locale for combating Iranian launches was in Poland and the Czech Republic (later Romania). Russian saw this as an attempt to weaken the system of nuclear deterrence, since the MK-41 launch system used in the Aegis-Ashore system is also capable of launching Tomahawk cruise missiles against Russian ICBM sites.[99]

The second serious challenge is the US Prompt Global Strike Program (PGS). The US Air Force's Global Strike Command, headquartered in Barksdale AFB, was established in August 2009 with the mission of providing strategic nuclear deterrence and operational capability to carry out rapid precision conventional strikes. The Russians believe that PGS is designed to neutralize Russian military capabilities by eliminating their offensive and defensive strategic deterrent forces without using nuclear weapons. The result has been an expanded Russian program to hide and improve nuclear and nonnuclear strategic and operational systems.[100]

[99] Ibid.
[100] Ibid.

Chapter 6
Branches of Arms

Motorized Rifle Troops

Although I love the cavalry madly, although I am a horse soldier from my cradle, every time I watch the infantry advancing at a sure, firm pace, with fixed bayonets and menacing drum-roll, I feel an emotion which has something of both reverence and dread. I don't know how to express it. All that comes to mind at the sight of a formation of hussars or uhlans flying past is the thought of what gallant lads they are, how well they ride, how dashingly they cross sabers! Woe to the enemy, and this woe usually consists of more or less dangerous wounds or captivity, and nothing more. But when the columns of infantry rush toward the enemy with their rapid, smooth, disciplined motion, there are no more gallant lads, that's all over: these are heroes who bear inevitable death or go to inevitable death themselves—there is no middle ground. The cavalryman gallops up, gallops away, wounds, rushes past, turns back again, and sometimes kills. But his every motion is eloquent of mercy for the enemy: all this is merely the harbinger of death. But the infantry formation is death itself, dreaded inevitable death.

-Nadezhda Durova, <u>The Cavalry Maiden</u>, 1836

The Motorized Rifle Troops is the largest of the Branch of Arms in the Ground Forces, providing the foundation of the Ground Forces. In conjunction with Tank Troops, they perform the following tasks:

- <u>In the defense</u> – retain occupied areas, lines and positions, repulse the enemy's attacks and defeat its attacking groups
- <u>In the offense</u>– break through the enemy's defense, destroy enemy troop units, capture important areas, lines and objects, cross water obstacles, and pursue the retreating enemy
- <u>In meeting engagements and battles</u> – act as part of amphibious and airborne assaults and tactical landings.

The epitome of the Motorized Rifle Troops is represented by the motorized rifle brigades, with their high operational autonomy, versatility and firepower. They are able to conduct day/night combat under conventional and weapons of mass destruction conditions in different physical environments. They can quickly perform marches over long distances, rapidly deploy into combat formations, break through the enemy's defenses (prepared or hasty), conduct a broad variety of maneuver on the battlefield, develop the offensive rapidly and advance to significant depths, ford water barriers, strengthen and retain captured lines, and quickly transition to a stable defense.

In terms of modernization and capability development, the Motorized Rifle Troops will increase their capabilities for airlift deployment; conducting independent, high maneuver combat in remote areas; transitioning rapidly from one form of warfare to another; rapidly changing directions and areas of action; and rapidly concentrating and dispersing units.[1]

In general, each motorized rifle brigade has three motorized rifle battalions, based upon a BMP, BTR, or MT-LB chassis (in tank brigades, there is one motorized rifle battalion). Motorized rifle battalions based upon BTRs and MT-LBs are slightly larger than units based upon BMPs. These units are larger because they have dedicated antitank units, a capability battalions based upon BMPs do not require, because of the BMPs greater firepower. The accompanying

[1] "Motorized Rifle Troops," *Ministry of Defense of the Russian Federation* Website, <http://eng.mil.ru/en/structure/forces/ground/structure/motorised.htm>, accessed 1 May 2016.

Motorized Rifle Battalion (on BTRs)

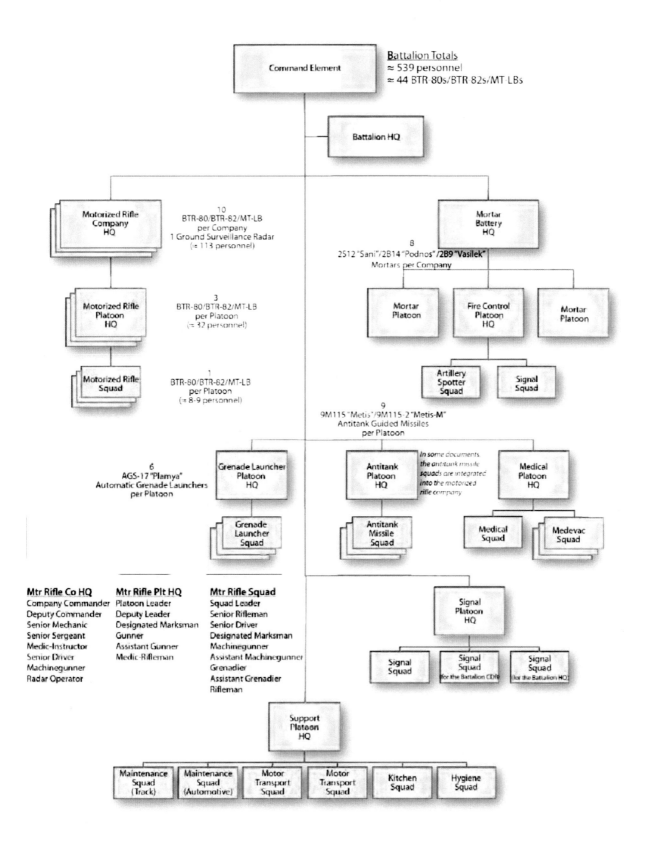

Battalion Totals
≈ 539 personnel
≈ 44 BTR-80s/BTR-82s/MT-LBs

Command Element

Battalion HQ

Motorized Rifle Company HQ

10 BTR-80/BTR-82/MT-LB per Company
1 Ground Surveillance Radar
(≈ 113 personnel)

Motorized Rifle Platoon HQ

3 BTR-80/BTR-82/MT-LB per Platoon
(≈ 32 personnel)

Motorized Rifle Squad

1 BTR-80/BTR-82/MT-LB per Platoon
(≈ 8-9 personnel)

Mortar Battery HQ

8 2S12 "Sani"/2B14 "Podnos"/2B9 "Vasilek"
Mortars per Company

Mortar Platoon

Fire Control Platoon HQ

Mortar Platoon

Artillery Spotter Squad

Signal Squad

9 9M115 "Metis"/9M115-2 "Metis-M"
Antitank Guided Missiles
per Platoon

6 AGS-17 "Plamya"
Automatic Grenade Launchers
per Platoon

Grenade Launcher Platoon HQ

Antitank Platoon HQ

In some documents, the antitank missile squads are integrated into the motorized rifle company

Medical Platoon HQ

Grenade Launcher Squad

Antitank Missile Squad

Medical Squad

Medevac Squad

Mtr Rifle Co HQ
Company Commander
Deputy Commander
Senior Mechanic
Senior Sergeant
Medic-Instructor
Senior Driver
Machinegunner
Radar Operator

Mtr Rifle Plt HQ
Platoon Leader
Deputy Leader
Designated Marksman
Gunner
Assistant Gunner
Medic-Rifleman

Mtr Rifle Squad
Squad Leader
Senior Rifleman
Senior Driver
Designated Marksman
Machinegunner
Assistant Machinegunner
Grenadier
Assistant Grenadier
Rifleman

Signal Platoon HQ

Signal Squad

Signal Squad (for the Battalion CDR)

Signal Squad (for the Battalion HQ)

Support Platoon HQ

Maintenance Squad (Track)

Maintenance Squad (Automotive)

Motor Transport Squad

Motor Transport Squad

Kitchen Squad

Hygiene Squad

Motorized Rifle Battalion (on BMPs)

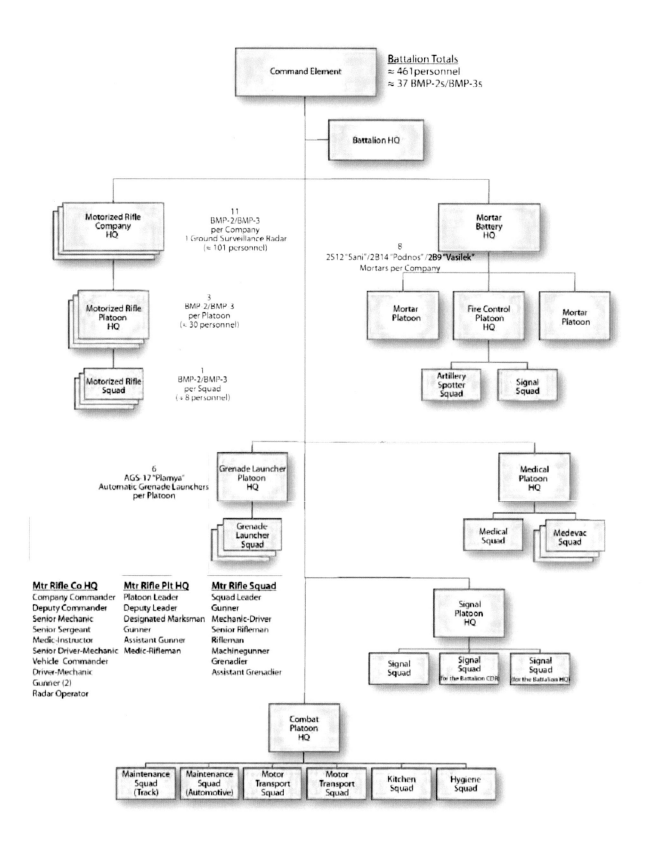

Battalion Totals
≈ 461 personnel
≈ 37 BMP-2s/BMP-3s

Mtr Rifle Co HQ
Company Commander
Deputy Commander
Senior Mechanic
Senior Sergeant
Medic-Instructor
Senior Driver-Mechanic
Vehicle Commander
Driver-Mechanic
Gunner (2)
Radar Operator

Mtr Rifle Plt HQ
Platoon Leader
Deputy Leader
Designated Marksman
Gunner
Assistant Gunner
Medic-Rifleman

Mtr Rifle Squad
Squad Leader
Gunner
Mechanic-Driver
Senior Rifleman
Rifleman
Machinegunner
Grenadier
Assistant Grenadier

graphics illustrate the differences between the two motorized rifle battalion types.

Russia is strong and respected when it has a strong, respected ground force and a strong, charismatic leader. Historically, Russian infantry has been the foundation of its ground force and has a long history of toughness, endurance and discipline. Modern Russian infantry is shaped by the concepts of reliable transport, tactical drills, terrain appreciation, and overmatching fire.

Reliable Transport
The vast Russian landmass has few high-capacity, all-weather roads and little year-round navigable terrain. Infantrymen are of little value if they are late to the battle, tired when they arrive, hungry and short of ammunition, unable to keep up with the tanks or committed piecemeal. During the 1930s, the Soviet Union realized the value of moving ground forces to the battlefield and having them arrive fit and provisioned to fight, but World War II broke out before it was able to implement its military motorization program fully. The Soviets were quick to grasp the value of the tank and the truck, which, coupled with the railroads and river barges, could move impressive combat power across the plains and marshes of Russia and beyond. Although during World War II Russian infantry rode on trucks and tanks when it could, most of Russian infantry was foot mobile and slow to mass and disperse. The Soviet Army began mounting its infantry on armored personnel carriers in the 1950s and succeeded in creating a 100% motorized ground force. This continues to this day. Even airborne, air assault, and special purpose (spetznaz) infantry are all mechanized forces. Airborne, riverine, amphibious and airmobile insertions include purpose-built infantry carriers, assault guns, artillery and transport. There is no light infantry in the Russian Army; it is all mechanized or motorized, in the Russian vernacular. In fact, in the Russian Army, Infantry is referred to as Motorized Rifle Troops and all these forces ride to combat in tracked or wheeled infantry fighting vehicles and armored personnel carriers.

Tactical Drills
The Russians expect motorized rifle subunits to perform to a standard and to produce a quantifiable amount of combat power that can produce a mathematical certainty of success when applied correctly. Too much combat power is a waste of effort and resources and too little is a guarantee of defeat. How does one train to a standard to produce a quantifiable amount of combat power? The answer is tactical drills. Football teams and SWAT teams use drills to speed up the orders process and to make complicated tasks quick and simple. Every U.S. Army infantryman knows how to do the four-man stack to enter a room. The Russian Ground Forces have a series of such tactical drills that they practice over and over and over until they become embedded muscle memory. The drill may be as simple as exiting a combat vehicle and going into an assault line. The continued practice of these drills makes them swift and smooth and gives the soldier something to focus on in the midst of the noise, confusion and terror of the battlefield. The drills replace thought when the soldier is cold, tired, hungry, and frightened, and perhaps is a reservist mobilized 15 years after his initial service.

The Russian commander is aided by these drills and a collection of tactical calculations and nomograms, which help him mathematically determine the length and duration of a march, the time it will take to cross a river, the time it will take to catch up to a retreating enemy, fuel consumption of a column, degree of destruction expected from an artillery strike, the optimum duration of fire before weapons should switch firing positions, and so on. These formulae and nomograms speed up planning and execution. They also add a tactical predictability (and rigidity) that provides operational flexibility. During World War II, German tactical units were more effective than comparable-sized Soviet (and US) units, but the Soviets were far more effective at the operational level and the Germans were never able to shift their operational reserve in time to block the Soviet penetration. The variety of battle drills available to the Russian commander allows sufficient flexibility to not disclose his game plan, while providing a quantifiable amount of combat power that can produce a mathematical certainty of success. The Russians use military history as operations research and have developed a mathematical system of comparing opposing forces and war-gaming courses of action. The study of the Correlation of Forces and Means determines the combat power of friendly and enemy weapons systems based on a selected Russian weapons system, which becomes the measurement standard. The system is assigned a value, and other similar friendly and enemy systems are rated against this measurement standard based on weapons, armor, on-board munitions, speed, range, and the like. Dissimilar systems (e.g., an infantry fighting vehicle versus the measurement-standard tank) are also compared and assigned values based on the standard measurement. These values are rolled into TO&Es to find the combat power of a unit. This is good as long as the fight is between equally-trained and experienced units fighting on a featureless plain. Variables ("K" values) are then entered to adjust the combat powers to reflect the terrain, the state of unit training, the number of days of combat experience that the unit has, maintenance standards, logistics support, the nationality and ideological/religious fervor of the soldiers, and whether the unit is fighting on its own or foreign soil. This system was developed during Soviet times and has been upgraded and revamped to take advantages of improved computer capabilities and the introduction of new weapons systems, improved electronic warfare (EW), and improved weaponry.

Terrain Appreciation
Much of the terrain on which Russia has fought its major wars is open plain, woodland and marshland intersected by large and small rivers. Maneuvering over this terrain has given the Russian commander a good eye for finding high ground and concealed avenues of approach. During World War II, German commanders frequently commented on the almost fanatical zeal that Russian forces displayed in order to seize a seemingly inconsequential piece of high ground. High ground is like a magnet to the Russian commander. This terrain has influenced Russian equipment design. Tanks and infantry fighting vehicles have much lower silhouettes than their Western counterparts. Tracks are much wider and vehicle clearance is much higher. Most vehicles are fitted with a self-recovery system. Most vehicles have an amphibious or fording capability. This terrain has also influenced Russian warfighting. Russian military history emphasizes large turning movements, highly mobile operations in the enemy depth, use of massed artillery fires in areas where the impacts cannot be observed to be adjusted, use of rivers as barriers and lines of communication and the use of winter for decisive actions.

SBR-3 Ground Surveillance Radar

Image Courtesy: Vitaly Kuzmin

213

Overmatching Fire

Americans enjoy the tradition of the frontiersman and his Kentucky rifle, who boasted of "one shot, one kill." Although marksmanship is a recognized sport in Russia, suppression of enemy small-arms fire is valued over accuracy. At the start of World War II, the Russian infantry was armed with the Model 1891, five-shot, 7.62mm Mosin-Nagant bolt-action rifle. It could kill at over 800 meters and was accurate to 500 meters. It could fire a maximum of ten rounds per minute (rpm). The problem was that the Germans brought the MG-34 7.92mm machine gun (800-900 rpm), the 9m MP-40 submachine gun (500-550 rpm) and the M1898, five-shot, 7.92mm Mauser bolt-action rifle (12 rpm) to the infantry fight. The rates of fire of the MG-34 and MP-40 kept the Soviet infantrymen's heads down while the M1898 picked them off. The Soviets needed to suppress the German rates of fire. Their answer was to develop and issue their own 7.62mm submachine guns, the PPD-40 and the PPSh-41. They could fire over 900 rpm, but were only accurate out to 100 meters. The Mosin-Nagants were pulled out of infantry units as the submachine guns became available. Now the Soviets had infantry weapons that could provide suppressive fire while they advanced close enough to kill the enemy. The problem was that if the enemy was over 100 meters away, the infantry could get badly hurt while trying to get into range. The Soviets began reissuing the Mosin-Nagants - this time with improved optics and an effective range of 1000 meters.

The Russians believe in suppressive fire. The famous Kalashnikov selector switch goes from safe to automatic to semiautomatic. Automatic is the preferred mode of fire. The US M16 selector switch goes from safe to semiautomatic to automatic, reflecting the US belief in marksmanship. Despite this, both armies fire thousands of small-arms rounds to inflict a single casualty. This Russian preference for suppressive fire extends to artillery, where massed artillery fires still hold a major place in maneuver warfare planning.

Small Arms Characteristics

	Makarov Pistol	AK-74 Automatic Rifle	RPK Machinegun	PKM Machinegun	RPG-7 Grenade Launcher	SPG-9 Recoilless Rifle	AGS-17 Grenade Launcher
Caliber (mm)	9	5.45	7.62	7.62	40	73	30
System Weight (kg)	.81	3.6	6.8	15.5	6.3	47	31
Max Effective Range (m)	50	500	1000	1500	300	1300	800
Rate of Fire (per min)	30	650	600	650	4-6	6	350-400
Initial Velocity (m/s)	315	900	745	825	300	700	185
Rounds per magazine	8	30	40; 75	100-200	3	6	29
Cartridge Weight (g)	10	10.2	16.2	21.8	2200	4400	350
Armor Penetration (mm)	—	—	—	—	260	400	—
Crew	—	—	—	—	2	4	2

Small Arms

AK-74 Automatic Rifle

Image Courtesy: Vitaly Kuzmin

The venerable AK-74 is available in quantity and will be the standard for years to come. Still, there is competition, as the AK-12, A-545 and AN-94 look to replace this 42-year-old weapon. The AK-74 is part of the Kalashnikov family of small arms. A lineal descendant of the 7.62X39mm AK-47 and AKM, the AK-74 joined the small bullet craze introduced by the Colt M-16 during the Vietnam War. The 5.45x39mm cartridge fires a lightweight, high velocity bullet at the rate of 600 rpm and is effective out to 500 meters, although the maximum range is over 3000 meters. It is not particularly accurate, but since its primary role is suppressive fire, it is suited to its role.

The RPK squad automatic weapon is a rugged veteran performer that has been around since the 1960s. It has a longer, heavier barrel than the standard Kalashnikov and fires the 7.62x39mm round effectively out to 1,000 meters. Squad engagements normally extend from 10 to 800 meters, so the RPK covers the gap between the suppressive fire of the AK-74 (effective to about 300 meters at burst rate) and the limits of normal

RPK Machinegun

Image Courtesy: http://www.defenselink.mil/

squad engagements. The Russians have also fielded an RPK-74, which fires the 5.45X39mm, which has the same improved range and accuracy of the RPK, but the effectiveness of the lighter bullet falls off significantly over 500 meters, so the older 10-pound RPK remains in active service.

PKP Machinegun

Image Courtesy: Vitaly Kuzmin

The PKP Pecheneg 7.62X54mm medium machine gun may be issued in lieu of the RPK squad automatic weapon. Like the RPK, it has a bipod, but it has an increased effective range of 1500 meters and a carrying weight of 18 pounds.

The RPG-7V2 is the most widely used anti-armor weapon in the world. Its ruggedness, simplicity, low cost, and effectiveness have kept it in the Russian motorized rifle squad and elsewhere since 1961. It has a HEAT, tandem HEAT, fragmentation and thermobaric round, with an effective range of 200 meters and a maximum range of 920 meters.

RPG-7 Grenade Launcher

Image Courtesy: U.S. Airforce

The round detonates at 920 meters - a feature that has even enabled it to be used as an air defense weapon.

The Dragunov SVD-63 is a semi-automatic sniper/designated marksman rifle that is chambered for 7.62x54mm ammunition and is found in the scout platoon. It was originally designed as a squad support weapon because the squad's long-range engagement ability was lost when submachine guns and assault rifles (which are designed for close-to-medium-range, rapid-fire combat) were issued as the primary infantry weapon. The Dragunov is accurate to 800 meters. The Soviet TO&E had a sniper per platoon, but the "sniper" was really a designated marksman. The scouts are also designated marksman. Russia has world-class snipers and world-class sniper weapons in the military and state security *spetsnaz*, internal security forces, river police and the new presidential guard. Some of their newer weapons are replacing the Dragunov in motorized rifle forces.

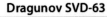
Dragunov SVD-63

Image Courtesy: Vitaly Kuzmin

Combat Gear and Load-Bearing Equipment

Dismounted troops carry too much weight. The Russians have introduced new load-bearing equipment and combat gear. The new combat gear (Ratnik) is an integration of protection, destruction, life support, and energy supply systems. Ratnik envisions the use of a total of more than 150 components. A variety of helmets and body armor, combat overalls, a headset with a hearing protection system, protective glasses, and a knee and elbow joint protection set are included. One can use a grenade launcher, an assault rifle, or a sniper rifle. Ammunition, a combat multifunction knife, standard reconnaissance instruments, small binoculars, a light signal flashlight, a shock-resistant and waterproof watch, winter and summer two-sided camouflage kits, and standardized optical and thermal-imaging gun sights supplement the new gear. There is also an autonomous heat source, assault pack, individual water filter, and lung protection, decontamination, and first aid equipment.

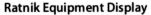
Ratnik Equipment Display

Image Courtesy: Vitaly Kuzmin

Soldier Wearing Ratnik Kit

Image Courtesy: Vitaly Kuzmin

Ground Troops Commander-in-Chief General Oleg Salyukov stated that the Ratnik (Warrior) system has reduced the weight of individual equipment by nearly 1.5 times, from 34 to 24 kilograms (75 pounds to 53 pounds). Furthermore, the effectiveness of the small arms that are part of Ratnik (the A545 assault rifle) has increased by 1.2 times. The designers have doubled the protection of the integrated body armor. However, perhaps the main thing is that they have managed to integrate the new combat gear's command and control system and communications systems with its other elements. This will permit soldiers to accomplish combat missions at any time of day and under various climactic conditions. Experts expect that the effectiveness of their actions will increase by at least 1.5-2 times.

Crew-Served Weapons

The AGS-17 automatic grenade launcher (Plamya) fires linked 30mm grenades from a tripod or vehicle mount to a maximum range of 1700 meters. The maximum effective range is 800 meters and it fires at the rate of 400 rpm (practical rate of fire is 50-100 rpm). It is used for direct and indirect fire and fires fragmentation and smoke rounds. It weighs a hefty 31 kilograms (68 pounds) and is being replaced by the AGS-30, which weighs 16 kilograms (35 pounds) and has a maximum range of 2100 meters.

AGS-17 Grenade Launcher

Image Courtesy: Vitaly Kuzmin

PKM Machinegun

Image Courtesy: Vitaly Kuzmin

The PKM machine gun fires the 7.62x54mm round at a rate of 600 rpm (250 practical rpm) to a distance of 3800 meters, with a maximum effective range of 1500 meters. It has a bipod and tripod mount. The weapon is found throughout the motorized rifle battalion. The vehicle mounted variant is the PKT.

The 9P151 antitank wire-guided missile launcher fires the 9M115 Metis (AT-7 Saxhorn) or the Metis-M 9M131(AT-13 Saxhorn-2) missile. It has an engagement range of 40-1000 meters and can engage targets traveling up to 37 miles per hour. It carries a HEAT warhead. The weapon is found in the motorized rifle antitank platoon.

9M115 Metis

Image Courtesy: Vitaly Kuzmin

Portable ATGM Characteristics

	9M111 "Fagot"	9M113 "Konkurs"	9M115 "Metis"	9M115-2 "Metis-M"	9M133 "Kornet"
NATO Designation	AT-4 Spigot	AT-5 Spandrel	AT-7 Saxhorn	AT-13 Saxhorn-2	AT-14 Spriggan
Caliber (mm)	120	135	93	130	152
Maximum Range (m)	2,000	4,000	1,000	2,000	5,500
Minimum Range (m)	70	70	40	80	UNK
Armor Penetration (mm)	400	600	460	1000	1300
Guidance System	SACLOS	SACLOS	SACLOS	SACLOS	SACLOS
Launcher Weight (kg)	22.5	22.5	10.2	10.5	26
Rocket Weight (kg)	11.5	14.6	6.3	13.8	29
Crew	2	2-3	2	3	UNK
Unit of Fire	8	UNK	8	UNK	UNK

BTRs and BMPs

Motorized riflemen ride into combat on the wheeled BTR-80 or BTR-82, the tracked BMP-3 or, in the northern latitudes, the MT-LB. The BTR-80 is an 8x8 wheeled amphibious armored personnel carrier, and is the most common chassis found in the Russian Ground Forces, entering service in 1986. It has a crew of two and carries a motorized rifle squad of eight. It has a turret-mounted KPVT 14.5x114mm heavy machine gun (.57 caliber) with a coaxial 7.62-

BTR-80

Image Courtesy: Vitaly Kuzmin

54mm PKT machine gun. The KPVT has a maximum effective range of 3000 meters and a range of 4000 meters. Seven firing ports enable the squad to fire from within the vehicle. It has a top speed of 50 mph and a combat radius of 375 miles. Some models mount the 30mm 2A72 automatic cannon, which fires the 30x165mm round to an effective range of 4000 meters. It fires HE-T and AP-T rounds up to 550 rpm. The infantry squad exits the BTR-80 through the roof hatches or from the two side doors. This arrangement has been criticized, since the squad is exposed to fire while dismounting, vice dismounting through (nonexistent) rear doors.

The BTR-82 is an upgraded version of the BTR-80. It was first fielded in 2011 and now can be found in the Russian Ground Forces, Naval Infantry, and Airborne. It is manufactured at the 81st Armored Vehicle Repair Plant in Armavir, Russia, and differs from the BTR-80 due to a 300-hp engine in place of the BTR-80's 260-hp engine, and a number of design features to protect the crew from mines and small-arms fire. The bottom of the vehicle is designed with a new two-level system for absorbing blasts, and all internal parts of the armored body are covered

BMP and BTR Characteristics

	BMP-2	BMP-3	BTR-80
System Weight (t)	14	18.7	13.6
Crew	3	3	2
Dismounts	7	7	8
Autocannon	2A42 30mm	2A70 100mm 2A72 30mm	—
Machinegun	PKT 7.62mm	PKT 7.62 (2)	PKT 7.62mm KPV 14.5mm
ATGM	9M111 "Fagot"	9M117 "Bastion"	—
Land Speed (kph)	68	70	90
Water Speed (kph)	7	10	10
Maximum Range (km)	600	600	600
Horsepower	402	494	256

by a special spall liner to provide better protection from shrapnel and other projectiles. These modifications reportedly give the BTR-82 a twenty percent higher survival rate than the BTR-80.

BTR-82A

Versions of the BTR-82 are equipped with air conditioning, digitally-encrypted R-168 radios, and the Trona-1 topographic navigation system. Although Russia will field the new wheeled "Bumerang" BTR in the next few years, the BTR-82 will likely still be in production for the foreseeable future, as its designation refers to not only newly produced vehicles, but also BTR-80s that have been upgraded to the BTR-82

Image Courtesy: Vitaly Kuzmin

standard. (The BTR-82 is also finding success on the export market; versions of it can be found in found in the armies of Azerbaijan, Kazakhstan, and Syria.) Common variants of the

Бронетранспортер (БТР)

Armored Personnel Carrier (BTR)

BTR-82 include the BTR-82A, armed with a 30-mm cannon and coaxial 7.62-mm machine gun; the BTR-82AM, designation of a BTR-80 after upgrade to the BTR-82A standard; the BTR-82A1, equipped with an unmanned turret that has a 30-mm cannon and coaxial 7.62-mm machine gun; and the Taifun-M reconnaissance vehicle, developed as an escort vehicle for intercontinental ballistic missile launchers. Russian efforts to build and/or modernize the BTR-82/BTR-80 line, while simultaneously fielding a new system (the "Bumerang" BTR), parallel Russia's modernization of the T-72 line of tanks while fielding the T-14 tank. Russia sees no need to completely change out its inventory of older vehicles, and instead has adopted a hybrid approach towards modernization. The Russian Armed Forces have chosen to approach institutional modernization by modernizing older platforms, while simultaneously fielding new platforms. This practice allows them to significantly enhance their combat power through wide-scale modernization, while developing new technologies at a sustainable cost. This approach is far from perfect, but it appears to be a long standing practice, instituted well before the time of current financial difficulties.[2]

MT-LB

Image Courtesy: Vitaly Kuzmin

The MT-LB was originally designed as an armored, amphibious artillery tractor. It has excellent marsh and snow mobility and has become a motorized rifle carrier (BTR), particularly for brigades in the northern latitudes. It has a crew of 2 and can carry up to 11 passengers. The squad mounts and dismounts through two rear doors. Some MT-LB carry the 12.7x108mm (.50 caliber) NSVT heavy machine gun, which has a rate of fire of 780 rpm and a maximum effective range of 1500 meters.

BMP-3

Image Courtesy: Vitaly Kuzmin

The BMP-3 is an amphibious, tracked infantry fighting vehicle that is fitted with a low-velocity 2A70 100 mm rifled gun, which can fire conventional shells or 9M117 ATGMs (AT-10 Stabber). It also has a 2A72 30 mm dual feed and a 7.62mm PKT machine gun. These are all mounted coaxially in the turret. There are also two 7.62mm PKM bow machine guns. The BMP-3 is capable of engaging targets out to 5000–6000 meters with its ATGM weapon system 9K116-3 "Basnya." The BMP-3 has a crew of three and carries a motorized rifle squad of seven. The squad dismounts out of the vehicle rear doors. It has a top speed of 45 mph and a combat radius of 370 miles.

Боевая машина пехоты (БМП)

Infantry Fighting Vehicle (BMP)

---

[2] Charles K. Bartles, "The BTR-82 and the Implementation of Modernization," *OE Watch* Online, August 2016. "BTR-82: Armored personnel carrier" as found on the website *Military-Today* <http://www.military-today.com/apc/btr_82.htm>, accessed 1 May 2016.
Igor Melnikov, "Military Motor Transport Operator Day" *Voyennyy Vestnik*, 24 May 2014.
"Baltic Fleet Naval Infantry is Mastering the New BTR-82A Armored Personnel Carrier," *Ministry of Defense of the Russian Federation*, 11 June 2013, <http://structure.mil.ru/structure/okruga/west/news/more.htm?id=11773465@egNews>, accessed 1 May 2016.

Modernization and Modularity

In Western Armies, the term "motorized" refers to wheeled vehicles and units, while "mechanized" refers to tracked vehicles and units. In the Russian Army, "motorized rifle" refers to any infantry unit mounted on tracked or wheeled vehicles. Russia's modernization and standardization efforts have included the creation of not only the Armata tracked heavy chassis, but also the Kurganets-25 tracked utility chassis and the Bumerang wheeled chassis. Interestingly, these three chassis types, made by three different manufactures, are all designed to accept the same turret, the "universal combat module" known

New Russian BTRs with "Epoch" Module

Images Courtesy: Russian Ministry of Defense

"Epoch" Universal Module

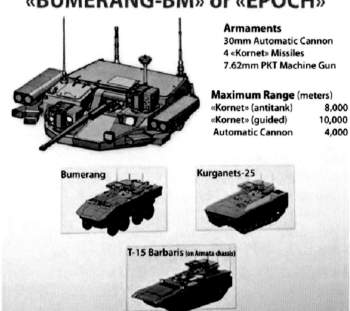

at the "Epoch" or "Bumerang-BM," made by a fourth company. (The universal combat module consists of a 30mm automatic cannon, four "Kornet" antitank missiles, and a 7.62mm PKT machine gun.)

This level of interoperability is unheard of in Western defense industries, where proprietary technology and financial considerations would make the pursuit of such an effort difficult. The imposition of such a standard must have been implemented several years ago, as some reports have implied the BTR-82A (armored personnel carrier) and BMD-4 (infantry fighting vehicle for the Airborne) have already entered service, and may also be capable of mounting the "universal combat module." Russia has put great stock in the concepts of interoperability and modularity. Russian media have reported that the "Armata" chassis (and likely the other two as well) will serve Russia throughout the 21st century. Russia appears to believe that although the chassis may be suitable throughout the 21st century, the weapons systems which it carries will not. After these three chassis are fielded, Russia will likely

221

pursue capability improvements through upgrading the turrets for the foreseeable future (not by the purchase of completely new vehicles). Other more novel innovations involve giving the Kurganets-25 vehicles a Sony PlayStation-like controller for steering to ease driver training and facilitate future automation. Aside from the obvious cost savings due to the economies of scale and the ability to relatively quickly repurpose equipment as needed, this development will also likely spur innovation. Weapons manufactures will now only have to design for one turret specification, which could lead to significant cost savings. This could be especially significant if these chassis enter the export market, as they likely will. The Russian military and Russia's export customers will be able to "plug-n-play" a variety of capabilities, based upon turret design, with their particular desired chassis type. Perhaps one of the most interesting implications of these universal chassis and turret specifications is that manned vehicle turrets may be a thing of the past, and the terms "infantry fighting vehicle" (IFV or BMP) and "armored personnel carrier" (APC or BTR) may become unimportant when describing these vehicles, as the only difference is the turret type.[3]

Barrel-Launched ATGM Characteristics

	9K116 "Kastet"	9K116-1 "Bastion"	9K116-2 "Sheksna"	9K116-3 "Basnya"	9K119 "Svir"	9K119M "Refleks"
NATO Designation	AT-10 Stabber	AT-10 Stabber	AT-12 Swinger	AT-10 Stabber	AT-11 Sniper	AT-11 Sniper-B
Caliber (mm)	100	100	115	100	125	125
Penetration (mm)	500-550	500-550	500-550	500-550	900	900
Range (m)	5,500	5,500	5,500	5,500	5,000	5,000
Guidance	Laser	Laser	Laser	Laser	Laser	Laser
Platform	MT-12	T-55	T-62	BMP-3	T-72B/T-72S/ 2A45 Sprut	T-80B/T-80U/ T-90/T-72B3

*The 9K119M "Refleks" ATGM system may fire missiles designed for the 9K119 "Svir," but not vice versa

T-90SM   T-80U

Images Courtesy: Vitaly Kuzmin

[3] Charles K. Bartles, "Modularity Facilitates Russian Armored Vehicle Innovations," *OE Watch* Online, October 2015. "BTR 'Kurganets-25': The Little Brother of the New Infantry Fighting Vehicle," *Interpolit* Online, 9 September 2015, <http://interpolit.ru/blog/btr_kurganec_25_mladshij_brat_novoj_boevoj_mashiny_pekhoty/2015-09-12-5605>, accessed 1 May 2016.
Yuriy Belousov, "Only an Armata is More Awesome than an Armata," 3 July 2015,
Krasnaya Zvezda Online, in Russian 03 July 2015, <http://redstar.ru/index.php/newspaper/item/24718-kruche-armaty-tolko-armata>, accessed 20 September 2015.

Tank Troops

Tank Troops are a Branch of Arms, and the main strike force of the Russian Ground Forces. They are used in conjunction with the motorized rifle units and perform the following tasks:

- <u>In the defense</u> – direct support of the motorized rifle units in repelling the enemy's offensive and the conduct of counterattacks and counterstrikes
- <u>In the offence</u> – deep strikes, development of success, and defeat of the enemy in meeting engagements and battles.

Tank Characteristics

	T-72B	T-72B3	T-80U	T-90
System Weight (t)	41	45	46	46.5
Crew	3	3	3	3
Main Gun (mm)	125	125	125	125
Main Gun Ammo Load	39	45	45	43
Machinegun	PKT 7.62mm KPV 14.5mm	PKT 7.62mm KPV 14.5mm	PKT 7.62mm KPV 14.5mm	PKT 7.62mm KPV 14.5mm
ATGM	9M119 "Svir" (AT-11 Sniper)	9M119 "Svir" or 9M119M "Refleks"	9M119 "Svir" or 9M119M "Refleks"	9M119M "Refleks" (AT-11 Sniper-B)
Land Speed (kph)	60	70	70	60
Maximum Range (km)	500	500	335	550
Horsepower	840	1140	1250	840

Russian Tank Troops are found in tank brigades and divisions, and in the tank battalions of motorized rifle brigades. Armor units are resistant to the effects of nuclear weapons, provide good firepower and protection, and have high mobility and maneuverability. Russian armor capabilities enable them to lead active combat operations, day and night, independent of other elements. They can also overcome NBC-contaminated areas and surmount water barriers, and are able to quickly form a solid defense to successfully resist enemy attacks. In terms of modernization and capability development, Russia is improving organizational issues by continuing the development of combined arms doctrine using armor, enhancing the firepower, protection, and maneuver capabilities of existing weapons platforms (primarily T-72), and developing new systems.[4] It is important to note that Russians

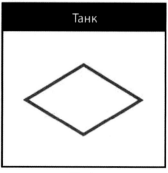

Танк

Tank

[4] "Tank Troops," *Ministry of Defense of the Russian Federation* Website, <http://eng.mil.ru/en/structure/forces/ground/structure/tank.htm>, accessed 1 May 2016.

Tank Battalion

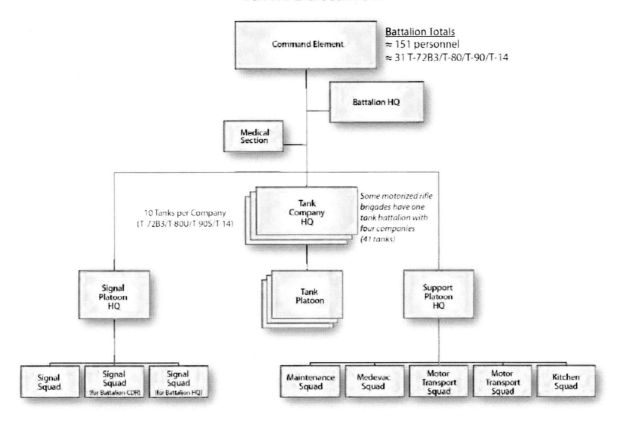

Battalion Totals
≈ 151 personnel
≈ 31 T-72B3/T-80/T-90/T-14

do not view future war solely as counterinsurgency, counterterrorism and area control, but also consider high-intensity maneuver warfare as an equally likely form of future war. Despite economic difficulties since the collapse of the Soviet Union, the Russians have developed three new tanks and are fielding two (T-90 and T-14). In terms of the maneuver brigades, there is one tank battalion (31 tanks) in each motorized rifle brigade, and three tank battalions in each tank brigade. Some motorized rifle brigades have one tank battalion with four companies (41 tanks).

The Armata Chassis and T-14 Tank

Russia has been experimenting with a common heavy tracked chassis for tanks, armored personnel carriers, infantry fighting vehicles, and other tracked vehicles standard in the Russian Ground Forces TO&E. The Russian Ground Forces took its first deliveries of T-14 tanks and T-15 heavy BMPs (mounted on the Armata chassis) early in 2015, and there have been unsubstantiated claims that the Armata entered serial production in March 2016.[5] If the Armata chassis proves successful,

T-14

Image Courtesy: Vitaly Kuzmin

[5] "Tanks A Lot: Russia's Advanced Armata T-14 'Already in Serial Production,'" *Sputnik* Online, 14 March 2016,

T-14

Image Courtesy: Vitaly Kuzmin

it could become the basis of many other Russian vehicle types.[6] Russia is considering the following Armata based variants:

- T-14 Tank
- BMP-T (T-15) infantry fighting vehicle
- BREM-T recovery vehicle
- USM-A1 general-purpose mine-laying system
- 2S35 Koalitsiya-S 152-mm self-propelled howitzer
- BMO-2 transport vehicle for shoulder -fired rocket-propelled flamethrower operators
- TOS BM-2 launch vehicle in a system for heavy rocket-propelled flamethrowers
- TZM-2 support vehicle in a system for heavy rocket-propelled flamethrowers
- MIM-A multipurpose engineer vehicle
- MT-A armored bridge layer
- UMZ-A general-purpose minelayer and obstacle clearer
- SPM special firefighting vehicle
- PTS-A amphibious transport vehicle.

<http://sputniknews.com/russia/20160314/1036238101/russia-armata-production.html>, accessed 20 March 2015.

[6] Charles K. Bartles, "Russia Considers Standardized Chassis for Most Tracked Vehicles," *OE Watch* Online, March 2015.

"Uralvagonzavod to deliver 20 new tanks and heavy infantry fighting vehicles in Feb-March," 28 January 2015, <http://www.interfax.com/>, accessed 1 May 2016.

Aleksandr Kurennoy and Aleksey Naryshkin: "Vyacheslav Khalitov, Deputy Director of the Uralvagonzavod Science and Production Corporation Open Joint-Stock Company for Specialized Technology," transcript of *Arsenal* radio program posted on *Ekho Moskvy* Online, 26 January 2015, <http://m.echo.msk.ru/interview/detail.php?ID=1480668>, accessed 1 May 2016.

The Russian Armed Forces consider the T-14 tank, a medium tank, as it weighs approximately 50 tons, but it has a chassis that supports approximately 65 tons, likely to allow for future modifications. The road wheels are reportedly based upon the T-80 tank. They were used because they were significantly lighter than the T-72 wheels (120 kilograms vs. 194 kilograms, resulting in an approximately one-ton savings in weight). The T-14 tank will be equipped with an adjustable suspension capable of adapting to varying relief, terrain type, and vehicle speed, resulting in increased speed while moving in columns, as well as over rugged terrain. The suspension system will also alleviate crew fatigue, while assisting the fire control system to deliver accurate fire while on the move. Unlike previous Soviet/Russian vehicles, crew safety (survivability) and comfort appear to be a concern. The crew is in an armored capsule that is somewhat roomy, compared to other Soviet/Russian tanks. The composite multilayered passive armor protection

Tank Gun Characteristics

	L/55 Rheinmetall	2A82-1M	2A83
Caliber (mm)	120	125	152
Tube Length (calibers)	55	56	52
Tube Length (mm)	6,250	7,000	7,200
Weight (kg)	3,200	2,700	>5,000
Tube Pressure (atm)	7,000	—	7,700
Muzzle Energy (mj)	12.7	15.24	>20
Muzzle Velocity (m/s)	1,700	—	1,980
Effective Range (m)	4,000	4,700	5,100
Sabot Penetration (mm)	800	1,000	1,100
ATGM Penetration (mm)	800	950	1,400
Effective ATGM Range (m)	8,000	8,000	20,000
Rate Of Fire (rounds/min)	6-8	12	15
Ammo Load	42	45	40
Auto Loader	No	Yes	Yes

of the T-14 tank is built with steel made by electroslag remelting and is combined with new composites to protect it against the most advanced modern weaponry. It also has the Afganit active protection complex, capable of intercepting shaped-charged grenades, antitank missiles, and subcaliber projectiles.

The tank's main armament is the 2A82-1M 125mm smoothbore cannon, capable of firing high-powered munitions, including armor-piercing discarding sabot, guided missile, and shaped-charge, as well as other types. There are also plans to equip versions of the T-14 with the 2A83 152mm gun. This gun can fire a heavier projectile that has greater range, and is more powerful in terms of explosive and kinetic energy; and allows the firing of a larger barrel launched antitank guided missile (ATGM), which most modern Russian tanks and infantry fighting vehicles (BMPs) can fire.[7] The T-14 is equipped with the Chelyabinsk A-85-3A X-diesel engine capable of producing up to 1500 hp. The tank also has a Tank Information Control System (TICS), which monitors all assemblies and components, diagnoses malfunctions, and controls onboard systems, andwill receive a new protection system.[8] One interesting

[7] Vladimir Tuchkov, "The Armata Penetrates One and a Half Meters of Armor," *Svobodnaya Pressa* Online, 24 November 2016, <http://svpressa.ru/war21/article/161227/>, accessed 19 December 2016.
[8] Charles K. Bartles, "Technical Specifications of Russia's T-14, 'Armata' Chassied Tank," *OE Watch* Online, March 2015.
"Can't Touch This! Russian Armata Tanks to Get New Active Protection System," *Sputnik* Online, 15 March 2016, <http://sputniknews.com/military/20160315/1036302986/armata-active-protection-system.html>, accessed 1 May 2016.
Sergey Ptichkin, "The Tank Maintains a Circular Defense: New T-14 Tank will Become the Sensation of the Year," *Rossiyskaya Gazeta* Online, 03 February 2015, <http://www.rg.ru/2015/02/02/tank.html>, accessed 1 May 2016.

Tank Characteristics Comparison

	T-72	T-72B3	T-90
Entered service	1973	2013	1993
Crew	3 men	3 men	3 men
Dimensions and weight			
Weight	41 t	~ 45 t	46.5 t
Length (gun forward)	9.53 m	9.53 m	9.53 m
Hull length	6.86 m	6.86 m	6.86 m
Width	3.46 m	3.46 m	3.46 m
Height	2.19 m	2.2 m	2.23 m
Armament			
Main gun	125-mm smoothbore	125-mm smoothbore	125-mm smoothbore
ATGW		9M119 Svir or 9M119M Refleks	9K119M (AT-11 Sniper-B)
Machine guns	1 x 7.62-mm, 1 x 12.7-mm	1 x 7.62-mm, 1 x 12.7-mm	1 x 7.62-mm, 1 x 12.7-mm
Elevation range	- 5 to + 14 degrees	- 5 to + 14 degrees	- 6 to + 14 degrees
Traverse range	360 degrees	360 degrees	360 degrees
Ammunition load			
Main gun	39 rounds	45 rounds	43 rounds
Machine guns	2 000 x 7.62, 300 x 12.7	2 000 x 7.62, 300 x 12.7	2 000 x 7.62, 300 x 12.7
Mobility			
Engine	V-46 diesel	V-92S2F diesel	V-84MS diesel engine
Engine power	780 hp	1130 hp	840 hp
Maximum road speed	60 km/h	~ 70 km/h	60 km/h
Range	500 km	~ 500 km	550 km
Maneuverability			
Gradient	60%	60%	60%
Side slope	40%	40%	40%
Vertical step	0.85 m	0.85 m	0.8 m
Trench	2.8 m	2.8 m	2.85 m
Fording	1.2 m	1.2 m	1.2 m
Fording (with preparation)	5 m	5 m	5 m

http://www.military-today.com/

development is that plans to affix a tethered UAV to the T-14 tank. Due to the T-14's main gun having a range of up to 8km, but only a sighting capability of up to 5km, the advantages of the T-14 are not fully realized. A tethered drone would provide a field of view of up to 10km, and would allow the tank to sit in covered positions while surveying the battlefield. This line of development is in sync with other Russian developments to provide improved and decentralized C4ISR assets. These UAVs are also likely intended to be networked together to augment the "netcentric" warfare concept that the Russian Armed Forces are pursuing.[9] Russia plans on attaining 2,300 vehicles on Armata chassis by 2025, a prospect that seems unlikely considering past procurement endeavors and the state of the Russian economy.[10]

Modernization of the T-72

Although there has been much hype about the introduction of the Russian T-14 tank, the bulk of Russia's armored power will still reside in the T-72 series of tanks.[11] This means that when considering the Russian Ground Forces' combat power, one should primarily focus on modernized T-72s, not T-14s, for the foreseeable future. Although Russia is adopting the T-14, at no time has it stated the desire to completely

T-72B3M

Image Courtesy: Vitaly Kuzmin

[9] Aleksey Moiseyev, "They Will Equip the Armata with a Reconnaissance Drone," *Izvestiya* Online, 18 November 2016, <http://izvestia.ru/news/645502>, accessed 19 December 2016.

[10] Sergey Ishchenko, "Assault Tanks Will Support the Armata," *Svobodnaya Pressa* Online, 15 December 2016, <http://svpressa.ru/war21/article/162629/>, accessed 27 December 2016.

[11] Russia does have T-80s and T-90s in its inventory, but the vast majority of Russian tanks are T-72s.

replace its tank fleet with T-14s, and there have been pronouncements that the T-14s would only be found in the 1st Tank Army and the 20th Combined Arms Army. Although the T-72 will still be the backbone of most Russian maneuver formations. Current Russian T-72s are much different than the ones that rolled of the assembly lines when the system was first produced in the early 1970s. Russia has embarked on a massive modernization program for the venerable T-72 that involves a frame-off refurbishment of the chassis and the additions of new cannons, engines, machine guns, optics, stabilization systems, reactive armor, and electronics. After this modernization the T-72 is redesignated a "T-72B3," and is essentially a new tank. In terms of characteristics, the T-72B3 has much more in common with the T-90 than with older T-72s, and it is almost certain that that many T-72s can be refurbished for the price of one T-14.[12] The Russian media reported that Russia had upgraded approximately 1,000 T-72Bs to the T-72B3 standard, and there are plans to upgrade 300 more.[13]

Tank Combat Support Vehicle (BMPT)

Russians consider tanks essential to warfighting, but in order for tanks to dominate the future battlefield, they must survive. One idea is that the BMPT Terminator could be reborn, but this time on an Armata chassis.[14] Despite the closeness of the acronyms, the BMPT is not classified by Russia as an Infantry Fighting Vehicle (BMP), but instead as a Tank Combat Support Vehicle (BMPT) [боевая машина поддержки танков (БМПТ)]; it is also sometimes referred to as a Combat Fire Support Vehicle (BMOP) [боевая машина огневой поддержки (БМОП)].[15] The concept of a Tank Combat Support Vehicle is not a new one in the Soviet/Russian experience.

In theory, mechanized infantry, self-propelled artillery, and armored forces are mutually supporting. Artillery rains destruction onto the front and flanks as infantry personnel carriers and dismounted infantry protect tanks from enemy antitank systems and enemy infantry. Simultaneously, tanks protect the personnel carriers and dismounted infantry from enemy tanks and strong points. In practice, personnel carriers have problems keeping up with

[12] Charles K. Bartles, "More Bang for the Buck: The Modernized T-72," *OEWatch* Online, February 2016.
"Oldies but Goodies: Upgraded 'Invulnerable' T-72 Tanks Join Russian Army," *Sputnik* Online, 20 December 2015, <http://sputniknews.com/russia/20151220/1032041217/russia-tanks-upgrades.html>, accessed 15 January 2015.
Oleg Valentinov, "With Tank Through Life: Servicing of Arms and Military Equipment Remains A Big Problem," *Voyenno-Promyshlennyy Kuryer* Online, 28 October 2015, <http://www.vpk-news.ru/articles/27722>, accessed 1 May 2016.

Dave Majumdar, "Russia's Cold War T-72 Tank Set for a Big Upgrade," *The National Interest*, 31 March 31, 2016, <http://www.realcleardefense.com/2016/03/31/russia039s_cold_war_t-72_tank_set_for_a_big_upgrade_280588.html>, accessed 1 May 2016.
[13] "On the Order of a Thousand T-72B3 Tanks have been Modernized by 'Ulralvagonzavod,'" *RIA Novosti* Online, 9 September 2016, <https://ria.ru/defense_safety/20160908/1476388731.html>, accessed 1 October 2016.
"The Armed Forces Will Receive More than 300 Modernized T-72B3 Tanks," RIA Novosti Online, 9 September 2016, <https://ria.ru/defense_safety/20160909/1476498530.html>, accessed 1 October 2016.
[14] Expert "Alexei Xlotov: The Syrian War, The BMPT [Tank Combat Support Vehicle] and BAM [Combat Artillery Vehicle] on the Armata Chassis," *MyInforms* Online, 2 April 2016, http://myinforms.com/ru-ru/a/16171669-ehkspert-aleksejj-khlopotov-o-sirijjskojj-vojjne-bmpt-i-bam-na-baze-platformy-armata/, accessed 1 May 2016.
"Russia Unveils 'Terminator-2' Tank Support Vehicle" *Sputnik News* Online, 25 September 2013, <http://sputniknews.com/military/20130925/183720985.html>, accessed 10 April 2015.
[15] Lev Romanov, "Recall the 'Terminator,'" *Oborona*, March 2015, <http://www.oborona.ru/includes/periodics/armament/2015/0216/180015213/detail.shtml>, accessed 1 May 2016.

fast-moving tanks, their armor protection is too thin to survive at the point of the attack, and battle drills between tanks and mechanized infantry frequently break down due to the lack of sufficient team training prior to combat. Artillery fire may be on or off target, or too early or too late. The bottom line is that there is often too great a gap between the tanks and the mechanized infantry at the crucial point, and artillery may not bridge that gap.[16]

Despite the impressive technology and tactics, tanks still tended to separate from BMPs and artillery during the advance. The 1973 Arab-Israeli War proved the value of the RPG and antitank guided missile (ATGM) to the defender. Tanks had to fight as a combined arms team to survive, but could not afford to slow down and lose the momentum of the attack. The answer appeared to be better combined arms training. In the late 1980s, the Soviets began forming combined arms battalions, which had organic tanks, BMPs, and artillery. The

Tank Combat Support Vehicle (BMPT) "Terminator-2"

Image Courtesy: Vitaly Kuzmin

combined arms battalion allowed units to train for mutual support continuously, instead of only during scheduled exercises. However, the combined arms battalion required seasoned commanders who could deal with the training, supply, and maintenance demands of this complex unit. Soviet junior officers were usually younger and less experienced than their Western counterparts when they commanded at various levels, although they tended to command longer during a career. The combined arms battalion experiment initially failed due to its complexity, internal turmoil in the army, and leadership challenges, but is now a well established institution in the Russian Armed Forces, being the most common formation type battling in Eastern Ukraine.

The proliferation of rocket-propelled grenade RPG-7 antitank grenade launchers and antitank missiles has complicated the task of tanks and mechanized infantry working together. The Soviet-Afghan War and the Chechen Wars emphasized the tactical gap for the Soviets and the Russians. The enemy was not modern, nor mechanized, nor arrayed in a defense in-depth. His RPG gunners knew where the soft spots were on the various Soviet/Russian vehicles.[17] The terrain worsened the problem of the tactical gap and, in the areas where the tanks could go, tanks and BMPs were often separated and unable to support each other. In the mountains of Afghanistan, tanks were often left behind and BMPs, and BTRs had to accomplish an independent mission they were not designed for. The Russians decided that the tactical gap between tanks and mechanized infantry is almost inevitable. The battle of Grozny on New Year's Eve 1994 provided the impetus to develop a heavily armored close combat system. The Russians discovered that the thinly armored ZSU 23-4 self-propelled antiaircraft gun was the

[16] Lester W. Grau, "Preserving Shock Action: A New Approach to Armored Maneuver Warfare," *Armor*, September-October 2006, < http://fmso.leavenworth.army.mil/documents/Preserving%20Shock%20action.pdf>, accessed 10 April 2015. Much of the following seven paragraphs has been extracted from that article.
[17] Lester W. Grau, "Russian-Manufactured Armored Vehicle Vulnerability in Urban Combat: The Chechnya Experience," *Red Thrust Star*, January 1977.

Tank Combat Support Vehicle (BMPT) "Terminator-2"

Image Courtesy: Vitaly Kuzmin

optimum system for tank support in city fighting, but its vulnerability offset the efficiency of its four 23mm automatic cannons.[18]

To ensure the survivability of tanks, they needed a new system that was built like a tank, but provided mutual close combat support. The new system had to provide protection against enemy antitank weapons, infantry, strong points, helicopters, and fixed wing aviation. It needed to be an integral part of the armored unit, but it could not be a modern T-35 with five turrets and multiple weapons. The Russian answer was the BMPT tank support vehicle.[19] It was not an infantry fighting vehicle (BMP), and the Russians were not discounting the value of mechanized infantry in the combined arms team. They were recognizing that the mechanized infantry may not be at the critical point at the critical time to support tank operations in traditional and urban combat roles. Russia's first BMPT was nicknamed the "Terminator," due to the anti-personnel capabilities of the system. It was built upon a T-72 or a T-90S tank chassis.[20] The BMPT has the armored protection, maneuverability, and ruggedness to maneuver directly with the tank platoon, has laminated and reactive armor, weighs 47 tons and carries a 5-man crew with a low-profile turret, housing a 30mm automatic cannon with a coaxial AG-17D grenade launcher, an AT-14 Kornet ATGM, and a 7.62mm machine gun.[21]

The most recent version of the BMPT has been renamed as a Combat Fire Support Vehicle (BMOP) and nicknamed the "Terminator-2." Despite the name change, the Terminator-2 fulfills the same role as originally intended, and was also built upon the T-72 or T-90S chassis. However, Russian Deputy Prime Minister Dmitry Rogozin, who oversees the Russian defense industries, suggests that the Terminator-2 could also be built upon Russia's newest heavy chassis platform, the Armata.[22] The Terminator-2 is primarily intended to destroy personnel, antitank grenade launchers and antitank missiles, but also has capabilities to destroy lightly armored vehicles, tanks, BMPs, fortified structures, and low flying aircraft. The system is equipped with dual 2A42 30mm automatic cannons with 1700 rounds of ammunition

[18] Dmitriy Litovkin, "Battlefield Combine. Tank Support Combat Vehicle to Enter Service Soon," *Izvestia* Online, 15 March 2005, <http://izvestia.ru/news/300570>, accessed 10 April 2015.
[19] Sergey Severinov, "Homeland Armor," *Red Star* Online, 10 September 2005, <http://old.redstar.ru/2005/09/10_09/1_01.html>, accessed 10 April 2015.
[20] Sergey Mikhaylov, "The Armed Forces Are on the Upswing: Marginal Polemical Notes on the Speech by CINC RF Ground Troops Colonel-General Oleg Salyukov," *Stoletiye* Online, 8 October 2014, <http://www.stoletie.ru/obschestvo/armija_na_podjeme_129.htm>, accessed 10 April 2015.
[21] Russian Ministry of Defense, pp. 208-213. The Russians have developed a variety of thermobaric munitions for bunker busting, minefield clearing and artillery preparation. See, Lester W. Grau and Timothy Smith, illustrated by John Richards and Ivan Pavlov, "A Crushing Victory: Fuel-air Explosives and Grozny 2000," *Marine Corps Gazette*, August 2000, pp. 30-33.
[22] "Russia Unveils 'Terminator-2' Tank Support Vehicle" *Sputnik News* Online, 25 September 2013, <http://sputniknews.com/military/20130925/183720985.html>, accessed 10 April 2015.

capable of destroying lightly armored vehicles and low-speed air targets (2500 meters) and ATGM systems, personnel, and other unarmored objects (4000 meters); a PKTM 7.62mm coaxially mounted machine gun with remote loader and 2100 rounds of ammunition capable of destroying personnel and unarmored targets (1600 meters);[23] and two AG-17D automatic grenade launchers with 600 rounds of ammunition capable of destroying lightly armed targets (1400 meters). The BMPTs antitank capability comes from four Ataka-T guided missiles with general purpose (9M120-1F) and antitank (9M120-1) warheads (5000 meters).[24] These weapons can reportedly clear the enemy from a city block at a distance of three kilometers.[25] The Terminator-2 has a five-man crew consisting of a vehicle commander, gunner, driver-mechanic, and two grenadier gunners. It is designed to let the crew fight from the safety of the vehicle, and does not require any exiting for any weapons operation or routine reloading. All weapons systems are remote controlled, and there is an optical system to assist the weaponeers with target acquisition. The vehicle has an aerosol capability (presumably smoke) to obscure its location from target acquisition systems, and when lased, the commander's panoramic sight will acquire the offending laser to readily direct fires. The vehicle's chassis will also permit the vehicle to be mounted with mine or obstacle plows to facilitate maneuver.

Hopes for fielding the BMPT were dashed in 2010, when the Russian MoD announced that funding for it had been cancelled. Despite this setback, the manufacturer, *Uralvagonzavod*, did not give up and began to look for customers in the export market. In 2012, Kazakhstan, a country with a post-Soviet Army that somewhat resembles the Russian military in force structure and tactics, signed an agreement to purchase nine BMPTs on T-72 chassis, with deliveries starting in 2013.[26] Apparently, the BMPT was perceived as a great success, and in April 2014 Kazakhstan signed another contract with *Uralvagonzavod* to produce the BMPT in Kazakhstan under a licensing agreement.[27] In 2013, Rogozin's statement that the Terminator-2 could be built on the Armata chassis may be seen as evidence that the BMPT program was not cancelled by Russian MoD, but was instead put on indefinite hold until a new universal chassis was put into production.[28]

[23] Anatoli Antipov, "Tanks Need Support," *Red Star* Online, 22 December 2004, <http://old.redstar.ru/2004/12/22_12/7_03.html>, accessed 10 April 2015.
[24] "Russia Unveils 'Terminator-2' Tank Support Vehicle" *Sputnik News* Online, 25 September 2013, <http://sputniknews.com/military/20130925/183720985.html>, accessed 10 April 2015.
[25] Dmitriy Litovkin, "Battlefield Combine. Tank Support Combat Vehicle to Enter Service Soon," Izvestia Online, 15 March 2005, <http://izvestia.ru/news/300570>, accessed 10 April 2015.
[26] Kazakhstan Purchased Unique Tank Combat Support Vehicles from Russia, *Interfax-Kazakhstan* Online, 5 May 2012, <http://tengrinews.kz/kazakhstan_news/kazahstan-zakupil-rossii-unikalnyie-boevyie-mashinyi-195486/>, accessed 10 April 2015.
[27] "In 2015, Kazakhstan will build BMPT 'Terminator,'" *Meta.kz* Online, 10 April 2014, <http://meta.kz/novosti/kazakhstan/879813-v-2015-godu-v-kazahstane-nachnut-sborku-bmpt-171terminator187.html>, accessed 10 April 2015.
[28] Anton Valagin, "Terminator on Armata Chassis Will Be Armed with Two Guns," *Rossiyskaya Gazeta* Online, 23 November 2016, <https://rg.ru/2016/11/23/reg-urfo/terminator-na-baze-armaty-vooruzhat-dvumia-pushkami.html>, accessed 19 December 2016.
Dr. Les Grau and Charles K. Bartles, "New System Preserves Armor Dominance of Future Battlefield: BMPT 'Terminator-2'" *Armor* Online, April-June, <http://www.benning.army.mil/armor/eARMOR/content/issues/2015/APR_JUN/Apr-Jun_2015_edition.pdf>, accessed 1 May 2016.

Artillery Troops

The Missile and Artillery Troops is a Branch of Arms in the Ground Forces, which is the primary means of destroying the enemy by conventional and nuclear fires during conduct of combined arms operations. They are designed to perform the following main tasks:

- achieve and maintain fire superiority
- defeat of the enemy's means of nuclear attack, manpower, weapons, military and special equipment
- disrupt troops and command and control, reconnaissance, and EW systems
- destroy permanent defense installations and other infrastructure
- disrupt the enemy's operational and tactical logistics
- weaken and isolate the enemy's second echelons and reserve
- destroy enemy tanks and other armored vehicles that breach the defense
- cover open flanks and junctions
- participate in the destruction of enemy aircraft and the amphibious assault forces
- conduct remote mining operations
- provide illumination to troops maneuvering at night
- provide smoke screens and blind enemy targets
- distribute propaganda materials.

Self-Propelled Artillery Characteristics

	2S5 "Giatsint-S"	2S1 "Gvozdika"	2S19 "Msta-S"	2S3 "Akatsiya"	2S9 "Nona"
Caliber (mm)	152.4	122	152.4	152.4	120
Max Range (km)	28.4-33	15.2	29	17.3-20	12.8
Rate of Fire (min)	5-6	4-5	7-8	3-4	8-10
Shell Weight (kg)	46	14.1-21.8	42.9-43.6	43.6	17.3
System Weight (kg)	28,200	15,700	42,000	27,500	8,000
Crew	5	4	5	4	4
Chassis	Object 123	MT-LB	T-80/T-72	Object 123	BRDM
Ammo Load	30	40	50	45	40
Set Up Time (min)	3	.3	2-2.5	.5	—
Unit of Fire	60	80	50	60	80

Towed Artillery Characteristics

	2A18 "D-30"	2A65 "Msta-B"	2A19 "MT-12 Rapira"	2A36 "Giatsint-B"
Caliber (mm)	122	152.4	100	152.4
Maximum Range (km)	15.3	8.1	3	28.3
Direct Fire Range (m)	870	2130	1850	1530
Armor Penetration (mm)	450	350	400	350
Traverse	360°	54°	52°	50°
System Weight (kg)	3200	3100	2750	9500
Set Up Time (min)	2.5	1	2-2.5	4
Rate of Fire (min)	8	6	7	6
Tow Vehicle	Ural	MT-LB	KrAZ	KrAZ
Tow Vehicle Range	850	500	800	800
Crew	6	6	6	8
Unit of Fire	80	80	60	60

The Missile and Artillery Troops consist of missile, rocket, and artillery brigades, including high-power mixed units (tube and rocket), artillery battalions, rocket artillery regiments, and separate artillery reconnaissance battalions, as well as artillery units of combined arms brigades and military bases. In terms of modernization and capability development, the Missile and Artillery Troops will increase their capabilities by creating reconnaissance-fire units, including on interim basis; ensuring defeat of targets in real time; fielding more precision weapons; and increasing weapons' firing ranges, the power of the ammunition, and the automation of the processes for preparation and firing.[29]

Maneuver with Fire and Maneuver by Fire

Artillery has always held pride of place in the Russian and Soviet Armies. Imperial Russian Artillery officers enjoyed a reputation for intellectual and professional excellence above the other branches.[30] The Soviet Army was an artillery army with many tanks. The Soviets

[29] "Missile Troops and Artillery," *Ministry of Defense of the Russian Federation* Website, <http://structure.mil.ru/structure/forces/ground/structure/rvia.htm>, accessed 1 May 2016.

[30] Top graduates of the Artillery School were commissioned with seniority over graduates of the Infantry school and the Aristocratic Corps of Pages. Count Leo Tolstoy, the author of *War and Peace*, was a professional artillery

Self-Propelled Howitzer Battalion

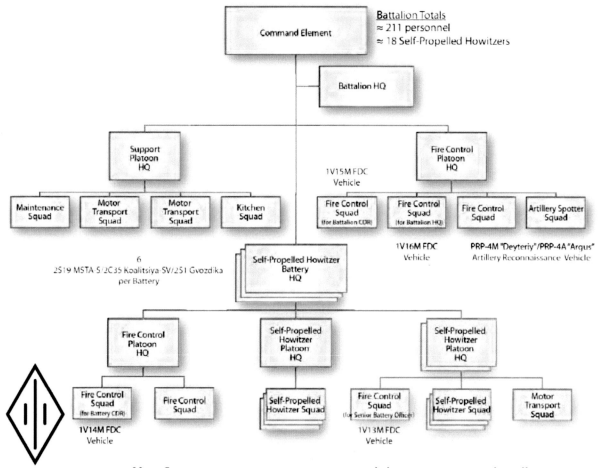

Battalion Totals
≈ 211 personnel
≈ 18 Self-Propelled Howitzers

Msta-S

Image Courtesy: Vitaly Kuzmin

structured their army around artillery.

The Russian Army is also artillery-centric. Fire and maneuver is a common concept among militaries, as artillery fire removes or suppresses opposing enemy groupings, which allows the supported maneuver element (infantry or tanks) to advance simultaneously without incurring heavy casualties. The artillery is lifted and shifted shortly before the maneuver element closes with the enemy being pummeled by artillery and direct fire.

Maneuver by fire is a Russian concept whereby fire is shifted from one target, line or sector without moving the firing positions of the artillery pieces. It is used in battle to cause mass destruction of important targets in a short period of time. All of the fires can be conducted officer who served in the Caucasus and at Sevastopol during the Crimean War. He authored technical papers on artillery issues as well as his more-famous literary works.

against one target simultaneously or conducted against that target and then other targets one after another. Maneuver by fire may also be used to redirect fire from one axis of advance to another.[31] In this way, the physical effects of artillery destruction may be maneuvered to achieve the effects of a maneuver force. Maneuver by fire is used to achieve fire superiority rapidly over an enemy while putting one's own artillery at risk; therefore, it is a massed artillery gambit. The Russian Army still believes in the efficacy and effectiveness of massing the effects of massed artillery fire to achieve maneuver and to support maneuver.

2S1 "Gvozdika"

Image Courtesy: Vitaly Kuzmin

Brigade and Battalion Artillery

The post-Soviet Russian Army has undergone the most sweeping reform in over a century. The new-model Russian Army has restructured around the brigade. A motorized rifle (mechanized infantry) or tank brigade has four maneuver battalions, four artillery battalions, two air defense battalions, a logistics battalion, a maintenance battalion, a signal battalion, an engineer battalion, an electronics warfare company, an unmanned aerial vehicle (UAV) company, an NBC company and a medical company. The artillery battalions are two howitzer battalions, a Multiple Launch Rocket System (MLRS) battalion and an antitank artillery battalion.

Thirty-six 2S19 Msta-S 152mm self-propelled, tracked howitzers form the firing base of the modern brigade's howitzer battalions (eighteen in each battalion). The 2S19 was introduced into the Ground Forces in 1989, just before the collapse of the Soviet Union. It has seen action in the Second Chechen War and in the current fighting in Eastern Ukraine. It is built on the T-80 tank chassis and is powered by the T-72 tank engine. It has an automated fire control system, automatic loader, NBC protection system, passive night vision device for the driver, wading kit, dozer blade, smoke generator and 81mm smoke launchers and a generator. The

2S3 "Akatsiya"

Image Courtesy: Vitaly Kuzmin

152mm barrel fires HE, HEAT-FS, HE-BB, HE-RA, smoke, chemical, nuclear, illumination and improved conventional munitions (ICM) rounds, as well as the laser-guided "Krasnopol" round. The 2S19 has been upgraded several times since its introduction, and is also produced in a towed, wheeled and export variant. It has a range of 29 kilometers (18 miles) using standard base-bleed ammunition and 36 kilometers (22 miles) using rocket-assisted ammunition. It can fire

---

[31] Institute of Military History of the Russian Federation Ministry of Defense, *Military Encyclopedic Dictionary* in two volumes [Военный Энциклопедический Словар в двух томах], Volume II, Moscow: Ripol classic, 2001, 27.

MLRS Battalion

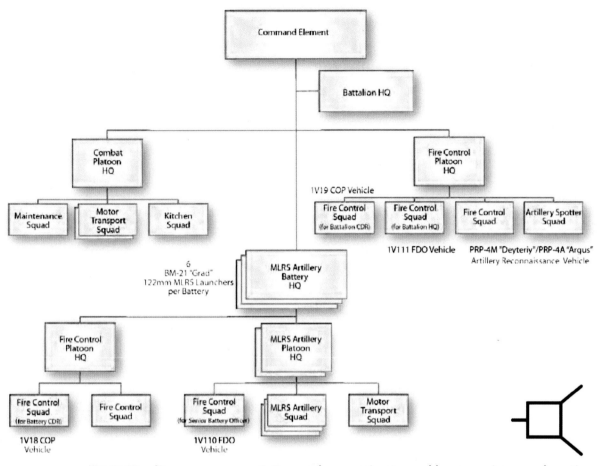

BM-21 "Grad"

Image Courtesy: Vitaly Kuzmin

6-8 rounds per minute and has a main gun elevation of 4° to +68° and a 360° weapon's traverse. Some brigades may still have the older 2S3 self-propelled 152mm howitzers.

Eighteen truck-mounted BM-21 122mm MLRSs form the firing base of the brigade's MLRS battalion. Each one of these Grad launchers carries 40 122mm rockets, which can be launched individually or in salvo. The original rockets are capable of engaging targets up to 20 kilometers, and a 720 rocket battalion salvo impacts an area of approximately 10 square acres. The BM-21 is an old design that first appeared in the Soviet Army in 1963, and it is a veteran of combat from Vietnam to Ukraine. Russia has engaged in a number of improvements to enhance its capabilities. A new generation of rockets have increased ranges, are GPS/GLONASS-capable, and field a variety of warheads, including High Explosive (HE), smoke, radio jamming, mines, and cluster munitions. Some new rockets for the BM-21 Grad reportedly have a range of up to 45 kilometers.

Antitank Battalion

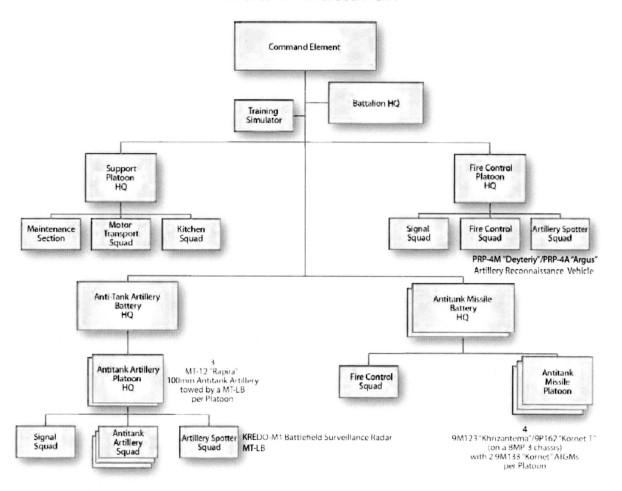

The brigade MLRS battalions are being refitted with the 9A52-4 Tornado, built upon a Kamaz-63501 chassis, which will reportedly be able to launch rockets/missiles of any of the three Russian MLRS calibers. The BM-27 220mm Uragan rockets carries HE-FRAG, chemical, ICM or scatterable mine warheads out to 35 kilometers (22 miles). The BM-30 300mm Smerch rocket carries HE-FRAG, antitank and antipersonnel ICM and thermobaric warheads out to 90 kilometers (56 miles). The Tornado will, for the first time, use guided missiles, instead of unguided rockets, which will improve capabilities significantly.

The brigade's fourth artillery battalion is the antitank artillery battalion. It has an antitank artillery battery of six MT-12 Rapira antitank cannons and two ATGM batteries of six each 9M123 Khrizantema or 9P162 Kornet-T tank destroyers, both of which mount two 9M133 Kornet ATGM launchers. The towed MT-12

9M123 "Khrizantema"

Image Courtesy: Vitaly Kuzmin

antitank cannon fields a 100mm smoothbore cannon that has a six-man crew (commander, driver of the towing vehicle, gun layer, loader, and two ammunition handlers). When the MT-LB is used as the tow vehicle, 20 rounds are typically carried (10 APFSDS, 4 HE-Frag, 6 HEAT). The standard equipment consists of the panoramic PG-1M sight for indirect fire and an OP4M-40U telescope for direct fire. The APN-5-40 or APN-6-40 night sight is used for direct fire. The gun can be fitted with the LO-7 ski gear for travel across snow or swampy ground.

The armored, tracked, amphibious Krizanterna or Kornet-T antitank destroyers' 9M133 Kornet ATGM rails have a range of 100-10,000 meters. The Kornet is a laser-beam rider with a HEAT warhead designed to defeat reactive armor and a thermobaric round designed to defeat bunkers.

2S12 "Sani"

Each motorized rifle battalion has its organic artillery battery of eight 2S12 Sani towed 120mm mortars. In the Russian Army, mortars belong to the artillery and so all the mortar battery are branched artillery. The 2S12 has a range of 0.5 (.31 miles)-7100 meters (4.4 miles). It fires HE, smoke, illumination and incendiary rounds, as well as a laser-guided round and a rocket-assisted round which fires over 13 kilometers (8 miles). A trained crew can fire 15 rounds per minute.

Image Courtesy: Vitaly Kuzmin

Mortar Characteristics

	2S12 "Sani"	2B14 "Podnos"	2B9 "Vasilek"
Caliber (mm)	120	82	82
Maximum Range (m)	7100	4270	4270
Minimum Range (m)	460	87	800
Traverse	10°	360°	60°
System Weight (kg)	210	42	662
Set Up Time (min)	3	1.3	2
Rate of Fire (min)	12	24	Cyclic
Base	Gaz-66	Portable	Gaz-66
Crew	5	4	4
Unit of Fire	48	120	300

2B14 "Podnos"

Image Courtesy: Russian Ministry of Defense

2S9 "Nona"

Image Courtesy: Vitaly Kuzmin

The 2S9 Nona tracked, lightly armored, amphibious, breech-loading 120mm mortar/cannon is incorporated in some motorized rifle battalions instead of the 2S12 Sani. The Nona also comes in a wheeled BTR chassis variant (2S23 Nona-SVK) and in a towed version (2B16 Nona-K). The system is unique in that this mortar/cannon has a direct-fire capability and has an antitank round available for it. When used as a cannon, it has a range of 13 kilometers (8 miles). The Nona may be replaced by the 2S31 Vena, which has been designed and tested but not put into full production. There is some speculation that the system is intended for the export market.

2B9 "Vasilek"

Image Courtesy: Russian Ministry of Defense

The advent of UAVs heralds a new age of Russian artillery, providing real-time, accurate targeting, fire adjustment and post-strike assessment. The UAV is an enabler, while artillery remains the all-weather means of Russian destruction and maneuver support. Currently the Russian Army is assigning a UAV company to each maneuver brigade. The brigade has four artillery battalions, but organic artillery can be reinforced with attached, reinforcing or supporting artillery from artillery or MLRS brigades from an Army Group. The UAV company is not assigned to any of the artillery battalions, but is a separate brigade unit, since the UAV company has several types of short- and medium-range UAV systems and a variety of UAV missions, including artillery support, EW and communications retransmission. A more detailed discussion can be found in chapter eight, "Russian UAV Developments."

MT-12 "Rapira"

Image Courtesy: Vitaly Kuzmin

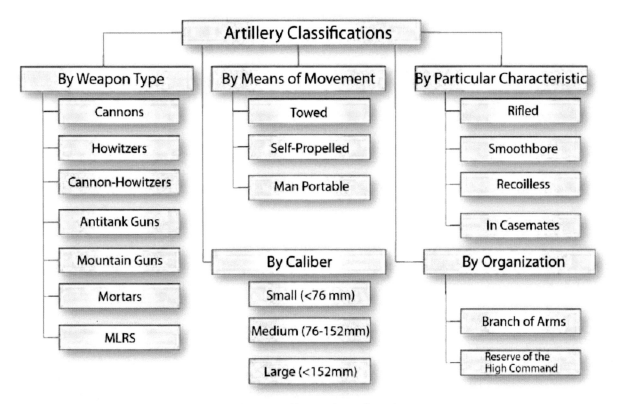

Russian Artillery Classifications

Artillery Terms and Concepts

Although the Russians have precision-guided munitions for their artillery, they still believe in the effectiveness of massed artillery fire. Tactical EW systems may jam or prematurely detonate electronic VT fuses, but the mechanical fuses of conventional artillery rounds cannot be jammed by electronic signals. There are occasions that call for the use of surgical, precision fires, but massed artillery fires carry a mathematical probability of kill with which it is easier to predict tactical success. Artillery missions include annihilation, destruction, neutralization/suppression and harassment of a target. Missions are assigned according to the nature of the target, overall mission and type of target.

BM-30 "Smerch"

Image Courtesy: Vitaly Kuzmin

Annihilation [уничтожение] inflicts such losses or damage on a target that it completely loses its combat effectiveness. In the annihilation of unobserved targets, fire is conducted until a mathematically determined number of rounds are expended that assures a 70-90% kill probability of individual targets or the mathematical expectation of 50-60% of targets destroyed in a group target. The implication is that the target is so damaged that it cannot be reconstituted and is incapable of even token resistance.

Destruction [разрушение] puts a target into an "unfit" condition. It is so damaged that it cannot be reconstituted without a significant expenditure of time and resources, and is capable of only sporadic, uncoordinated resistance.

Neutralization/suppression [подавлениие] inflicts such losses and creates such conditions that the target is temporarily deprived of its combat effectiveness, its maneuver is restricted or prohibited or its control is disrupted. In neutralizing an unobserved group target, the expenditure of a norm of rounds assures the mathematical expectation of 30% of the targets destroyed. The implication is that the target is severely damaged, but would be capable of eventual coordinated resistance once the suppressive fire is lifted.

Harassment [изнурение] involves a limited number of artillery tubes and a specified number of rounds fired within a prescribed time to exert moral-psychological pressure on enemy personnel in defensive positions, in assembly areas, at control points or in logistics areas. Firing platoons or batteries normally conduct harassing fire from temporary firing positions or positions previously occupied by a larger artillery unit.[32]

2S5 "Giatsint-S"

Image Courtesy: Vitaly Kuzmin

Much of the terrain in which Russia may fight is fairly flat; consequently, it is difficult to get forward observers into good positions to spot artillery targets. Hence, Russian artillery planning involves the expenditure of significant amounts of artillery ammunition. Annihilation artillery missions against unobserved targets involve the physical removal of hectares. However, the availability of a UAV company may significantly diminish artillery ammunition expenditure. UAVs can identify targets, adjust artillery fire and perform post-strike damage assessments.

Artillery fire is further classified as fire against an individual target, fire concentration, standing barrage fire, defensive rolling barrage fire, successive fire concentration, offensive rolling barrage fire, and massed fire.[33] UAV support will prove most effective in supporting the first two classifications, since the rest are predetermined and fired against a schedule.

One of the problems with Soviet artillery was that it was not always able to conduct split-battery fires, since the battalion fire direction center could only conduct a limited number of fire missions simultaneously. Now, with improved communications and computer technology, split-battery fire is possible and common. Each battery now has its own fire direction center (FDC).

---

[32] G. E. Peredel'skiy and M. P. Pankov, *The Artillery Battalion in Combat* [Артллерийский Дивизион в Бою], Moscow: Voyenizdat, 1989, 20-21.
[33] Ibid.

Positioning of Artillery

In the offensive, a howitzer battalion is commonly attached to or put in support of a maneuver battalion.[34] Howitzer battalions are also incorporated into Brigade Artillery Groups (BrAG), which include gun and multiple rocket launcher battalions. Surface-to-surface missile battalions (Iskanders and Tochkas) are not incorporated into BrAGs, but remain in support of the Army Group. In the defense, artillery battalions are more often placed in support of forward maneuver battalions.[35] Gun and howitzer batteries are positioned astride armored axes of approach in

ATS-59G Artillery Tractor

Image Courtesy: Vitaly Kuzmin

order to employ their direct fire capability. Mortar batteries and multiple rocket launcher batteries are located in areas inaccessible to tanks. Firing positions are located away from prominent features which would aid the enemy in registration. Intervals of 20-40 meters are maintained between guns, howitzers and mortars, while a 50-60-meter interval is maintained between multiple rocket launcher platforms.[36]

An artillery battalion has one primary and one or two alternate positions. A battalion may have a temporary firing position in the security zone, in defending a forward position, when conducting fire against distant targets or when acting as a roving battalion. Each battery has a primary and one or two alternate positions in a battalion area. In addition, a battery may have a temporary firing position when serving as a roving battery or duty battery.[37] Batteries normally shift positions following a fire mission.[38]

Artillery reconnaissance is conducted from the battalion artillery command/observation post (COP) and the battery COPs. Normally the artillery battalion commander collocates

---

[34] Attached artillery [приданная артиллерия] is directly subordinated to the commander of the force to which it is attached. Attached artillery is normally exclusive and fires only those missions assigned by the force commander. In an emergency, fire missions for a senior commander may be fired. Supporting artillery [поддерживающая арттллерия] is under the command of the senior artillery commander and fires assigned missions established by the combined arms commander. Thus, a supporting artillery battalion may be in support of several maneuver battalions, whereas an attached artillery battalion will fire exclusively for one maneuver battalion/brigade. Usually a supporting artillery battalion will be in support of one specific maneuver unit and will collocate its headquarters with that of the maneuver unit, but will take its firing mission from the senior artillery commander. V. Y. Lebedev, *Field Artillery Officer's Handbook* [Справочник Офицера Наземной Артеллерии], Moscow: Voyenizdat, 1984, 8. UAV will doubtless be attached or supporting to artillery units in the same manner.

[35] Peredel'skiy, 10-11.

[36] Ibid, 18-19.

[37] Ibid, 194-195. A roving battery is used to engage targets of opportunity without disclosing the location of the main battalion firing positions. It moves after firing. It uses the battalion FDC and battalion and battery forward observers. Logically, it will use a UAV in a supporting role. A duty battery is the fire unit designated to return enemy artillery H & I fire, engage enemy reconnaissance efforts and ground probes, conduct harassing fire and serve as first responder when artillery is needed.

[38] Lester W. Grau, "Soviet Artillery Planning in the Tactical Defense," Soviet Army Studies Office, Fort Leavenworth, Kansas, September 1990, 11.

himself and his COP with the maneuver battalion command post. Battery commanders are often collocated with maneuver company commanders. The artillery battalion may also establish forward and lateral observation posts to provide complete observation. With sufficient time, artillery observation posts and supporting vehicles are dug in with overhead cover. Radio intercept and radar intercept provide target intelligence to the artillery. Sound-ranging platoons and ground reconnaissance patrols provide target locations as well.[39] The battalion FDC is located near one of the artillery batteries. The battalion chief of staff controls the battalion's fires, since the battalion commander is forward at the COP. Ideally the UAV operator control station for the medium-range Orlan-10 would be located with the battalion FDC, if its electronic signature does not attract enemy fire. The UAV operator control station for the short-range Granata-1 will probably be located with the battery COP.

Revitalization and Downsizing the Reconnaissance-Fire Group

In the mid-1980s, the Soviets developed and fielded a first-generation reconnaissance-fire complex - a tactical range system linking a real-time reconnaissance/target designation/vectoring system with an intelligence fusion center and an FDC. In turn, this was linked to dedicated, precision weaponry which could destroy the target in near-real time. The targets were tactical nuclear delivery systems, self-propelled artillery and mortar batteries, FASCAM (family of scatterable mines) delivery systems, command posts, reconnaissance systems, aircraft parked on airfields and carrier decks and other high-value targets.[40] The reconnaissance-fire group (разведывательно-огневая группа) consisted of

2S4 "Tulpan" (240mm mortar)

Image Courtesy: Vitaly Kuzmin

several artillery battalions, a dedicated artillery reconnaissance platoon, a group headquarters and often a helicopter. The assets normally came from division assets. With the brigade as the primary maneuver unit, this mission would now become a brigade mission. The UAV capability should greatly enhance the reconnaissance element for the BrAG.

Artillery Fire Planning

On a map or plotting screen, Russian maneuver forces are depicted in red, enemy forces in blue and Russian artillery in black. Russian artillery planning initially identifies targets and plots them as artillery concentrations on the map or screen. The artillery concentration identifies the firing batteries and number and type of rounds required for each concentration. Then the concentrations are connected by lines. In the attack, these lines are fired consecutively to insure that no identified targets are missed or that they are fired at out of turn, giving the survivors the opportunity to recover and fight advancing maneuver forces. Artillery fire is further classified as fire against an individual target, fire concentration, standing barrage fire, defensive rolling barrage fire, successive fire concentration, offensive rolling barrage fire, and massed fire.[41]

[39] A. I. Kirillov, V. P. Kuznetsov, V.I. Agafonov, *Preparation of the Reserve Officer* [Подготовка офицера запаса], Moscow: Voyenizdat, 1989, 250.

[40] Ibid, 15.

[41] Peredelskiy, 10-11. Remainder of Artillery Fire Planning section is extracted from Peredelskiy, 20-32.

Fire against an individual target

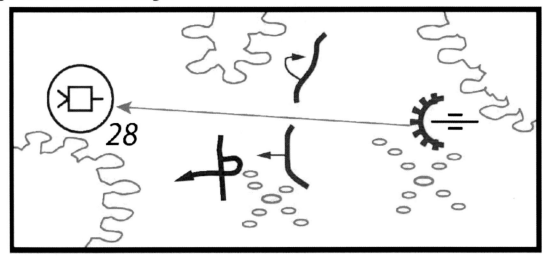

(Above) Fire against an individual target is most often conducted against single targets that are discovered during the course of an attack and are addressed promptly. In the accompanying figure, the Russians are advancing against a withdrawing enemy. An enemy ATGM is covering the withdrawal and has disrupted the advance of the northern Russian attack. The enemy location is now known and identified as target 28. One or more platoon fires may be directed to deal with a newly discovered target. In this case, an individual Russian howitzer is directed to eliminate the target using direct fire (firing over open sights).

Fire concentration

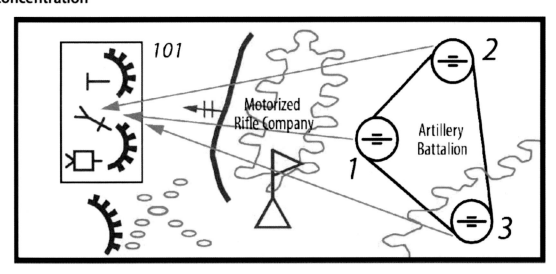

(Above) Fire concentration is used against an attacking or defending enemy. It is depicted with a black rectangle (square for MLRS) and delineates the physical area of impact. The fire concentration is conducted by several batteries or battalions simultaneously against one target box. Fires are planned to provide an even distribution of rounds within the target box. The accompanying figure depicts a howitzer battalion supporting an attacking motorized rifle company as it advances against a prepared enemy defense. An enemy machine gun, antitank weapon and ATGM have been identified within fire concentration 101. As usual, the artillery battalion command post is collocated with the maneuver battalion command post.

Standing barrage fire

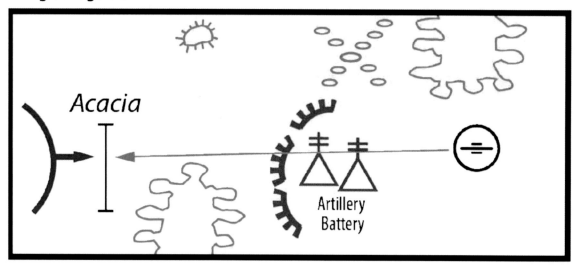

(Above) Standing barrage fire is a single wall of fire planned on an enemy axis of advance or counterattack axis. It is designed to inflict such casualties on the enemy so as to stop his advance, destroy his combat formation and create the conditions to facilitate the destruction of his antitank systems. Standing barrage fire is planned on avenues of approach and placed where it can be observed from command and observation posts. Sometimes, by necessity during the course of combat, they must be planned outside of direct observation. Standing barrage fires are fired by howitzer and cannon artillery, since the desired effect is a curtain of fire, not an area of destruction. The accompanying figure shows a standing barrage fire Acacia (standing barrages are named after flowers or trees) that is conducted by an artillery battery against an enemy axis of advance. A standing barrage fire is normally planned no closer than 300-400 meters in front of forward defending Russian soldiers, and its width is usually no wider than 50 meters per participating artillery piece. Thus, an 18-gun artillery battalion could have a standing barrage of up to 900 meters.

Protecting one's own troops from friendly artillery is an important planning factor. Charges are selected which provide minimum dispersion, mixed ammunition lots are not fired in the proximity of friendly troops and fragmentation rounds are fired in lieu of HE when close to friendly troops.

The Russians do not plan standing barrages along tree lines, hill crests, trench lines or the outskirts of populated areas, since an enemy approach to these features may not be detected and 60-70 seconds will pass from detection to first round impact, allowing the enemy to advance 120-150 meters past these features. Consequently, standing barrage lines are planned 150-200 meters from these features. A standing barrage can consist of more than one line.

A deep standing barrage

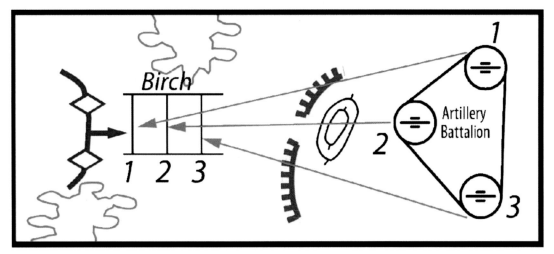

(Above) A deep standing barrage can by fired by a single howitzer battalion on a narrow approach (300 meters with an 18-gun battalion) or by several battalions on a regular approach. All the lines of the deep standing barrage are fired simultaneously and continuously throughout the duration of the fire mission. Line three is planned 300-400 meters from forward defending Russian soldiers. The deep standing barrage is named after a tree. The accompanying figure shows a defending artillery battalion firing a narrow deep standing barrage against an enemy on an armor axis of advance. Each battery is firing a separate line within the standing barrage.

A double moving barrage

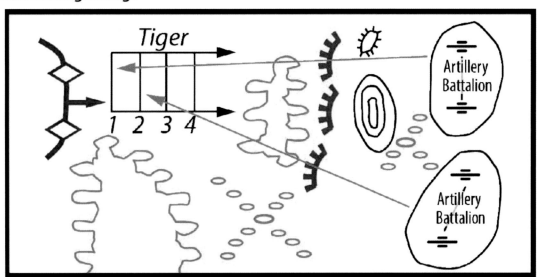

(Above) A double moving barrage may be planned, particularly on enemy armor avenues of approach. Figure 6 shows two howitzer battalions positioned to fire the Tiger moving barrage. As the enemy approaches Tiger, one artillery battalion will fire Tiger 1 and the other will fire Tiger 2 simultaneously. This will continue until the enemy column is exiting Tiger 1 or the enemy column is approaching Tiger 3. The lead battalion commander lifts and shifts the fires from Tiger 1 to Tiger 3. The second battalion commander will then follow his lead and shift to Tiger 4. Tiger 4 may become a standing barrage, reinforced with the fires of the lead defending motorized rifle or tank battalion. Both battalions are laid out for direct fire should the enemy penetrate the forward defenses.

Moving barrage

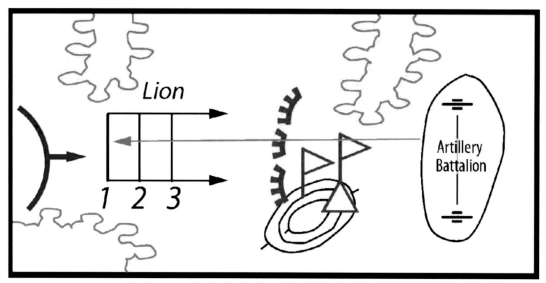

(Above) A moving barrage is located on an enemy axis of advance and named after a predatory animal. The lines are fired sequentially ("Lion 1", "Lion 2", "Lion 3"). The first line is 2-4 kilometers from the forward edge of one's own troops. At this point, the attacking enemy is expected to be moving in platoon column. The second line is 700-1000 meters from the forward edge of one's own troops at the point where the attacking enemy is expected to move from platoon column to attack formation. The last line is 400-600 meters from the forward defense and is that point where the enemy infantry will probably dismount for the assault. Danger close is 300 meters from one's own troops dug into prepared positions and 400 meters from one's own troops in a hasty defense. MLRS is not planned closer than 1000 meters from one's own troops. The moving barrage may have a standing barrage fire line positioned at the end of the moving barrage, or the last line of the moving barrage may become that standing barrage. The accompanying graphic shows moving barrage Lion planned on an enemy avenue of approach. The artillery battalion is positioned on line so that it can shift to direct fire in case of an enemy breakthrough. There is no standing barrage line at the end of the moving barrage, so Lion 3 will become the standing barrage line.

Successive concentrations of fire

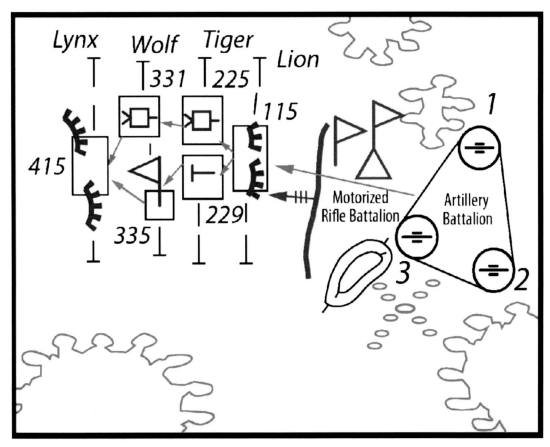

(Above) Successive concentrations of fire are planned on the axis and flanks of a Russian attack. Artillery planners plot artillery concentrations on defending enemy positions and systems and link them in firing lines. Each concentration is numbered and each firing line is named after a different predatory animal. The accompanying graphic shows an artillery battalion attached to a motorized rifle battalion attack. The artillery battalion will first destroy defensive positions in concentration 115 on Line Lion. It will then attack an ATGM position (concentration 225) and machine gun position (concentration 229) on Line Tiger. Subsequently it will attack another ATGM position (concentration 331) and a command post (concentration 335) on Line Wolf, and then attack company reserve positions (concentration 415) on Line Lynx. Targets that are discovered during the attack will be addressed during the course of the attack.

Offensive rolling barrage

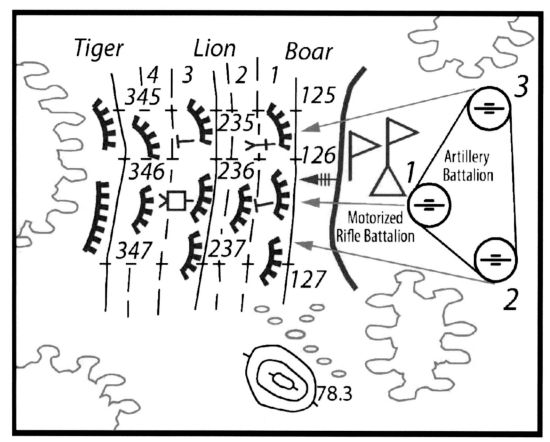

(Above) The offensive rolling barrage is used to support a Russian attack when the enemy is in a strong point defense or a fortified region that is well dug in, with ample trenches, communication trenches, bunkers and fortified fighting positions. The density of the defense hinders precisely determining the location of strong points. The offensive rolling barrage is a solid curtain of fire shifted ahead of attacking maneuver subunits to neutralize enemy personnel and weapons. One or two lines of fire can be fired simultaneously. The first line is planned along the first trench of the enemy defense. Intermediate lines are planned to neutralize the enemy located between the primary lines and to prevent his maneuver along communication trenches. The distance between intermediate lines (named after predatory animals) is 100-300 meters apart, depending on the enemy strength, positions, geography and expected rate of advance. The barrage is walked forward by incremental extensions of range. Each battery has a numbered section of the moving barrage that it is responsible for firing. Each artillery piece has a frontage of 15-25 meters, depending on its caliber. The barrage moves at least 500 meters in front of friendly forces and is designed to destroy the enemy in his positions. MLRS fire is conducted beyond the first wall so that it is no closer than 1000 meters to its own troops. The maneuver commander shifts the primary firing line when his troops reach the troop safety line. The artillery commander shifts the intermediate line at the end of the prescribed time for fire, which is normally 2-3 minutes. Due to the restricted frontages and anticipated ammunition expenditure, the offensive rolling barrage is normally an artillery brigade mission. This figure shows an artillery battalion supporting a motorized rifle battalion with a single rolling barrage where the enemy has a dense trench network. Artillery fire planners usually assign sector lines, which are solid black arrows to mark the area of fire and planning responsibility for the artillery unit. Black interrupted arrows depict additional areas of fire and planning areas that may be assigned under certain contingencies.

Massed fire

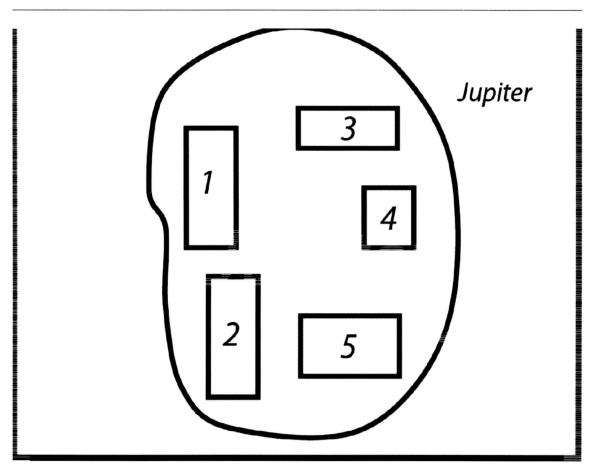

(Above) The massed fire graphic is used to plan a simultaneous massed fire strike against an area target executed in a short period of time. Usually battery or battalion concentrations are plotted within the area of massed fire and the concentrations are numbered to correspond to the battalion (battery) assigned to the mission. Cannon/howitzer targets are indicated by rectangles and MRLS targets by squares. The massed fire graphic is designated by a planetary name. Number and type of rounds to be expended and the duration of the strike are assigned to each firing unit. This graphic is not widely used today, but can still be expected against high-value targets whose exact locations are unknown. This graphic shows a simultaneous fire strike by five cannon/howitzer battalions and an MRLS battalion. This massed fire strike is designated "Jupiter".

Artillery Fire Control

The Russian and Western systems for the command and control of artillery differ substantially. In the Russian system, the artillery commanders do not sit with their artillery pieces. Instead, artillery battalion and battery commanders are typically collocated with the supported maneuver commander in order to relay calls for fire to the artillery; or they are on the battlefield, calling for fire on targets of opportunity. Artillery commanders have Command Observation Post (COP) vehicles with appropriate communications, navigation, and sighting gear to fulfill this function.[42] The fire control for artillery units is provided by the chief of staff for battalions, and senior battery officer (the senior platoon leader) for batteries. These officers, not the commanders, are the ones actually collocated with the artillery, providing them with fire solutions. They man Fire Direction Center (FDC) vehicles to fulfill this function.[43] The FDC vehicles are similarly equipped as the COP vehicles, but are designed to function as FDCs, and so they usually have less or no sighting equipment, more fire control equipment, and may be on a chassis more suitable to functioning as a FDC, than a COP that is conducting artillery reconnaissance on the battlefield. The Russian Armed Forces use a variety of artillery fire control systems, but they all generally follow this described scheme, the following three systems, and their derivatives, are most common in the Russian Ground Forces.

1V12 "Kharkov" Artillery Fire Control System

The 1V12 Kharkov artillery fire control system is based upon the MT-LBu chassis, and is primarily designed to service self-propelled howitzer units. A battalion level set consists of eight vehicles: three 1V13 battery FDC vehicles, three 1V14 battery COP vehicles, one 1V15 battalion COP vehicle, and one 1V16 battalion FDC vehicle. The 1V12M Faltset artillery fire control system is a modernized version of the 1V12 Kharkov, and its constituent vehicles follow the same naming convention as the 1V12 Kharkov system, except with an "M" suffix (IV13M, IV14M, IV15M, IV16M).

IV13M Fire Direction Center Vehicle

Image Courtesy: Vitaly Kuzmin

<u>The IV13 functions as the FDC for the battery</u>, and is manned by the senior officer of the battery (typically the first platoon leader). It has direct radio communications with the battery COP (IV14), the battalion COP (IV15), and the battalion FDC (IV16).
<u>The IV14 functions as the COP for the battery</u>. The IV14 is typically collocated with the COP of

---

[42] Antitank artillery units typically do not align to this command and control scheme. This difference is likely due to the different role that antitank units fill in the Russian Armed Forces, and the fact that the antitank artillery does not need as sophisticated system for command and control since targets are generally within line of site. In terms of reconnaissance assets, most antitank artillery units have portable ground surveillance radars instead of artillery reconnaissance vehicles. These radars are appropriate for the antitank units' primary mission, securing enemy high-speed avenues of approach.

[43] One of the differences between NATO-standard and Russian designed fire computation is that the NATO-standard circle has 6400 mils, while the Russian-standard has 6000 mils. The computing results of each will differ slightly due to this basic difference in standards.

the supported maneuver unit commander so targets can be relayed from the supported unit to the artillery, or is on the battlefield calling for fire. It has direct radio communications with the battery FDC (IV13), the battalion COP (IV15), and the battalion FDC (IV16).

The IV15 functions as the COP for the battalion. The IV15 is typically collocated with the COP of the supported maneuver unit commander so targets can be relayed from the supported unit to the artillery, or is on the battlefield calling for fire. It has direct radio communications with the battery FDCs (IV13), the battery COPs (IV15), and the battalion FDC (IV16).

The IV16 functions as the FDC for the battalion, and is manned by the battalion's chief of staff. It has direct radio communications with the battery FDCs (IV13), battery COPs (IV14), and the battalion COP (IV15).

1V17 "Mashina-B" Artillery Fire Control System

The 1V17 artillery fire control system was developed to service towed and MLRS artillery units. Unlike the 1V12 system that has all vehicles built upon one chassis (MT-LBu), the IV17 uses several different chassis types. The BTR-60 chassis is used for the COP vehicles, the GAZ-66 chassis for the battery FDC vehicles, and a ZiL-131 chassis for the battalion FDC. In most units, these chassis have likely been upgraded to newer BTR-80, KamAZ, or Zil chassis as appropriate. A battalion level set consists of eight vehicles: three 1V110 battery FDC vehicles, one 1V111 battalion FDC vehicle, three 1V18 battery COP vehicles, and one 1V19 battalion COP vehicle.

The IV110 functions as the FDC for the battery, and is manned by the senior officer of the battery (typically the first platoon leader), on a BTR-60/BTR-80 chassis. It has direct radio communications with the battery COP (IV18), the battalion COP (IV19), and the battalion FDC (IV111).

The IV111 functions as the FDC for the battalion, and is manned by the battalion's chief of staff, on a Zil-131 chassis. It has direct radio communications with the battery FDCs (IV110), battery COPs (IV18), and the battalion COP (IV19).

The IV18 functions as the COP for the battery. The IV18 is typically collocated with the COP of the supported maneuver unit commander so targets can be relayed from the supported unit to the artillery, or is on the battlefield calling for fire. It is built upon a GAZ-66 chassis, and has direct radio communications with the battery FDC (IV110), the battalion COP (IV19), and the battalion FDC (IV111).

The IV19 functions as the COP for the battalion. The IV16 is typically collocated with the COP of the supported maneuver unit commander so targets can be relayed from the supported unit to the artillery. It is built upon a GAZ-66 chassis, and has direct radio communications with the battery FDCs (IV110), the battery COPs (IV18), and the battalion FDC (IV111).

IV110 Fire Direction Center Vehicle

Image Courtesy: Vitaly Kuzmin

1V126 "Kapustnik-B" Artillery Fire Control System

The 1V126 artillery fire control system was developed to service a variety of artillery systems for the domestic and export markets. The 1V152 is the designation for the battalion and battery COP vehicles, and is often mounted on a BTR-80 chassis. The 1V153 is the designation for the battalion and battery FDC vehicles, and is often mounted on a Ural-4320 chassis. The battalion COP and FDC vehicles can support up to four batteries, while the battery COP and

Model of the IV126 Artillery Fire Control System

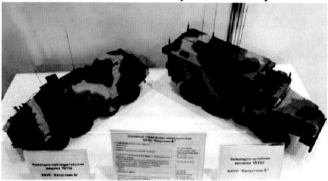

Image Courtesy: Vitaly Kuzmin

FDC can support up to eight artillery pieces. The 1V126M Kapustnik-BM (1V152M, 1V153M) is a modernized version of the 1V126 Kapustnik-B. The 1V127 Kapustnik-C modification is designed for self-propelled artillery systems.

The IV153 functions as the FDC for the battery, and is manned by the senior officer of the battery (typically the first platoon leader). It has direct radio communications with the battery COP (IV152), the battalion COP (IV152), and the battalion FDC (IV153).
The IV153 functions as the FDC for the battalion, and is manned by the battalion's chief of staff. It has direct radio communications with the battery FDCs (IV153), battery COPs (IV152), and the battalion COP (IV152).
The IV152 functions as the COP for the battery. The IV152 is typically collocated with the COP of the supported maneuver unit commander so targets can be relayed from the supported unit to the artillery, or is on the battlefield calling for fire. It has direct radio communications

with the battery FDC (IV153), the battalion COP (IV152), and the battalion FDC (IV153). The IV152 functions as the COP for the battalion. The IV152 is typically collocated with the COP of the supported maneuver unit commander so targets can be relayed from the supported unit to the artillery. It has direct radio communications with the battery FDCs (IV153), the battery COPs (IV152), and the battalion FDC (IV153).

1V118 Reostat/1V119 Spektr Artillery Fire Control System

The 1V118 Reostat/1V119 Spektr artillery fire control system was developed to service self-propelled, towed, and MLRS artillery and mortar units in Airborne (VDV) and Naval Infantry units. This system is built upon BMD-1 chassis. The 1V118 Reostat is the COP vehicle, while the 1V119 Spektr is the FDC vehicle. The 1V118-1 Reostat/1V119-1 Spektr is a modernized version of the 1V118 Reostat/1V119 Spektr artillery fire control system. The Russian Armed Forces are currently testing the "Zavet-D" system as a possible replacement.

IV119 Fire Direction Center Vehicle

Image Courtesy: Vitaly Kuzmin

The IV119 functions as the FDC for the battery, and is manned by the senior officer of the battery (typically the first platoon leader). It has direct radio communications with the battery COP (IV118), the battalion COP (IV118), and the battalion FDC (IV119).
The IV119 functions as the FDC for the battalion, and is manned by the battalion's chief of staff. It has direct radio communications with the battery FDCs (IV119), battery COPs (IV118), and the battalion COP (IV118).
The IV118 functions as the COP for the battery. The IV118 is typically collocated with the COP of the supported maneuver unit commander so targets can be relayed from the supported unit to the artillery, or is on the battlefield calling for fire. It has direct radio communications with the battery FDC (IV119), the battalion COP (IV118), and the battalion FDC (IV119).
The IV118 functions as the COP for the battalion. The IV118 is typically collocated with the COP of the supported maneuver unit commander so targets can be relayed from the supported unit to the artillery. It has direct radio communications with the battery FDCs (IV119), the battery COPs (IV118), and the battalion FDC (IV119).

Brigade-Level Artillery Fire Control & Reconnaissance Systems

Maneuver brigades usually have a deputy commander for artillery. The brigade's fire control battery [батарея управления и артиллерийской разведки] is commanded by, or reports to this officer. As would be expected, the fire control battery contains assets for detecting, determining coordinates, and the transmission of targeting data and orders. The typical configuration for brigade-level fire control batteries include platoons for: artillery spotting (PRP-4A Argus), radars (1RL232-2M SNAR-10M1 and 1L219M Zoopark-1), listening posts, geodesy, and communications. UAVs now regularly supplement artillery fire control, for a detailed discussion of this issue, see the "UAV Development" section in *Chapter 9*.

Fire Control Battery

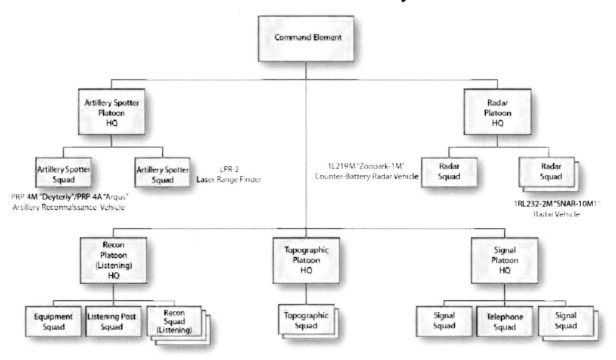

PRP-4A "Argus" Artillery Reconnaissance Vehicle

Weight (tons)	14
Max speed on paved roads (kph)	65
Travel range along a paved road (km)	550
JTD-20S1 Engine (horsepower)	300
Optical-electronic detection range of a tank type target (km):	
During the day	≥8
At night	≥3
Detection range of a cool, tank type target under a camouflage net (km)	≥2
Radar detection range of a moving, tank type target (km)	≥12
Median error of target coordinates (m):	
Optical-electronic instruments	≤20
Radar	≤40
Set up time (min)	2

Image Courtesy: Vitaly Kuzmin

The PRP-4A Argus artillery reconnaissance vehicle is used to conduct artillery reconnaissance of point and mass, fixed and moving, and open and camouflaged targets, and process, store and transmit this data to artillery units. It is equipped with optical, electro-optical, and radar siting devices, a GLONASS enabled navigation system, and radios. The PRP-4A has two workstations and an equipment set for a remote observation post.[44]

[44] Yuriy Avdeyev, "The New Capabilities of Artillery Reconnaissance," *Krasnaya Zvezda* Online, 7 November 2016,<http://www.redstar.ru/index.php/news-menu/vesti/tablo-dnya/item/31079-argus-neusypnyj-strazh>, accessed 20 December 2016.

1RL232-2M "SNAR-10M1" Radar Vehicle

Weight (ton)	12.7
Crew	4
Field of view:	
Range (km)	.2-40
Azimuth (degrees)	12-360
Moving target detection range:	
Personnel (km)	15
Tanks (km)	35
Shell/mortar detonation- ground surface (km)	10
Shell/mortar detonation- water surface (km)	20
Median error for moving target coordinates:	
Range (m)	10
Azimuth (degrees)	.12

Image Courtesy: Vitaly Kuzmin

The SNAR-10M1 is a battlefield surveillance radar vehicle used to locate moving ground and sea-surface targets. The SNAR-10M1 is designed to locate convoys, ground targets, sea-surface targets, and low-flying aircraft and UAVs. The system is also used to locate shell bursts in order to adjust friendly artillery fire. The SNAR-10M1 is equipped with modern radios and communications systems to facilitate the automated data transmission. It also has a GLONASS enabled navigation system and digital terrain map.[45]

1L120 "Kredo-M1" Portable Radar

Field of view:	
Range (km)	.2-32
Azimuth (degrees)	12-180
Elevation (degrees)	±18
Detection range for moving targets:	
Personnel (km)	≤15
Tanks (km)	≤30
Trucks (km)	≤32
155mm shell detonations	≤10
Median error for moving target coordinates:	
Range (m)	25
Azimuth (degrees)	.3
Weight (kg)	51

Image Courtesy: Vitaly Kuzmin

The Kredo-M1 Portable Radar is designed for the detection of moving surface targets. It is also used to adjust friendly artillery fire, especially for antitank units. The Kredo-M1 is a man-portable system capable independent operation, but it can be networked with other systems.[46]

---

[45] "Russian SNAR-10M1 battlefield surveillance radar," as found at: *Army Recognition*, <http://www.armyrecognition.com/weapons_defence_industry_military_technology_uk/new_snar-10m1_1rl232-2m_battlefield_surveillance_radar_unveiled_at_oboronexpo_2014_in_russia_1408145.html>, accessed 20 December 2016.

[46] "Kredo-M1," as found at *Almaz-Antey* [The manufacturer's website], <http://www.almaz-antey.ru/en/catalogue/millitary_catalogue/1219/1242/1331>, accessed 20 December 2016.

1L219M "Zoopark-1M" Counter-Battery Radar Vehicle

Scanning Range (degrees)	90
Number of Targets Simultaneously Tracked	12
Set-up/Tear-down time (min)	5
Detection of Launch Position Range (km):	
Mortars	20
Field Artillery	15
MLRS	30
Tactical Missiles	40
Fire Correction Range (km):	
Mortars	22
Field Artillery	20
MLRS	35
Tactical Missiles	40

Image Courtesy: Vitaly Kuzmin

The Zoopark-1 counter-battery radar vehicle is designed to determine the coordinates of enemy artillery positions (field artillery, MLRS, mortars,) and tactical missile launch positions in order to provide targeting information for counterbattery missions, and to adjust friendly artillery fire. The Zoopark-1 can reportedly determine the coordinates of 60 batteries in a minute, and the position of a concealed mortar in an urban environment. The Russians consider the Zoopark-1 to be an equivalent of the AN/TPQ-36.[47]

1L271 "Aistenok" Portable Counter-Battery Radar

Field of view:	
Range (km)	.2-20
Azimuth (degrees)	360
Median error, subject to positioning deviance of no more than 3.5m (m):	
Mortar (ascending path)	30
Mortar (descending path)	200
Mortar (Point of impact)	30
Moving ground targets	40
Artillery shell burst	40
Minimum range for target detection (m):	
Mortar firing positions	750
Moving ground targets	200
Weight (kg)	135

Image Courtesy: Vitaly Kuzmin

The Aistenok is primarily a counter-battery radar designed to determine the coordinates of 81–120mm mortar firing positions and monitoring their flight trajectories. It is also capable of monitoring 122–155mm artillery shell bursts, and determining the coordinates of "tank" type moving surface targets.[48]

---

[47] Sergey Ptichkin, "Our Army Has the Best Artillery Reconnaissance Complexes in the World, but Cannot Effectively Utilize Them," *Rossiyskaya Gazeta* Online, 2 October 2008, <https://rg.ru/2008/10/02/zoopark.html>, accessed 20 December 2016.
[48] "Syrian Army Receives Advanced Mobile Radar System from Russia," as found at *SouthFront*, <https://southfront.org/syrian-army-receives-advanced-mobile-radar-system-from-russia-photos/>, accessed 20 December 2016.

(Right) The graphic on the facing page shows a motorized rifle battalion in the defense, with the battalion scheme of fire and artillery plan incorporated on the same map. The planners have determined the coordinates and distance to various visual benchmarks within the security zone. These are used to determine company sectors of fire, as well as reference points for designated weapons systems that can engage them or nearby targets. The green positions are deception positions designed to disguise the true front-line trace and in-depth positioning. The deception front-line trace is held by a minefield, temporary positions for the AGS-17 grenade-launcher platoon, the bronegruppa, the antitank reserve and the reserve. The mortar battery is temporarily forward to cover the forward position in the forward defensive zone.[49] The battalion is defending, with two motorized rifle companies forward and one back. There is an attached tank company which has attached a platoon to each of the forward motorized rifle platoons and has a platoon in the security zone. This last platoon will join the bronegruppa upon withdrawal. Artillery planning has determined several possible enemy axes of advance throughout the security zone. The planners expect the enemy to move from company to platoon column at the limits of the security zone and have plotted some artillery concentration boxes on the expected deployment line. The battalion has the second echelon company forward holding the forward position in the security zone. The forward position is protected by a minefield and obstacles. The artillery planners have plotted moving barrages Lion and Snow Leopard on the flanks of the forward position to assist in its withdrawal.

The artillery planners have plotted artillery concentrations on the lines where they expect the enemy platoons to move from platoon column to platoon line. Concentrations for tank fire platoons are also plotted in red. The final dashed blue lines are where enemy troops are expected to dismount and form into assault lines. Moving barrages Fox and Wolf are plotted before and after this line. Sectors of concentrated company fire (divided into platoon sections) are plotted before the expected dismount lines. The artillery planners have plotted standing barrage lines Acacia, Birch, Oak and Pine between the expected assault lines and the forward deception positions. Behind the deception positions is the third minefield and forward edge of the defense. Should the enemy penetrate the forward defense, there is an antitank ditch, antitank reserve, bronegruppa, and the reserve firing lines, as well as a firing line from the brigade's tank battalion. At this point, the artillery will be firing missions within the fallen defensive area and may be deployed in a direct fire role. The artillery may also deploy to alternate or reserve firing positions.

[49] This graphic shows a forward position in a rather shallow forward defensive area. The Russians prefer having a security zone of at least 15 kilometers depth. With a deep security zone, the mortar battery would deploy into it and have at least three firing positions. Artillery firing platoons or roving guns would also deploy into the security zone.

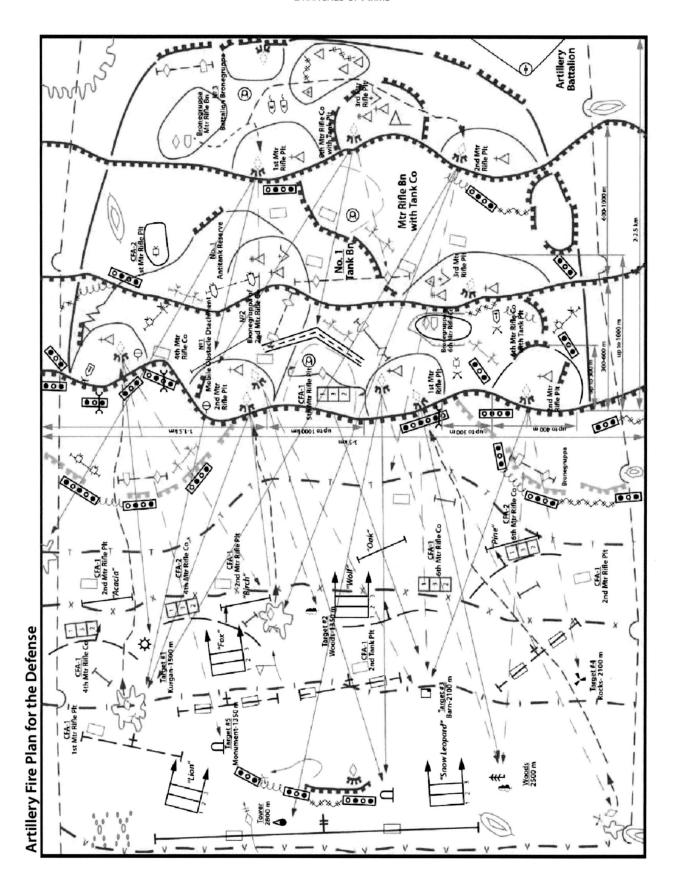

Artillery Fire Plan for the Defense

Artillery Modernization

In the U.S. military, the infantry is often referred to as the "Queen of Battle," but in the artillery-centric Russian Army, the artillery is often referred to as the "God of War." In keeping with this theme, Russia has put a great emphasis on the modernization of artillery pieces to project combat power more effectively. In terms of tube artillery developments, Russia is pursuing two lines of effort. The first is the creation of a new howitzer, the 2S35 Koalitsiya-SV 152mm self-propelled howitzer. The Koalitsiya-SV is a new howitzer design, with an unmanned turret, capable of firing 16 shells per minute, allowing each Koalitsiya-SV to achieve the same effects as an artillery battery (with 6 howitzers) using older guns. Although it is currently mounted on a T-90 based chassis, there are plans for it to also be fielded on the Armata chassis. As with other technological innovations, it will be modified and used by other branches of service, namely the Navy's Coastal Defense Troops. The Coastal Defense Troops are considering a wheeled variant that the Ground Forces is testing for use by "mountain" designated units. This capability, to be mounted on different chassis, suggests the Koalitsiya-SV is following the same design pattern as other Russian military combat vehicles, i.e., the turret may be attached to a variety of tracked and wheeled chassis, likely an innovation furthered for the benefit of the Russian Defense Ministry, but also as a selling point on the lucrative international arms export market.

2S35 "Koalitsiya-SV"

Image Courtesy: Vitaly Kuzmin

Another Russian artillery combat vehicle innovation pattern is fielding a small number of new systems, while conducting a major refurbishment of existing systems. Unlike the U.S. system, Russia does not find a need to retire functioning equipment, but rather prefers to refurbish this equipment at a fraction of the price of purchasing new systems. Although these refurbished systems have less impressive capabilities as newly purchased systems, these refurbished assets are a great bargain and deliver more "bang-for-the-buck." This institutional practice allows Russia to upgrade existing capabilities for a majority of the force, while buying a few expensive new technologies. Since Russia pursues a more "evolutionary" than "revolutionary" approach to arms procurement and utilizes only a few equipment manufacturers, there is substantial overlap in parts and components that are used in new and refurbished vehicles. This use of a combination of refurbished and brand new equipment does not cause the logistical headaches which would be expected from the increased production load list required for brand new systems using different parts and components. Thus, while Russia is preparing to field the Koalitsiya-SV, it is also modernizing its predecessor, the 2S19 (Msta-S) 152mm self-propelled howitzer, which reportedly boasts a firing rate of 10 rounds per minute and is designated the Msta-SM after refurbishment. Russian commentators have mentioned the possibility of these systems being capable of functioning in a "simultaneous fire assault" mode, a practice where both types of howitzers fire at different trajectories on the same target, causing the rounds to land on the target at

BM-27 "Uragan"   9A53 "Uragan-1M"

Images Courtesy: Vitaly Kuzmin

the same time. Russia's efforts to modernize tube artillery are in sync with efforts to develop a "reconnaissance-fire delivery system," a system for the rapid integration of targeting, fire control, and fires. As with other Russian developments, current innovations focus upon modularity and interoperability. The 9A53 Uragan-1M, a modernized version of the Uragan, has recently passed state trials. Instead of a rack of 16 rockets that the Uragan sports, the Uragan-1M has 2 pods of 6 rockets each. This pod system is intended to increase firing rates by speeding the replenishment process. The Uragan-1M will be reloaded by removing an empty pod and replacing it with a full one, which is presumably quicker than loading one rocket at a time. In addition, a pod system will allow the "Uragan-1M" to fire rockets of varying calibers. This pod system is being incorporated into Russia's next generation of MLRS launchers, the "Tornado" family. One member of this family, the 9A52-4 Tornado, built upon a Kamaz-63501 chassis, will reportedly be able to launch pods of any of the three caliber types, albeit of fewer number for the larger caliber rockets.

9A52-4 "Tornado"

Russian capability improvements have not stopped at material improvements, but also include doctrinal improvements. The Russian Army has been experimenting with the use of MLRS systems in direct fire roles and has recently changed doctrine (field regulations) for engaging observable targets from unprepared positions.[50] Russia is not only modernizing tube and MLRS platforms, but also pursuing modernization plans for automated command and control and fire control systems, with a keen interest in the integration of UAVs.

Images Courtesy: Vitaly Kuzmin

[50] Charles K. Bartles, "Russia Increasing Already Robust MLRS Capabilities," *OE Watch* Online, January 2016. Sergei Ptichkin, "A Younger Katyusha," *Rossiyskaya Gazeta* Online, 20 November 2014, <http://www.rg.ru/2014/11/20/katyusha.html>, accessed 15 December 2014.
Ilya Shchegolev, "Bi-caliber MLRS "Uragan-1M" Passed State Tests," *Rossiyskaya Gazeta* Online, 24 August 2015, <http://www.rg.ru/2015/08/24/uragan-site-anons.html>, accessed 15 December 2015.
"Troops in Western Russia to be reinforced with 50 MLRS systems by year end," I *Interfax-AVN*, 2 December 2015.

MLRS Characteristics

	BM-21 "Grad"	BM-27 "Uragan"	BM-30 "Smerch"
Caliber (mm)	122	220	300
Number of Rockets	40	16	12
Maximum Range* (km)	20.7	34	70
Minimum Range* (km)	—	—	20
Minimum Time To Fire All Rockets (s)	20	20	38
Rocket Weight (kg)*	66	280	800
System Weight (kg)	10,700	20,000	30,000
Crew	3	4	4
Chassis	Ural-375A	Zil-135	Maz-543A
Vehicle Speed (kph)	75	65	90
Reload Time (min)	3	3	2
Unit of Fire	120	48	24

* With Standard Rockets

The end state of these endeavors is to acquire targets more rapidly and appropriately task decisive fires.

Another interesting aspect of Russian artillery developments is the topic of relative cost. Consider the Russian 152mm GPS/GLONASS-enabled artillery shell in relation to the U.S./ NATO 155mm M982 Excalibur artillery shell. Reportedly, the Russian shell costs about $1000, while the U.S./NATO shell costs about $80,000 to manufacture. Issues of cost and affordability have always been top concerns in the Soviet, and later Russian, arms production cycles. In the Russian system, the cost of a given technology is one of the first criteria checked for feasibility, not the last. For Russia, it would be far better to use a less capable technology that can be used as desired than a more capable technology seldom used due to cost issues.[51]

[51] Charles K. Bartles, "Innovation, Cost, and Compromise Regarding the 'God of War,'" *OE Watch* Online, June 2016. "Advanced Self-Propelled Russian Rifle Gets Satellite-Navigated Shells," *Sputnik* Online, 24 April 2016, <http://sputniknews.com/russia/20160424/1038522310/russiagunmissilesatellite.html>, accessed 20 May 2016. "Fast and Accurate: Best-Kept Secrets of Russia's 'Sniper' Howitzer Revealed," *Sputnik* Online, 20 December 2015, <http://sputniknews.com/russia/20151220/1032044882/russiahowitzerdetailsvideo.html>, accessed 20 May 2016.

The 9K720 Iskander System

Although Russian maneuver brigades do not have organic Short-Range Ballistic Missile (SRBM) systems, they can be expected to support maneuver brigade commanders in high intensity conflict situations. The Missile and Artillery Troops operate these systems in dedicated missile brigades at the Army Group level. The Iskander missile system is a significant improvement over its predecessors (Tochka and Oka) and fills an important niche in Russian force projection. Tactical and theater ballistic missiles are far more important for Russia than for the U.S./NATO. In general, Russia believes that the U.S./NATO will maintain air superiority, and so has heavily invested missile technologies to fill a niche that air power fills for the U.S./NATO. For similar reasons Russia has also heavily invested in EW and air defense capabilities.

In terms of capabilities, the Iskander missile system has little in common with its predecessors. The system is capable of not only transporting and launching two missiles, but also firing two different types of missiles. The Iskander, which Russia classifies as a tactical-operational missile system, can fire two SRBMs (SS-26 Stone) or two ground-launched cruise missiles (referred to as the R-500 or Iskander-K in Russian), and possibly could fire a combination of these missiles. These missiles can carry a variety of payloads weighing 480-700 kilograms, including cluster warheads (antipersonnel/antimateriel), fragmentation submunitions, area denial submunitions, HE, thermobaric, high explosive earth penetrators for bunker busting, and electromagnetic pulse, decoy, and nuclear warheads. The Iskander's missiles are reportedly compliant with the 1987 Intermediate-Range Nuclear Forces (INF) Treaty, but there are allegations that these missiles could be easily modified to violate the 500-kilometer lower limit of the treaty.[52]

Perhaps the biggest difference between the Iskander and its predecessors, is its accuracy. While the Circular Error Probability (CEP) of the Iskander's predecessors was often estimated in hundreds of meters, the Iskander reportedly has a CEP of 10-30 meters. The warheads have an inertial unit with a terminal guidance electro-optical seeker and topographic data for finding targets. Some versions reportedly have guidance systems capable of GPS/GLONASS satellite navigation and active radar and/or infrared imaging seekers. A CEP of 10-30 meters may not seem impressive in the days of GPS, but it is important to note that Russians believe that GPS/GLONASS signals will not be available (jamming, spoofing, or other denials of service) in a conflict with a peer such as the U.S. or China. Although the warheads equipped with GPS/GLONASS systems are likely to have a better CEP than their non-GPS/GLONASS-equipped brethren, Russia appears to be betting that these types of systems will only be feasible in an engagement with a less capable opponent.

Russia touts the capability of the Iskander's missiles to evade missile defense systems by being able to vary their flight paths and deploy various countermeasures. Russia has stated on several occasions that one purpose of the Iskander missile system is to destroy U.S.

"Packing a Punch: A Self-Propelled Gun That's Worth a Whole Battery," *Sputnik* Online, 22 November 2015, <http://sputniknews.com/military/20151122/1030528826/russiakoalitsiyaartillery.html>, accessed 20 May 2016.
[52] One of the Iskander's predecessors, the Oka, was decommissioned due to the provision of the INF Treaty that the missile range is limited to 500-5500 kilometers.

9K720 "Iskander"

Image Courtesy: Russian Ministry of Defense

strategic missile defense assets at their launch sites which are located in Eastern Europe. The first combat use of the Iskander was during the 2008 Russo-Georgian War. Iskander SRBMs armed with cluster and high-explosive warheads reportedly destroyed most of a tank battalion and an ammunition depot. The Iskander is forward deployed in the Kaliningrad enclave in Eastern Europe and has also been deployed to Syria.

Iskander brigades consist of three Iskander battalions, with each battalion having two Iskander batteries. Each Iskander battery has two transporter erector launcher (TEL) vehicles, two reload vehicles, a command and control vehicle, a maintenance vehicle, and a support vehicle. In total, an Iskander brigade has 51 vehicles, consisting of 12 launchers, 12 transporter-loaders, 11 command and control vehicles, 14 support vehicles, 1 servicing and maintenance vehicle, and 1 information preparation vehicle.[53]

Iskander is a tactical-operational artillery asset that can support the maneuver brigade through long-range fires and interdiction, but it also has a nuclear capability, which raises issues of area denial and possible conflict escalation whenever it is employed.

---

[53] Mikhail Barabanov, "Iskander the Great," *Moscow Defense Brief*, Issue #4, 2008.
Charles K. Bartles, "Russia Touts Roles, Capabilities, and Possible Targets for the Iskander," *OE Watch* Online, January 2015.
"America in Shock: All Europe in Iskander-M's Sights," *Zvezda* Online, 13 November 2014, <http://tvzvezda.ru/news/forces/content/201411121543-iiyl.htm>, accessed 1 May 2016.

Conclusion

The Russians have continued to upgrade their artillery systems and bring new systems on line. Many of the improvements have been in the range, type and lethality of artillery ammunition. The Russians appreciate the potential for surgical strikes with precision munitions and have developed their own precision systems. However, they also believe that massed artillery fires will continue to hold pride of place in future maneuver combat and are effective when precision fires are not. Improvements in EW and the need to establish fire superiority at war's onset confirm their belief that quantity has a quality of its very own. Florent-Jean de Vallière (1667-1759), Director-General of the Battalions and Schools of Artillery, standardized French artillery sizes, making it less expensive and more abundant. On his largest cannon, the 24-pounder, was inscribed the Latin phrase "Ultima Ratio Regum." The Russians subscribe to this thought: artillery remains the "Last Argument of Kings."

9K720 "Iskander" Conducting Launch Operations

Image Courtesy: Russian Ministry of Defense

Air Defense Troops

The Air Defense Troops are a Branch of Arms of the Russian Ground Forces. They are intended to protect troops and facilities from different means of air attack (strike aviation, cruise missiles, UAVs) in a combined arms combat environment and on the march. They perform the following tasks:

- air defense combat
- detection of enemy aircraft and warning the troops covered
- destruction of the means of an enemy air attack
- theater missile defense support.

Anti-Aircraft Missile Battalion

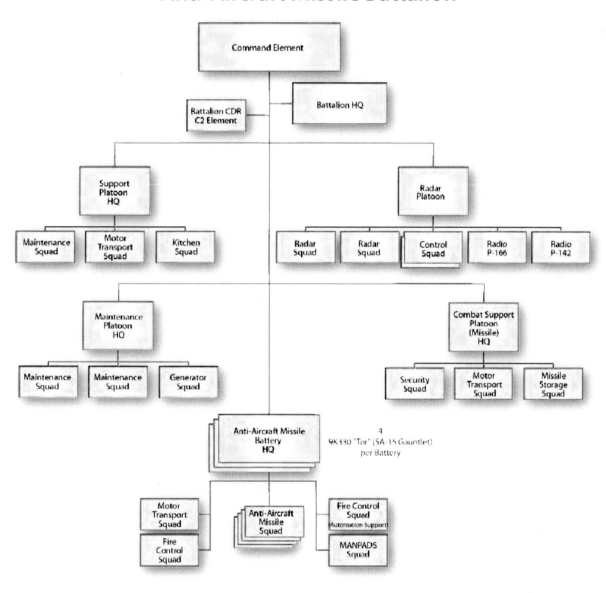

Anti-Aircraft Missile-Artillery Battalion

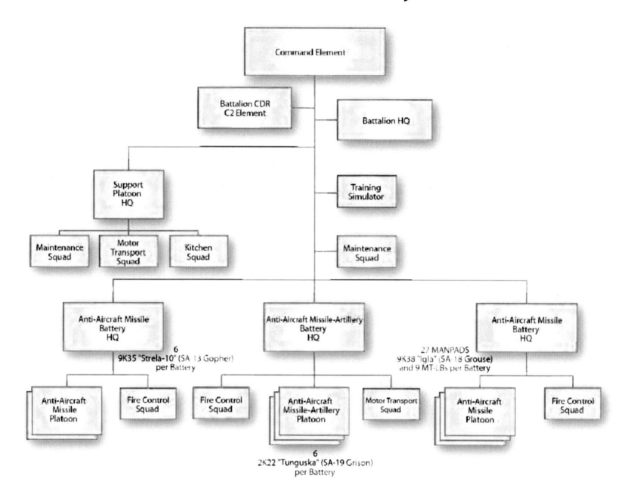

Organizationally, the Air Defense Troops consist of military control bodies, command points, anti-aircraft missile (rocket-artillery) and radio-technical formations, military units and subunits. They are capable of destroying enemy means of air attack throughout the range of altitudes: extremely low (up to 200 m), low (200-1000 m), medium (1000-4000 m), high (4000-12,000 m), and in the stratosphere (above 12,000 m), and at different flight speeds. The Air Defense Troops are equipped with anti-aircraft missiles, anti-aircraft artillery, anti-aircraft gun-and-missile systems and portable anti-aircraft missile systems. These systems have differing ranges, channeling ability and means of missile guidance. Depending on the range of destruction of aerial targets, they are divided into the systems of near range (up to 10 km), short range (up to 30 km), medium range (up to 100 km), and long range (more than 100 km). In terms of modernization and capability development, the Air Defense Troops are interested in improving mobility, survivability, covertness of operation, degree of automation, fire efficiency, expansion of denial areas, reduction of response times, and improvement of the weight and size characteristics of missiles.[54]

---

[54] "Air Defense Troops," *Ministry of Defense of the Russian Federation* Website, <http://eng.mil.ru/en/structure/forces/ground/structure/vpvo.htm>, accessed 1 May 2016.

Although there has been much discussion of Russia's long-range operational/strategic air defense assets (S-300, S-400, S-500, etc.) found in the Aerospace Defense Forces, the vast majority of Russian air defense assets are of the short-/medium-range variety and are found in the Air Defense Troops of the Russian Ground Forces. Russia has long been a strong proponent of Air Defense at all levels, due to fears of U.S./NATO air superiority. It has continued this tradition into the present and has expanded air defense capabilities to counter not only hostile airplanes and helicopters, but also cruise missiles and UAVs. The Russian Ground Forces have medium- and short-range air defense assets in dedicated air defense brigades, but maneuver brigades also have significant organic short-range air defense capabilities. These capabilities reside in the maneuver brigade's two air defense battalions, with four different air defense systems that provide the brigade an overlapping zonal defense. Although these capabilities are formidable, they are not the sole means of air defense for the brigade. Russian maneuver brigades have substantial EW capabilities that complicate attack aviation targeting, and Russia has touted the abilities of its "Vikhr" and "Ataka" missiles to hit relatively low- and slow-flying aircraft. In addition, Russia's fielding of small, unmanned turrets, which will be mounted as secondary weapons on heavy weapon platforms and as the primary weapon on armored cars and support vehicles, will also have a limited air defense capability for low- and slow-flying aircraft.[55]

Commonly Found Organic Air Defense Assets in a Maneuver Brigade

The 2K22 Tunguska (SA-19 Grison) is a short-range missile-gun heavy tracked, lightly armored system that has twin 2A38M (30 mm) guns and 8 short-range missiles designed to engage low-flying aircraft and cruise missiles at a distance of up to 8 km and flight ceiling of 3.5 km. The twin 2A38M (30 mm) guns are useful for engaging extremely close targets, where the expenditure of a missile would be uneconomical (such as a small UAV), targets that are have EW protection capabilities (that missiles cannot engage), and, when necessary, ground targets. Each maneuver brigade typically has six launcher vehicles within a battery of the air defense missile-artillery battalion. Russia is now planning on developing a successor to the Tunguska, equipped with a 57mm autocannon.

2K22 "Tungunska"

Image Courtesy: Vitaly Kuzmin

[55] Charles K. Bartles, "Flying the Unfriendly Skies: Air Defense in the Russian Ground Forces," February 2016.
Charles K. Bartles, "Unmanned Turrets to Increase ISR Capabilities and Lethality," *OE Watch* Online, November 2015.
Dmitry Fedyushka, "Secrets of a Deserted Tower," *Voyenno-Promyshlennyy Kuryer* Online, 7 October 2015, <http://vpk-news.ru/articles/27399>, accessed 1 May 2015.
Aleksandr Luzan, "The Fight above the Forwardmost Defensive Positions- Part I," *Voyenno-Promyshlennyy Kuryer* Online, 18 November 2015, <http://vpk-news.ru/articles/28054>, accessed 1 May 2016.
Aleksandr Luzan, "The Fight above the Forwardmost Defensive Positions- Part II," *Voyenno-Promyshlennyy Kuryer* Online, 25 November 2015, <http://www.vpk-news.ru/articles/28156>, accessed 1 May 2016.

The Brigade's Organic Air Defense Units

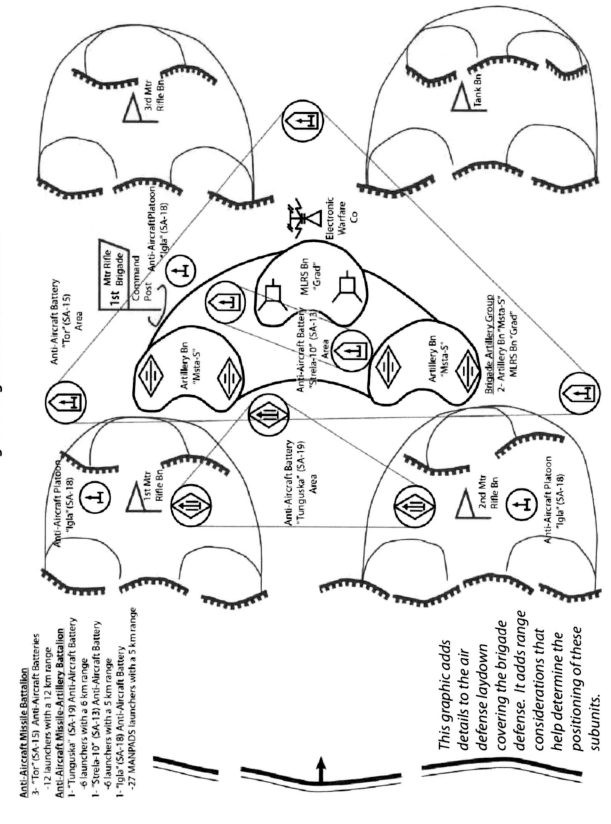

Anti-Aircraft Missile Battalion
3- "Tor" (SA-15) Anti-Aircraft Batteries
-12 launchers with a 12 km range
Anti-Aircraft Missile-Artillery Battalion
1- "Tunguska" (SA-19) Anti-Aircraft Battery
-6 launchers with a 6 km range
1- "Strela-10" (SA-13) Anti-Aircraft Battery
-6 launchers with a 5 km range
1- "Igla" (SA-18) Anti-Aircraft Battery
-27 MANPADS launchers with a 5 km range

This graphic adds details to the the air defense laydown covering the brigade defense. It adds range considerations that help determine the positioning of these subunits.

9K35 "Strela-10"

The 9K35 Strela-10 (SA-13 Gopher) is a close-(very short) range missile system, usually built upon a MT-LB (light tracked) chassis. It has four close-range, visually sited missiles capable of engaging targets at a distance of up to 5 km and flight ceiling of 3.5 kilometers. The system was reportedly designed to complement the Tunguska, as the Strela-10 costs less and is much less susceptible to EW countermeasures, due to its targeting system. Each maneuver brigade typically has six launcher vehicles within a battery of the air defense missile-artillery battalion.

Image Courtesy: Vitaly Kuzmin

9K310 "Igla"

Image Courtesy: Vitaly Kuzmin

The 9K310 Igla (SA-18 Grouse) is a close-(very short) range, man-portable air-defense system (MANPADS), capable of engaging targets at a distance of up to 5 kilometers and flight ceiling of 3.5 kilometers. Each maneuver brigade typically has 27 MANPADS within a battery of the air defense missile-artillery battalion. It is being replaced by the 9K333 Verba, which has similar characteristics as its predecessors, but has a better guidance system and increased abilities to circumvent EW countermeasures.

The 9K330 Tor (SA-15 Gauntlet) is a short-to-medium-range heavy tracked, lightly armored, platform that packs 8 missiles that are primarily designed to engage cruise missiles and other precision guided weapons at a distance of up to 12 kilometers and flight ceiling of 6 kilometers. It is being replaced by the Tor-M2, which sports 16 missiles with an increased flight ceiling (10 kilometers) and can engage up to 4 targets simultaneously, while firing on the move. Each maneuver brigade typically has 12 launcher vehicles within the batteries of the air defense missile battalion.

9K330 "Tor"

Image Courtesy: Vitaly Kuzmin

Modernization of Russian Ground Force's Air Defense Assets

Russian Ground Forces are in the midst of a mass modernization of air defense systems. These upgrades include systems that carry more missiles, have better radar and C2 capabilities, and have missiles with greater ranges and better abilities to circumvent EW countermeasures. These modernizations include:

The 9K330 Tor (SA-15 Gauntlet): The Tor is being replaced by the Tor-M2, which sports 16 missiles with an increased flight ceiling (10 kilometers) and can engage up to 4 targets simultaneously, while firing on the move.

The 2K22 Tunguska (SA-19 Grison): The 96K6 Pantsir-S1 (SA-22 Greyhound) was initially thought to be the successor to the Tunguska, as it has a similar missile-gun combination, but is armed with 12 short-range missiles designed to engage low-flying aircraft and cruise missiles at a distance of up to 20 kilometers and flight ceiling of 15 kilometers. Despite similar appearances, the Pantsir-S1 does not appear to be the successor to the Tunguska. Instead, The Pantsir-S1 is being used to protect strategic (long-range) air defense assets of the Aerospace Defense Forces, such as the S-300 and S-400. The role of the Pantsir-S1 as a strategic protection asset may be one reason that the system can be provided on a wheeled chassis. Russia is now planning on developing a successor to the Tunguska, equipped with a 57mm autocannon.

The 9K35 Strela-10 (SA-13 Gopher): The Strela-10 is being replaced by the Luchnik-E, which has 8 missiles with a 6-kilometer range and 3.5-kilometer flight ceiling, with the most important capability improvements being the addition of all weather and day/night firing capabilities. There are also reports that the Strela-10 could be replaced with the Sosna that has twelve Sosna-R missiles with a 10-kilometer range and 5-kilometer flight ceiling.

Luchnik-E

Image Courtesy: Vitaly Kuzmin

- The 9K310 Igla (SA-18 Grouse): a close- (very short-) range MANPADS, capable of engaging targets at a distance of up to 5 kilometers and flight ceiling of 3.5 kilometers. It is being replaced by the 9K333 Verba, which has similar characteristics as its predecessors, but has a better guidance system and increased abilities to circumvent EW countermeasures.

- The 9K37 Buk (SA-11 Gadfly): is not a part of Ground Forces maneuver units, but is instead found within the Ground Forces' air defense artillery brigades. It is a short-to-medium-range missile system on a heavy tracked platform that has 4 missiles with a range of up to 30 kilometers and flight ceiling of 14 kilometers. It is being replaced with the 9K317M Buk-M3 (SA-17 Grizzly), which is equipped with 6 missiles that have ranges of up to 70 kilometers and flight ceiling of 35 kilometers. The most interesting purported capability is being able to engage not only air targets, but also ground targets.

Chapter 7
Specialty Branches

Reconnaissance, Spetsnaz, and SOF

Reconnaissance units are a branch of the Russian Ground Forces. These units are intended to perform a wide range of tasks in order to ensure commanders and their staffs receive accurate and timely information about the enemy, terrain and weather, to support decision making and prevent surprise enemy action. Reconnaissance units [разведывательные воинские части] and formations [разведывательные соединения] may consist of any of the following: combined arms, spetsnaz, signals intelligence, or dedicated TO&E reconnaissance subunits [подразделения] and units [воинские части].

Reconnaissance units fulfill the following objectives, in preparation for, and during, the conduct of combined arms operations:
- determining the enemy's order of battle, immediate preparations for battle, and warning signs of surprise attack
- identifying the enemy's composition, position, echelonment, status and capabilities of forces, system of command and control
- determining which targets to engage and their locations
- finding significant enemy theater-level weapons and equipment, detecting enemy engineer field fortifications and his integrated obstacle network
- determining the difficulty of crossing terrain, the status of communications, the nature of water obstacles, the boundaries and size of areas of destruction, fires and floods, disease-contaminated areas, and the possible axes of overcoming or bypassing them
- identifying new enemy weapons and methods of warfare, as well as the conduct and measures required for the 360° security of the operation or combat
- determining the morale of enemy troops and the local population, and the economic status of the area of operations.

Intelligence units and formations collect intelligence by:
- monitoring and eavesdropping
- ground and air photography
- signal intercept, to determine object coordinates
- conducting search, raid, ambush, reconnaissance missions
- questioning local residents, and interrogating prisoners and deserters
- analysis of captured enemy documents, equipment and weapons.

In terms of modernization and capability development, the reconnaissance units will increase their intelligence capabilities by developing new and/or improved: means of technical intelligence, including ones based on new physical principles; tactical reconnaissance complexes, that utilize unmanned aerial vehicles; and automated collection, processing and that will bring intelligence to the commander (commander) and headquarters in real-time.[1]

Relationship of Reconnaissance and Intelligence
In the Soviet/Russian system, the term for intelligence [разведка] can mean "intelligence" or

"reconnaissance" or a combination of both these terms. In a military context, especially at the tactical levels, the term usually refers to reconnaissance activities. In the Russian system, the intelligence staff section directly commands dedicated reconnaissance units and other intelligence assets. At the battalion level (of maneuver units), the officer in charge of the intelligence staff section is also in charge of reconnaissance, but since at the battalion level most maneuver units do not have dedicated reconnaissance assets, regular units from the battalion are assigned for this purpose on an *ad hoc* basis. This officer is a career (branched) maneuver officer (as appropriate to the type of unit), whose primary responsibility is determining the position of the enemy through the personnel and assets under his direct control. In the US/NATO system, the officer in charge of the intelligence staff section (S-2) is usually a career (branched) intelligence officer, and is primarily responsible for analyzing and presenting information about the enemy and environment to the commander. A U.S./NATO S-2 typically does not command reconnaissance units (reconnaissance teams, Long Range Reconnaissance Patrols, etc.) as does his Russian counterpart. In the Western system these assets are typically directly controlled by the operations section. In short, at tactical levels, the Soviet officer in charge of the intelligence staff is a maneuver officer, a fellow "meat eater" that works closely with the commander, functioning as his eyes and ears by deploying his own subordinate assets on the battlefield. This is in stark contrast to most U.S./NATO battalion S-2s that are relegated to purely staff work, and having a much more distant relationship with their commanders. The implication of this systemic difference between the Russian and Western acquisition of intelligence is that Soviet/Russian reconnaissance units, such as spetsnaz, would be normally associated with the intelligence staffs, as opposed to the operations staff as in most Western Armies.

Tactical Reconnaissance

Russia broadly views military intelligence at the strategic, operational-tactical, and tactical levels. Operational-tactical and tactical military intelligence are divided into five function-based spheres: ground, air, sea, space, and "special." Military intelligence conducted at the tactical level for ground forces focuses on determining the position of the enemy, finding strong and weak points in the defense, and uncovering obstacles to maneuver. The term "tactical reconnaissance" best describes the military intelligence activities occurring at the tactical level of ground operations. Tactical reconnaissance is doctrinally divided into several categories including: combat reconnaissance, signals intelligence, radar, electro-optical, artillery, engineer, medical, route, and nuclear, biological and chemical detection. Tactical reconnaissance is performed by intelligence, motorized rifle, tank, airborne, air assault, and spetsnaz units; and is conducted through observation, signal intercept, search, raid, ambush, and patrol.

Task Organized Reconnaissance Elements by Echelon

Since most Russian units do not have dedicated reconnaissance units below brigade/division level, Russia has a well-defined system for task organizing units for this purpose. The following lists each maneuver echelon with its typically associated task organized reconnaissance elements. It is important to remember that these elements will not be found on standing TO&Es, but will be encountered in the field.

<u>Brigades/Divisions</u> - reconnaissance detachments [разведывательные отряды], reconnaissance patrols [разведывательные дозоры], reconnaissance groups [разведывательные группы], leader's reconnaissance [офицерские разведывательные дозоры], search units [подразделения для проведения поисков], ambush units [подразделения для устройства засад], reconnaissance in force [подразделения для проведения разведки боем], observation posts [наблюдательные посты].

<u>Regiments (in a division)</u> - reconnaissance detachments [разведывательные отряды], reconnaissance patrols [разведывательные дозоры], leader's reconnaissance [офицерские разведывательные дозоры], search units [подразделения для проведения поисков], ambush units [подразделения для устройства засад], observation posts [наблюдательные посты]

<u>Battalions</u> - combat reconnaissance patrols [боевые разведывательные дозоры], ambush units [подразделения для устройства засад], patrol squads [дозорные отделения], observation posts [наблюдательные посты]

<u>Companies</u> - patrol squads [дозорные отделения], observation squads [наблюдателие отделения], combat reconnaissance patrols [боевые разведывательные дозоры], Platoons- patrol squads [дозорные отделения], observation squads [наблюдателие отделения]

Task Organized Reconnaissance Elements

<u>Reconnaissance Detachment [разведывательный отряд]</u> - Reconnaissance detachments are typically mounted reinforced companies that are capable of conducting observation, searches, raids, ambushes, installing/removing observation equipment, and, if necessary, engaging the enemy. They move on primary axes in advance of a march, meeting battle or offensive and are normally proceeded by a Reconnaissance Patrol (platoon). The standard operating range of a Reconnaissance Detachment varies by mission, but an operational depth of 50 kilometers for company-sized units and 80 kilometers for battalion-sized elements is common.[2]

Reconnaissance Detachment

<u>Reconnaissance Group [разведывательная группа]</u> - Reconnaissance groups are typically motorized rifle or spetsnaz squads dispatched to reconnoiter in the enemy rear area to locate nuclear delivery systems, enemy forces, headquarters, airfields, signal sites and other important targets. Reconnaissance groups are capable of conducting observation, raids, ambushes, and installing/removing observation and communication equipment.

Reconnaissance Patrol or Group

275

They may be inserted by helicopter, vehicle or on foot.[3]

Reconnaissance Patrol [разведывательный дозор] - Reconnaissance patrols are typically platoon-sized elements, reinforced with engineers and other specialists, that reconnoiter up to 10 kilometers ahead of the parent unit. Reconnaissance patrols can be combat, officer reconnaissance, NBC or engineer.[4]

Reconnaissance Units in the Brigade and Division
The "New Look" reforms downsized reconnaissance battalions to companies, when the maneuver divisions transitioned to brigades. The Russian Ground Forces are now in the process of reversing this reform, as brigade commanders complained that reconnaissance companies are insufficient for the brigade's required ISR tasks.[5] (The accompanying graphics depict both the company and battalion structures, as Russia is still in the process of this transition.) Unlike the personnel in other Ground Forces' Branches of Arms or Specialty Branches, most personnel serving in these reconnaissance battalions and companies are usually motorized rifle troops, in terms of military occupational specialty. Reconnaissance personnel typically conduct reconnaissance with BTRs, BMPs, Combat Reconnaissance Patrol Vehicles (BRDMs), or Tigr/Tigr-M reconnaissance vehicles.

Reconnaissance Company

Combat Reconnaissance Vehicle (BRDM-2)

Image Courtesy: Vitaly Kuzmin

The Combat Reconnaissance Patrol Vehicle (BRDM-2) is designed to perform enemy and terrain reconnaissance while in combat conditions, performing march security, and monitoring lines of communication. The amphibious BRDM is capable of overcoming ditches and water obstacles, and is equipped with an environmental system to protect the crew from NBC threats. The BRDM is typically equipped with radios, night vision devices, navigation equipment and other reconnaissance related equipment. The vehicle is manned by four personnel, is relatively light, (seven tons) and has two crew-served weapons, 14.5mm KPVT and 7,62mm machine guns.

The GAZ-2330 Tigr is a 4x4 multi-role, all-terrain light armored vehicle that serves as a reconnaissance vehicle. The vehicle is primarily operated by Russian Defense Ministry and Ministry of the Interior forces, and can be found conducting escort and reconnaissance missions, patrols, and counter-terrorist operations. The Tigr resembles a HMMWV, and has engine forward, crew cab in the middle and a troop section in the rear. The modular design of the Tigr allows the conversion of the base vehicle platform into 11-passenger, armored or cargo vehicles. The Tigr's crew-served weapon is mounted on the roof, and can be a 7.62mm or 12.7mm machine gun, or 30mm automatic grenade launcher.[6] The GAZ-233114 Tigr-M is an improved version of the Tigr.[7]

Combat Reconnaissance Patrol Vehicle

GAZ-2330 "Tigr" with ATGMs

Taifun-M

What is Spetsnaz?

In the West, the terms "spetsnaz" and "special operations" are used as synonyms. In Russia, these terms are related but different terms. The word *spetsnaz* [**спецназ**] is a Russian abbreviation of the words *spetsialnovo naznacheniya* [**спец**иального **наз**начения], a term which can roughly be translated as "special designation" referring to troops with a special purpose. The word "special" is used in a very broad way that can indicate that the unit has a very narrow area of specialization, such as signals intelligence, engineering, reconnaissance, etc.; or the unit is experimental or temporary in nature; or the unit conducts tasks of special importance such as sensitive political or clandestine operations.[8] This broad usage of the term means that "spetsnaz" cannot be thought of as equating to the Western concept of Special Operation Forces (SOF).

Soviet Roots of Spetsnaz

The Soviets started experimenting with elite reconnaissance and sabotage units in the Spanish Civil War, and employed such units in the Soviet-Finnish War, and in Romania, Yugoslavia, and Belarus during the Second World War. But modern usage of the term spetsnaz started in the 1950s. The development of modern spetsnaz was the direct result of the US introduction of tactical nuclear weapons systems into the European theater. The United States employment of tactical missiles was problematic for the Soviets. U.S. tactical nuclear weapons in the 1950's had relatively short ranges (Little John-19 kilometers, Honest John-25 to 50 kilometers) but could rapidly deploy and deliver a devastating payload. Conventional Soviet forces were ill equipped to handle such a threat, so spetsnaz reconnaissance companies were formed to identify and neutralize such targets quickly, while operating at ranges up to 200 kilometers in the enemy rear. As the range of U.S. tactical missiles increased throughout the 1950s and 1960s, so did the Soviet need for spetsnaz forces capable of actions at greater operational depths. Spetsnaz battalions were formed later for missions up to 400 kilometers in the enemy rear, and eventually in 1962, in response to the Lance, Sergeant, and Pershing missile systems, spetsnaz brigades were established to operate up to 750 kilometers in the enemy rear. Although the primary driving force for the creation of the spetsnaz had been finding and eliminating tactical nuclear weapons, the spetsnaz also retained an important secondary mission, related to its roots in the Spanish civil-war, identifying and destroying other key objectives behind enemy lines.[9]

> "The evolution of the Spetsnaz, after the war, was directly connected to the development of nuclear weaponry, although eliminating these weapons and their delivery systems has never been our only task. We have also been trained for pure reconnaissance and for guiding artillery and aviation."
>
> Spetsnaz Colonel Vassily Kolesnik[10]

Command & Control of the Spetsnaz

Emblem of the GRU Spetsnaz

In the pre-Cold War years, reconnaissance and sabotage units that were formed under the Main Intelligence Directorate of the General Staff, were typically operationally controlled by the intelligence sections of the respective Front Commanders. In the post-Cold War years, proponency passed from the Second Directorate to the Main Intelligence Directorate of the General Staff (GRU)[11], and the operational control of the spetsnaz companies passed from the Fronts to the intelligence sections of their subordinate Army Groups. The spetsnaz's primary mission of nuclear weapon destruction would become the main factor driving how the units were operationally controlled. The relatively short range of early U.S. tactical nuclear weapons (20-50 kilometers) placed the launch vehicles well within the Army Groups's area of responsibility. Since the

Image Courtesy: Russian Ministry of Defense

tactical nuclear weapons were within the 1st echelon Army Group's area of responsibility, it was logical that the spetsnaz companies be assigned directly to these Army Groups. As the effective ranges of tactical nuclear weapons increased, command and control passed from Army Group, with an area of responsibility of up to approximately 100 kilometers. (spetsnaz companies), to Fronts with the responsibility for an operational depth of several hundred kilometers (spetsnaz battalions), and finally, with the introduction of the Pershing system, with a operational-strategic level reach, to the General Staff (spetsnaz brigades).[12]

Spetsnaz in the Post-Soviet Era

By the time of the collapse of the Soviet Union, the term "spetsnaz" when used in reference to the Soviet Union's elite combat units usually referred to the GRU's *Spetsnaz* Brigades and Combat Swimmer units (roughly the GRU's naval reconnaissance force with a saboteur/anti-saboteur capability) , the Russian Airborne's 45th Spetsnaz Regiment (later brigade), or select elite anti-terrorist units. (such as the FSB's Alpha and Vympel). In a more general context, the term "spetsnaz" also found use while referencing special purpose units such as certain signals intelligence, experimental, or other atypical sorts of troop formations. (In these instances perhaps a better translation would be "special troops" instead of "spetsnaz" to differentiate.)

> … various armed units subordinated to Russia's numerous government agencies began
> to borrow the word Spetsnaz for their own titles so as to sound more important, even though
> in many cases these units were just glorified guard and protection squads. The term was
> also borrowed by some highly trained and well-armed police units, the Russian equivalent
> of America's SWAT teams[13]

In the post Soviet era, the term spetsnaz grew considerably in usage and were increasingly found in a wide range of titles of units with diverse, and sometimes relatively mundane, missions in a variety of ministries. In all, Russia has an estimated 50,000 personnel in "spetsnaz" designated units. It is important to note that in the West, the term "military" is typically associated with uniformed serviceman, whose primary occupation is war fighting, that serve under the Ministry or Department of Defense. In Russia the term "military" has a much broader context, due to the militarization of the police (internal security services) and intelligence services. This means that many of these 50,000 spetsnaz personnel were not necessarily found within the Ministry of Defense, but also found throughout the other Russian security services.

Russian Spetsnaz within the Hierarchy of Elites

Perhaps the biggest difference between American/Western SOF and Russian Spetsnaz, referring specifically to personnel serving in the GRU Spetsnaz brigades, is the perception of these forces as elites. In the U.S., SOF have the highest prestige, and are considered the crème de crème of trigger pullers. This is in marked contrast to the Russian system, where the true elite "trigger pullers" are members of the Russian Airborne (VDV). One of the best examples of how Russia values these units is in terms of manning. In the Russian system units are manned with a combination of officers,

BRM-3K Combat Reconnaissance Vehicle

Image Courtesy: Vitaly Kuzmin

contract soldiers, and conscripts, the more elite the unit, the higher percentage of contract personnel *vis-à-vis* conscripts. Currently, the Russian VDV is manned with approximately 80% contract, a far higher percentage than the GRU Spetnaz.[14] In general, this difference between American SOF and Russian Spetsnaz can be attributed to very different origination stories, namely American SOF growing out of the U.S.'s Vietnam experience as direct action forces, training guerillas, and conducting COIN versus the Russian usage of GRU spetsnaz as primarily ISR assets.

Differentiating American SOF from Russian Spetsnaz

Perhaps the biggest difference between the U.S. and Russian system is the idea of specialization. In the U.S. system, Navy SEALs may be found conducting a hostage rescue in an urban area, providing ISR on a remote mountain in the middle of Afghanistan, performing sniper duties in Iraq, or acting in a more traditional frogman role placing or removing explosives in a naval setting. In the Russian system, spetsnaz and SOF appear to much more rigidly stick with their areas of expertise. GRU Spetsnaz conduct ISR for conventional forces, Russian frogman work exclusively with naval missions, elite FSB units conduct hostage rescue operations, elite MVD units conduct SWAT and riot control missions. Although these units may conduct direct action missions, they are in no way seen as a substitute for the Ground Forces, VDV, or Naval Infantry. Russian Spetsnaz are elite, but the main instrument for projecting combat power is seen as the conventional forces, even if Russia is engaged in what the West would consider Military Operations Other Than War (MOOTW) or low intensity conflict. This manner of thinking explains why the Russian Federation has made great increases in her conventional capabilities, but has shown little interest in increasing her spetsnaz/SOF capabilities. These capabilities are seen as important, but they are seen as enablers for conventional forces, not means of conducting war in themselves.

Russian Special Operations Forces

"Having studied international practice in creating, training and using special operations forces, the Ministry of Defense has started to build a similar force…We have set up a special command, which has already begun to put our plans into practice as part of the Armed Forces training program. We have also developed a set of key documents that outline the development priorities, the training program, and the modalities of using these new forces… "
- General Valeri Gerasimov

General Valeriy Gerasimov,
Chief of the Russian General Staff
March 6, 2013[15]

In 2013, The Russian Federation announced the creation of a Special Operations Command.[16] Although it may be tempting to assume this Russian Special Operations Command will resemble its Western brethren, it important to remember some differences between the organizations. According to some reporting the command was partially activated in 2009, due to the aftermath of the 2008 Russo-Georgian War, where the GRU Spetsnaz had a few high-profile gaffes. There was also speculation that the command was formed due to the new Defense Minister's interest in creating a more "Western" military, with an emphasis on quality instead of quantity. Whatever reason the command was stood up, it appears to have no Western or Russian equivalent. The most striking aspect of the command is that it appears more of a branch proponent than an actual functional command. The command (в/ч 92154 HQ & Doctrine Development) will reportedly standardize doctrine and capabilities for Russia's premiere SOF units in all military forces, and have the capability to provide command and control for these units in wartime.[17] The premier elite units are found in the:

- Ministry of Defense
- Federal Security Service
- Ministry of Internal Affairs
- Federal Protection Service
- Federal Penal Service
- Federal Narcotics Trafficking Control Service

The command also provides day-to-day control of a Training Center (в/ч 99450) and MoD unit (в/ч 01355 Operational Detachments & Support). From a Russian view, the most interesting aspect of the command is that it reports to the General Staff, but not the Main Intelligence Directorate (GRU) as do the spetsnaz brigades. Although the exact directorate has yet to be named, it is likely the operations directorate. If this is true, this would be a major doctrinal change, and

Lieutenant Colonel Boris Nikolaev
Commander of the "Saturn" Spetsnaz Detachment of the Federal Penal Service
Image Courtesy: Vitaly Kuzmin

suggests that the unit could have a much more of a direct action, as opposed to ISR role. There has been some reporting that the unit is intended to conduct peacetime missions such as hostage rescue, evacuation of civilians from war zones, and operations against criminal groups, and in wartime missions such as destruction of enemy strategic weapons, command and command, and disrupting communications and logistics.[18]

There have been few details about the structure or manning of the command, but the command reportedly has about 1000 personnel, roughly half in the headquarters and training center, and the rest in a newly created MoD unit (with personnel recruited from GRU Spetsnaz Brigades). In some aspects, this new unit will closely resemble other Russian Spetsnaz units, and is likely structured on the basis of a GRU regiment, consisting of saboteur reconnaissance teams equipped with armored vehicles. Unlike other spetsnaz units, that are seen as elite forces that perform missions (reconnaissance, direct action, etc.) for the sole purpose of furthering the movement and maneuver of the conventional Armed Forces, this new MoD unit's structure suggests that it is intended to act independently. The command has a dedicated special aviation brigade that is responsible for the coordination of, or directly controls, Army combat aviation assets at Torzhok, and a squadron of the Il-72 transporters at the Migalovo airfield near Tver, and the command has supporting elements that provides Combat Support and Combat Service Support functions.[19] These developments coincide with legislative changes that provides a legal mechanism for certain extraterritorial deployments, as there has been some interest in deploying the elite counter narcotics unit to Central Asia for narcotics interdiction mission.[20]

Although Russia has established a special operations command and is experimenting with SOF forces in a way more accustomed to the ways they are used in the West, Russia does not appear interested in the U.S./Western model of SOF employment. Russia appears to have more faith in its conventional forces, than the West has in its own. Russia used spetsnaz and SOF in the Crimea, but the vast majority of the "polite people" were almost certainly from elite conventional units. Russia executes operations in this manner, not due to the lack of special operations forces, but simply because many missions that the West would consider "SOF missions," are missions that Russia performs with her elite conventional forces such as the Airborne, Naval Infantry, or even elite conventional motorized rifle or tank units. In the Russian system, direct action is conducted primarily by the conventional warfighter, not the special operator.

Signal Troops

The Signal Troops are intended to deploy communications systems, and support the command and control of Ground Forces units in war and peacetime. They are also responsible for operating automated command and control systems. Signal Troops may be found in regular line units and technical support units, operating automated command and control systems, in the signal communications security and postal-and-courier communications services, and in other places. Signal Troops are equipped with a variety of mobile and reliable equipment related to: radio relay, tropospheric and satellite communications, telephony, tone telegraphy, television, photography, signal switching, and cryptography. In terms of modernization and capability development, the Russian Federation is interested in equipping the Signal Troops with modern means of signal communications, as well as automated command and control systems that provide reliable, fast, encrypted communications throughout the chain of command in war and peacetime conditions, even in the most difficult physical and climatic conditions. Particular emphasis is being made on automated command and control systems that function at the tactical level, that provide individual troops with secure, jam-resistant means of communication.[21] In terms of the maneuver brigades, each has a signal battalion. Since Russian brigades are garrisoned individually, the signal battalion supports both tactical and garrison communications.

Network-Centric Warfare

Command and control (C2) has long been a problem in both the Soviet and Russian militaries. At the tactical level, radio technology was generally lacking, and the ability to transmit digitally nonexistent. In the last few years, this has begun to change. The Russian Federation has made a great effort to develop a "network-centric" command and control system. The Signal Troops are at the center of this effort that is one the main components of the Russian Armed Forces' 2008 "New Look" reforms. Network-centric warfare can roughly be described as the wide-scale use of networked

Platoon/squad leader tablet PC

Image Courtesy: Vitaly Kuzmin

electronic reconnaissance and targeting systems (satellites, unmanned aerial vehicles, etc.) coupled with mobile formations that can be quickly deployed throughout the entire theater of military operations to deliver decisive strikes on the enemy's flanks and rear, as quickly and efficiently as possible. The Signal Troops appear to be the key to implementing this program, as they man the automated command and control systems, radios, and landline infrastructure required for this endeavor. At the highest levels, this concept has led to the establishment of a national command center that will reportedly be connected to subordinate command centers at the operational strategic command (military district) and Army Group levels. At the tactical level, the Armed Forces are overcoming C2 problems and implementing network-centric warfare through a variety of new technologies including: new tactical radios, a tactical digital mobile subscriber system (roughly a military digital cell phone and data system), and tactical laptops and tablets. Despite these advances, Russia has still had difficulties fielding a modern, unified C2 system for tactical units. The answer to this problem is the fielding of the 'Andromeda' C2 system, which has been in development for several years. This system is in many ways similar in purpose and capabilities to the US's Force XXI Battle Command Brigade and Below (FBCB2) system. The Andromeda is intended to provide situational awareness to the commander and allow for the real-time exchange of information

Laptop

Image Courtesy: Vitaly Kuzmin

from the highest commander down to the squad, and even individual soldier. The Andromeda can reportedly interface with space based networks and has extensive counter electronic warfare capabilities. The system utilizes digital mapping technologies, allowing terminal operators to annotate the positions of troops, armaments, and equipment. Vehicles, and in some reports eventually even individual Soldiers, will be automatically tracked via a GPS/GLONASS connection. If the fielding of the Andromeda is deemed a success for the Russian VDV, it is very likely the system would also be adopted by the Russian Ground Forces. Even if the 'Andromeda' C2 system is not ultimately adopted throughout the Russian Armed Forces, Russia will likely continue to experiment with command and control systems to unify the information space, integrate fires and effects, manage robotics and other unmanned technologies to ultimately more efficiently mass, and then apply combat power.[22]

Tactical Radio Communications

The Russian Federation has made great efforts in transitioning away from Soviet era analog based equipment, to digital equipment with substantial data transmission, encryption, and anti-jamming capabilities. The Russian Ground Troops, the Aerospace Forces, and the Navy have been receiving fifth generation R-168 Akveduk radios for the last few years. The entire Russian Ministry of Defense, as well as Russia's other militarized intelligence and security structures appear to be transitioning to the same radios for interoperability reasons. The

R-168 Radio

Image Courtesy: Vitaly Kuzmin

R-142N Command Vehicle

Image Courtesy: Vitaly Kuzmin

Russian Federation has also started introducing the sixth generation R-187 Azart radio series. The compact, frequency hopping VHF capable, Azart made its first public appearance in 2014 when carried by the "polite people" that occupied the Crimea in early 2014. These radios reportedly implement a Software-Defined Radio (SDR) technology that replaces some of the radio's components (mixers, filters, amplifiers, modulators/demodulators, detectors, etc.) with software solutions. The manufacturer of these radios, the United Instrument Manufacturing Corporation

R-149 Command Vehicle

Image Courtesy: Vitaly Kuzmin

(UIMC), has stated that the SDR technology allows the radios to have features such as multitasking, multiple waveband capability, and better protection against surveillance and jamming. These sixth generation radios are capable of self-testing communication links and self-rebooting. Due to the high degree of automation and "smart" technology, these radios will lower the probabilities for operator error. Russia's sixth generation radios will provide faster and more secure communications, and offer a software based upgrade capability. The Soviet Army lagged greatly behind the U.S./NATO in terms of

tactical radio communications, the Armed Forces of today's Russian Federation do not.[23]

Electronic Warfare Troops

The Russian Federation has made Electronic Warfare (EW) capabilities a high priority for development. Although EW was considered vital even in Soviet times, the impetus for recent developments likely stems from the aftermath of the 2008 Russo-Georgian conflict, when Russia lost five aircraft in the first two days of fighting. Only after the arrival of Russian EW troops were Georgian air defense systems suppressed. This lesson was not lost on the Russian Federation. Not only would EW be important for countering the capabilities of technologically advanced opponents, but it is also useful for combatting technologically less advanced opponents. After the conflict, Russia allocated funds for the development of new EW systems, and made organizational, personnel, and industrial changes. The result of these endeavors was the emergence of a Russia's next generation of electronic intelligence and jamming systems. These new systems, with some rather ominous sounding names, include the: President-S, Leer-3, Moskva, Krasukha-4, Leyer-2 , Rtut-BM, Rychag, Lorandit, Infauna, Borisoglebsk-2, and Khibiny.

These "next generation" defensive and offensive EW systems are found throughout the Russian Armed forces. Like the U.S. Navy and Air Force, Russia's Navy and Air Force have significant EW capabilities. Where Russian and U.S. EW capabilities radically differ are the use of these systems by the fighters on the ground. While the U.S. Army and Marine Corps have few EW assets, the Russian Ground Forces, and to a lesser extent Airborne (VDV) and naval infantry, have dedicated EW companies, battalions, and brigades. The Russian Ground Forces even appear to be EW's main proponent in the Russian Armed Forces. Russia's largest and most powerful EW systems such as the Murmansk-BN, Krasukha, Leer-3, and Moskva, are found in the Ground Forces' EW brigades. EW brigades have capabilities to work at the tactical, operational, and arguably strategic levels. These capabilities include

Electronic Warfare Company

wide area cellular communications jamming, GPS location spoofing, reconnaissance and communication satellite jamming, and disrupting early warning aircraft such as the E-3 Sentry (AWACS). While the EW brigades are capable of fulfilling operational and strategic objectives, each Russian maneuver brigade has a dedicated EW company with tactical capabilities. On order, these EW companies are capable of jamming communications (R-934B/ R-378B/ R-330B Mandat/Borisoglebsk-2), interfering with radio controlled artillery fuses (SPR-2 Rtut), and jamming GPS signals that are essential for precision weapons (R-330ZH Zhitel/Borisoglebsk-2) [24] In terms of organization and function within the maneuver brigades, Russian EW companies could be equally at home in the U.S. warfighting function of Fires, Protection, and Intelligence. In general, at the tactical level, most systems have varying capabilities to interfere with hostile communications, disrupt precision targeting, and determine the location of the sources of hostile emissions. There appears to be a close relationship between artillery, signal, and electronic warfare in the Russian Armed Forces. EW units not only protect the artillery from hostile targeting, but also perform a signals intelligence (SIGINT) function that tips and cues artillery and air defense units to the locations of potential targets. Most tactical Russian EW systems provide an azimuth to a potential target (within 1-2 degrees), and these systems can provide a general position of a given target (through triangulation) when connected to a command center, such as the R-330K Mobile Command Post.

It is also very likely that there is a strong relationship of EW with the Signal Troops. Although the Russian military presumes that GPS and GLONASS signals will be disrupted by Russia's own EW units in a combat situation with a near peer, they assume radio communications will be available, and so there is likely much coordination with signal units to ensure friendly communications are not disrupted.[25] In sum, Russia believes that EW capabilities are essential for victory with technologically unsophisticated, as well as technologically sophisticated opponents. These capabilities will create a contested environment for any adversary utilizing terrestrial or satellite radios, GPS-based positioning, navigation, and timing (PNT) information, and especially precision guided munitions.

Russian Concept of the Aspects of Electronic Warfare

Russian EW Systems Organic to Maneuver Brigades

R-378AM Automated HF Communications Jammer System

The R-378AM High Frequency (HF) communications jammer is designed for the detection, finding direction, and of enemy HF radio frequencies. These HF frequencies may be tactical command and control links at fixed frequencies with conventional waveforms, in programmable and automatic frequency tuning modes, as well as for transmitting short encoded messages. The jammer also provides analysis and selection of emitters' signal parameters.

Operating frequency range	1.5 – 30 MHz
Panoramic scan rate	480 MHz/s
Jamming output power	1.0 kW
Narrowband	3.0; 10.0; 20.0; 50.0
Response rate (from detection to jamming)	15 ms
Multitarget jamming capability	up to 5
Deployment time	less than 40 minutes
Scan rate	up to 7,000 MHz/s
Detection-to-suppression time	less than 5 ms
Frequency hopping signal detection	up to 300 hop/s
Crew	4
Truck chassis	Ural-43293

RP-377L (LORANDIT) Compact Multifunctional Radiomonitoring, Direction-Finding And Jamming Complex

The RP-377L (LORANDIT) Compact Multifunctional Radio monitoring, Direction-Finding and Jamming Complex provides for the search of, position location, and jamming of VHF/UHF radio electronic communications. The RP-377L complex can be vehicle mounted or placed in two cases and four canvas bags, and be carried by 2-3 persons. Depending on mission requirements, multiple complexes can work together, with one complex configured as a command post.

Frequency range (search and detection)	20-2000 MHz
Frequency range (direction and finding)	25-2000 MHz
RMS direction-finding error	not more than 3 degrees
Instant monitoring bandwidth	180-1200 kHz
Types of searching signals	FM, AM, SSB, FSK, PSK
Transmitter output	greater than 100 W
Deployment time	15 minutes

R-330B/R-330T Automated VHF Jamming System

The upgraded R-330B/R-330T Very High Frequency (VHF) jamming system is designed for detection, direction finding and jamming of VHF communications. The jamming system provides analysis and selection of emitters' signal parameters. The R-330B/R-330T VHF jamming system consists of an equipment vehicle on a wheeled (R-330T) or tracked (R-330B) chassis, a diesel electric power station mounted on a two-axle trailer (R-330T), or MT-LBu armored tracked chassis (R-330B).

Frequency range	30–100 MHz
Transmitter power	1 kW
Jammed RF links (at fixed frequencies)	3
Jammed RF links (with frequency hop)	1
RMS direction-finding error	not more than 3 degrees
Azimuth search coverage	360 degrees
Types of received signals	AM, FM, CW, SSB, ISB, FSK, PSK, keying, PFT
Scan rate	up to 7,000 MHz/s
Detection-to-suppression time	less than 5 ms
Frequency hopping signal detection	up to 300 hop/s
Crew	4
Truck chassis	Ural-43293

R-934B VHF/UHF Aircraft Communications Automated Jamming Station

R-934B Automated VHF-UHF Aircraft Radio Communication Jamming Station is designed for detection, direction finding, position finding (using two jamming stations) and jamming of VHF-UHF aircraft radio communication means, tactical aircraft guidance systems in 100-150 MHz and 220-400 MHz frequency bands as well as terrestrial radio communications and mobile radios in 100-400 MHz that use fixed frequencies, frequency hopping and transmission of short telecode messages. R-934B AJS can operate under a command post or be remotely controlled.

Frequency range	100-400 MHz
Transmitter power	500 W
Jammed RF links (at fixed frequencies)	4
Jammed RF links (wit frequency hop)	1
RMS direction-finding error	not more than 3 degrees
Time of deployment	30 minutes
Crew	3

Types of jamming signals:
- high-frequency signal modulated in frequency by noise with deviation of 800 and 6000 Hz
- high-frequency signal modulated in frequency shift of 5, 10, 20 and 40 kHz and unit intervals of 150 and 800 μs
- high-frequency signal manipulated in phase (0–180°) with discretization of unit elements

P-330ZH "Zhitel" Automated Jamming Station

The P-330ZH "Zhitel" automated jamming station provides for the automated detection, direction finding and signal analysis of radio emission sources in the designated operating frequency range. The system is capable of disrupting finding mobile ground stations (user terminals) of the "INMARSAT", "IRIDIUM," and GSM-900/1800 satellite communication systems, and the "NAVSTAR" (GPS) satellite navigation system. and the base stations cellular communication system. These signals are completely suppressed within a radius of 20-30 kilometers from the operating station. The P-330ZH "Zhitel" can operate under an automated command post, or operate independently.

Frequency range	100-2000 MHz
Transmitter power	10 kw
Suppression range	20-30 km
RMS direction-finding error	not more than 2 degrees
Time of deployment	less than 40 minutes
Crew	4

Image Courtesy: Russian Ministry of Defense

R-330K Mobile Automated Command Post

The R-330K Mobile Automated Command Post is designed for centralized control of automated jamming stations, such as R-330T, R-378A, R-934B. The R-330K Automated Command Post consists of protected computers with special software in a local area network, radios, data transfer equipment to synchronize automated jamming stations cycles, an embedded electric generator, as well as life-support system.

Controlled jamming stations	up to 20 stations
Deployment time	less than 40 minutes
Crew	4
Communication links (radio relay)	2
Communication links (wire)	4
Transport chassis	Ural-43203 truck
Power consumption	not greater than 8 kW

SPR-2 (RTUT-B) Artillery Radio Proximity Fuse Jamming Station

The SPR-2 (Rtut-B) jamming station is designed to protect friendly troops and equipment against artillery fire equipped with radio proximity fuses by causing premature detonation. The station is powered by a dedicated generator (primary source) or onboard electric system (standby source). The SPR-2 station is mounted on a variety chassis, and can operate on the move.

Protected area	.5 km
Frequency range	95-420 MHz
Energy potential	not less than 300 W
Deployment times	less than 4 minutes
Crew	2

Borisoglebsk-2

The Borisoglebsk-2 is one of Russia's newest tactical EW systems, and started replacing the R-330 "Mandat" in 2012. Although there have been few published details about the characteristics of the Borisoglebsk-2, it reportedly can suppress twice the frequency bandwidth of its predecessor in the HF and UHF bands, 100 times faster. There are also reports that it has the capability to disrupt mobile satellite communications and radar navigation systems. The Borisoglebsk-2 consists of several different systems mounted on MT-LBu chassis.

(Right) The graphic on the facing page shows an enemy brigade has seized and occupies the high ground to the west of the city as well as four bridges on roads leading into the city. The enemy brigade is split by the east-west river and its feeders. Russian forces hold the east bank of the north-south branch of the river and one bridge on the north-south road to the city. They are contesting ownership of another bridge on the central east-west road. The Russians are conducting an advance to capture the northernmost east-west road bridges and attacking into the enemy brigade along the central east-west road.

Russian electronic warfare involves the normal missions of controlling and denying the enemy use of the electromagnetic spectrum through electronic attack (countermeasures), electronic protection (counter-counter-measures) and electronic warfare support (search, interception, location and identification measures). However, the Russians include physical destruction as an integrated part of electronic warfare. To do this, they will assign high-performance aircraft, helicopter gunships, artillery and mortars and ground assault to the assets included in an electronic warfare maneuver group. The electronic warfare maneuver group may be formed in support of an attack, withdrawal or march under threatened conditions. The Russian maneuver brigade's electronic warfare company is a central actor in this effort but the effort is controlled by the brigade.

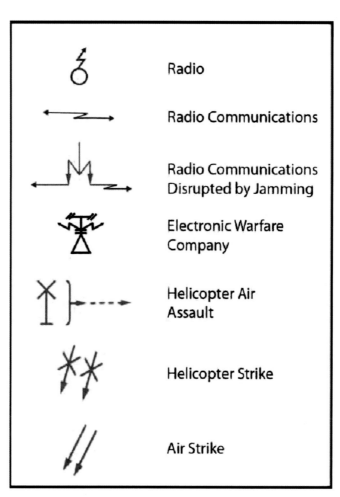

As the Russian forces attack out of the city going north, the electronic warfare company jams the enemy brigade communications between the brigade headquarters and its battalions, between the brigade and several bridge and road intersection sites, and between controlling headquarters and bridge sites. Fighter-bomber and helicopter gun ship strikes launch against critical communications sites. Air assault landings are conducted against the enemy brigade headquarters and one of its battalion headquarters. The brigade artillery group and battalion mortars are involved with supporting the ground attack, however, these assets may also be attached or tasked for electronic warfare physical destruction missions.

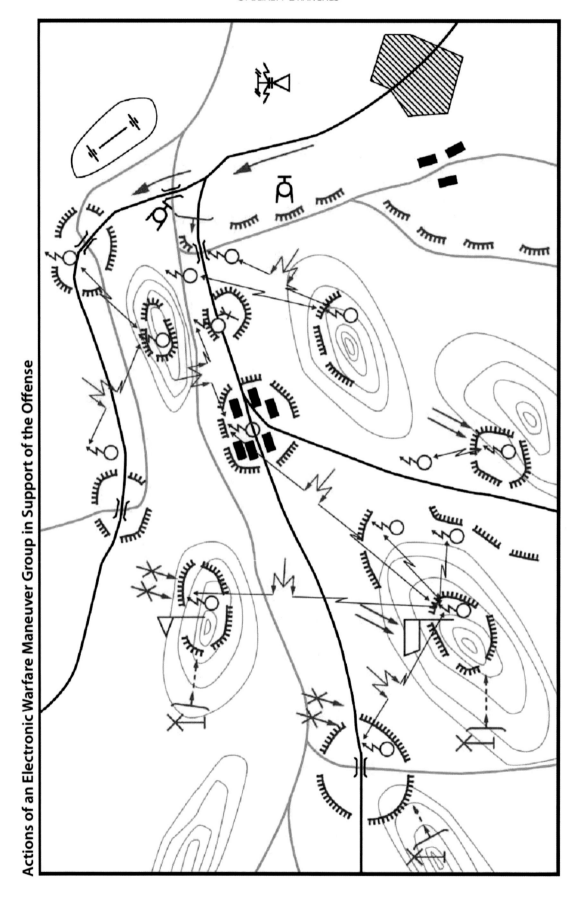

Actions of an Electronic Warfare Maneuver Group in Support of the Offense

RB-531B Infauna

The RB-531B Infauna is intended primarily to provide protection from radio controlled mines and explosive devices, and disrupt enemy tactical communications. The RB-531B Infauna is mounted on a modified BTR-80 chassis, has a crew of two, operates in the 20-2020 MHz frequency range, and is in use by the Russian VDV.

Engineer Troops

The Engineer Troops is a Specialty Branch in the Ground Forces formed to accomplish complex engineering missions in support of combined-arms operations and combat that require specialized training of personnel and the use of engineer equipment, as well as inflicting casualties on the enemy through the use of engineer charges and explosives. The engineers are organized into formations, units and subunits for various purposes: engineer reconnaissance, combat engineering, obstacle construction and clearing, engineer assault, road construction, pontoon bridge construction, river assault-crossing, camouflage, engineering technology, field water supply, etc.

- engineer reconnaissance of the enemy, terrain and features;
- construction (layout) of field fortifications (firing positions, ditches and communication trenches, shelters, bunkers, dugouts, etc.) and the layout of field troop installations (residential, logistical, medical);
- the planning and layout of engineer obstacles, including installation of mine fields, demolition work, the planning and layout of non-explosive obstacles (anti-tank ditches, scarps, counterscarps, stakes, etc.);
- clearing mines from areas and key points;
- preparing and maintaining march routes and roads;
- equipping and maintaining ferries across water barriers, including the construction of bridges;
- extracting and purifying water in the field and other tasks.

In addition, engineers are involved in countering the intelligence systems and targeting by the enemy's weapons (camouflage), creating the illusion of troops and facilities, providing misinformation and conducting actions to deceive the enemy as well as to eliminate the effects of enemy weapons of mass destruction.

In peacetime, military engineers carry out a number of important and socially significant missions: they clear areas of explosive hazards; they assist in the aftermath of man-made accidents, catastrophes and natural disasters; and they prevent the destruction of bridges and waterworks by floating ice. Engineer Troops are being equipped with new, high-quality, highly effective, versatile equipment. This equipment is built with standard components and modules and is replacing the redundant non-standardized equipment built for the same purpose.[26]

There is an organic engineer battalion in the maneuver brigade. Its function is to aid in the mobility of own forces and hinder or deny the mobility of enemy forces. In order to do so, the battalion provides route clearing, construction and maintenance; engineer reconnaissance; water crossing support; camouflage/deception; water supply; mine field and other obstacle breaching; mine field and other obstacle construction and preparation of defenses.

Russia has a less-developed road system than in the West. Paved, multi-lane roads in good condition are less common, particularly away from the urban centers. Dirt roads are common in the countryside and Russian engineers are skilled in route clearance, maintenance and

construction. Russian combat engineers classify roads as directional (frontal-leading to the combat front; lateral-running parallel to the line of contact); primary (march column route, supply route, evacuation route) or auxiliary (access road, detour road, reserve road and dummy road); and by the nature of the traffic (wheeled, tracked or combined wheel and track). They may be further classified/restricted as battalion, brigade (division), army and military district roads. Military roads and march column routes will incorporate existing roads and build new ones using locally-available material. They must support the prescribed rate of movement, pass through the locale with the best defensibility and concealment, do not require an excessive amount of preparation, have sections where they can bypass narrow sites that might hinder the spacing of the column, and bypass those areas that are subject to enemy interdiction.[27]

Movement

During a march, the engineer commander will constitute a movement support detachment [отряд обеспечения движения] (OOD) for each column. The mission of the OOD is to move behind the advance guard or forward detachment (about two hours ahead of the main body) to conduct engineer reconnaissance and to improve the axis of advance by filling in craters, constructing bypasses, improving rugged sections, bridging minor gaps or repairing bridges and clearing paths through minefields. The OOD will have a force of motorized rifle or tank troops to protect its bulldozers, cranes, dump trucks, tank or truck-launched bridges, mine clearers as well as trucks carrying explosives and pierced steel plating (PSP).[28] Should the march culminate in an attack, the OOD then moves behind the attacking first echelon or prepares a route for the commitment of the second echelon. OODs are primarily used in the attack for mine and obstacle breaching. OODs may also be constituted in the defense to prepare concealed counter-attack routes.

The engineer battalion route construction and clearing equipment includes four BAT-2 combat engineer vehicles. The battalion also has two DZ-180A wheeled road scrapers and a KRAZ-257B wheeled crane. The battalion's four TMM-3 or TMM-6 truck-launched bridge sets are each capable of laying down a 10 meter span. The spans can be connected. This gives the option of a 10.5 meter, 21 meter, 31.5 meter or 42 meter bridge that is 3.8 meters wide.[29] Depending on the terrain, all or most of these are part of the OOD. The BAT-2 combat engineer

BAT-2 Combat Engineer Vehicle

Image Courtesy: Vitaly Kuzmin

vehicles are almost always included. These armored tracked bulldozers have an adjustable width dozer blade and a two ton crane with a maximum 7.3 meter boom reach. It has a 700 horsepower diesel engine, can ford up to 1.3 meters of water and can winch up to 25 tons.

UR-77   KDMB Armored Wheeled Bulldozer

Images Courtesy: Vitaly Kuzmin

Elements or all of the mine clearing platoon may accompany the OOD. The platoon has two UR-77 mine clearing vehicles and two IMR-3M combat engineer vehicles. The UR-77 "Dragon" (ustanovka razminirovaniya) is a mine clearing vehicle with two launch ramps on its turret mounted on the same chassis as the 2S1 Gvozdika self-propelled howitzer. The ramps fire rockets towing line charges of explosive hose. A single line charge will clear a path of 90 meters by 6 meters. The UR-83 is a similar system, but is not mounted on a vehicle chassis. The IMR-3M is a combat engineer vehicle built on the T-90 tank chassis. It has a multipurpose bulldozer blade as well as a mine plow. It has a telescopic boom with an 8.15 meter reach that can be fitted with a manipulator. The boom can lift 2.2 tons.

Obstacles

Neither the United States nor Russia are signatory to the Ottawa Convention that bans the ownership and use of anti-personnel mines. The United States has agreed to abide by the treaty except in defense of South Korea. Russia continues to stockpile and train in the use of anti-personnel and anti-tank land mines and has not announced any plans to sign the Ottawa Convention. Land mines still constitute a significant part of Russian defensive and offensive actions. Land mines can be emplaced manually or by minelaying vehicles/trailers, helicopters, artillery fire and

IMR-3M Combat Engineer Vehicle

Image Courtesy: Vitaly Kuzmin

aviation bombs. The Russian engineer commander will normally constitute a mobile obstacle detachment [подвижный отряд заграждений] (POZ) that can quickly emplace mines to protect a flank or block an attack or support a counterattack. The POZ normally works with a flank security detachment or the anti-tank reserve to lay rapid minefields and create other obstacles, primarily against an armored thrust. Besides mine-laying vehicles and trailers, the POZ may use ditching machines and explosives to create craters and downed tree obstacles. Anti-tank mines are usually laid by vehicles and trailers or helicopters whereas anti-personnel land mines are normally laid by hand. The Russians have a variety of enemy-triggered and command detonated mines. Howitzers and MLRS can lay both anti-tank and anti-personnel scatterable mines.[30]

GMZ-3 Tracked Mine Layer

Image Courtesy: Vitaly Kuzmin

The Russians prefer short, but deep, minefields to long, shallow ones which may lack stopping power. Brigade armored minelayers can lay a quick 1000 meter minefield in three panels of approximately 3,000 meters, 1000 meters and 300 meters from the forward edge of the battle area in under ten minutes. The three GMZ-3 tracked mining vehicles of the obstacle platoon can lay a 1,200-meter, three-row minefield, containing 624 mines, in 26 minutes. The Russians prefer to lay minefields shortly before an enemy advance to prevent enemy knowledge of their location. Defensive antitank minefields laid out sometime before the battle are normally 200-300 meters wide and 60-120 meters in depth with four rows per minefield. These minefields are carefully surveyed and placed on likely avenues of approach. Antipersonnel minefields are placed on likely dismounted infantry avenues of approach. They are located in front of fighting positions or in gaps between fighting positions and are 30-300 meters wide and 10-50 meters deep. They usually contain a mixture of blast and fragmentation mines. Placing mines by hand is time-consuming and the Russians employ the UMZ-3 remote mine delivery system for deploying antipersonnel mines, as well as antitank mines. UMZ stands for *universal'nogo minnogo zagraditelya* (universal mine-layer). The UMZ consists of six firing modules mounted on the back of a ZiL-131 truck. Each module has thirty firing tubes, so the UMZ has 180 firing tubes. Depending on the type minefield desired, the UMZ can lay from 180 to 11,520 mines without reloading. The UMZ can launch an antitank or antipersonnel minefield 30-60 meters from itself while the truck is driving from 10 to 40 kilometers per hour. It takes two men from one and a half to two hours to reload the UMZ. One UMZ can lay a three row minefield stretching from 150 to 1,500 meters long, depending on the mine that is used. The UMZ can be used to restore a breached or depleted minefield during combat.[31] Command detonated mines are often placed directly in front of fighting

Uran-6 Mine Clearing Robot

Image Courtesy: Vitaly Kuzmin

positions. As time and resources permit, Russian engineers construct minefields within the defensive positions to slow and canalize an enemy attack, support a fire line or protect the flanks of the defense or a counterattack. Engineers also mine roads, bridges and fords and likely water crossings.[32]

Defensive positions
When on the defensive and time permits, Russians dig in. They start with crew-served weapons positions and two-man fighting positions, then connecting fighting trenches and bunkers. Much of this work is done by soldiers with shovels, however most combat vehicles are equipped for self-emplacement and engineer bulldozers and trenching machines supplement these efforts. The priority field construction tasks for the engineers are security zone or forward positions, CPs, artillery firing positions, artillery ammunition storage, artillery transport and communication trenches.

(Right) The graphic on the facing page shows the 1st Motorized Rifle Brigade defending in two echelons with a forward position. The enemy is defending along an international boundary, so the Russian Army is apparently constituting a defense before the outbreak of hostilities. In the forward position, the 7th and 8th Motorized Rifle Companies from the 3rd Motorized Rifle Battalion (second echelon) plus a tank company from the tank battalion (second echelon) are establishing defensive positions opposite the international border. A tank ambush and a motorized rifle ambush cover gaps in the forward position. The engineers may assist these companies in digging in. Each of the company positions require constructing 11 dug-in vehicle fighting positions, a personnel bunker, three command bunkers, 13 covered trenches, five observation posts, and 11 squad fighting positions (except for the tank company). Behind the forward positions is a stream crossed by two bridges, the bridge to the north runs over the top of a dam. The annotation "time" would indicate the time by which the construction would be completed.

Two motorized rifle platoons from the 1st and 2nd Motorized Rifle Battalions are dug-in forward of the main defense. Their purpose is to provide cover for the withdrawal of the companies of the forward position, deceive the enemy as to the location of the main defense and to canalize the attacking enemy into the fire sac between the 1st and 2nd Motorized Rifle Battalions. Each platoon position requires the construction of three dug-in vehicle fighting positions, one command bunker, four covered trenches, five observation posts and three squad fighting positions.

The first echelon defense is manned by the 1st and 2nd Motorized Rifle Battalions. The 1st and 2nd MRBs have two companies forward and one back and defends in two echelons. There is a dummy platoon position between the two battalions. It is manned by a platoon from the 2nd MRB and has a fallback fighting position behind it. The purpose of this position is to create a penetration point for the attacking enemy. The enemy will attack, thinking that the two forward platoons are the forward edge of the defense. The southern bridge and main defense fire will guide the enemy to the false position. After a fight, the platoon will fall back to its actual position, creating a fire sac and blunting the penetration. The advancing enemy will then be caught in flanking cross fire. The 2nd MRB/s northern company is short one platoon (the one in the false position) and so

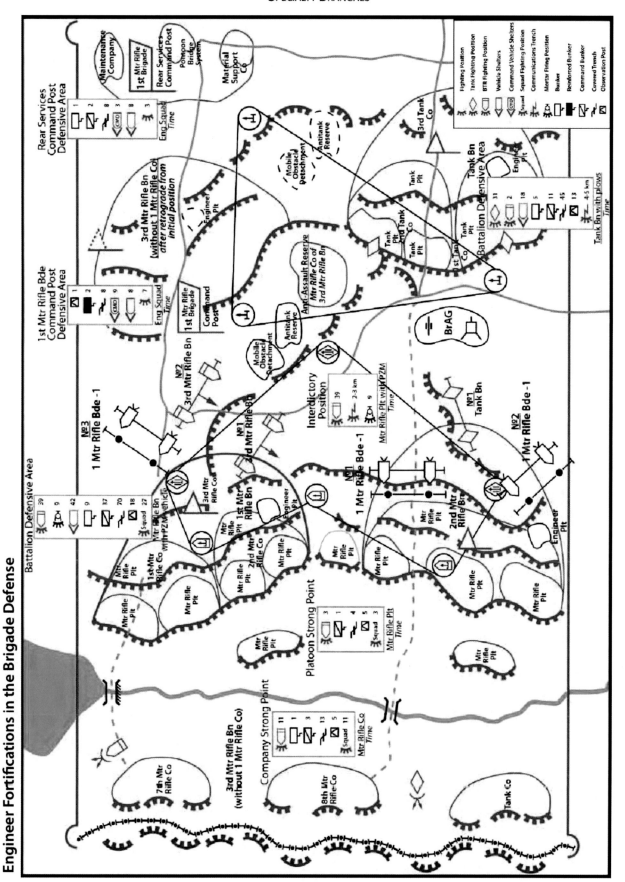

Engineer Fortifications in the Brigade Defense

defends with one platoon forward and one back (when it pulls back from the forward position). The two platoons have been incorporated into the defense of its southern neighboring MRC and comes under its temporary command. The northern company commander will fight the fire sac fight. The southern MRC commander will fight the forward platoon fight and then withdraw it to his second echelon position. Both forward MRBs have an engineer platoon assigned to help with fortifications. Field fortifications in both forward battalions will require construction of 39 BMP fighting positions, 9 mortar firing positions, 42 vehicle shelters, 9 personnel bunkers, 37 command bunkers, 70 covered trenches, 18 observation posts and 27 squad fighting positions.

Behind the first echelon battalions, the brigade commander has established three stop lines for the antitank reserve. Number one covers the southern bridge approach and fire sac. Number two covers the brigade southern flank. Number three covers the brigade northern flank. All require dug-in positions in advance. The brigade commander also established two fortified firing lines –both containing and firing into the fire sac created by the false position in the first echelon defense. Number one tank is the tank battalion line to the rear of the 2nd MRB. Number two mrb is for two companies of the 3rd MRB. Number one mrb is also a firing line for the 3rd MRB as is

Lieutenant General Yuriy Stavitskiy
Chief of the Russian Armed Forces' Engineer Troops
Image Courtesy: Russian Ministry of Defense

advances to occupy prepared positions to block the fire sac if needed. Construction of fortifications to support the anti-tank stop line number three and the three firing lines and positions to deal with the fire sac includes 39 vehicle fighting positions, 2-3 kilometers of communications trenches and 9 mortar firing positions. A PZM trenching and digging machine and a platoon are assigned to this effort.

The brigade artillery group's howitzer and MLRS battalions are dug in at primary and alternate firing positions in the area between the two defensive echelons. That also contains the assembly area for the antitank reserve, the mobile obstacle detachment (POZ) and the anti-assault reserve (a motorized rifle company from the 3rd MRB). Air defense elements are dispersed across both echelons with MANPADS and anti-aircraft guns forward and missiles further back. The brigade command post is located just in front of the second echelon defense. Construction of the brigade command post entails 1 observation post, 2 reinforced bunkers, 8 covered trenches, 9 vehicle shelters for the command post vehicles, 8 vehicle shelters for other vehicles, and 7 fighting positions.

The second echelon defense will be manned by two companies of the 3rd MRB and the tank battalion. The 3rd MRB defends with two companies forward and a platoon-sized reserve. An engineer platoon will assist the battalion after it completes other work. The tank battalion defends with two companies forward and one back. An engineer platoon assists the tank battalion in constructing 31 tank fighting positions, 2 BMP shelters, 18 truck shelters, 5 personnel bunkers, 11 command bunkers, 45 covered trenches, 13 observation posts and 4-5 kilometers of

communications trenches. The battalion will use its tank dozers for much of this effort.
The brigade rear services area (this graphic is not to scale) is located further back and contains the
alternate brigade command post, the material support company, the pontoon bridge set and the
maintenance company. It requires the construction of 1 personnel bunker, 2 command bunkers, 8
covered trenches, 3 vehicle shelters for CP vehicles, 8 vehicle shelters and 3 fighting positions. An
engineer squad assists the rear area units in this effort. The Russian Army is a digging army and a
brigade has an abundance of engineer equipment to help it.

Camouflage

The purpose of camouflage is to conceal soldiers, weapons, positions and movement quickly;
disorient the enemy and create an advantage for the force. It is an ongoing process that
includes hiding the force; portraying another force using mockups, dummy equipment and
positions, and corner reflectors; using smoke, light and noise discipline and signals deception.
Soldiers are responsible for camouflaging themselves, their weapons and their positions.
Engineers advise and inspect camouflage and conceal large and important facilities and
important points such as river-crossing sites, roads, road traffic, command posts and fueling
areas. Engineers create phony positions within and outside the defensive area.[33]

Hydrology

Large rivers and lakes dominate Eurasia and
have served as major arteries of industry
and commerce, defensive barriers, lines of
communication and avenues of advance.
Armies are more accustomed to solving
the problem of crossing rivers rather than
controlling stretches or the entirety of the
river or lake. Yet control of the river or lake
is often more decisive to a campaign than
a crossing. In Russia, the Volga, Vistula,
Danube, Dnieper, Oder and Amur Rivers form
operational/strategic barriers. The Danube,
Dnieper, Oka, Koma, Neman, Don and Amur

TMM-3 Bridge Layer

Image Courtesy: Vitaly Kuzmin

Rivers form avenues of approach. Lakes Ladoga, Onezh, Beloye, Il'men, and Chyda may serve
as barriers or avenues of approach. During conflict, control of the rivers and lakes is often
vital to controlling a country. A brigade may engage in riverine combat and operations to
deal with significant bodies of water.

Rivers start on high ground and run to lower. Upriver, the river is normally deeper, narrower
and faster. The river valley is V-shaped and the river forms waterfalls, rapids, gullies, and
potholes. River erosion is primarily at the river bottom. Mid-river, it widens and slows as
the slope lessens. The river valley widens and forms a flood plain. Erosion is from the river
bottom and banks. Downriver, it widens more, becoming shallower and slower. The river
slope is gradual. The erosion is primarily from the banks. At places the river may split or bend
(meander). The river may form terraces, levees, and swamps. Where the river meets the sea or

River Bend and Crossing Sites

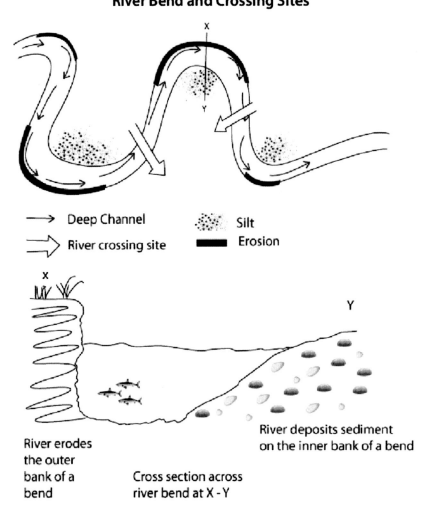

→ Deep Channel

⇒ River crossing site

∴ Silt

▬ Erosion

River erodes
the outer
bank of a
bend

Cross section across
river bend at X - Y

River deposits sediment
on the inner bank of a bend

lake, the river may braid over its flood plain, forming multiple channels and islands.

River bottoms tend to change depending where they are on the river. Upriver, the bottom is usually bed rock, and boulders. Mid-river, the bottom is usually gravel and sand in the channel with fine sandy mud over older sediment closer to the banks. Downriver, the bottom is usually mud and fine sand. Where the river meets the sea or lake, the river bed rises and the river becomes shallower from the built-up sediment. River aquatic vegetation increases mid-river and downriver.

Rivers are best crossed at bends which loop into the side of the crossing element. This means that the channel runs next to the bank held by the crossing party and the deepest part of the river is closest to the crossing party. Further, the opposite bank is the shallowest part of the river. Thus the crossing party can deal with the hardest part of the crossing from the adjacent, friendly shore and land on the shallowest. Crossing at bends which loop into the side of the crossing element may also provide the opportunity to cut off an enemy force defending along the river bank.

Canals are manmade, generally straight, of uniform depth, and have steep sides. They are difficult to cross due to the high, steep, often-concrete banks. They have less current than nearby rivers and are primarily located on flat ground. Special locks and other devices are sometimes needed to deal with changes in elevation.

Lake and inland sea shores vary from shallow and sediment-covered to steep and inaccessible due to prevailing winds and geologic formations. Large lakes and inland seas can be treacherous during harsh weather and high winds. Key terrain in riverine operations includes population centers, industry, bridges, fords, dams, headwaters, river junctures, levees, canals, pumps, effluent stations, and dominating ground that threatens primary movement on or adjacent to the waterway.

Riverine operations are axial or trans-sectional. They can deal with control of the entire length of a waterway (axial) or with a slice of it, usually for water-crossing (trans-axial).[34] The Russian experience with axial riverine operations is to constitute a naval river flotilla, with a strong naval infantry contingent, which is subordinated to the operational ground commander. The Russians have spent a great deal of time and resources on developing trans-axial capabilities. In Eastern and Central Europe, an advancing or retreating army can expect to meet a six-meter wide water obstacle every 20 kilometers, up to a 100 meter-wide water obstacle every 35-60 kilometers, a 100 to 300 meter wide obstacle every 100-150 kilometers and a water obstacle over 300 meters wide every 250-300 kilometers.[35] River crossing capabilities depend, of course, on the width, current, banks, river bottom and surrounding terrain of the river crossing site. The optimum way to cross a river is over an established heavy-duty

PTS-2 Tracked Amphibious Transport

bridge or in the dead of winter when the river is frozen over solid. The Russians have amphibious personnel carriers, artillery, air defense, and antitank combat vehicles. Tanks are equipped with snorkels and can cross rivers with good bottoms and not-too-much depth (5.5 meters). The Russians have truck-launched and tracked launched bridges for narrow waterways. They have vehicle ferries, prefabricated bridges and assault boats for major waterways. Russian engineers can also construct bridges using local materials (trees, stone). During World War II, the Russians were skilled at building underwater bridges-bridges that were a foot or so under the water so they could not be detected by aircraft, but could easily be driven over by trucks.

TMM-6 Bridge Layer

Image Courtesy: Vitaly Kuzmin

MTU-90 Heavy Bridge Layer

Image Courtesy: Vitaly Kuzmin

The Russian Army conducts two types of river crossing-unopposed and opposed. The unopposed river crossing [переправа через реку] is conducted against little or no effective opposition. The opposed river crossing [форсирование] is conducted against an effective opposition on the obstacle line. The attack from the march (hasty attack) is the preferred method of conducting an opposed river crossing. Should that fail, a deliberate attack will be considered.[36] The brigade's engineer battalion has the previously mentioned four TMM-3 or TMM-6 truck-launched bridge sets and a PP-61 pontoon bridge company capable of spanning 268 meters. A 268 meter long bridge can carry 60 tons, a 165 meter bridge can carry 90 tons while a 141 meter bridge can carry 120 tons. It takes under an hour to emplace with a well-trained engineer company.[37] It has six BMK-255-1 cutter vessels to help in the assembly and in maintaining its position in the current. In addition it has seven PTS-2 tracked amphibious transports. Each can carry up to ten tons. Not part of the engineer battalion, but available in the tank brigade is the MTU-90 heavy bridge layer. Based on the T-90 tank chassis, the vehicle can lay a 25 meter bridge in under three minutes. It can support 50 tons.[38]

A hasty attack across a water obstacle from the march is conducted to maintain the high tempo of the advance, seize bridgeheads, rapidly develop the opposite shore or secure an assembly area for an upcoming operation. Water crossings differ by season and weather. In the winter, crossing depends on the strength and stability of the ice. In the spring, there is drifting ice and flooding. In the summer and fall, TO&E and attached crossing equipment can be used. If the water obstacle is less than five meters deep, and the river banks and bottom are suitable, tanks can snorkel across. Crossing on a wide front at a quick tempo using a forward detachment or advanced guard is preferred. The crossing plan designates the crossing sector, the departure area, the attack crossing line (1 to 2 kilometers from the water's edge), the troop embarkation or cargo loading area (5 to 6 kilometers from the water's edge) and the tank sealing area for snorkeling (also 5 to 6 kilometers from the water's edge). Air defense assets will cover the crossing and preparation areas. If possible, an air assault may conduct a landing to seize the far shore.[39] A deliberate attack will normally involve far more artillery and aviation preparation and involve an attack from the march through friendly forces in contact with the enemy. Smoke, air defense and counterbattery efforts will be particularly critical.

Pontoon Bridging Operations

(Right) The graphic on the facing page provides further details of engineer support to the above brigade defense when the enemy attacks and the brigade conducts one of its counterattacks. In this instance, the enemy attacked with two reinforced mechanized battalions reinforced with a reinforced tank company. The two battalions were stopped by the brigade defense, but the enemy forced his way through the false position into the fire sac. The brigade commander committed the antitank reserve to "Stop Line Number 3." The brigade commander decides to commit his northern counterattack from the 3rd MRB position to drive the remaining enemy from the fire sac and restore the main defense. There is a small lake and a stream in front of the 3rd MRB position that has two bridges over the stream (this was not shown on the previous graphic). The engineers installed 25 corner reflectors on the northern and southern counterattack routes to conceal movement from enemy radar. They also installed two phony radar transmitters on the northern and southern routes. They also provided overhead screening over part of both routes. At the deployment line, the engineers installed laser reflectors to defeat beam-riding artillery and aviation ordnance. The engineers installed reflective markers of different colors marking the deployment routes for the motorized rifle and tank platoons to the counterattack line.

While war gaming the counterattack, the brigade determined that the weak points were the two bridges that the counterattack force would have to use. The brigade posited that the enemy might attack the northern bridge with scatterable mines (FASCAM) and destroy the southern bridge with air strikes. The counterattack went over these bridges. Engineer reconnaissance determined new routes for the counter attack and, in the north, laid a tank-launched bridge. In the south, the engineer reconnaissance determined a new counter attack route across a stream ford. Continuing to war game the counterattack, the brigade determined that the enemy could fire FASCAM to block the counterattack during the enemy withdrawal. The engineer battalion alerted and positioned minefield clearing assets (UR-77, BAT-2, IMR-3M) to deal with such an eventuality. Some of the tanks of the tank battalion are equipped with mine plows and could also be used if needed.

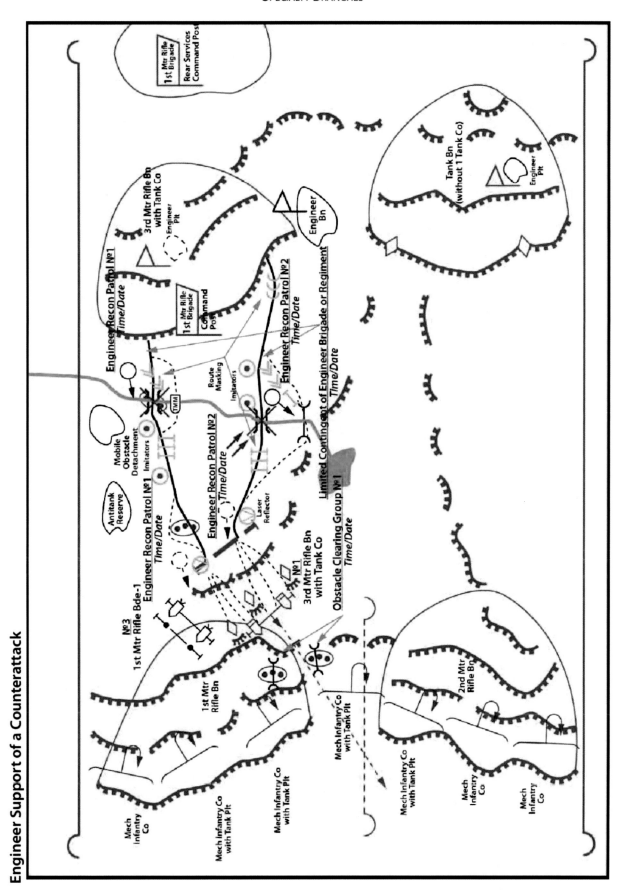

Engineer Support of a Counterattack

NBC Defense Troops

The Radiological, Chemical and Biological Defense (NBC) Troops of the Russian Ground Forces are intended to mitigate the Ground Forces losses associated with environments that are contaminated with radioactive, chemical and biological contaminates. The NBC Troops ensure that the Ground Forces can fulfill their combat tasks in NBC contaminated environments, as well as enhancing their survivability and protection from high-precision weapons and other weapons.

The basis of the NBC Defense Troops are multipurpose NBC brigades that have subunits capable of performing NBC tasks, these tasks include:
- identification and assessment of the radiological, chemical and biological environment, the scale and effects of radiological, chemical and biological damage;
- the protection of units from radiological, chemical and biological contamination;
- reducing the visibility of troops and facilities;
- disaster (damage) recovery;
- use of flame and thermobaric weapons.

The NBC Defense Troops are organized and conduct operations in normal and NBC conditions, and in hostile and non-hostile environments, and includes:
- nuclear detection;
- NBC reconnaissance and control;
- the collection and processing of data and information on radiological, chemical and biological environments;
- the notification of troops about NBC contamination;
- conducting special treatment (decontamination, degaussing and disinfection) of armaments, military and special equipment, buildings and other objects, as well as the decontamination of personnel;
- aerosol countermeasures against the enemy's reconnaissance and targeting means.

Russia is concerned about defense against nuclear weapons as well as reconstituting the force and fighting on after nuclear exchange has begun. Military equipment is designed with overpressure systems to keep out chemical and radioactive material and the NBC Defense troops are practiced in vehicle, weapons and personnel decontamination. The NBC Defense Troops are a dual-purpose force that have both war and peace time missions, such as NBC contamination resulting from industrial accidents. In terms of modernization and capability development, the NBC Defense Troops are interested in increasing their capabilities to: identify and assess the extent and effects of weapons of mass destruction; integrate automated control systems; and developing strong electronic countermeasures. The Russian

RXM-6 NBC Reconnaissance Vehicle

PXM-6

Image Courtesy: Vitaly Kuzmin

NBC Defense Company

Federation is equipping units with: new means of NBC reconnaissance, including new NBC reconnaissance vehicles; new means of individual and collective NBC defense; means of reducing the visibility and masking; thermobaric weapons; as well improving the materials, formulations, methods and technical means of decontamination.[40]

In general, Russian NBC Defense Troops are in many ways very similar to their Western counterparts. They are tasked with identifying NBC threats in the environment, performing decontamination of troops and equipment, but they also deploy aerosols and flame weapons to engage the enemy.[41] (In most militaries, flame weapons have traditionally belonged to the NBC Troops.) The popularity of such weapons has waned significantly throughout the world, but not so in the Russian Armed Forces. While the utility of NBC Troops in today's asymmetric warfare is questioned in other armies, Russian NBC Troops firm grasp of flame weapons keeps them relevant, engaged, and makes them an important asset in the Russian maneuver commander's toolbox. The term "flamethrower" itself conjures ideas of the Second World War, with soldiers carrying backpack mounted aerosol tanks spewing flame from hand-held wands, or the M-67 flame throwing tank that was utilized by the U.S. Army and Marine Corps in Vietnam. In current Russian military parlance the term "flamethrower" usually refers to projectile launched flame, smoke and thermobaric weapons.[42]

The Rocket Propelled Infantry Flamethrower (RPO)

The Rocket Propelled Infantry Flamethrower (RPO), colloquially known as the Shmel, Russian for bumblebee, is a family of multi-use firing devices that fire expendable rocket-assisted projectiles, but with a substantially different design than its prototype, the *Rys*. The RPO Shmel was first fielded in the 1980s, and proved to be a great improvement over both the *Rys* and the traditional back packed LPO-50, both of which the Shmel quickly replaced. The Shmel is lighter, has a longer range, and packs far more of a punch than the *Rys*. The RPO

Shmel proved very effective while being deployed in urban and mountainous terrain, and even earned the nickname "Satan Pipe" among the Afghan Mujahedeen. The thermobaric warhead of the Shmel was expected to kill all personnel within a 50 meter radius in an open area, and within an 80 cubic meter area in a closed structure. Due to the thermobaric properties of the warhead, it is estimated to have about the same amount of energy as a 107 mm artillery shell on impact. The RPO Shmel is capable of firing three types of munitions. The RPO-A is thermobaric, and is most often used for the destruction of buildings, bunkers, and personnel in enclosed areas. The RPO-Z is an incendiary munition, and the RPO-D is for smoke. The RPO Shmel was used extensively in the First and Second Chechen Wars, and its performance was much lauded. In 2003, The RPO Shmel-M entered service, the Shmel-M, also known as the RPO PDM (Increased Range and Lethality), has improved characteristics (weight, range, strength of blast, etc.), reportedly having about the same amount of energy as a 152 mm artillery shell on impact, and is replacing the RPO Shmel as inventories are depleted.[43] The newest addition to the family is the MRO Borodach, (Small Caliber Infantry Flamethrower), which was fielded in 2013 and has reportedly seen service in Eastern Ukraine. The Borodach is not replacing the Shmel-M, but instead is likely to be a special version of the RPO family designed for urban warfare. The Borodach is smaller and lighter than both the Shmel and the Shmel-M, has a much shorter range, causes less blast damage, and has a different, easier to use, optical system. In terms of munitions, the projectiles are similar to the rest of the family: thermobaric (MRO-A), incendiary (MRO-Z), smoke (MRO-D), smoke/incendiary (MRO-DZ).[44]

Rocket Propelled Flamethrower Characteristics

Employment of the RPO

The Russian Federation believes that rocket propelled flamethrowers are best employed by NBC troops. Although promotional materials for these weapons tout them as "easy to use," there is apparently a great deal of training provided to their operators, including a virtual training simulator, the 9F700-2M. The conditional usage of the thermobarics may be another reason they are used almost exclusively by the NBC troops, although Russia does field thermobaric munitions for other rocket propelled grenade systems. A Russian motorized rifle brigade typically has one flamethrower platoon in its NBC Defense Company. Flamethrower platoons usually consist of three six-man squads mounted on specialized BMP-2 (BMO-1) or T-72 (BMO-T) chassised transport vehicles capable of carrying their 6 man squad (vehicle driver included) and 30-60 Shmel or Shmel-Ms.[45] Depending on circumstances, the platoon may be attached as a platoon, squads, or as individual members as needed to the supported unit, usually a motorized rifle battalion. A common scenario for the employment of flamethrowers against an entrenched conventional enemy would involve a flamethrower platoon being attached to a motorized battalion, the flamethrower platoon advancing to within 1.5 to 2.0 km of the enemy line, dismounting and with each soldier carrying two RPOs, advancing to within 600 meters of enemy positions (the maximum effective fire rage within the Shmel-M), discharging their weapons, and then returning to their vehicles for replenishment. Aside from the flamethrower platoons found in the motorized rifle brigades, the Russian Federation also has flamethrower battalions in NBC Defense Brigades and Regiments. These assets can be attached as needed to support maneuver units and would almost assuredly be assigned (if available) to any maneuver commander expecting urban warfare [46]

RPO Shmel-M

Heavy Flamethrower System

The Heavy Flamethrower System (TOS-1), colloquially known as the *Burantino*, Russian for Pinocchio, was the Soviets first attempt to field a heavy, rocket propelled, flamethrower system in the 1980s. The TOS-1 is a heavy flamethrower system that consists of two different vehicles (a launcher and support vehicle), but in common usage, the launch vehicle itself is often referred to as the "TOS-1." The TOS-1 system consists of a Combat (launch) Vehicle (BM-1/Object 634B) equipped with 30 220mm rocket tubes mounted on top of a T-72 tank chassis,

TOS-1A Heavy Flamethrower

Image Courtesy: Vitaly Kuzmin

and a Transport-Loader Vehicle (TZM-T), also on a T-72 chassis, that carries an additional set of rockets and a loading boom. Doctrinally, the TOS-1 was envisioned to decimate a large area, by charging ahead, while under the protection of tanks, launching its rockets in rapid succession (all 30 rockets in 7.5 seconds), and then returning to the rear for rearmament and redeployment. The TOS-1 has a much shorter range (approximately 3.5km), and its rockets were substantially less accurate than conventional artillery systems, but the combined blasts of the thermobaric rockets produce mutually reinforcing shockwaves that have an impressive effect that has been described as appearing as a nuclear explosion. The TOS-1 saw its first action in Afghanistan, where it was very effective in mountainous terrain, as gorges and valleys are favorable environments for the use of thermobarics.[47]

During combat actions in Afghanistan, some deficiencies were identified with the TOS-1. The 30 barrel rocket housing proved vulnerable to rocket propelled grenades, a dangerous proposition considering the volatile cargo, so the employment of the TOS-1 always required a substantial covering force. To correct this deficiency, Russia developed a second version of the TOS-1, the TOS-1A *Solntsepek*. The TOS-1A has an added heavy housing to protect the rocket tubes from premature detonation; this armor has reduced the rocket capacity from 30 to 24 rockets. In order to increase mobility, the T-72 chassis has an upgraded engine that produces 800 more horsepower than the TOS-1. The TOS-1A saw combat in Chechnya, its performance was well lauded in mountainous and urban environments alike.[48]

Organizationally, the TOS-1 series of heavy flamethrowers are organized in a similar fashion as Russian artillery units, batteries generally consisting of six TOS-1 or TOS-1As (six BM-1s launch vehicles and six TZM-T support vehicles), with each battalion having three batteries.[49] In general, the TOS-1 or TOS-1As fills the same niche as the RPO series flamethrowers, but on a much larger scale. They will most often be utilized in urban warfare settings, bunker busting, and clearing light infantry. Although the TOS-1/TOS-1A are not organic to Russian maneuver brigades, they are a likely attachment, especially if the brigade is operating in urban areas, or engaging an enemy that is entrenched.

The Future of Flame and NBC Defense Troops

From a Russian military perspective, flamethrowers are not seen as weapons simply to be handed out to the rank-and-file for any *ad-hoc* use, but instead are seen as a mature weapon system that fills specific capabilities gaps in the Russian Armed Forces force structure. While maneuver units do have limited flamethrower assets in their NBC defense units, all heavy flamethrowers and flamethrower battalions reside in NBC Defense Regiments and Brigades. At a time when other armies are reevaluating the role of NBC troops in their militaries, the Russian NBC Troop's

BMO-T Heavy Combat Vehicle for Flamethrower Operators

Image Courtesy: Vitaly Kuzmin

monopoly on flame, and its usefulness for urban and mountain warfare, bunker busting, and clearing light infantry has required the expansion of NBC troops in the Russian military with the creation or reconstitution of at least four NBC Defense Regiments in 2014.[50]

Although Russia is expanding her flame capabilities for urban warfare and other niche purposes, Russia's expansion of her NBC Troops may also be due to concerns about conventional maneuver warfare. The Russians still plan and practice for surviving and conducting tactical nuclear battle. This is in stark contrast to Western military exercises and wargames, where a tactical nuclear exchange is usually the culminating event. In Russian exercises and wargames a tactical nuclear exchange can be an early or mid-point event as they wrestle with the problems of survival, force reconstitution and maneuver in future war. The NBC Defense Troops have a clear role in "thinking the unthinkable." In sum, Russian concerns about urban warfare and the effects of nuclear weapons on conventional maneuver will likely cause Russia's flame wielding NBC Defense Troops to continue to be a high priority for development.[51]

Material Technical Support Troops

In the Russian Armed Forces, logistics is referred to as "Material Technical Support" (MTO). Despite the different naming, the Material Technical Support Troops have the same function as their Western counterparts, essentially provisioning and maintaining the force to help ensure constant readiness. Organizationally, MTO structure parallels the echelons of command. In terms of the Ground Forces, at echelons below brigade there are no dedicated MTO units, MTO functions at this level (supply, unit maintenance) are provided by units' organic or attached assets, typically in the form of a support platoon or squad. The lowest echelon MTO unit is the MTO Battalion, which is found in all Ground Forces maneuver brigades. At the Army Group level, MTO Brigades are found. Dedicated supply depots and refurbishment plants are at the Military District/Operational Strategic Command level. Responsibility for logistic issues culminates at the Ministry of Defense, with a dedicated Deputy Defense Minister. The incumbent, General Dmitri Bulgakov, is Russia's top Russian logistics officer. In terms of organic MTO support in the maneuver brigades, two dedicated battalions were typically found: a logistic battalion (primarily a motor transport unit) and a maintenance battalion which provides organizational-level maintenance for the brigade. These battalions are now being combined into a 'MTO Battalion'. The Russian Federation is still in the process of transitioning to this new system, so both systems may be found.

Material Technical Support activities include:
- provisioning the Armed Forces with weapons and military equipment;
- providing fuel;
- clothing and feeding personnel;
- providing issue items (uniforms, equipment, household items, etc.);
- providing stations for changing, washing and repairing clothes in garrison and field conditions;
- repairing and restoring road and rail access;
- organizing the transportation of military cargoes and personnel;
- receiving, accounting, and issuing material warehouse resources;
- organizing the maintenance and repair of weapons, military equipment and supplies;
- servicing and repairing buildings and public utilities on military installations;
- ensuring the accuracy and reliability of standards of measurements;
- training military personnel for MTO related military occupational specialties;
- providing controls for food and fire protection at military installations.

The Material Technical Support system includes:
- The Material Technical Support Headquarters of the Russian Armed Forces;
- Department of Transportation Support of the Russian Armed Forces;
- Department of Maintenance and Security of the Public Utilities of Military Units and Organizations of the Ministry of Defense of the Russian Federation;
- Main Armor Directorate of the Russian Armed Forces;
- Main Missile and Artillery Directorate of the Russian Armed Forces;
- Main Directorate of the Railway Troops;
- Department of Meteorology of the Russian Armed Forces.

Logistic Battalion (old system)

Maintenance Battalion (old system)

The Material Technical Support main activity areas are:
- planning the state arms program;
- organizing the supply of products, works and services;
- controlling MTO personnel, weapons, military equipment and other materiel;
- ensuring quality standards;
- providing regulations about MTO processes;
- developing the equipment needed for the provision of MTO services;
- training military personnel for MTO related military occupational specialties.[52]

Perhaps one of the most controversial of the "New Look" reforms was the reform of the Russian logistics system. Russia inherited its military logistics and combat service support system from the Soviets. The Soviet system was based upon the idea of mobilizing the whole societal and economic potentials of the Soviet Union for the conduct of war.[53] In practice, this meant that all civilian resources could and would be used in the event of war. In particular, civil manufacturing and transportation/infrastructure were designed to also facilitate the conduct of war. In recent years, the Russian Federation has come to the conclusion that mass mobilization, and its required logistics requirements, is no longer desired nor sustainable. The Soviet logistic system was based upon several "Rear Services," material support organizations, and a separate armaments branch to sustain the force in war and peace. In order to streamline or right size some of the massive logistics capabilities, the "New Look" reforms merged these various organizations into the Material Technical Support (MTO) structure.

> "The new superstructure, aimed at simplifying the system, merged numerous preexisting organizations. The MTO Department of Planning and Coordination includes departments of resource and transport support, the former Main Directorate of the Railway Troops, the Main Vehicle, Armoured Vehicle and Tank Directorate, the Main Missile and Artillery Directorate and the Metrological Service. Within the military districts MTO bases and brigades were formed, as well as arsenals for the storage of missiles, ammunition, and missile and artillery weapons. Moreover, within the combined-arms brigades, MTO battalions were created; these include separate logistics and maintenance battalions in each brigade…Underlying the reform of the structure of the rear services system, according…was an effort to combine rear services with various material support structures and the Deputy Defence Minister post into one 'MTO' organization."
>
> - Roger N. Mc Dermott[54]

There has been some up and downs, but this reform has generally been successful, and is still in the process of being tweaked.[55] Other logistic reforms have had varying degrees of success. Russia briefly attempted "outsourcing" the maintenance component of its logistics system, an effort that was unsuccessful. Commanders complained about the level of service and feasibility of contractor-provided maintenance services on the battlefield. In current practice, operator, unit, and organizational maintenance is provided by uniformed servicemen, while depot-level maintenance is provided by contract labor (usually by way of a state owned company) at a maintenance depot or by the equipment manufacturer.[56] Other logistic problems related to the "New Look" reforms, have not been the result of the logistic system itself, but of the personnel system. In general, most contract NCOs fill "trigger puller" positions, and positions requiring advanced skills and training. This means that combat support and service support roles have a lower percentage of contract NCOs. This is occurring at the same time the Russian Armed Forces are procuring more technologically advanced equipment, which subsequently require more maintenance support. This situation has resulted in maintenance issues being one of the top complaints of Russian maneuver commanders.[57]

Deploying and provisioning forces in the field and abroad is supported by the Department of Transportation Support, an entity in the Russian General Staff. The Department of Transportation Support is roughly a Russian equivalent of the U.S. Transportation Command (USTRANSCOM), albeit much smaller, that is responsible for:

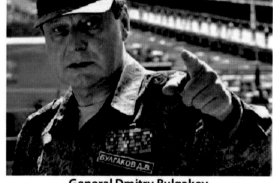

General Dmitry Bulgakov
Deputy Minister of Defense of the Russian Federation, Chief of Logistics
Image Courtesy: Russian Ministry of Defense

- development of a military shipping system for the Armed Forces using general use transport;
- placement of orders for military shipments and performance of other transport services for the Armed Forces;
- development of plans for military shipments by common carrier, finalizing these by established procedures, and facilitation, execution, and control of these shipments;
- establishing oversight over the preparation of common carrier transport to carry out military shipments; and
- planning and disbursement of funds for military transport, and monitoring such expenditures.[58]

The Department of Transportation Support is the Ministry of Defense's authorized representative for common carrier rail, air, sea, and inland water transport intended for military shipments. In general, the department is responsible for the coordination and/or contracting of commercial transport.[59]

In terms of force projection, perhaps the most important logistical asset in the Russian toolbox is the nation's massive railroad system. The vast majority of personnel and cargo are transported via rail for civil and military purposes. Rail transport is the primary means of logistical support for most military operations (including current operations in and around Eastern Ukraine) and is an absolute necessity for any type of large-scale movement throughout the great expanse that is the Russian Federation. Due to the importance of rail for military operations, the Russian Federation has a separate branch, the Railroad Troops, dedicated to protecting, servicing, and maintaining rail service in combat and

MTO Soldiers Laying Pipe
Image Courtesy: Russian Ministry of Defense

austere conditions for the Russian Armed Forces. They consist of ten brigades and several independent battalions scattered throughout the Russian Federation which are operationally attached to their respective military districts. These units provide rail-related logistical support for military operations to include repair, bridge building, and concealment.[60]

The Unfinished Debate

During the 1920s and 1930s, a far-reaching debate on the nature and conduct of future war was conducted by the leading theorists of the Soviet Red Army. Mechanization of war meant that the stationary warfare of World War I probably would not be repeated. Two schools of thought emerged, that of the attrition and the offensive. The attrition school, led by General-Major Aleksandr A. Svechin posited that the Soviet Union's vast expanse should be used to draw attacking armies deep within the territory of the country, and, once the enemy was overextended, counterattack and destroy him. Marshal of the Soviet Union M. N. Tukhachevsky led the offensive school which held that if the Soviet Union were attacked, the Soviets should launch a swift, decisive mechanized counterstrike at the enemy country, restricting the ravages of warfare to the territory of the enemy. The debate was more complicated than this and eventually led to debates by the protagonists. Tukhachevsky's side prevailed and Svechin was branded as a class enemy. When Germany invaded the Soviet Union, the Soviet counterstrike fizzled and the forward Soviet armies were surrounded and lost. Svechin was right, but neither he nor Tukhachevsky were alive, as they both were executed as part of Stalin's purges of the Red Army officer corps in the late 1930s[61]

The nature of future war and the best strategy to resolve it was not resolved in 1931. Will Russia be faced with a large-scale World War III, requiring millions of soldiers? What is Russia's

Comprehensive Support

Comprehensive Support

- Combat Support
- Moral Psychological Support
- Technical Support
- Rear Support

best strategy to maintain the nation? Svechin has been officially exonerated and is a favorite theorist of many of today's Russian military leaders. However, the distance between the Estonian border and St. Petersburg is under 100 miles. In this case, attrition may be an unacceptable strategy. The West is fearful of a Russian offensive strategy, but this is usually viewed in Russia as a counterstroke following a Western provocation. The Russians have transitioned to a brigade structure with divisions planted on critical directions of advance. Brigades are far more mobile, but lack the long-term combat power of divisions. A major change in the nature and conduct of future war is the presence and role of nuclear weapons and a major concern is accidental war and the role of nuclear weapons. Although the West is concerned with NATO's Eastern border, Russia is also concerned with defending its vast land mass along the Black Sea, the troubled Caucasus, an increasingly unpredictable Central Asia, the long border with China, the Pacific Coast-and the Arctic. What does all this have to do with logistics? Plenty. Russia has to defend in 360°. It is heavily dependent on barge and rail movement. It does not have the manpower of Soviet times. It cannot be strong everywhere at once and has gone to highly mobile brigades so that it can rapidly assemble forces where needed. It is a regional power, not a super power-but it still has the nuclear power to drastically reshape the world.

Tactical Logistical Theory

The Russian Ground Forces, and to a similar extent the Russian Airborne and Naval Infantry, utilize six principles of tactical logistics support.[62]

Centralized Control. The bulk of supplies and transport resources are held at army and higher level. This enables commanders to focus support where it is needed. Support can be shifted rapidly from one area to another if needed. This is not "everyone gets a fair share." At times, a unit may have to live on what it has or what it can forage since the priority has shifted elsewhere.

Combat Support

- Combat Support
  - Reconnaissance
  - Security
  - Electronic Warfare
  - Tactical Maskirovka
  - Engineer Support
  - NBC Defense

Forward Delivery. Higher commanders are responsible for keeping their subordinates supplied. Higher delivers to lower-either to dumps or directly to the brigade. Military Districts manage in-area railheads and have transportation brigades of trucks for delivery. In terms of

Moral Psychological Support

fuel distribution, the Army Groups have dedicated field pipeline units that are capable of tapping into the national infrastructure's civil pipelines, and then piping the fuel to rear service areas. This may then be trucked from the rear service areas up to the end user.

Maintenance of Stockage. A combined arms brigade carries three to five days of supplies as mobile stocks on its organic vehicles. The Russian Army uses a push system for tactical logistics. The logisticians have determined brigade consumption rates for combat and heavy combat. These consumption rates are determined for expected ammunition, POL, parts and food expenditure and constitute "push packages" of supplies that are pushed forward. The familiar Western "requisition and receive" model does not apply for these classes of supply, however, the Russian logisticians keep the rear area logisticians apprised of combat and maintenance losses of vehicles, weapons and personnel, as well as unusual consumption of ammunition and fuel. The Military District maintains "float" vehicles and weapons and would push part of this float forward to the Army logisticians in wartime. This push system enables the brigade to weather a temporary disruption of its lines of communication and continue fighting. This is "timely logistics" rather than "just in time logistics".

Technical Support

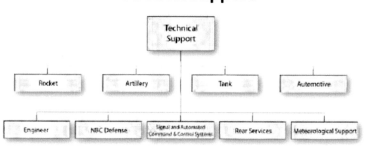

Supply Priorities. Ammunition, POL, technical supplies, rations, non-technical supplies. Non-essentials will not be delivered if it will reduce the provision of essential combat supplies. In a pursuit, ammunition and POL may switch priority. Ammunition is accounted for and issued in units of fire. For example, a unit of fire for each AK-74 assault rifle is 400 rounds, for each mortar it is 80 rounds, for each T-72 tank main gun it is 40 rounds and for each 152mm howitzer it is 60 rounds. Since the brigade has 36 howitzers, the brigade composite unit of fire for 152mm howitzer is 2160 rounds. The brigade will have normally have six composite units of 152mm howitzer ammunition or 12,960 rounds. The number of composite units of fire in the brigade varies by weapons type. For example, the composite unit of fire for tank main gun ammunition is four. POL is calculated in refills. A refill is the amount required to fill each vehicle in the brigade (one fill

Rear Support

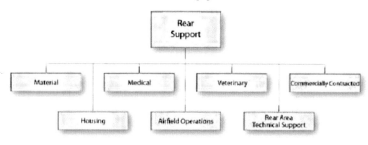

provides a 500 kilometer range on roadways for most vehicles). A brigade starts with three refills, one in the vehicles and the rest on transport.

Forward Positioning of Support Elements. Army and brigade medical, equipment recovery, and repair elements will keep up with the advance. They move forward to the last area of combat to treat the personnel and equipment casualties on site. Priority is given to returning lightly wounded soldiers and lightly damaged equipment to battle and evacuating the seriously wounded and heavily damaged to the rear for extensive healing and repair.

Force Restoration. In the past, the Soviet and Russian practice has been to replace depleted units, not individuals. Depleted units were reorganized as smaller units, combined with other depleted units or reconstituted with healed hospital patients and repaired equipment. There has been no move to adopt the Western system of individual replacement. However, the strategic reserve system is no longer built around the "cadre unit" mobilization concept, which involved a small cadre maintaining equipment until the unit was fleshed out with personnel in the strategic reserve, since Russia is no longer preparing for a long war scenario. The military districts will likely constitute replacement units of reservists who will be grouped by military occupational specialty and organized into platoon or company-sized subunits for further deployment where needed. First priority, however, may go to transferring subunits from an uncommitted brigade to a depleted brigade. The longer-term goal of converting

Organization of Ammunition Distribution for a Motorized Rifle Battalion in the Defense

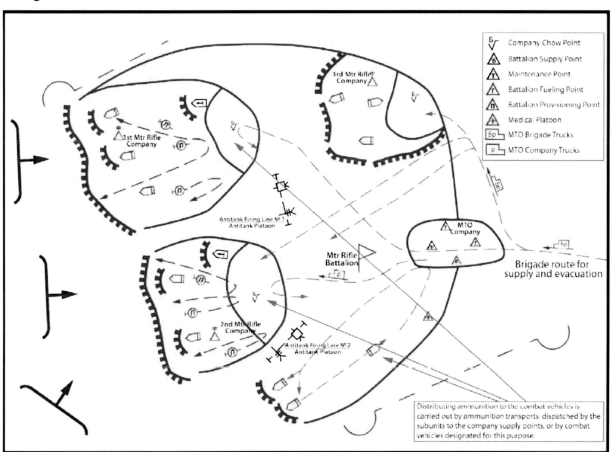

all maneuver battalions in a brigade into battalion tactical groups would support this replacement scheme optimally. It would also provide a trained combined arms team that could readily integrate into a different brigade with a minimum of adjustment and stand-up time.

Material-Technical Support Units (MTO)

In terms of organization, the system of material technical support of the Russian Armed Forces is divided by the scale (tactical, operational, and strategic) and type of support provided. The types of support include: national level support, support for branches of service and arms, support for forces in a theater of military activity (TVD), fleets, armies (combined arms armies, rocket armies, etc.), long-range aviation, military-transport aviation, naval bases, divisions, brigades, regiments and battalions. MTO support for the Ground Forces, Airborne (VDV), and Naval Infantry units is generally provided in the following manner. Military districts and army groups are supported by MTO brigades, divisions by MTO battalions, brigades by MTO battalions or MTO companies (depending on brigade type), and regiments by MTO companies. The most important change regarding recent MTO reforms is the relationships of the battalions' material support (logistic) platoons to their battalions. Previously, these platoons were organic to the battalions, now it appears these platoons will be organic to the MTO battalion, and attached as needed. The following description of a MTO battalion, describes a MTO Battalion that is supporting a Motorized Rifle Brigade mounted on BTRs (approximately 4,500 personnel). Although MTO battalions vary in size and structure depending on the supported brigades type and size, this description provides a reasonable baseline for the function, size and capabilities for other MTO battalions that may be encountered. There is one discrepancy that should be noted. In current Russian logistical training materials, the MTO Battalion has platoons that are attached to the maneuver brigade's subordinate battalions, but when attached these platoons are often depicted as companies for unknown reasons. These apparent discrepancies were likely not done in error, as they were found in several different sources. We have not discovered the reasoning behind this practice, and have elected to present the information as found.[63]

Material Technical Support Brigade (variant)

MTO Brigade

MTO brigades support Military Districts and Army Group level organizations. MTO brigade capabilities differ substantially, but there is a concerted effort to develop a somewhat standardized TO&E that would give every MTO brigade: a command and control element, two motor transport battalions, a maintenance battalion, a pipeline battalion, road-commandant battalion (traffic/movement control), warehouses, a field refueling company, a motor transport company (water), a general support company, bath and laundry services, and mobile bakeries. Any of these assets may be attached to a particular brigade or division to support operations as needed.

MTO Battalion

The MTO battalion consists of approximately 1000 personnel and 408 transport vehicles (148 general freight/260 specialized/48 trailers), and can reportedly haul 1,870 tons of cargo (1190 tons of dry cargo, 680 tons of liquid). MTO battalions typically have a: command and control element, motor transport companies (general cargo, ammunition, and POL), a maintenance company, and support companies. The majority of the battalion's personnel (672) are located in the MTO battalion's two support companies and support platoon. Since maneuver battalions have relatively few organic logistical assets, these units rely on logistic and maintenance assets provided by MTO battalions to conduct operations. During operations, the MTO battalion's support companies are detached and their subordinate platoons are attached to the maneuver and fires battalions. The MTO battalion's support platoon detaches its subordinate squads to support the engineer battalion and brigade headquarters. Typically, each maneuver or fires battalion has a dedicated support platoon, with motor transport and maintenance squads. The mission of these subunits is to haul materiel from the depots of the logistic support battalions or companies directly to the units at the front line and provide limited maintenance support or evacuate inoperable vehicles as needed. In non-combat/field/expeditionary conditions, typically only 10-12 trucks of the MTO battalion are involved in supporting a maneuver brigade's daily needs. The remaining vehicles wait at depots, fully loaded, fueled, but with batteries removed.

Support Platoon (for a Motorized Rifle Battalion)

Field Fueling Operations
Image Courtesy: Russian Ministry of Defense

A maneuver brigade's logistics subunits may spread over an area of 40-70 square kilometers and may move twice in 24 hours if the brigade advance is rapid. Normal logistics activities will include supply points, ammunition points, POL points, assembly points for damaged vehicles, technical inspection points, a repair and evacuation group (REG) and medical aid posts. Medical aid posts will be 10-20 kilometers from the forward edge of the fight. Ammunition and POL points will be 20-40 kilometers from the fight in an advance and 35-50 kilometers in the defense. Supply points are generally further back. The Russians hope to hold the battle area at the end of the day since it contains the disabled Russian and enemy vehicles and weapons, they also hope to maintain equipment strengths with float vehicles and rapid repair. During 1944-1945, 25% of Soviet tank losses were unrepairable, but 80-90 % of the remainder were returned to service within two days. If Russia does move to three standard chassis, common turrets and PLL, Russia will likely speed vehicle repair times.

Organization of the MTO Battalion in the Defense
The defense is one of the primary forms of combined arms combat, which has the goal of destroying the advancing superior enemy force, inflicting maximum damage on him, while retaining important regions or lines of territory and establishing advantageous conditions for the conduct of further actions. Preparation of units and subunits of MTO support is conducted simultaneously with the preparation of combat subunits of the brigade and begins with the receipt of the commander's orders for material-technical support and directives of the senior MTO chief.

Preparations include:
- receipt of the decision on material-technical support;
- establishing the fire and maneuver subunits missions involving MTO issues and also the MTO subunits' missions;
- conducting a reconnaissance of the rear area;
- organizing all the types of MTO support;
- planning material-technical support;
- organizing coordination and deployment of control systems of MTO support;
- organizing the protection, defenses, security and camouflage of MTO units and subunits;
- controlling the preparation and readiness of MTO subunits for combat, as well as the readiness of MTO units and subunits to fulfill established missions under combat.

The MTO Battalion area must support:
- the smooth placement of battalion subunits considering mission accomplishment;
- the dispersion and concealed placement of the combat equipment and personnel of MTO subunits;
- the rapid assembly of battalion subunits, the timely exit of battalion wheeled vehicle columns, the transport of supplies, the deployment and redeployment of the battalion to a new area using existing roads and trail spurs;
- meeting the requirements to safeguard the various types of supply dumps;
- ideal conditions for protection from air attack and battalion command and control;
- nearby access to an area suited for a transport assembly or waiting area that can be used as a battalion arrival and departure area;
- nearby access to a water source of sufficient size;
- a sufficient separation distance from large industrial centers and inhabited regions which may be the target of enemy strikes.

The total operating area of an MTO battalion is up to 80km^2, or if subordinate MTO companies are not present (i.e. deployed forward) 40km^2. During the conduct of a brigade defense, the MTO battalion is situated according to the brigade plan in a designated area at a safe distance from the forward edge of the defense, taking in account the enemy use of nuclear and NBC weapons and the nature of the terrain. If the defending brigade is in the first echelon-the MTO battalion is located away from the main enemy avenue of attack. If the brigade is in the second echelon (or is the reserve) the battalion deploys behind the brigade second echelon or reserve.

Naval Infantry Medics
Image Courtesy: Russian Ministry of Defense

The MTO support companies are located in corresponding regions to support the brigade combat subunits. The MTO battalion of a second echelon brigade (or combined arms reserve) in the defense is located behind the combat formation (in an assembly area) prepared to move to support brigade subunits in a counterattack or to carry out the commander's decision regarding a short-notice mission. The senior commander orders the movement from the MTO battalion's designated area. In the event of the surprise enemy use of weapons of mass destruction, high-precision weapons, incendiary weapons or FASCAM mines, and if the senior commander cannot be informed expeditiously, the MTO battalion commander may make the movement decision. However, the battalion commander must follow this up with a report to the senior commander.

The deployment and redeployment of the MTO battalion depends on the combat formation and mission of the supported brigade; the safe distance from the supported subunits; the NBC situation; the terrain; if the brigade is in the first echelon-the battalion is located away from the main enemy avenue of attack; or if the brigade is in the second echelon (or is the reserve). In that case, the battalion deploys behind the brigade second echelon or assembly area. The battalion may deploy in two parts assigned to two planned axes of advance by friendly forces, but in areas not accessible from all directions and behind natural or manmade barriers.

MTO battalion support companies may be deployed into adjacent regions supporting combat subunits of the brigade. Primarily this will be in support of a security zone or forward position. Trucks from the transport company may haul ammunition and engineer obstacle material. Repair personnel may be deployed to combat subunits defending the forward position. The MTO battalion designates main and reserve areas for support. They are located 5 to 7 kilometers apart. The total MTO battalion support area is up to 80km² or if subordinate companies are not present (i.e. deployed forward) 40km². The MTO deployment area is selected by the senior

Vehicle Maintenance
Image Courtesy: Russian Ministry of Defense

commander or by the battalion commander in agreement with the brigade staff.

The battalion truck companies transport material to the subunits:
- during a positional defense, the battalion provides the primary forces and means and supports maneuver (if necessary);
- during maneuver defense, part of the cargo and repair subunits may be detached to strengthen the first echelon brigade;
- including ammunition transport, delivery to the designated points and to points separated from the firing positions; to the point of material transfer with an ammunition reserve and the redeployment of it during battle. On the return trip, the trucks are used to evacuate the sick and wounded and shuttle supplies.

Refueling is based upon the brigade commander's decision (which establishes the order, times, the routes used by the supporting units, refueling the units and the strict observance of camouflage discipline):

- at occupied positions, refill vehicles move to the military equipment under the cover of darkness;
- in the depth of the defense, refill at the end of the end of the day's fighting using a combination of methods, depending on the situation (the refueling trucks can move to the combat vehicles or vice versa. Also, refueling can use the field refill points);
- refill tanks, BMPs, BTRs moving in the combat formation, artillery tractors and specialized vehicles at the place of their deployment;
- refill combat equipment supporting subunits within the second echelon (combined arms reserve), and the subunits of the MTO supporting subunits at the place of their deployment.

The battalion commander organizes the provision of bread. Bread is delivered according to plan, twice in a 24-hour day. Bread is baked at a central location. In some cases, subunits send vehicles back to pick up bread. The bakery squad usually distributes bread to one area and then another or brings all deliveries to a single central area. The battalion commander organizes the shower and laundry support. The shower and laundry point personnel are protected by the military unit being supported. The repair and evacuation of armored vehicles, trucks and rocket and artillery vehicles, weapons and military equipment is provided by the repair companies.

Mobile Bakery
Image Courtesy: Russian Ministry of Defense

Evacuation of armored vehicles and weapons includes:
- Dragging out stuck, overturned, buried and sunk equipment;
- Restoring that equipment to a transportable state and transporting the damaged (nonfunctioning) equipment from the combat area or from the place it broke down to the evacuation route and then to the repair site at the damaged equipment collection point.

Organization of the MTO Battalion in the Offense
The advance is one of the primary forms of combined arms combat, which has the goal of destroying the resisting enemy and seizing designated lines or regions and establishing the conditions for the conduct of further actions. The preparation of MTO units and subunits of is conducted simultaneously with the preparation of combat subunits of the brigade and begins with the receipt of the commander's orders for MTO support and directives of the senior MTO chief.

Preparations include:
- receipt of the decision on MTO support;
- establishing the fire and maneuver subunits missions involving MTO issues and also the MTO subunits' missions;
- conducting a reconnaissance of the rear area;
- organizing all the types of MTO support;
- planning MTO support;
- organizing coordination and deployment of control systems of MTO support;
- organizing the protection, defenses, security and camouflage of MTO units and subunits;
- controlling the preparation and readiness of MTO subunits for combat, as well as the readiness of MTO units and subunits to fulfill established missions under combat.

The MTO Battalion area must support:
- the smooth placement of battalion subunits considering mission accomplishment;
- the dispersion and concealed placement of the combat equipment and personnel of MTO subunits;
- the rapid assembly of battalion subunits, the timely exit of battalion wheeled vehicle columns, the transport of supplies, the deployment and redeployment of the battalion to a new area using existing roads and trail spurs;
- meeting the requirements to safeguard the various types of supply dumps;
- ideal conditions for protection from air attack and battalion command and control;
- nearby access to an area suited for a transport assembly or waiting area that can be used as a battalion arrival and departure area;
- nearby access to a water source of sufficient size;
- a sufficient separation distance from large industrial centers and inhabited regions which may be the target of enemy strikes.

The total operating area of an MTO battalion is up to 80km^2, or if subordinate MTO companies are not present (i.e. deployed forward) 40km^2. During the conduct of a brigade attack from

the march (or departure area or assembly area), against a defending enemy, the MTO battalion is situated on a designated area at a safe distance from the forward edge of the enemy defense. During the brigade movement from a departure area or assembly area to the line of attack, the MTO battalion follows the second echelon combat formation. The senior commander orders the movement from the MTO battalion's designated area. In the event of the surprise enemy use of weapons of mass destruction, high-precision weapons, incendiary weapons or FASCAM mines, and if the senior commander cannot be

Soldiers' Mess
Image Courtesy: Russian Ministry of Defense

informed expeditiously, the MTO battalion commander may make the movement decision. However, the battalion commander must follow this up with a report to the senior commander.

Organization of the MTO Battalion on the March

Military equipment is refueled in rest stop areas and in the assembly area at the end of the march. However, tanks and other equipment with smaller fuel tanks are fueled additionally at a stop during the second half of a 24-hour march day. With this goal in mind, the senior commander designates brigade refueling areas along the march route where he will concentrate transport subunits with fuel reserves ahead of time and deploy fueling systems of the higher commander. If the refueling systems of the brigade are stationed forward with the MTO subunits, then they will move to the refueling areas ahead of time and deploy to conduct a mass refueling of the entire brigade in a short time. The Russian Federation currently utilizes the PZP-10, PZP-10A, PZP-14, and PZP-20 field fueling systems.

Field Fueling Systems

	PZP-10	PZP-10A	PZP-14	PZP-20
Trailer Chassis	1-AP-1,5	1-AP-1,5	1-AP-1,5	2-PN-4
Fuel Storage Type	Collapsible bladder	Tanker Truck	Collapsible bladder	Tanker Truck
Output (liters per minute)	1,000	1,000	1,470	2,600
Fuel stations	10	10	14	20
Nozzels per station	2	2	2	2
Distance between stations (m)	10	10	10	10
Deployed length (m)	90	90	130	190
Weight (kg)	800	1,395	2,140	1,600

The norms for refueling equipment at a field refueling point (using the PZP-10A) are:
- Motorized rifle company-10 minutes
- Motorized rifle battalion-30 minutes
- Motorized rifle brigade-2-2.5 hours

Hot food is prepared at TO&E food preparation points and is fed to personnel at stops lasting up to two hours, at a stop during the second half of a 24-hour march day and at the day (night) lager. When it is not possible to feed three hot prepared meals in a day, two are provided. The first at the start of the march and the second, after completing a 24-hour march, at the day (night) lager. During the interval, the personnel are provided dry rations (bread, sugar, tea, cans of meat, fish or fruit compote) to provide the complete daily food ration. Under circumstances where hot meals cannot be provided, the brigade commander

MTO Brigade on the March

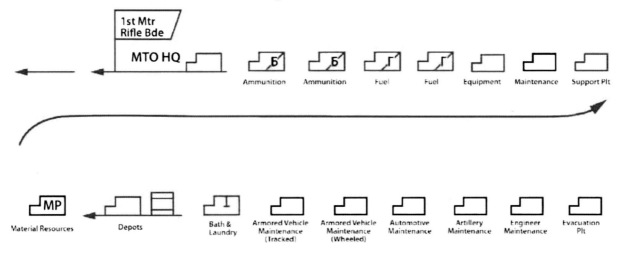

will order the issue of individual combat field rations (similar to MREs) from the emergency ration reserve. Water reserves are established to the degree determined by the brigade's location relative to a water spring or water supply point (where all the water tanks can be refilled).

Transport of material supplies is organized considering not only how the MTO battalion will routinely transfer the reserve military supplies to the combat subunits, but also how to accomplish this when in regions not directly contiguous with the rest areas or if out of direct contact with their higher formations and units. Usually, the MTO transport companies move to the rest stops of the subunits ahead of time, issue the required supplies and then replenish their reserve stores from those of the MTO organs of their higher headquarters.

Field Fueling System

Image Courtesy: Russian Ministry of Defense

MTO technical support is organized and conducted to provide repair and maintenance to sustain readiness and support required work using the MTO systems and proper technical service, maintenance, upkeep, scheduled services and evacuation. During the march, technical support is provided in the rest stops and day (night) lager. At the rest stops, only a general inspection and the elimination of detected faults is conducted. During the march, missions for technical support by the MTO march column are conducted by the technical maintenance section (usually at the tail end of the column).

Technical support for vehicles that breakdown during the march is usually accomplished by pulling the vehicles over to the right onto the road shoulder where the technical maintenance section and drivers work on them. If it is impossible or inadvisable to fix the vehicle on site, the vehicle is towed to the nearest damaged vehicle collection point. This is usually located at the day (night) lager and sometimes on the march route itself where organized by the brigade or army. Unit and medium repairs are primarily conducted at the damaged vehicle collection point. Vehicles requiring a major overhaul are evacuated to a final collection and restoration area after the conclusion of the march. During the preparation of units (subunits) of the MTO brigade, the battalion undertakes the following measures to fulfill their missions during the march:

- finish bringing up to strength the MTO subunits with personnel, equipment and parts;
- implement technical services, repairs and preparations for MTO technical services, tables of equipment and material services reserves;
- evacuate MTO technical service equipment that cannot be repaired before the start of the march on the order of the senior commander for dispatch to the higher level repair facilities;
- organize training for personnel on embarking on vehicles and on loading parts and supplies on trucks or railroad cars (or ships, aircraft and helicopters);
- instruct personnel in the warning signals and vehicle assignments and loading order;
- instruct drivers on march preparation and main features of the march, march route and safety measures;
- where necessary, provide additional measures (outfit vehicles with entrenching tools and drivers instruments, provide sketch maps showing the march route and the more dangerous sections on it).

The MTO battalion preparations must include its own road march, transport on train, ship, river transport, aircraft, helicopter or any combination of these. The battalion must be intact with its required load of supplies and material, on time at the designated area and fully prepared to undertake its required mission. The MTO battalion preparations take place as part of the brigade or independently, concluding with assembly at the designated area. Orders for the battalion preparations for the march are issued by the Brigade Deputy for MTO Support (the battalion commander may be dual-hatted in this position in some brigades). Subunits of the battalion move on one or two march routes some 5 to 10 kilometers from the brigade main body.

Depending on the situation, the battalion column may have various compositions. During a march that will terminate in combat, the battalion column, as a rule, has battalion subunits transporting ammunition reserves well forward and during marches that will last more than 24 hours and have little expectation of meeting the enemy, fuel reserves will travel well forward. The distance between the day (night) lagers may extend 250-300km.

Distances during the movement of a march column:
- 2-3 km between company columns and various battalion subunits;
- 0.5-1km between platoon columns and their various subunits;
- 25-50m between vehicles.

Average speed of battalion subunits:
- 20-25kph for a mixed column of wheeled and tracked vehicles;
- 25-30kph for a wheeled vehicle column.

Methods of Supply Delivery

Pushed from Higher Echelons

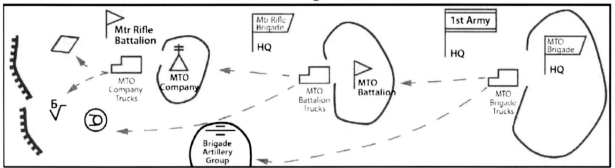

Supply delivery is accomplished by "pushing" supplies to subordinate units. This method is used while in the offense for the supply of first echelon and artillery units and subunits when the higher echelon unit has a sufficient number of vehicles for the task. *The above graphic depicts supplies being pushed from the depots of the MTO brigade, to the MTO battalion, to the MTO company, and eventually to the end user.*

Pulled from Higher Echelons

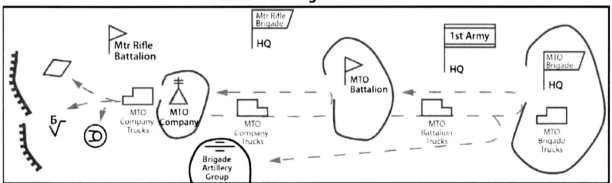

Supply delivery is accomplished by subordinate units "pulling" supplies from higher echelon units. This method is used in the initial period of the war; during the preparation for the offensive; during the defense, before the enemy's attack; by units conducting actions on secondary axes; units in the second echelon or reserve; and/or when the higher echelon unit does not have a sufficient number of vehicles for the task. *The above graphic depicts supplies being pulled from the depots of the MTO brigade, to the MTO battalion, with the MTO company pulling supplies from the MTO battalion pushing them to the end user.*

Pushed and Pulled from Higher Echelons

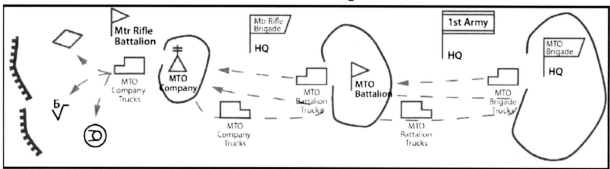

Supply delivery is accomplished by higher echelon units "pushing" supplies to subordinate units and subordinate units "pulling" supplies from higher echelon units. This method is used when higher echelon units do not have sufficient capabilities to solely supply subordinate units. Usually, the higher echelon will provide the majority of support in this situation. *The above graphic depicts supplies being pushed from MTO brigade, the MTO battalion pulling supplies from the MTO brigade and pushing supplies to the MTO companies, and the MTO company pulling supplies from the MTO battalion and pushing them to the end user.*

Pushed, Bypassing Intermediate Echelons

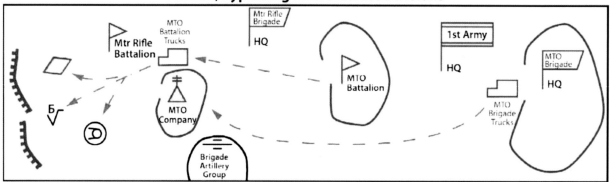

This method of supply delivery is conducted by "pushing" supplies from higher level unit to lower level units by bypassing intermediate echelons. *The above depicts supplies being pushed from the depots of the MTO brigade directly to the MTO company, bypassing the depots of the MTO battalion.*

(Right) The graphic on the facing page depicts a standard motorized rifle brigade defense defending with two motorized rifle battalions forward in the brigade first defensive echelon and a motorized rifle battalion and tank battalion in the brigade second defensive echelon. The brigade has its artillery battalions, air defense battalions, antitank reserve and mobile obstacle detachment deployed primarily between the brigade first and second defensive echelons. There is a well-defined fire sac between the brigade first and second defensive echelons. The MTO battalion is in the rear. The brigade has two main east-west roads and two north-south connecting roads. Route and Traffic control points limit the amount of traffic and vehicle spacing on the roads to prevent vehicles from bunching up in observable target sets. The brigade headquarters has a forward and alternate CP location as well as a main CP location in the rear area. The MTO battalion has a forward and alternate command post location in the area between the brigade first and second defensive echelons and a main CP in the rear area. There is a reserve rear area services location.

Each battalion has its organic support platoon which provides vehicle evacuation, messing, motor transport, laundry and bath support and limited vehicle maintenance. This platoon remains with the battalion when it is detached on separate missions such as forward detachment, advance guard, flanking detachment, rear guard or raiding detachment. An organic medical platoon is also a permanent part of the battalion, but is separate from the organic support platoon. The support platoon belongs to the battalion, but it is also part of an MTO company. The MTO companies deploy forward to the rear of the fire and maneuver battalions during the defense and provides additional maintenance, fueling, food service, supply, ammunition and transport support.

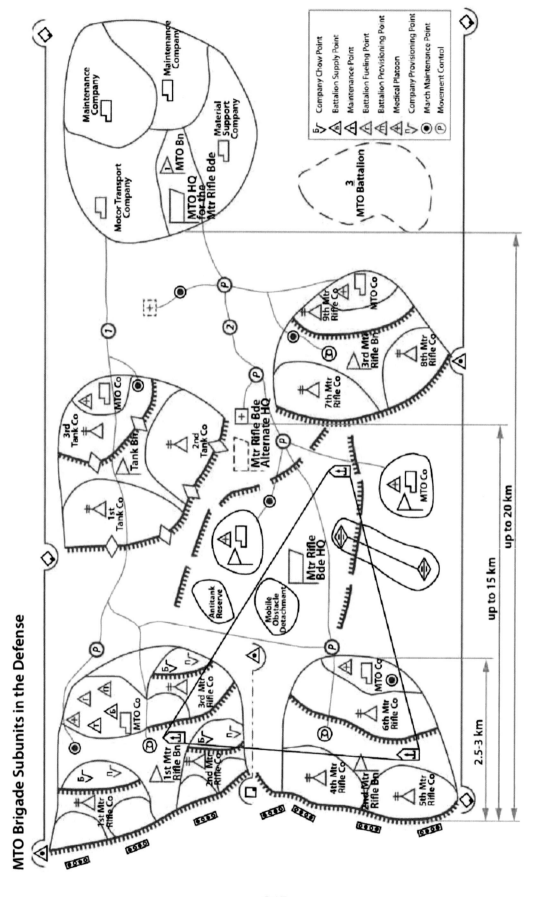

MTO Brigade Subunits in the Defense

(Right) The graphic on the facing page shows the location of MTO subunits during the phases of a motorized rifle brigade attack from the march. The brigade attacks with three motorized rifle battalions on line. Either the tank battalion has detached a company to each of the attacking motorized rifle battalions and is not depicted or the tank battalion is following as a second echelon attack battalion. The artillery and air defense battalions and other supporting elements are not depicted. The graphic shows the location of MTO subunits during seven time hacks. Conveniently, there are three east-west roads running through the attack area.

The first time hack occurs while the entire brigade is in an assembly area 20-40 kilometers from the enemy front line defense. The MTO subunits are busy filling, feeding and maintaining the brigade in preparation for the attack.

The second time hack occurs while the artillery conducts preparatory fires and the maneuver battalions form into march columns and advance toward the enemy. As they advance the battalions deploy into battalion precombat, company precombat and platoon precombat formations, each carefully choreographed with the phases of artillery preparatory fires. The platoons go on line and conduct the assault. During this time, the organic battalion support platoons and medical platoons accompany the battalions. The MTO companies cross the start line and follow well behind the attack. The rest of the MTO subunits load and prepare to leave the assembly area.

The third time hack occurs when the battalions achieve their immediate objective and usually commit or prepare to commit their second echelon attack subunits. Artillery is beginning to displace forward while the rest of the artillery conducts supporting fire. As the MTO companies move, they begin evacuating or repairing damaged maneuver battalion vehicles and weapons. The MTO subunits in the assembly area finish loading up and move to the start line.

The fourth time hack occurs when the first echelon battalions achieve their subsequent objective. Artillery continues to displace forward and the BrAG is reconstituted forward. Other artillery continues to move forward. The MTO companies move forward, collecting and repairing as they go. The remainder of the MTO subunits and command elements have crossed the start line and are marching toward the initial attack line.

The fifth time hack is the Brigade immediate objective and is practically identical to the first echelon battalions' subsequent objective. The sixth time hack is the subsequent objective of the second echelon battalions. The BrAG is reconstituted forward. The MTO companies have formed vehicle collection and supply points and have pushed subunits forward to join the battalion organic supply platoons to refit, refuel, feed and evacuate casualties. The MTO headquarters and battalion CP have formed a rear area supply and repair area short of the first echelon battalion immediate objective. The seventh time hack is the Brigade subsequent objective and is practically identical to the second echelon battalions' subsequent objective. This is also referred to as the objective of the day and is often the time for a pause in the brigade's offensive to refit while a follow-on brigade is committed to continue the attack.

MTO Brigade Subunits in the Offense

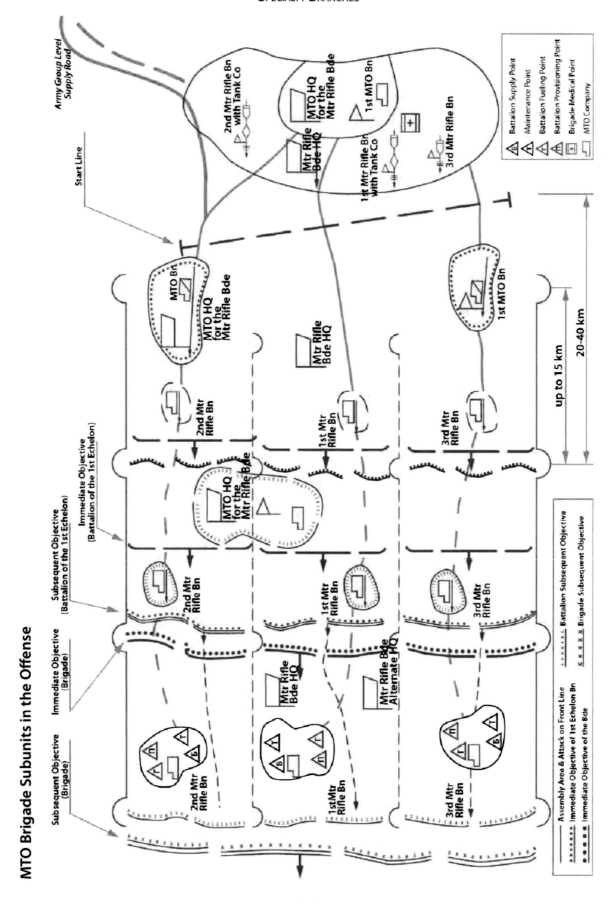

Logistic Vehicle Modernization

The Russian Armed Forces are not only incorporating interoperability and modularity into combat vehicles, but also into logistical vehicles. This goal has presented some significant difficulties as the Russian Federation inherited Soviet logistical vehicles made by six different manufactures: Kama Automobile Plant (KamAZ), The Urals Automotive Plant (Ural), the Likhachov Plant (ZiL), Gorky Automobile Plant (GAZ), Kremenchuk Automobile Plant (KrAZ), and the Minsk Automobile Plant (MAZ). By the mid-1990s, the Russian Federation had stopped the procurement of most now "foreign" vehicles produced by MAZ (Belarus) and KrAZ (Ukraine). Even though the number of manufacturers of logistical vehicles had decreased, there were still significant problems.

Russian Logistic Vehicle Families

'Motovoz' Family   'Mustang' Family

Images courtesy: Vitaly Kuzmin

Russia's four domestic manufacturers of vehicles (KamAZ, Ural, Zil, GAZ) each had their own subcomponents and parts, that were not interchangeable. Some vehicles, such as the ZiL-131, were gasoline powered, while the vast majority of the fleet was diesel powered. For these reasons they decided to adopt a single manufacturer, and family of vehicles, to fulfill logistical duties. In 1998, The Urals Automotive Plant was selected to produce the "Motovoz" family of trucks. The Motovoz consists of three chassis, the Ural 43206 (4x4), Ural-4320-31 (6x6), and Ural-5323 (8x8). These vehicles reportedly share 95% of their components. Due to financial difficulties, only one vehicle of the Motovoz family, the Ural-43206 (4x4), was fielded in large numbers from 2006-2008.

Former Defense Minister Anatoliy Serdyukov decided to shift course on the logistical vehicle modernization effort by abandoning the Ural's Motovoz family in favor of the KamAZ's Mustang family. The Mustang family also consists of three chassis, the KamAZ-4350 (4x4), KamAZ-5350 (6x6), and KamAZ-6350 (8x8). There is some speculation about the cause of this shift ranging from corruption to production problems at the Urals plant, but it is most likely that the transition was due to KamAZ being part of the State Corporation for Assisting the Development, Production, and Export of High-Tech Industrial Products (Rostekh). Currently, the Russian Armed Forces have almost completely retired their Ural-4320s, ZiL-131s, and GAZ-66s. The Motovoz trucks are still in service, and will remain in service for the foreseeable future, but are small in number. But the vast majority of logistical vehicles in service with the Armed Forces are of KamAZ's Mustang family, the KamAZ-4350 is now the standard vehicle found in the battalion's logistical support platoons.

In terms of capabilities, the Mustang family has about the same payload capacities as the Motovoz family of vehicles, but Russian logisticians point out other differences between the families. In general, most Russian logisticians are of the opinion that the KamAZ Mustang family is best suited for over-the-road hauling at distances of over 500-600 km, while the Ural Motovoz family is best in more austere environments where off road characteristics are most important. Another difference is technical complexity, the Mustangs are substantially more complex than the Motovoz vehicles, preventing operators and organizational level mechanics from conducting many repairs on the Mustang vehicles that they could otherwise perform on the Motovoz family of vehicles. Due to this situation, the brigades' MTO battalions, and army group and military district MTO brigades have greatly increased their lift capacities, but are not always capable of delivering materials directly to the subunits at the forward edge of the battle area. In general, The Russian Armed Forces and military forces of the Interior Troops (MVD-VV) appear to be integrating both the Mustang and Motovoz family of vehicles as they complement each other.

In terms of standardization, reportedly 90-95% of logistical vehicle components (including POL) are now interchangeable. These vehicles not only have components interchangeable with other KamAZ vehicles, but also interchangeable with subcomponents and parts of other manufacturers such as engines produced by the Urals Automotive Plant (Ural) and cabs produced by the Italian firm Industrial Vehicles Corporation (Iveco). This line of effort towards interoperability and modularity is paralleled throughout the Russian defense industry and is most apparent in combat vehicle development. Although the Mustang family is currently Russia's solution for interoperability, Russia has already started its next generation of logistic vehicles, the Tayfun and Platforma families. These vehicles will take integration one step farther, by utilizing a common chassis for logistic and some combat vehicles.[64]

Logistic Vehicle Characteristics

Russian Logistic Vehicles

ZiL-131

The ZiL-131 is a 6x6 general-purpose military truck that has an all-metal cab which provides seating for the driver and two passengers. Its production commenced in 1966, as a replacement for the ZiL-157. Production of the ZiL-131 ceased in 1994 after the production of nearly 1,000,000 vehicles. The baseline model of the ZiL-131 is a cargo truck with a payload capacity of 5,000 kg on hard surface roads and 3,500 kg off-road, often being used to carry troops, cargo and other military equipment. The cargo area can be covered with bows and canvas. The ZiL-131 can tow trailers or artillery pieces with a maximum weight of 6,500 kg on hard

ZiL-131

Image Courtesy: Vitaly Kuzmin

surface roads and 4,000 kg off-road. The ZiL-131 is powered by a 150 hp V8 gasoline engine with a 5-speed manual gearbox. The vehicle is all-wheel drive, however the front axle can be disconnected on hard surface roads, and is equipped with a central tire inflation system. Some models are equipped with a self-recovery winch. Variants of the ZiL-131 include a ZiL-131V tractor truck for towing semi-trailers, ZiL-131D dump truck and fuel and water tankers. It is used as a chassis for the Grad MLRS system. An improved variant, the ZiL-131N, was introduced in 1986. A civilian version of this truck, the ZiL-130 with 4x4 configuration was also produced in large numbers. In 1995 a new ZiL-4334 was proposed as a replacement of the ZiL-131N. A small number of these trucks are in service with the Russian Army.[65]

GAZ-66

The GAZ-66 is a 4x4 light general-purpose truck with a cab over engine design that has seating for the driver and one passenger. Production of the GAZ-66 commenced in 1964 at the Gorkiy Automobile Plant, as a replacement for the GAZ-63. The design follows the usual Soviet guidelines of relative simplicity, strength and versatility, being produced for both civilian and military use. There are no design frills on the GAZ-66, it can be produced in, or modified into, many different versions. Production ceased in 1999, after almost 1,000,000 were built. The GAZ-66 is simple and easy to maintain, with a 2,000 kg payload capacity. The

GAZ-66

Image Courtesy: Vitaly Kuzmin

basic cargo/utility model has an all-steel cargo body with an optional bow and canvas cover mounted on a chassis frame that can be arranged to carry any number of body styles. The GAZ 66 is powered by a 115 hp 4.2-liter V8 gasoline engine. The vehicle is all-wheel drive, and has superb cross-country mobility characteristics, some models have a winch. Models produced from 1968 have a central tire pressure system and may feature a soft-top cab. The vehicle can operate in climatic conditions ranging from -50°C to +50°C. The GAZ-66 is still used by the Russian Army, many ex-Warsaw Pact armed forces and wherever Soviet influence had spread. Many are used throughout the Middle East and nations in Africa. A follow-on version was developed, the GAZ-3308 Sadko, but it was abandoned in favor of the KamAZ-4350. The GAZ-66B is the modified version for the airborne forces. It is air droppable, and has an open cab with a canvas cover. Its windshield can be folded over the hood. The GAZ-66-40 was the final production model. It is powered by a 123 hp GAZ-5441 turbocharged diesel engine. There are numerous variants of the GAZ-66 including models for: NBC decontamination, POL distribution, supply, command and control, and communications. The GAZ-66 is used to carry the 2B19 Podnos and 2B9 Vasilek mortars.[66]

Ural-43206

The Ural-43206 4x4 light general-purpose truck is a member of the Motovoz family of vehicles produced by the Ural Automotive Plant. Other family members include the Ural-4320 (6x6) and Ural-5323 (8x8). The Ural-43206 reportedly shares 95% of its components with the other vehicles in the Motovoz family, and was developed from the larger 6x6 Ural-4320. The Ural-43206 uses the same cab as the Ural-4320 and provides seating for the driver and two passengers. It was accepted into the Russian Armed Forces in 1996, often being used for troop or cargo transport. The Ural-43206

Ural-43206
Image Courtesy: Vitaly Kuzmin

has a payload capacity of 4,200 kg, and can carry up to 24 troops in the rear cargo area. The cargo area can be covered by bows and canvas, and has drop sides and tailgate. It is capable of towing trailers or artillery pieces with a maximum weight of 7,000 kg. The Ural-43206 is powered by a 180 hp YaMZ-236M2 turbocharged diesel engine with a 5-speed manual gearbox. It is an all-wheel drive vehicle that is designed to operate on and off road, and has a central tire pressure system. The Ural-43206 comes in several body types and variants. The Ural-43206-41 has a more powerful 230 hp YaMZ-236NE2 turbocharged diesel engine. The Ural-43206-0551 has a four-door cab, which accommodates the driver and 5 passengers, but only has a payload capacity of 3,650 kg. The Ural-43206-47 has an Iveco cab, and a 250 hp YaMZ-236BE2 turbocharged diesel engine, with a 5,200 kg payload capacity.[67]

Ural-4320

The Ural-4320 6x6 medium general-purpose utility truck was designed to supersede the Ural-375D, and is a member of the Motovoz family of vehicles, which it reportedly shares 95% of its components. It is produced by the Ural Automotive Plant. Other family members include the Ural-43206 (4x4) and Ural-5323 (8x8). The cab of the Ural-4320 provides seating for the driver and two passengers and can be equipped with an add-on armor kit to protect the cab and engine from small arms fire and artillery shrapnel. Production commenced in 1976, and is still ongoing. Since then the Ural-4320 has assumed many of the roles previously filled by the Ural-375D. The Ural-4320 is in service with the Russian military as well as the militaries of many other countries. It has a conventional design and is easy to repair. It has a payload capacity of 4,500 kg off-road and 6 tons on hard surfaced roads. A standard troop/cargo platform has drop sides, drop tailgate and removable tarpaulin and bows. In the troop carrier configuration it accommodates 27 troops. This military truck also tows trailers or artillery pieces with a maximum weight of 12 tons. The Ural-4320 was first powered by 210 hp YaMZ-740 10.85-liter V8 diesel engine, then a 220 hp diesel engine, and is currently being produced with a 240 hp

Ural-4320

Image Courtesy: Vitaly Kuzmin

YaMZ-238M2 engine. Some models have even been equipped with Caterpillar engines, but all have a standard 5-speed manual transmission. The Ural-4320 is an all-wheel drive vehicle equipped with a centralized tire pressure system, which can operate in climatic conditions, ranging from -50°C to +50°C. There are many versions of the Ural-4320, including: Ural-4420 tractor truck for towing semi-trailers. The Ural-4320-0911-30 is a large wheelbase model with a payload capacity of up to 10 tons that can carry up to 39 troops.[68]

Ural-5323

The Ural-5323 is the 8x8 heavy general-purpose truck member of the Motovoz family of vehicles produced by the Ural Automotive Plant. Other family members include the Ural-43206 (4x4) and Ural-4320 (6x6). The vehicle has a cab over engine design that provides seating for the driver and one passenger. The Ural-5323 was specifically developed in the early 1990s for military service. It has a relatively simple design, and it is easy to maintain, using a number of components from other Ural and KamAZ trucks. The Ural-5323 was designed to be a heavy transport for troops and supplies. It has a payload capacity of 9,000 kg, with

Ural-5323

Image Courtesy: Vitaly Kuzmin

some versions having a payload capacity of up to 12,000 kg, and can tow a trailer with a maximum weight of 16,000 kg. The cargo bed has hinged side benches for troop transport of up to 39 troops, and can be covered with bows and a tarpaulin. The Ural-5323 can also mount various heavy weapons systems. The standard engine is a 260 hp KamAZ-7403 turbocharged diesel. Other engine options are available, including the 290 hp Ural-745 and 320 hp Ural-746 air-cooled diesels. The vehicle is equipped with a central tire inflation system and has a climatic operational range from -50°C to +50°C.

The Ural-5323 has many variants. The Ural-5323-20 is fitted with KamAZ cab, Ural-5323-21 is fitted with Iveco cab, and the Ural-5323-23 is fitted with armored cab. The Ural-5323-41, -42, -61 and -62 models are intended to mount various heavy weapon systems. The Ural 5423 is a tractor truck for towing semi-trailers. The Ural-E5323D is fitted with an armored cab and armored body with a V-shaped hull, providing protection against small arms fire, mine blasts, and IEDs. The Ural-5323 serves as the chassis for the KET-T recovery vehicle and the REM-KL repair and recovery vehicle.[69]

KamAZ-4350

The KamAZ-4350 is the 4x4 light general-purpose truck member of the Mustang family of vehicles produced by the KamAZ Corporation. Other family members include the KamAZ-5350 (6x6) and KamAZ-6350 (8x8). The KamAZ-4350 has the same three-person cab with a sleeping compartment as the rest of the Mustang family that can accept an add-on armor kit. It traces its origins back to the KamAZ-4310, launched in 1981. The KamAZ-4350 was accepted into service with the Russian Armed Forces in 2002, with small-scale production commencing in 2003, as a replacement for the GAZ-66 light utility truck. It has a conventional

KamAZ-4350

Image Courtesy: Vitaly Kuzmin

design with a payload capacity of 4,100 kg and can tow trailers or artillery pieces with a maximum weight of 7,000 kg. It can be fitted with a variety of body types, as well as shelters and removable containers. The standard troop/cargo version carries up to 30 troops, is fitted with drop sides and tailgate with removable bows and tarpaulin. The KamAZ-4350 is powered by a 240 hp KamAZ-740.11.240 turbocharged diesel engine that is compliant with EURO II emission requirements, and equipped with a cold weather starting device that allows operation at temperatures down to -50°C. The KamAZ-4350 is an all-wheel drive vehicle that is equipped with a central tire inflation system. The KamAZ-4350 comes in several variants, including the Airborne Troops' KamAZ-43501, nicknamed "Flying KamAZ," that has a shorter wheelbase and can be airdropped using a parachute.[70]

KamAZ-5350

The KamAZ-5350 is the 6x6 medium general-purpose utility truck member of the Mustang family of vehicles produced by the KamAZ Corporation. Other family members include the KamAZ-4350 (4x4) and KamAZ-6350 (8x8). The KamAZ-5350 has the same three-person cab with a sleeping compartment as the rest of the Mustang family that can accept an add-on armor kit. This general utility truck is a further development of the KamAZ-4310, which was launched in the early 1980s. The KamAZ-5350 was accepted into service with the Russian Armed Forces in 2002, with small-scale production commencing in 2003, as with

KamAZ-5350

Image Courtesy: Vitaly Kuzmin

other members of the Mustang family. The KamAZ-5350 has a conventional design with a payload capacity of 6,000 kg, and it can also tow trailers or artillery pieces. It can carry a variety of shelters or container-type loads. A standard troop/cargo platform has drop sides, drop tailgate and removable bows and tarpaulin. The KamAZ-5350 is powered by a 260 hp KamAZ-740.13.260 turbocharged diesel engine that is a compliant with EURO II emission requirements, and equipped with a cold weather starting device that allows operation at temperatures down to -50°C. The KamAZ-5350 is an all-wheel drive vehicle that is equipped with a central tire inflation system. There are numerous variants of the baseline model, including the KamAZ-53501 bridge transporter and the KamAZ-53504 tractor truck for towing semi-trailers.[71]

KamAZ-6350

The KamAZ-6350 is the 8x8 heavy general-purpose truck member of the Mustang family of vehicles produced by the KamAZ Corporation. Other family members include the KamAZ-4350 (4x4) and KamAZ-5350 (6x6). The KamAZ-6350 has the same three-person cab with a sleeping compartment as the rest of the Mustang family and can accept an add-on armor kit. The development of the KamAZ-6350 began in 1987, with the first prototypes being completed in the early 1990s. The KamAZ-6350 was accepted into service with the Russian Armed Forces in 2002, with small-scale production commencing in 2003, as with

KamAZ-6350

Image Courtesy: Vitaly Kuzmin

other members of the Mustang family. The vehicle has a conventional design with a payload capacity of 10,000 kg and can tow trailers or artillery pieces with a maximum weight of 12,000 kg. It can carry a variety of shelters or container-type loads. A standard troop/cargo platform has drop sides, drop tailgate and removable bows and tarpaulin. It is powered by a 360 hp KamAZ-740.50.360 turbocharged diesel engine that is a compliant with EURO II emission requirements, and equipped with a cold weather starting device that allows operation at temperatures down to -50°C. The KamAZ-6350 is an all-wheel drive vehicle that is equipped with a central tire inflation system. There are numerous variants of the baseline model, including the KamAZ-63501 that has a payload capacity of 15 000 kg. The KamAZ-6450 is a tractor truck for towing semi-trailers and artillery pieces. The KamAZ-6350 serves as the chassis for the Pantsir-S1 air defense system; the Semser 122mm truck-mounted howitzer; and the 9A52-4 Tornado, Naiza, and Lynx MLRS systems[72]

BREM-1

The BREM-1 armored repair and recovery vehicle [бронированная ремонтно-эвакуационная машина] was developed to support a fleet of T-72 main battle tanks and its derivatives. The main role of this vehicle is to recover damaged tanks and other armored vehicles from the battlefield. It tows damaged vehicles to the nearest shelter, assembly point, maintenance unit or repair depot. The BREM-1 also recovers stuck, swamped or overturned vehicles, and assists field repairs and servicing of armored vehicles. The BREM-1 is based on a modified T-72A main battle tank chassis. The turret has been removed and new superstructure fitted. It is fitted with a front-mounted dozer blade, crane, winch and other specialized equipment. The BREM-1 is operated by a crew of three, including commander, driver and handler. The BREM-1 is fitted with a 4.4 meter crane. It has a 19 ton capacity at 2 meters and 3 ton capacity at 4.4 meters. It is used to lift damaged or stuck vehicles. Also the crane can be used to lift vehicle for access and repair. The main winch has a 25-ton capacity that can be increased

BREM-1

Image Courtesy: Vitaly Kuzmin

to 100 tons using snatch blocks. The cable is 200 meters long. It can be also used for self-recovery. There is also a 530 kg capacity auxiliary winch with 425 meters of cable. The BREM-1 can tow a vehicle of up to 50 tons over a prolonged distance. There is also a 3.1 meter-wide bulldozer blade that can be used for excavation, rubble clearing, and filling ditches. It also carries various tools for tank repair and servicing, including welding equipment. The BREM-1M is an improved version with a 840 hp V-84MS or 1,000 hp V-92S2 engine. The BREM-L is based on a BMP-3 chassis. There are also reportedly plans to create versions based on the Armata and Kuganets chassis.[73]

MTO-UB1

The MTO-UB1 Universal Maintenance Vehicle is the designated system for the maintenance and routine repair of weapons and equipment found in motorized rifle and tank battalions, and can service tanks, BMPs, BTRs, MT-LBs and logistic vehicles. The system consists of the Ural-4320 chassis, workshop, and 2.5-ton crane. It has a crew of five: squad leader/mechanic, crane operator, mechanic, machinist, and driver. An MTO-UB1 crew can detect and repair minor faults in vehicle and weapon systems and has the capability to perform metal work, arc welding, battery maintenance, lubrication and tire servicing, filter replacement and painting as needed.[74]

MTO-UB1

Image Courtesy: Vitaly Kuzmin

Chapter 8
Other Tactical Considerations

Airborne (VDV)

Although the Russian Airborne, and to similar extent Naval Infantry, are not a part of the Russian Ground Forces, they are significantly different than their Western counterparts and have much in common with their land-based brethren. Structurally, the Russian Airborne is a heavily mechanized force and is divided between parachute and air assault units. In terms of function, the Russian VDV fulfills many of the same roles as those in the West, but also fills another niche not filled by Western airborne forces, that of a reliable enforcer for politically sensitive operations. This role began in Soviet times, with the Soviet invasion of Hungary in 1956 to quell the Hungarian uprising. VDV units began quietly occupying Hungary weeks before overt Soviet action began, and after the commencement of hostilities they gained a reputation for quickly and efficiently seizing objectives in an urban battle space to which conventional Soviet commanders were not accustomed.[1] Although exact details have yet to emerge, reportedly VDV units were involved in operations in Crimea, and if previous behaviors are indicators of the operational tactics in the recent campaign, it will likely be discovered that the VDV elements began arriving there well before masked gunmen started showing up on the streets of Crimea.[2] It is also likely that the vast majority of "polite people" and "little green men" seen in Crimea were VDV and Naval Infantry troops, not special operations forces as many analysts have speculated. In terms of training, Russian experts estimate that around 40 percent of specialties require significantly more training than elsewhere in the Russian military, increasing the requirement for contract personnel.[3] In the Russian system, the best and brightest often vie for careers in the VDV, and not in the various spetsnaz units.

Colonel General Andrei Serdyukov
VDV Commander-in-Chief
Image Courtesy: Russian Ministry of Defense

Russian Airborne Dispositions

Airborne Dispositions

The Russian Airborne (VDV) has been one of the biggest beneficiaries of the Russian Federation's efforts to increase conventional military capabilities. The VDV's 38th Signal and 45th Spetsnaz regiments have been upsized to brigades; a third parachute/air assault regiment will be added to each division; and a new maneuver brigade (345th Air Assault Brigade) will be created; and there are plans to reactivate the 104th Air Assault Division. This increase in forces is in addition to current plans to add a tank battalion to each division and brigade.

BTR-MDM   BMD-4M

Airborne Equipment and Modernization

The VDV is a mechanized force for several reasons. The Soviets believed in the concept of "deep battle" which required high levels of mobility, leaving no place for any infantryman without vehicle transportation. Other reasons stem from the lethality of the modern battlefield, and NBC protection, which the Soviets believed would be a factor in any conflict with NATO. Today, Russia still believes in the importance of battlefield field mobility, and has all infantryman mounted on wheeled or tracked vehicles, including its special operations forces and airborne

2S25 "Sprut-SD"

Image Courtesy: Vitaly Kuzmin

infantryman. But, in order to be "airmobile," and mechanized, the VDV has had to utilize substantially lighter vehicles. The VDV's newest 13.5 ton Infantry Fighting Vehicle (BMD-4M) and 13 ton Armored Personnel Carrier (BTR-MD) weigh several tons less than their cousins in the Ground Forces. In order to maintain an airmobile tank capability, the VDV has fielded light tanks capable of being transported, and air dropped with crew, by the IL-76 transport aircraft. (As mentioned earlier, the VDV is also now fielding non-airmobile T-72B3s). The amphibious 2S25 Sprut-SD is a 125mm tank turret mounted on a BMD chassis. The Sprut-SD has a three-man crew, and is equipped with an autoloader, capable of firing 4-6 APFSDS, HE-Frag, HEAT and ATGM per minute. Reportedly, new versions of the Sprut (Sprut-SDM1) will be placed on

2S36 "Zauralets"

Image Courtesy: Vitaly Kuzmin

a BMD-4M chassis, and be equipped with new electronics, targeting, and fire control capabilities that will give the Sprut roughly the equivalent firepower of a T-90 tank. The Russian Federation was also developing another "big gun on a little chassis," the 2S36 "Zauralets" artillery system. The Zauralets was intended to replace the 2S9 Nona-S, reportedly being capable of functioning as a field gun, howitzer, and mortar, and was chambered in 120 and 152 millimeter versions. Development of the Zauralets system has been suspended in favor of a similar system known as the "Lotos." The amphibious and air droppable Lotos will be capable of being mounted on a BMD-4M or a wheeled armored car (Volk-3) chassis. In general, airmobile operations require vehicles of lighter weight, the VDV has faced this reality, as the BTR-MD, BMD-4M, Sprut-SD, Zauralets, and Lotos exemplify, by sacrificing lots of armored protection, but very little lethality.[4]

361

Coastal Defense Troops

The Russian Coastal Defense Troops consist of two separate organizations, the Coastal Defense Artillery Troops and the Naval Infantry. In terms of command and control, the Coastal Defense Troops are part of the Russian Navy. The Navy's command and control of these forces is exercised through the four fleets and one flotilla, where the commander of the Coastal Defense Troops units in each of these commands serves on the fleet (flotilla) staff.

Naval Infantry

The Naval Infantry garners much less coverage in the Russian media than the Russian Ground Forces and VDV, but still is a major beneficiary of efforts to reform and modernize the Russian Armed Forces. The Naval Infantry is undergoing an overhaul to improve equipment and training and has recently expanded the Third Naval Infantry Regiment of the Pacific Fleet and the Sixty-First Naval Infantry Regiment of the Northern Fleet into full-fledged brigades.[5] It

Lieutenant General Alexander Kolpachenko
Coastal Defense Troops Commander-in-Chief
Image Courtesy: Russian Ministry of Defense

is important to note that the Russian Naval Infantry is not the United States Marine Corps (USMC), having only an estimated 8,000-9,000 personnel. Since the Naval Infantry is much smaller than the USMC, and is subordinated to fleets/flotilla, the Naval Infantry is only capable of coastal defense missions and offensive missions at a tactical level, not large-scale (operational level) missions. Other differences involve the Naval Infantry's close relationship to the VDV. This relationship dates back to the Second World War, when certain Naval Infantry units were commanded by VDV officers.[6] These close ties continue today: Naval Infantry units have select units on jump status, and naval infantrymen routinely train at the VDV training center in Ryazan. The current commander of the Coastal Defense Troops, Major-General Aleksandr Kolpachenko, is a career VDV officer.[7] The Naval Infantry likely has a far different doctrine for amphibious landings than the USMC. Although Russia does have an impressive array of armed hover and landing craft, Russian doctrine for amphibious assault likely involves using aviation assets to air assault or parachute initial forces into a contested area to first neutralize coastal defenses and secure a beachhead for the landing of heavier follow-on forces, as each Naval Infantry brigade has an airborne/air assault battalion. The Russian

Russian Naval Infantry Dispositions

Naval Infantry Dispositions

Naval Infantry is a heavily mechanized force, and has much in common with the Russian Ground Forces and VDV in terms of tactics, doctrine, and equipment, including the fact that it does not possess its own organic aviation assets, relying on the Russian Aerospace Troops (Air Force) for all aviation support. These similarities make the practice of detaching units from one of these services, and attaching them to another, a routine practice in the Russian Armed Forces. The Russian Naval Infantry is considered an elite force in the Russian Armed Forces, regularly training and operating with the Russian Airborne Forces. Although the Naval Infantry are mostly formed into brigades, these brigades are significantly smaller, and subsequently have far less combat power than Ground Forces, and even Airborne brigades.

Coastal Defense Artillery Troops

The Coastal Defense Artillery Troops are responsible for manning fixed and mobile missile and tube artillery systems and protecting the State borders along Russia's 38,000 kilometers of coastlines. This unique mission has had a great impact on the Coastal Defense Artillery Troops' equipment and vectors for future development. Unlike the Ground Forces, Airborne, and Naval Infantry, the Coastal Defense Artillery Troops generally prefer wheeled vehicles (to more quickly traverse the vast coastlines) and artillery systems that provide good long distance stand-off capabilities. Many Russian artillery systems have specially modified versions for coastal defense use, such as the Koalitsiya-SV self-propelled howitzer and the BM-21 Grad 122mm MLRS. Although the Coastal Defense Artillery Troops protect ports, harbors, and other shore based facilities, it's most interesting capability is naval area denial, which is provided by tactical-operational missiles. Russia is currently fielding several tactical-operational missile systems, the Iskander surface-to-surface missile system is operated by the Russian Ground Forces, but the Bal and Bastion coastal missile defense systems are operated by the Coastal Defense Artillery Troops. One advantage of coastal missile defense systems, is that they are not subject to the Intermediate-Range Nuclear Forces Treaty (INF Treaty) that limits the Iskander and other surface-to-surface missile systems to a less than a 500 kilometer range.

The Bal is equipped with eight Kh-35 missiles with an approximately a 130 kilometer range. There are typically four systems in a battery. Interestingly, the same missile system used on the road-mobile Bal, may also be operated from a standard sized shipping container. Russia sells this "shipping container" missile system as the Club-K on the export market. The Russian Federation has recently increased the range of the Kh-35 to 300 kilometers (The Club-K can fire a variety of Kh-35 and 3M-54 missile types). Russia has been keen to tout the new range and concealability of the Kh-35 and the Club-K, and makes it very apparent that this system is intended to negate some of the U.S. Navy's overmatch of weaker navies. The modular design of the system allows for the missiles to be fired using their internal sensors for targeting, or they may use a similarly "containerized" C2/Radar system, or they may be directed from other target acquisition systems (AWACS, another vessel, etc.). Undoubtedly, an extended range Kh-35 and Club-K combo that can "hide-in-plain-sight," should be of some concern in increasingly crowded sea-lanes. Promotional materials for the Club-K also mention the possibilities of deploying the system on rail or on the back of a flatbed truck, a possibility that turns any common shipping container into a possible threat.[8]

"Bal-E" Coastal Defense Missile System

Image Courtesy: Vitaly Kuzmin

The "Bastion" coastal missile defense system was developed by the Machine-Building Science and Production Association for the 3M55 Onyx missile. (export designation Yakhont, NATO classification SS-N-26 Strobile). The Onyx is Russia's latest anti-ship missile that has a range of approximately 600 kilometers. The Bastion comes in two variants, the fixed-position "Bastion-S", and the mobile "Bastion-P". The Bastion-P is comprised of four mobile launchers (two missiles per launcher), a command vehicle, and loader/transporter vehicles. Vehicles mounted with the "Monolit-B" radars may also be employed to enhance targeting. The Onyx (Yakhont for exported systems,

"Bastion" Coastal Defense Missile System

Image Courtesy: Russian Ministry of Defense

with a 300 kilometer range) missile is a supersonic homing anti-ship missile developed to destroy surface ships of all classes, particularly vessels comprising: surface strike groups, carrier battle groups, amphibious assault forces, and convoys. The system can be situated up to 200 kilometers inland, and is capable of protecting a stretch of coastline measuring in excess of 600 kilometers against potential enemy amphibious landing operations. The manufacturer purports the time between receipt of a call for fire mission and full deployment of the system is five minutes, and that the system can remain in firing position 72-120 hours, depending on available fuel reserves.

Area Denial Capabilities

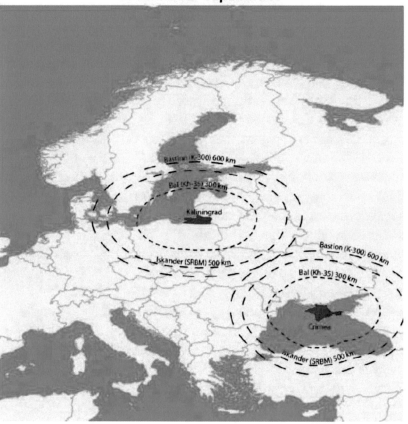

The Onyx/Yakhont anti-ship missile is stored inside a hermetically sealed transport and launch container. The missile is fully combat ready when it leaves the manufacturing plant, and is stored, transported, and mounted on the launcher inside this container. The missile's diagnostics can be monitored without opening the container. The Onyx uses a ramjet engine with a solid-propellant booster, allowing the missile to reach a cruise velocity of Mach 2.0-3.5 at an altitude of up to 20,000 meters. One of the Onyx missile's most interesting characteristics is its guidance system. The guidance system can purportedly work in tandem with other missiles, and can allocate and classify targets based on their importance, and then select an appropriate attack scheme. Following the destruction of the primary target, the remaining missiles attack other ships, so no target is attacked by more than one missile. After an initial target lock is achieved, the Onyx shuts down its radar and descends to a low altitude (5 to 10 meters), below the operational level of most air defense radars. Once the missile emerges from beneath the radar horizon, the missile radar is reactivated and locks back on to the target. This feature, in conjunction with the Onyx's high rate of speed, greatly complicates adversarial air defense and electronic warfare countermeasures.[9]

Military Police

The institution of a Military Police Corps is a relatively new concept in the Russian Armed Forces. The route security duties of U.S. Military Police are performed by Commandant Service or Road Commandant units in the Russian military, but the Russian military has never had a dedicated internal security apparatus until 2012. During Soviet times, the commander of a subunit or a unit had the authority to send subordinates to the local guardhouse (jail) for discipline infractions. This practice was subsequently abolished by the Russian Federation after the collapse of the Soviet Union, the reasoning being that only a judge had the right to imprison someone. Commanders were unhappy with this reform because according to the new rules, there is a required court proceeding, and only after due process could he send the soldier to jail. Since months could elapse between the discipline infraction and the punishment, few commanders were interested in pursuing charges. This reform left commanders without their most effective method for dealing with discipline problems. Only commanders that could find other means to enforce unit discipline maintained order. Some officers attributed the loss of their jailing authority as a reason that *"dedovshchina"*, or brutal hazing, became more problematic in the aftermath of the collapse of the Soviet Union. In order to impose discipline and decrease the number of embarrassing hazing and corruption problems, the establishment of a Military Police Corps was proposed by both civilian and the military authorities.[10]

Military Police Badge

Image Courtesy: Russian MoD

The path to the establishment of a Military Police Corps in the Armed Forces has been a long one. In 1992, the Russian Prosecutor General's Office proposed the creation of a Military Police Corps to conduct criminal investigations and combat economic crimes, but the State Duma did not pass the bill. In 1996, due to some embarrassing corruption incidents, the State Duma Committee for Defense again proposed the establishment of a Military Police Corps outside of the military's chain of command, but the proposal encountered resistance from the military and was eventually dropped to due to funding concerns. In 2005, Human Rights Commissioner Vladimir Lukin suggested creating a Military Police Corps to combat hazing, and in 2006 the high profile case of Private Andrey Sychev, a conscript who lost his legs from a severe hazing incident, caused President Vladimir Putin to back the idea. After a few more false starts, in 2012, former Chief of the Russian General Staff, General Nikolay Makarov announced that by December 1, 2012, Military Police units would begin operations, and that a Defense Ministry main directorate and units in the military districts and the fleets had already been established. In 2015, the charter defining the Military Police's structure, functions, and tasks was confirmed by Presidential Edict No. 161 on 25 March 2015.[11]

Military Police Officer

Image Courtesy: Russian MoD

In terms of function, Russian Military Police are intended to uphold law and order, provide physical security, conduct investigations into acts of disciplinary and general criminal misconduct, operate military jails, and ensure general traffic safety, but they do not provide route security.[12] In certain situations, the Military Police provide protection for victims, witnesses, and other participants in criminal proceedings such as service personnel, military court judges, and military prosecutors. The Military Police have assumed control of Ministry of Defense disciplinary units and garrison guardhouses (jails). Russian Military Police are also considered an agency of inquiry in the Armed Forces, which gives them the authority to conduct inquests. In the past, when commanders wanted to conduct an investigation, they appointed one of their subordinate officers as an investigating officer for the matter. Usually these officers have no investigative or legal experience, and would have to conduct an investigation with little guidance. Now, when an investigating officer is appointed, he may request assistance from the Military Police, with the eventual goal that all investigations in the Armed Forces will be conducted by the Military Police. Although this practice will relieve the commander of some administrative burdens, there is reporting that the intent of this reform is to remove any commander influence, to ensure a fair and thorough investigation. The approximately 10,000 strong Military Police Corps operates under the authority of the Russian Armed Force's Prosecutor General and his subordinate military prosecutors. This command relationship allows the Military Police to cordon off or blockade military garrisons and areas without consulting the unit commander.[13]

Arms Procurement Process

The Russian Federation has demonstrated an impressive capability to design and rapidly field new large end items such as tanks, BTRs, and BMPs, a process which takes substantially longer in the U.S. One example is the fielding of Russia's T-14 tank mounted on the Armata chassis. In March of 2016, Sergey Chemezov, head of the Russian state corporation Rostec, announced that the T-14 tank had already begun serial production.[14] If this statement is accurate, the T-14 and its Armata chassis have entered serial production less than five years after the May 12, 2011 announcement in *Rossiyskaya Gazeta* that Russia had abandoned development of the T-95 (object 195) tank in favor of the development of the Armata chassis and associated T-14 tank.[15]

Skorpion 2MB

Image Courtesy: Vitaly Kuzmin

The fielding of the Armata chassis appears not to be the exception, but the rule, as it apparently takes about five years from the beginning of the Russian design process until serial production begins for most major Ground Forces/Airborne end items, if the initial prototype is deemed viable. The Ground Forces' 2S35 Koalitsiya-SV howitzer (replacement for the Msta-S 2S19 howitzer), the Russian Airborne's 2S36 Zauralets-D mortar/howitzer (replacement for the 2S9 Nona) and the 2S25 Sprut-SD light tank have all took about five years to get from the issue of requirement/ initial design concept to the serial production phase.[16] Problems delaying the production of Russian armaments are usually in regard to the state's financial resources, and not due to bureaucratic, production, or parliamentary constraints.

The Russian Federation is able to enter serial production quicker than the U.S. due to a much different arms development cycle. Capability development questions are settled in the Russian General Staff with inputs from the branch chiefs (far fewer bureaucratic hurdles in the Russian system). There also appears to be no bidding process. A manufacture is simply assigned, and they build a few prototypes, if the prototype is unacceptable, the manufacture returns to the design phase. Innovations are accepted or rejected at the prototype phase, many designs make it no further than this phase. If the prototype is acceptable, improvements are made, and a test batch (approximately a battalion set) of vehicles is produced for field testing.[17] This field testing takes approximately a year or two, after which, the product is further refined and put into full serial production. If the initial prototype is deemed viable, serial production of a major end item can begin approximately five years after the receipt of requirement and the design process begins. This appears to be the case with the Armata. Prototypes of the Armata chassis (as a BMP and tank) participated at the May 9, 2015 Victory Parade. On November 17, 2015 *Interfax* announced that *UralVagonZavod*

was producing a test batch of 20 T-14s for government trials, and on February 29, 2016 *Interfax* announced these that 20 T-14s were undergoing state trials. Full serial production of the Armata was expected in 2017-2018, but the announcement that serial production had already begun in March 2016, earlier than anticipated, may have been due to many of the design problems being worked out during the course of the T-95 (object 195) project, which shares many features with the Armata, and likely had the same design team.[18]

Tigr-M SPN (with remotely operated 30mm cannon)

Image Courtesy: Vitaly Kuzmin

Another reason that Russia is able to reach serial production quickly is the emphasis on interoperability and modularity.[19] All new Russian designs for BTRs and BMPs (Armata, Kyrganets, Atom, BTR-82, BMD-4M) are manufactured to accept BMP-3 turret specifications. Manufactures only have to design for the weapon capability and turret specification. (mobility characteristics are determined by the chassis selected.) In situations where the chassis is not sufficient (such as ground pressure issues resulting from heavier loads), instead of developing a new chassis, the existing chassis are heavily modified. For example, the BMD-4M chassis had additional road wheels mounted to support the heavier components of the 2S25 Sprut-SD light tank, and the Armata chassis can have the engine situated in the front (BTR/BMP) or rear (tank) as needed. Russia's unified design standards make many combinations of turrets and chassis possible, despite being produced by different manufacturers, a beneficial situation for the export market. It appears that cost (both production and operation/maintenance) is a key factor that is considered from the very beginning of development. Innovations that are deemed too costly are weeded out early, the design must not only be combat effective, but also feasible in terms of cost.

In order to develop new technologies and control costs, Russia appears to pursue the incremental "evolutionary" approach, as opposed to "revolutionary" approach to development and design. Many of the design elements of the T-95 tank prototype are found in the T-14, to include the gun (2A82 125-mm smoothbore gun/ ATGM launcher), active defense system (Afganit), engine (Chelyabinsk A-85-3A X-diesel engine), and several other systems.[20] Russia can apparently overcome any proprietary issues and may "plug-n-play" options and features from different manufactures as desired. Although Russia will experiment with new innovations (such as double barreled howitzers), they will usually build these innovations on the backs of known and trusted components. For instance the 2S35 Koalitsiya-SV howitzer has a completely automated turret (new innovation) with plans to reduce the crew to two-three personnel, but this turret is on the same chassis that has reliably served Msta-S for many years. (there are plans that Koalitsiya-SV will eventually be on an Armata chassis) This system assures that Russian weapons manufacturers never really "start-from-scratch" and allows for the efficiency of smaller production runs. Russia is also pursuing this evolutionary strategy in terms of robotization. Instead of attempting to develop robotic combat vehicles from scratch, Russia is incrementally adding robotic capabilities (autoloaders, unmanned turrets, computerized steering, etc.) to existing systems and reducing crew sizes, with the desired end state of eventually eliminating the entire crew for some combat vehicles, including the T-14.[21]

One advantage that likely allows a quicker run to serial production is Russia's use of only a few manufacturers. Russia's primary manufactures of combat vehicles are *UralVagonZavod* (T-72,T-90, Armata) and *KurganMachineZavod* (BMP-1, BMP-2, BMP-3). These production lines may be kept "warm" through the steady production of new combat vehicles and the refurbishment of old combat vehicles. *UralVagonZavod* is currently conducting "frame-off" upgrades of Russia's entire T-72 fleet, converting them into T-72B3s. Russian manufacturers have also touted the capabilities of new computer software that more quickly facilitates production than traditional paper plans and have recently introduced 3D printing technology that has also sped development.[22]

UAV Development

UAV development is being pursued in the Russian Federation by all of the main and lesser branches (including the airborne forces) of the Ministry of Defense, in a variety of sizes ranging from smaller models, similar to the US "Raven," to larger models similar in size and purpose to the US "Predator." As for the Russian Ground Forces (GF) in particular, GF officials have mentioned that the UAVs will be used for communications, intelligence and electronic warfare tasks. [23] In practice, the Russian GF appear to be focusing on the use of UAVs as artillery spotters. Russia has fielded several models for this purpose (Granat, Eleron, Takhion, Orlan and Zastava), with maximum ranges of about 40 kilometers, appropriate for Russian artillery systems.[24]

In 2014, Russia added almost 200 UAVs to its inventory and activated 14 UAV companies, with plans that each of Russia's motorized rifle brigades will gain a dedicated UAV company in the next few years. The Russian Ministry of Defense has also announced plans to field its first UAV regiment and set up an inter-ministerial UAV training center.[25] At present, the Russian Federation has no capability for placing a weapon system on a UAV, but there are plans for the introduction of such a weapon in the next few years.[26]

Organization and Structure of Russian Ground Forces' UAV Units

There have been conflicting reports about how these assets would be controlled. Some reports have stated that UAVs would be considered a brigade-level asset and assigned to the brigade's reconnaissance company or intelligence support platoon (attached to subordinate units as required); other reports state these particular UAVs (artillery spotters) would be organic to the artillery companies' reconnaissance platoons. In the last few years this issue has apparently been resolved. Russia has decided the best way to organize its UAV fleet is by putting all of a brigade's UAVs in a single company. The companies are divided into platoons based on the size and range of the UAVs they operate. For instance, the "mini-platoon" operates the hand launched Granat-1, while the "short-range platoon" operates the larger Orlan-10 and Granat-4 airframes. One UAV company mentioned had six platoons, but this may be atypical as the unit was located at the 201ˢᵗ Motorized Rifle Division base in Tajikistan, and may have had a larger complement due to its unique status of serving a division in a geographically disparate location.[27] Russia likely places all of its UAVs in a single company and splits the companies into platoons based on size instead of function to more easily facilitate C2 and maintenance of these high value and limited assets. Since there is mention of "payloads" on the UAVs, there appears to be some capability for repurposing of mission if needed (artillery reconnaissance, electronic warfare, and communications, etc.). The Orlan-10 is used for both artillery reconnaissance and electronic warfare missions.[28]

UAV Company Personnel

In 2013, the Russian Air Force Academy accepted its first UAV class. Russian UAV officers will be trained in 4-5 year academies, which would resemble a combination of a U.S. service academy and an initial officer basic course for occupational training. Upon completion of the academy, graduates will be commissioned as lieutenants and be sent to their gaining units. Although the program is located at the Russian Air Force Academy, it would not be unusual for a Russian Ground Forces officer to attend such a program, as it is not uncommon for service members from other branches of service and even ministries to attend other service academies for certain "low-density" specialties such as UAV officer.[29] Since the first 62 graduates of the academy do not graduate until 2018, current UAV unit officer vacancies are being filled by officers from other branches with other specialties, with a preference for artillery officers. These "shake-n-bake" UAV officers are sent to the Russian Defense Ministry Interbranch Center for Unmanned Aviation in Kolomna, where they receive a short course on UAV operations.[30]

Orlan-10

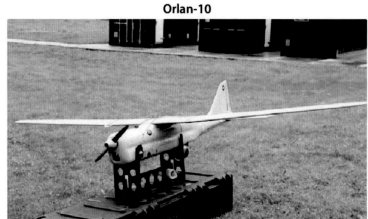

Range: 50 - 120 km
Flight Duration: 10 hours
Maximum Takeoff Weight: 15 kg
Maximum Payload: 5 kg
Wingspan: 3.1 m
Length: 1.8 m
Speed. 75-170 km/h
Maximum Altitude: 6000 m
Fuel: A-95 Gasoline
Operating Temperature: -35C to + 40C
Takeoff: Catapult
Landing: Parachute

Image Courtesy: Vitaly Kuzmin

It appears that enlisted personnel operate most UAVs, but officers do fly certain missions. Russia does practice a conscription system, but all UAV operators are "contract NCOs" that attend the UAV operator course at the Inter-Branch Center for the Training of Specialists for the Ground Troops in Kolomna, Russia. Conscripted soldiers do serve in the UAV companies, but they serve in support roles such as wheeled vehicle drivers.[31]

Artillery Spotting
Since artillery systems have ranges well beyond the line of sight, (the Russian Msta-S self-propelled howitzer has a range of 29-36 km) they rely on forward observers to find targets and adjust fire. In the Russian system, on the offensive, the artillery battalion commander's headquarters is collocated with the maneuver commander leading the offensive. The battalion commander's senior deputy (roughly equivalent to a chief of staff) is located with the artillery CP. In the batteries, the battery company commanders are in a forward observation posts directing fires, while the senior battery officer (roughly equivalent to an executive officer) is located with the battery.

The use of UAVs for artillery spotting significantly supplements forward observation capabilities, a very important technological development for an artillery-centric post-Soviet army. For artillery purposes, UAV support is provided by the "mini" and "short-range" UAV platoons.[32] Although Russia is experimenting with a number of airframes, the mini-class "Granat-1" and short-range "Orlan-10" are most frequently mentioned. It is clear from various video segments and articles that the UAVs do not usually directly communicate with the fire direction centers of the batteries.[33] Apparently, the UAV operators determine target coordinates and relay that information to forward observers on the Artillery Reconnaissance Vehicles (ARVs), who in turn relate the information to the fire direction centers[34]

Due to differing ranges, it is likely the Orlan-10 operators are collocated with the batteries and their accompanying ARVs. There have been some discrepancies about the range of the Orlan-10. The specifications list the range as 50-120 kilometers, while articles referring to use for artillery spotting mention 40-50 kilometers. This variance may have to do with the UAV's broadcast range of its gyro-stabilized Full Motion Video (FMV), which may not be possible with current capabilities at distances that exceed 50 kilometers.[35] Due to the relatively short range of FMV transmission for the Granat-1 (10 kilometers), it is very likely the Granat-1 operators are collocated with the battalion's forward observation post or battery COP. In addition to targeting, it was also mentioned the Granat-1 had a role in providing information for damage assessments.[36]

Methods of Target Acquisition
On July 7 2015, *TASS* news service published an article about the training of officers in the use of the Orlan-10 UAV for artillery spotting purposes. The following day, a Russian blogger posted his theory of how artillery spotting can be conducted with UAVs, and observed the Orlan-10 is only capable of conducting the two simplest methods of artillery spotting. (see graphic) The blogger appears quite knowledgeable about Russian UAV capabilities and the modern battlefield, and his observations agree with observed Russian artillery procedures as viewed on various online videos.

Although the Orlan-10 and Granat-1 are not capable of the more advanced methods of artillery spotting, they can still be quite effective. Although less desirable than some other methods, the capability to fix a target's location by relative terrain feature (method 1) is sufficient for many Russian artillery purposes. Russian artillery batteries and battalions annihilation and destruction missions make precise target information useful, but unnecessary. In addition, the Russian Federation has a strong cartographic tradition, undoubtedly any Russian serviceman referencing terrain features for targeting purposes would have access to high quality, large scale, digital maps of most places within the former Soviet Union. Although current UAV artillery spotting capabilities may be adequate for current purposes, these capabilities are very likely to continue to develop.[37]

Artillery Spotting Methods for UAVs

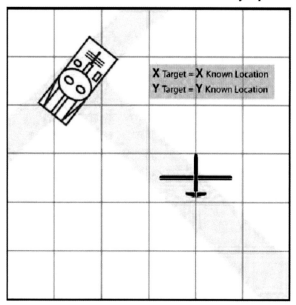

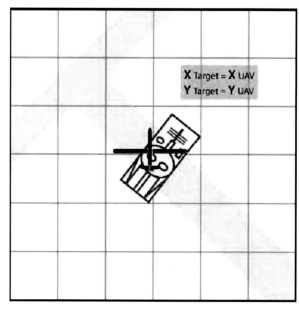

1st Method- Use of a reference point. This method can be used if the coordinates of a given reference point (landmark or intersection) are known. The disadvantage of this system is that the coordinates of the reference point must be known with certainty, requiring detailed maps and/or GIS data. In addition, target accuracy diminishes the farther the target is from the reference point. Conclusion: This method works, but is the least suitable for artillery spotting.

2nd Method- Fly above the target. The UAV flies above the target and its position is recorded. Target accuracy depends on the accuracy of the UAV's navigation system. The disadvantage of this is method is that it requires flying over the target, meaning that only a limited number of targets may be acquired and that the UAV is extremely susceptible to enemy fire. Conclusion: This method works, but is most suitable for less organized adversaries, such as insurgents.

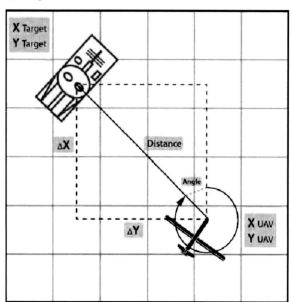

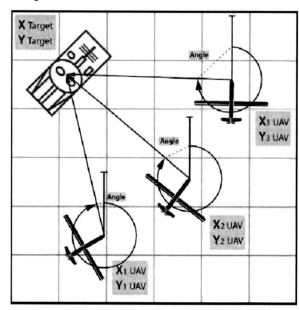

3rd Method- Use of range finder. Requires a gyro stabilized electro-optical system with a laser rangefinder. The coordinates of the target are calculated using basic trigonometry. The accuracy depends on the accuracy of the UAV's navigation system and rangefinder. This method provides good accuracy and the capability to acquire many targets, sufficient for several batteries or battalions. The disadvantage of this is method is the use of an active sensor (the laser) which can be easily detected by modern military equipment. Conclusion: This method is very effective, but requires a sophisticated UAV and would be more susceptible to enemy fire.

4th Method- Use of multiple azimuths. The UAV takes several azimuths on a given target, while in flight. Trigonometry is than used to calculate the position of the target. This method provides good accuracy and the capability to acquire many targets. This method requires a sophisticated UAV, but is completely passive, an advantage that can significantly increase the UAV's life expectancy above the modern battlefield. Conclusion: this is preferred method for UAV artillery spotting.

Artillery Spotting at Night

Russian UAVs reportedly have a night-targeting capability that operators regularly practice.[38] This capability is most likely provided by thermal imagers that are found in many short-range Russian UAVs, including the Orlan-10.[39] Thermal imagers are probably the most common since there was only one report of an infrared sensor, and no reports have mentioned or implied any radar capability.[40] Since terrain association with a thermal imager would be difficult at best, and the risk of the UAV being shot down at night is significantly reduced, it is likely the UAV operator uses the "fly-over-the-target" method (2nd method in the above graphic) to fix the target. Target acquisition with a thermal imager is also significantly more difficult due to the reduced spatial resolution of the technology in comparison to video. There is likely not much difference in signature between a BTR and a SUV when viewed through the type of thermal imagers that can be mounted to a small UAV. Since determining what exactly the imager is viewing is much more difficult, the acquisition of the wrong target is much more likely. Although identification of the wrong target is problematic, the Russian military does not have a "Zero Defect" view of various indiscretions, and any errors made in a combat situation with such a method of targeting would likely be looked upon as an accident due to the "fog of war."

Outlook for UAVs and Russian Artillery Spotting
Undoubtedly, Russia will continue to improve its UAV artillery spotting capabilities. Russia is heavily investing in UAVs in general, and have claimed they will spend 9.2 billion US dollars on the technology and overtake the U.S.'s position as the preeminent UAV power in the next few years.[41] The Russian Federation is also looking at ways of reducing prices for UAV technologies, and has expressed interest in using 3D printers to "bake" the next generation of Russian UAVs.[42] The most likely advancement will be the integration of the UAV directly into one of the new Russian C2 systems under development, the most likely of which is the "Andromeda" (the Russian version of FBCB2). Russia has made frequent comments about the need to "unify the information space" and the integration of UAVs into that space would be in furtherance of that goal. How likely this is to occur is anyone's guess, unsurprisingly marrying up differing technologies (Andromeda, the UAV, and the existing artillery fire control system) is difficult, time consuming and costly. One aspect of Russian artillery spotters that is not likely to change, is their size. Since the Orlan-10 and its cousins are attached to the units they serve and their ranges are more than adequate for the missions they support, developing larger airframes for fire control purposes would not be advantageous, as any requirement for a takeoff/landing area would be prohibitive.[43]

Robotics in the Russian Armed Forces

The Russian military, as many other militaries, is now seriously considering the role of robotics and artificial intelligence on the modern battlefield. Despite references to the Terminator® franchise, Russia does not appear to see a future, in the near term, where combat is conducted solely by autonomous robots. Instead remote controlled and semi-autonomous robotics will be integrated into conventional units, serving in the most dangerous roles as fire fighters, mine clearers, EOD technicians, armed sentries, and as the accompanying articles describe, cannon fodder for the

Image Courtesy: Vitaly Kuzmin

initial assaults on fortified positions. In keeping with these functions, and unlike many of the robots in Terminator®, Russian robots have a distinctively "mechanized" appearance, with most systems being found on tracked chassis. In fact, just as much discussion of robotics deals with automating existing platforms (such as the Armata, Kurganets, and even T-72 chassis) as with creating new systems. Russia's newest generation of light track chassis, the Kurganets, reportedly utilizes a Sony PlayStation® like controller for steering. Apparently, designers think that Russian soldiers of the future will be much more comfortable with this scheme of maneuver, than steering levers and a manual transmission. But these sorts of novel designs will also more easily facilitate the installation of automated control systems.[44]

In general, The Russian Federation has adopted an evolutionary, as opposed to revolutionary, approach to robotization. In practice, this means that instead of trying to develop completely new systems, a majority of Russian efforts in this area have focused on grafting robotic

"Crossbow-DM" Remote Controlled Turret

Image Courtesy: Vitaly Kuzmin

capabilities on to existing platforms. These efforts have not only included experimenting with remote controlled and semiautonomous heavy tracked platforms (such as the Armata, Kurganets, T-90, and even T-72 chassis), but have also included fielding small robotic turrets on traditional (manned) heavy and light chassis. These developments mesh well with Russia's considerable experience fielding auto loading tanks and self-propelled artillery systems, a necessity for fielding any robotized weapons platform. In general, most Russian robotics developments, and other "incremental"

378

technology advancements are useful not only for future robotic platforms, but also for current systems, supporting Russia's line of effort, to do more, with less personnel.[45]

Robotics utilization is not limited to unmanned platforms in the Russian Federation. The Russian Armed Forces is also developing small automated turrets for placement on manned armored personnel carriers, armored cars, support vehicles, and even used as secondary weapons on large weapon systems such as self-propelled artillery pieces. Russia believes that the era of the manned turret has come to an end, and is now fielding unmanned turrets. These turrets are not only viewed as beneficial for crew protection, but also from an Intelligence, Surveillance, and Reconnaissance (ISR) perspective. These Remote Controlled Turret Modules (DUBM) are equipped with a variety of sensors which far exceed the capabilities of the human eyes and ears of a manned turret. Other reports about these systems have touted their ability to engage low flying and low speed aircraft. This capability may be a result of the Russian belief that the battlefield of the future will increasingly involve more UAVs controlled by both state and nonstate actors. A limited ability for air defense, such as these Remote Controlled Turret Modules, would be a great benefit in such an environment. Most DUBM configurations involve the use of a a 12.7-mm 6P49 "Kord" machine gun, a rough equivalent to the U.S. Browning .50 caliber machine gun. If Remote Controlled Turret Modules become common place in the Russian military, even Russian armored cars and support vehicles would be equipped with about the same firepower as most U.S. Army Strykers, as Strykers are most often equipped with a .50 caliber machine gun as their main armament.[46]

Controlled Turret Module Workstation

Cold Weather and Arctic Combat

Russia has hard winters and the Russian military has long trained for and fought during the winter. A large portion of Russia lies north of the Arctic Circle and Russia is preparing seriously for conflict in this region. The land areas approaching and within the Arctic Circle provide unique challenges to military operations. In the Arctic, there are permanent ice and snow-covered areas, but much of this area is devoid of snow and cold during the summer thaw and movement and combat during the thaw can be quite difficult and requires different techniques and equipment.[47]

Significant, large-scale combat has taken place in the higher latitudes. The terrain, weather and limited infrastructure impose severe difficulties on untrained and non-acclimated soldiers. The prime concerns are mobility and shelter. Tactics and force structure require modifications and adjustments. Equipment does not run as efficiently and may require special lubricants, garaging, fuels and support. Everything takes more time.

On 30 November 1939, the Soviet Union attacked Finland in the Winter War that lasted until 20 March 1940. It was a short, brutal war that cost the Red Army 65,384 KIA or died of wounds, 14,142 MIA, 186,584 WIA, 5468 POWs and 9614 cold-weather casualties.[48] Finnish casualties were lower (some 26,662 dead and 39,886 wounded), but Finnish forces were much smaller and the Soviets won the 105-day war. Some of the fighting occurred on the Kola Peninsula within the Arctic Circle, but the main fight occurred in south and central Finland.[49] The Finnish forces were able to withstand the Soviet onslaught for as long as they did due to their specialized training, acclimation and familiarity with winter movement.

Ski Training

Image Courtesy: Russian Ministry of Defense

In October 1944 the largest Arctic ground operation in history occurred in Northern Finland and Norway between the Soviet 14th Army and the German 20th Mountain Army. The 133,500 men of the Soviet Army, supported by the Soviet Northern Fleet, faced some 45,000 *Wehrmacht* and German allies. The Soviet Petsamo-Kirkenes offensive forced the German Army to withdraw and captured the crucial Finnish nickel mines in Pechanga/Petsamo. The Soviets massed ski troops, naval infantry, artillery and tanks, supported by 30 engineer battalions, horse and reindeer transport companies and significant airpower. The Soviet advance was successful but limited by the retreating German destruction of the meager road network.[50] Soviet losses were 21,233 (6084 KIA and 15149 WIA) in the 23 days of fighting.[51] Soviet sources estimate German losses at 18,000 KIA and 713 POW.[52]

Arctic Sniper

Image Courtesy: Russian Ministry of Defense

In the northern sector during the Winter War and the Soviet-Finnish/German Continuation War, fought from 25 June 1941 –19 September 1944, the fights were in the forests and on the tundra for possession of the few east-west roads in the region. Down south on the Karelian Peninsula, defensive lines were continuous and tied in. Further north, open flanks were common by necessity and the fights were attempts to turn a flank while maintaining pressure along the road. Soldier survival was of paramount importance and, in winter, required nearby warming stations and living accommodations to keep soldiers alive. During the Continuation War, the Finnish efforts were directed to restoring territory lost to the Soviets during the Winter War, maintaining border integrity and interdicting Soviet railroad lines. Railroad was the most reliable means of transport in the far north and, along with the roads and population centers, represented key terrain.

Mobility and Maneuver

Vast swampy tundra, mountains, rivers, large quantities of boulders and limited roads complicate mobility and maneuver in the higher latitudes. It is a difficult region for even simple engineering projects, and, in winter, deep snow drifts, polar night and low temperatures add to the difficulty. Weather is always a complicating factor and radio communications are often interrupted by metrological conditions. The Russians consider

DT-30 Articulated Winter Vehicle

March/April through October as the best time for maneuver in the north. The snow melt starts in the spring and the "white nights" allow 24-hour observation.[53] Russia prefers the warmer weather with nearly 24-hour visibility, a reduced requirement for warming-up stations during operations, lessened chances of blizzards and other incapacitating weather for the trade-off of more difficult cross-country and road mobility. They build their wheeled and tracked vehicles with high-clearances for use in their native terrain. Their track width is usually broader than similar US tracked vehicles. Military advances and retreats normally follow roads, rivers, beach and trails across the tundra. Military objectives are frequently villages, road intersections, defiles, isolated heights, mountain passes, river crossing sites and water-landing points. Tracked vehicles are often optimum for movement, but they can tear up the rather delicate earth surface and create their own obstacles.

Amphibious landings and raids are often a major component of Arctic ground maneuver.[54] During the spring and summer, rivers and lakes provide the ability to move and maneuver using shallow draft boats with low overhead clearance. However, navigation of glacier-fed waterways can be treacherous due to the shifting channels, sand or gravel bars and other obstructions.

High-latitude combat is seldom settled over a single season. Simple tasks take longer in the higher latitudes and complex tasks may become impossible. The primary concern of high-latitude combat is to keep one's soldiers alive, disciplined and capable of coordinated combat.

Arctic Sledding

Image Courtesy: Russian Ministry of Defense

The critical component of arctic and subarctic combat is keeping the force alive and motivated. Snow and cold dictate a heating plan, establishing winter garrisons, warming stations and countering thermal and smoke detection sensors. Warming and maintaining warmth in normal tents requires inordinate amounts of fuel and are readily identifiable to heat sensors. Engineer support in constructing troop shelters is complicated by the cold and wind, reducing their effectiveness some 30%-50%.[55]

Eating, drinking, field sanitation and prevention of cold-weather injuries are difficult in the arctic, particularly for soldiers not trained and accustomed to working there. Poor morale and psychotic behavior can also break out quickly. Aggressive small-unit leadership can prevent or mitigate problems in these areas, but ground units need to plan frequent rotation of ground units to keep them combat effective.[56]

Ground combat in the Arctic often begins with the contending forces not in direct combat, and the depth of the objectives can be significant. This requires combined-arms task organization blending tanks, mobile infantry, mortars, artillery and engineers. If the region has lakes, amphibious vehicles may be needed in the summer, whereas skis will do as well in the winter. Flanking detachments frequently work with air assault forces to seize road junctions and bridges. Planning considerations for the scheme of maneuver include swamps, regions of deep snow pack, order of march, flank and rear security and increased combat support. Movement across snow may require marking the way with dye, coal dust or oil. Naturally, flank and rear attacks are better than frontal attacks. Ground combat may require movement during polar night, blizzards, fog, and snow storms. Most of this movement will be directed by compass azimuth or satellite signal. In many areas of the arctic, compasses and satellite signals are not reliable. Keeping units warm, intact and moving will be a challenge.[57]

Close Air Support

During World War II, Britain, the United States and Germany placed a great deal of confidence and resources backing the theory of the decisive nature of strategic bombing. Strategic bombing failed to deliver decisive victory. The terrorized urban populations did not overthrow their governments and demand peace at any price. Instead, the populations of England and Germany learned to survive bombing attacks and bonded closely to their governments until victory or the bitter end. The Soviet Union did not conduct a strategic bombing campaign although the Soviets had the world's largest multi-engine bomber fleet at the start of the war. Their experience in the Spanish Civil War convinced them that tactical air attack was far more effective than strategic. The Soviets believed that the war would be won by ground power and that air power could make its significant contribution by supporting ground operations. The Red Army Air Force was not an independent air arm, as were the Royal Air Force and the Luftwaffe, but, like the US Army Air Corps, the Red Army Air Force was an

Colonel General Viktor Bondarev
Aerospace Forces Commander-in-Chief
Image Courtesy: Russian Ministry of Defense

auxiliary of the Red Army and an essential part of the ground-air team. Air units were always subordinate to ground-force commanders, although there was a separate air force chain of command for administration, personnel, training and logistics.[58]

The Soviet Air Force became a separate service after World War II. Nuclear weapons were a major concern and long-range aviation and air defense aviation aircraft became a priority in the Soviet Union. Air defense became a separate service in 1949, combining aircraft, antiaircraft artillery and air defense missiles into strategic air defense and tactical air defense branches. The Soviet Air Force had a long range aviation branch, military transport branch

Mi-24PN

Image Courtesy: Vitaly Kuzmin

and an aviation of the front branch. The aviation of the front branch provided close air support to ground forces and had the largest number of aircraft in the Soviet Air Force-particularly as missiles took over as the primary nuclear weapons delivery means. Long-range aviation shrunk in importance after the Strategic Rocket Forces were formed in 1959. Aviation of the front assets included fighter bombers and army aviation. Army aviation were helicopters and Su-25 *Frogfoot* close air support aircraft

Mi-28N

Image Courtesy: Vitaly Kuzmin

flown by Air Force pilots. In the 1980s, the Soviet Union had the largest military aviation force (air force plus air defense force) in the world (some 10,000 aircraft).

In 2015, the Russian Aerospace Defense Troops and Russian Air Force were combined into a new branch of service called the "Aerospace Forces" branch. In the Russian system, the Aerospace Defense Troops are considered "troops," roughly a lesser branch of the Armed Forces, and are responsible for strategic air defense and the operation of military space assets. The Air Force is a considered a full branch of service, but has struggled in recent years to maintain operational control of its army aviation (ground attack aircraft and helicopters) and transport aviation from the Russian Ground Forces and Airborne (VDV), which have long desired to integrate these capabilities as organic assets into their own organizations. The "ground-centric" Russian Armed Forces consists of three branches – the Aerospace Forces, the Ground Troops, and the Navy; and two types of troops–the Strategic Missile Troops (RVSN) and Airborne Troops (VDV). Although the benefits of putting air force, strategic air defense, and space assets under a single unified command covering "air and space" are obvious, this reorganization also significantly weakens the position of the Aerospace Forces in the Ministry of Defense. It increases the probability that the Aerospace Forces could lose its ground aviation and some transport aviation assets, retaining operational control of relatively few assets.[59]

Air Support of Ground Troops

Aviation attack is closely integrated with artillery planning and priorities. Target priorities remain nuclear delivery systems, conventional artillery and air defense, attack groupings or defensive strong points, command and control, enemy air assault forces and assets, enemy penetrations, enemy reserves and logistics and illumination. Artillery remains the 24-7, all-weather primary fire support, but given sufficient visibility, the speed, flexibility, range and accuracy of aircraft can be decisive during a high-speed

Su-25SM

Image Courtesy: Vitaly Kuzmin

advance, particularly if artillery is unable to keep up. High-performance aircraft belonging to the aviation of the front will be involved in air superiority and interdiction missions, but will also provide close air support for difficult missions such as air assault, river crossings or breakthroughs. The helicopters and close air support aircraft of army aviation will routinely provide close air support.

During planning, aircraft are given point targets and missions for seeking out those targets outside of artillery range or not located with sufficient accuracy for an artillery strike. Fixed-wing aircraft attack deep targets while helicopters operate over their own force or the forward line of contact. Helicopters may also go deeper during meeting battles, air assaults or the pursuit. Helicopters are commonly employed in flank protection missions.

Coordination between ground and air is always a concern. The Russians address this through:
- shared frequencies and radio systems: This has long been a strength of the Soviet and Russian joint air-ground system. The ground soldier and the aircraft pilot can talk to each other directly over common radio systems and frequencies.
- liaison: Artillery, air and air defense staffs maintain close cooperation. The Russians primarily have ground FACs and some air FACs. Ground FACs are found at maneuver brigade and battalion level and are experienced pilots. The ground FAC controls both fixed and rotary-wing assets. Russians have employed air FACs, however, they consider that the ground FAC has much better situational awareness and understands the ground commander's intent more clearly.
- separation: Artillery, fixed wing and rotary-wing assets can be employed simultaneously in the same area. The strikes will coincide in time, however different target sectors will be assigned to each type of asset.
- "weapons tight": Ground-based air defense assets may be constrained in select sectors or along designated flight corridors during air missions.[60]
- minimum safe distances: The minimum safe impact distances of aerial ordnance near friendly forces are 1,000 meters for free-flight rockets, 500 meters for helicopter cannon and 300 meters for helicopter machine guns.[61]

The aviation preparation of the attack begins with joint planning at the Army or Military District level, with the second and third parts of the air strike planning conducted at maneuver brigade and battalion level. In the course of the air preparation of an attack, strikes are delivered at the targets chosen beforehand at designated times, either simultaneously or consecutively. In actions on predetermined targets, aviation units and combat control bodies are given the necessary time for a thorough preparation of crews and aircraft to strike after receiving mission assignments. Optimal means of destruction for specific targets and combat equipment are selected, the composition of an attack group is determined, as well as the method of attacking the target, the assigned direction and height of target approach, maneuvers in the vicinity of the target, and other key tactical options. The composition of support groups is also decided. The strike and support groups use various flight formations along the route and near the target, depending on the combat actions, conditions and tactical situation.

On call fires in the course of the aerial support of an attack deal with newly-discovered targets and are initiated by FACs. These are first serviced by available aircraft circling in an airborne alert area. If these are not available, the FAC contacts a duty officer at an airfield, preferably one with a 5 to 15-minute readiness standby unit. For on-call fires, army aviation units are usually only given information on the probable area of action and type of target. The strike group (usually a couple or a squadron of helicopters) act without support groups. Take-

Ka-52

Image Courtesy: Vitaly Kuzmin

off is made on command from the control post. If the helicopters are circling on aerial alert and are within the control area of the FAC, the command to attack is given by the combat actions control group or by a forward air controller upon target acquisition. The forward air controller corrects the targeting trajectory of helicopter gunships right up to the moment of target detection by the group leader.

Other missions of army aviation include air assault, mine laying and mine clearing from the air, control and communications assurance, correction of artillery fire, electronic countermeasures, resupply, as well as guarding troop rear areas, illumination, search and rescue and medical evacuation.[62]

Fighter bombers from the Aviation of the Front can effectively deliver ordnance in close air support. Minimum safe distances are increased over helicopter and Su-25 distances. In Afghanistan, fighter bomber pilots began dropping bombs and firing rockets on the same pass. They learned to make multiple passes with multiple planes from multiple headings. They learned to attack difficult targets in the mountains by developing diving attacks, pitch-up bombing and the carousel attack.[63] Support of ground forces remains a key mission of Russian military aviation. UAV are beginning to supplement this effort, however the Russians have been slow to arm their UAVs, using them primarily as reconnaissance and BDA assets.

Appendix
Russian Military Symbology

	Command Post of a Front, Fleet, Branch of Arms (with flag of corresponding branch color), Military District, Air Force Zone, Air Defense Zone, or Air Force and Air Defense Zone
	Command Post of a Army, Air Force and Air Defense Army, Flotilla, or Cosmodrome
	Command Post of a Corps, Air Defense Corps, Air Force and Air Defense Corps, Squadron, or Naval Base
	Command Post of a Division, Air Force Division, or Air Defense Division
	Command Post of an Important Site
	Command Post of a Brigade, or Fortified Area

	Command Post of a Regiment, Otriad (detachment), Psychological Operations Group for a Front or Float, or Kommandatura (military government headquarters)
	Observation-Command Post of a Battalion, Cartographic Detachment, Psychological Operations Detachment, Separate Squadron, or Radar Company
	Motorized Rifle Battalion on BTRs (on the March)
	Tank Company (on the March)
	Self-Propelled Field Gun Platoon (on the March)
	Motorized Rifle Squad on BMP

БХВТ ◁ M	Equipment and Armaments Base in Support of a Division **M** — Motorized Rifle **Т** — Tank **А** — Artillery **З** — Air Defense **Д** — Airborne
БХВТ Д	Equipment and Armaments Base in Support of a Brigade **M** — Motorized Rifle **Т** — Tank **А** — Artillery **З** — Air Defense **Д** — Airborne
ФРВБ	Command Post of a Rocket Maintenance Base
ФТБ	Command Post of Rear Services Hospital, Center, or Forward Operating Base for an Army or Front
★	Command Post of an Operational Group for a Front or Fleet
★	Command Post of an Operational Group for Nuclear Munitions Disaster Response

1 2	**Machineguns:** 1 - light machinegun *(RPK or PKP machinegun)* 2 - company machinegun *(PKM machinegun)*
1 2 3	**Grenade Launcher:** 1 - handheld, antitank *(RPG-7V2 rocket propelled grenade launcher)* 2 - automatic *(AGS-17 automatic grenade launcher)* 3 - heavy antitank recoilless rifle *(SPG-9)*
1 2 3 4	**Tanks:** 1 - general symbol *(T-72B3/T-80BV/T-90A/T-14)* 2 - tank of a battalion commander or tank battalion on the march 3 - amphibious *(PT-76/2S25 Sprut-SD)* 4 - equipped with mine plow
	Infantry Fighting Vehicle (BMP or IFV) *(BMP-2/BMP-3/T-15)*
	Armored Personnel Carrier (BTR or APC) *(BTR-82/BTR-82A/Bumerang/Kurganets)*
1 2	**Reconnaissance Vehicles:** 1 - reconnaissance vehicle (BRM) 2 - combat reconnaissance patrol vehicle (BRDM) *(BRDM-2)*
1 2 3	**Automobiles/Trucks:** 1 - general symbol *(Zil-131/Kamaz-6560)* 2 - ambulance 3 - automobile/truck with trailer
1 2 3	**Recovery Vehicles** 1 - heavy *(BREM-1)* 2 - tracked *(BREM-L)* 3 - automobile/truck *(Ket-T)*
	Motorcycle
1 2 3 4 5	**Field Guns:** 1 - general symbol 2 - calibers up to 122 mm *(D-30 towed howitzer)* 3 - calibers up to 155 mm *(Msta-B towed howitzer)* 4 - calibers over 155 mm 5 - nuclear munitions
1 2 3 4	**Antitank Guns:** 1 - general symbol 2 - calibers up to 85 mm 3 - 100 mm caliber *(MT-12 Rapira)* 4 - calibers over 100 mm
	General Self-Propelled Gun Symbol (exact gun symbol dependent on caliber) *(Msta-S self-propelled howitzer)*

	Antitank Guided Missiles (PTUR or ATGM): 1 - portable *(9M115 Metis)* 2 - mounted on a combat vehicle *(9M123 Khrizantema/9P162 Kornet-T)*
	Multiple Launch Rocket Systems (MLRS): 1 - general symbol or small caliber *(BM-21 Grad)* 2 - medium caliber *(BM-27 Uragan)* 3 - large caliber *(BM-27 Smerch)*
	Mortars: 1 - general symbol 2 - small caliber (up to 82mm) and medium caliber (up to 100mm) *(2B14 Podnos)* 3 - large caliber *(2S12 Sani)* 4 - self-propelled mortar (exact mortar symbol dependent on caliber) *(2S9 Nona)*
	Rockets in Launch Position: 1 - tactical *(Scud)* 2 - tactical-operational *(9K720 Iskander)*
	Anti-Aircraft Artillery: 1 - general symbol 2 - small caliber 3 - medium caliber
	Self-Propelled Anti-Aircraft Artillery System (ZSU) *(ZSU-23-4 Shilka)*
	Anti-Aircraft Rocket Systems (ZRK): 1 - general symbol 2 - close range (up to 10 km) *(Igla, Tunguska, Strela-10, Osa, Pantsir-S1)* 3 - short range (up to 30 km) *(Tor)* 4 - medium range (up to 100 km) *(S-300V, Buk)*
	Combat Vehicle with a Close Range Anti-Aircraft Missile System *(9K35 Strela-10)*
	Self-Propelled Anti-Aircraft Artillery and Missile System *(9K22 Tunguska)*

	The boundary line between Brigades
	The boundary line between Regiments
	The boundary line between Battalions
5 мсд / 5 мсд / 10.00 05.07	Area occupied by a given unit (dotted line indicating future location) *a given area occupied by the 5th Motorized Rifle Division at 10:00 A.M. on the 5th of July*
	Area occupied by a given unit *a given area occupied by a BMP mounted squad*
12 зрдн	Area occupied by a given unit *a given area occupied by the 12th Anti-Aircraft Missile Battalion*
12 зрдн	Air Defense Artillery in firing position (exact system symbol depedent upon system) *the 12th Anti-Aircraft Missile Battalion in firing position*
БрАГ / 10.00 01.12 / 1 садн	Artillery in firing position (exact system symbol depedent upon system) 1 - Brigade Artillery Group (BrAG) *a brigade artillery group in firing position at 10:00 A.M. on the 1st of December* 2 - artillery battalion *the 1st Self-Propelled Artillery Battalion in firing position*
	Artillery battery in firing position (exact system symbol dependent upon system)

	Mortar platoon in firing position (exact system symbol dependent upon system)
ТакВД / **2 мсб**	Landing area for an air assault *landing area for an air assault conducted by the 2nd Motorized Rifle Battalion*
2 мсб / **06.00 10.11**	Planned landing area for an air assault *landing area for an air assault conducted by the 2nd Motorized Rifle Battalion at 6:00 A.M. on the 10th of November*
	Subunits in the defense
N 2 / *мср* *N 1* / *тр* *N 3* / *БнГ* 1 2 3	On Order Firing lines (lines of counterattack) 1 - motorized rifle subunit on BMPs *(second firing line)* 2 - tank subunit *(first firing line)* 3 - bronegruppa *(third firing line)*
N1 / *птадн* 1 *N2* / *птв* 2	On Order Firing lines 1 - antitank reserve of a brigade *(first firing line)* 2 - antitank platoon *(second firing line)*
	Repelled attack
	Withdrawal
	Opposing fronts
	Boundary of a field of fire
	Additional boundary of a field of fire

1 2 3 4	**Ranges of Fire** 1 - antitank weapons 2 - tanks 3 - BMPs 4 - small arms
1 2 3 *CO-1* *мср*	**Concentrated Area of Fire (non artillery unit)** *Concentrated fire area "number 1" of a motorized rifle company*
1 2 3 *№ 1* *гв*	**Firing Lines for a Grenade Subunit** *Firing line "number 1" of a grenade launcher platoon*
28	**Target** *Target "number 28"*
1 2	**Concentrated Fire Area** 1 - tube artillery 2 - MLRS artillery
„*Волк*" „*Лиса*" 201 101 / 202 102 / 203 103 / 1 2	**Successive Concentrations of Fire** 1 - Successive concentration line "Wolf" 2 - Successive concentration line "Lynx"
„*Акация*"	**Standing Barrage Fire** *Standing barrage firing line "Acacia"*
„*Берёза*" 1 2 3	**Deep Standing Barrage** *Deep standing barrage firing line "Birch"*
„*Лев*" 1 2 3 4	**Double Moving Barrage** *Double moving barrage firing line "Lion"*
„*Юпитер*"	**Concentrated Area of Fire (artillery unit)** *Concentrated fire area "Jupiter"*

1 2		**Lines of Attack** 1 - general (battalion) symbol 2 - tank battalion
1 2		**Combat Missions of a Formation, Unit, or Subunit** 1 - immediate objective 2 - subsequent objective
1 2		**Immediate Objective** 1 - general (battalion) symbol 2 - motorized rifle battalion on BMPs
1 2		**Subsequent Objective** 1 - general (battalion) symbol 2 - motorized rifle battalion on BMPs
		Direction of Further Attack
		Direction of Attack or Counterattack of a Unit or Subunit
		Area of a Breakout
		The Starting Line, Starting Line for an Assault, Line of Regulation
1 2 3		**Lines of Deployment** 1 - platoon columns 2 - company columns 3 - battalion columns
1 2		**Lines of Deployment** 1 - dismounted motorized rifle troops 2 - troops dismounted from tanks

19.00 12.00 10.00 8.00	Description of Movement and Time Map symbols depicting action or locations of units at certain times. This system allows the description of time phased events on one graphic.
	Rocket Launched Mine Clearing System (UR-83)
1 2 3 4	Helicopters 1 - general symbol 2 - combat (Mi-24, Mi-28, Ka-50, Ka-52) 3 - electronic warfare (Mi-8MTPR) 4 - anti-submarine warfare (Ka-27)
1 2 3 4	Helicopters 1 - reconnaissance 2 - transport (Mi-8/Mi-17) 3 - medevac 4 - artillery spotting
1 2	Unmanned Aerial Systems 1 - short range (Granat-1, Orlan-10, Zastava, Eleron) 2 - medium range (Forpost)
1 2	Infantry Flamethrowers 1 - light (RPO Shmel) 2 - heavy (TPO-70)
1 2	Flamethrower Vehicle Systems 1 - heavy combat vehicle for flamethrower operators (BMO-T) 2 - heavy flame thrower (TOS-1, TOS-1A)
1 2	Artillery Reconnaissance Radars 1 - battlefield surveillance radar vehicle (SNAR-10M1) 2 - counter-battery radar vehicle (Zoopark-1M)

	Artillery Reconnaissance Vehicle *(PRP-4A Argus, PRP-4MU Deuterium)*
	Fighting Position
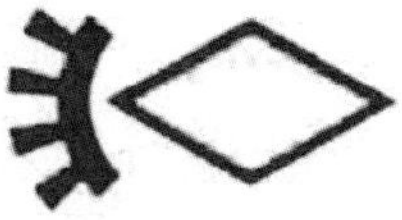	Tank Fighting Position
	BTR Fighting Position
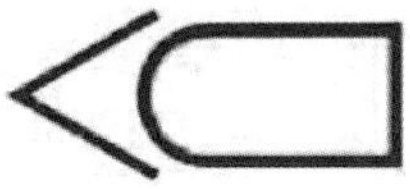	Vehicle Shelter
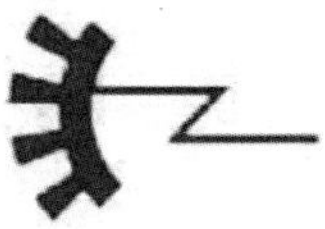	Communications Trench
	Mortar Fighting Position
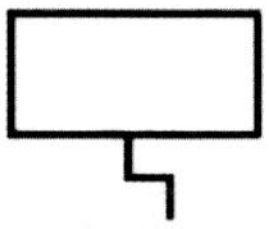	Bunker
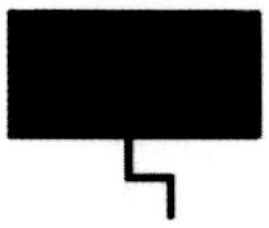	Reinforced Bunker
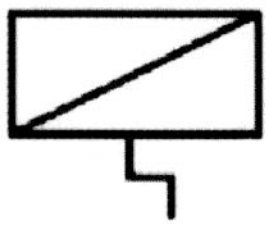	Command Bunker
	Covered Trench
	Observation Post

Combat Laser System (Peresvet) ————

Russian Laser Cannon

DESCRIPTION

In 2018, the Russian Defense Ministry released a video featuring the deployment process and combat preparations for the Russian combat laser system "Peresvet", which entered experimental combat service with the army on December 1.

Russian President Vladimir Putin has said that projects aimed at developing laser weaponry are extremely important to the country as this particular type of weaponry is expected to determine the combat potential of the Russian Armed Forces for years to come.

According to Deputy Defense Minister Yuri Borisov, "…weaponry based on new physics principles (beam, geophysical, wave, kinetic and other types of weapons) would define the shape of the Russian Armed Forces under the new state arms procurement program until 2025."

CAPABILITIES

The new weapon is apparently designed to track and shoot down hostile airborne targets, including aircraft, missiles and drones. Russia's new battle lasers are most likely designed with close-range air defense in mind, and specifically for the destruction of drones and cruise missiles.

The laser beam is far more economical than the use of standard anti-missile missiles and its accuracy is much greater. Even miles away traveling at supersonic speed, in the time it takes the laser light to reach the target, a missile will only have traveled less than an inch. It's not a question of whether you can hit the target. The question is what part of the missile do you want to hit? The payload at the tip or the engine and flight controls at the back?

REMARKS

High-energy laser (HEL) weapon systems compensate for atmospheric fluctuations using adaptive optics. The atmospheric compensation is usually done using a separate beacon illuminator laser to create a pseudo star on the target and sense the return in a wavefront sensor to drive the adaptive optics. The high-energy laser itself can be used as a beacon illuminator by turning it off periodically for a very short period giving the wavefront sensor and aim point sensor an opportunity to measure the return from the high-energy laser.

A laser weapon needs to be maintained on a specific area of the target for a period of time to be effective. Atmospheric compensation using adaptive optics reduces the time the high-energy laser must be maintained on a target. A tracker illuminator (TIL) is employed to measure the angle and range of the target relative to the ground-based HEL weapon system. A beacon illuminator (BIL) is used to create a pseudo star on the target. The BIL return signal is measured by a wavefront sensor to determine atmospheric turbulence between the weapon system and the target. This information is then used to drive adaptive optics (deformable mirrors) to vary the HEL beam to compensate for atmospheric disturbances. This reduces the time on target required to destroy the target.

T-14 Armata Main Battle Tank

T-14 Armata

Image from Russian MOD

DESCRIPTION

The Armata "is to be used as a main battle tank for Russia's ground troops; it boasts a new ammunition feed system as well as other brand new operational characteristics." The turret in the photo is covered with a case.

The Armata has a multi-layer armored capsule for the crew of just two operators and is expected to have the potential to evolve into a fully robotic battle vehicle. 2,300 units are estimated necessary for the Russian Army.

CAPABILITIES

The Armata is equipped with:

- remote-controlled 125mm smoothbore cannon

- 30mm sub-caliber ranging gun to deal with various targets, including low-flying aerial targets

- 12.5mm heavy machine gun with a turret, which can take out anti-tank missiles

- active-phased array antenna and a large variety of other sensors.

Armata T-14 (continued)

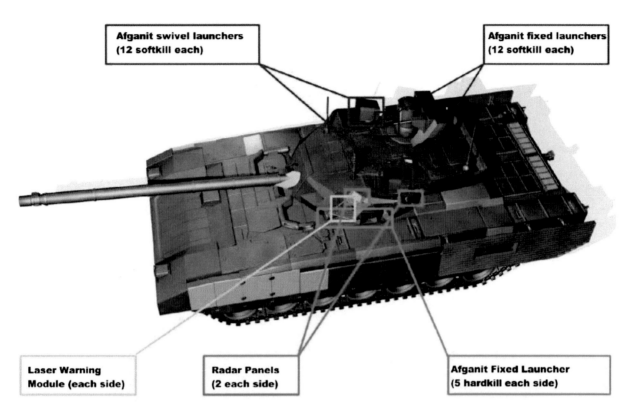

Afganit swivel launchers (12 softkill each)

Afganit fixed launchers (12 softkill each)

Laser Warning Module (each side)

Radar Panels (2 each side)

Afganit Fixed Launcher (5 hardkill each side)

T-15 Heavy Infantry Combat Vehicle

T-15 Armored Personnel Carrier

Image from Russian MOD

DESCRIPTION

T-15 (Object 149) heavy infantry combat vehicle based on the platform of the Armata main battle tank appears to have the same power plant and armor as Armata MBT, made of a 'cake layer' of newly-developed armor steels, ceramic and composite materials.

CAPABILITIES

The weapons mounted on T-15 unmanned turret, which unlike the Armata, is mounted closer to the rear of the vehicle, might consist of a 30mm automatic cannon, at least one machine-gun, automatic grenade launcher and antitank guided missile system.

Kurganets-25 Light Tracked Armored Vehicles ————

Kurganets-25

Image from Russian MOD

DESCRIPTION

The Kurganets-25 (Russian: Курганец-25) is a tracked, 25-ton modular infantry fighting vehicle and armored personnel carrier being developed for the Russian Army. The Kurganets-25 will evolve into various models, gradually replacing BMP, BMD, MT-LB and other types of tracked Soviet armored platforms. The Kurganets-25 will have modular armor that can be upgraded for specific threats.

CAPABILITIES

There are two versions of the vehicle: a heavily armed infantry fighting vehicle carrying 6-7 troops; and a lightly armed APC carrying 8 troops. Other variants proposed for the Kurganets include an armored ambulance, an 82 mm Vasilek mortar carrier, anti-tank vehicle, armored recovery vehicle, a reconnaissance vehicle, a command vehicle, and an armored engineering vehicle.

2S35 Koalitsiya-SV 152-mm Self-Propelled Howitzer ━━━

2S35 Koalitsiya-SV

Image from Russian MOD

DESCRIPTION

The 2S35 Koalitsiya-SV (Russian: 2C35 «Коалиция-СВ», lit. "Coalition-SV") is a Russian self-propelled gun first seen in public (initially with its turret covered) in 2015.

The 2S35 is expected to have a very high level of automation that will dramatically reduce the crew number, to perhaps just two or three people located in an armored capsule below the two front hull hatches.

CAPABILITIES

The main armament as a 2A88 152 mm gun with a range of up to 80 kilometers using precision-guided rounds and up to 40 km with standard rounds that are currently used on Msta-S. The claimed average rate of fire is around 16 rounds per minute, with a maximum rate of 20 rounds per minute. 2S35's rate of fire was improved due to the new pneumatic loader. Estimated ammunition load is around 60-70 rounds and using a special loader vehicle the recharge time for full ammunition load is 15 minutes

VPK-7829 Bumerang

DESCRIPTION

The VPK-7829 Bumerang (Russian: Бумеранг, Boomerang) is a modular amphibious wheeled infantry fighting vehicle and armored personnel carrier. Bumerang vehicle is based on Armata Universal Combat Platform. It is amphibious using two waterjets. The engine is located in the front so armed troops can exit at the rear.

CAPABILITIES

It has a crew of three consisting of the driver, gunner, and commander and holds seven troops. Protection includes ceramic armor to prevent shell splinters. Like BTRs, the Bumerang is an 8×8 wheeled vehicle, equipped with a 750 hp turbocharged diesel engine.

1K17 Szhatie (1• 17 • • • • •)

Russian "Stiletto" Laser Tank

DESCRIPTION

The 1K17 Szhatie (Russian: 1K17 Сжатие — "Compression") is a self-propelled laser vehicle of Soviet origin. The platform uses a Msta-S chassis with a battery of laser projectors mounted in the turret. It was developed by the Soviet Union in order to disable the optical-electronic equipment of enemy missiles, ground and aerial vehicles.

Western intelligence services code named it the "Stiletto".

CAPABILITIES

The "tank" used an intense laser beam to disable the optical-electronic equipment of the enemy vehicles. This was created by focusing light through 30 kg of artificial rubies which made the whole system very expensive to produce. The optics that produced the laser were placed at the end of a silver coated spiral which helped amplify the beam and increase convergence. The energy to power the laser was provided by a generator and an auxiliary battery system.

Other titles we publish on Amazon.com:

Russia Land-Based Electronic Warfare/RUMINT

RUSSIA MRAPs, ARMORED CARS, ARMORED PERSONNEL CARRIERS & ARMORED ASSAULT VEHICLES

Russia Surface-to-Air Missile Systems

Russia Ballistic Missiles

Other titles we publish on Amazon.com:

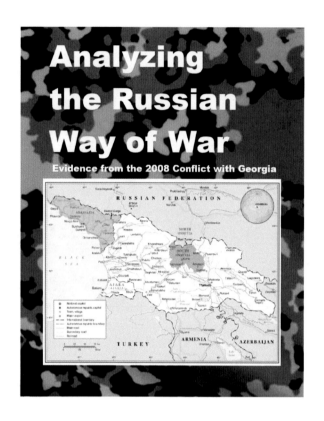

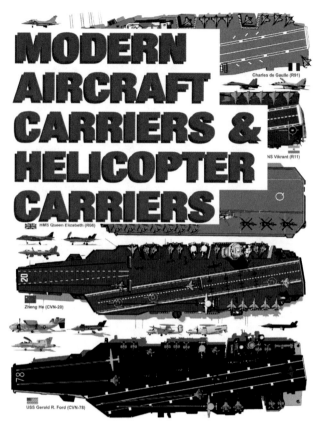

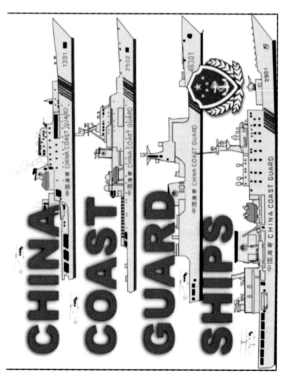

Other books we publish on Amazon.com

MODERN RUSSIAN TANKS

CHINA ELECTRONIC WARFARE WEAPONS/ RUMINT

People's Liberation Army Rocket Force

Luis Ayala

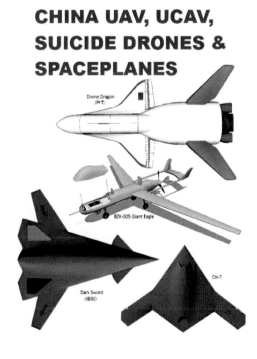

CHINA UAV, UCAV, SUICIDE DRONES & SPACEPLANES

Other books we publish on Amazon.com

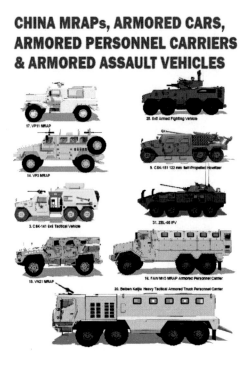

Made in United States
Orlando, FL
12 June 2025

62080634R00257